TRADITIONS OF PERTH

George Penny

CULROSS

Published facsimile in their 'Re-print Series
in 1986
by Wm. Culross & Son Ltd.
Coupar Angus
Perthshire

ISBN   0   900323   79   5

TRADITIONS OF PERTH,

CONTAINING SKETCHES OF

THE MANNERS AND CUSTOMS OF THE INHABITANTS,

AND NOTICES OF PUBLIC OCCURRENCES,

DURING THE LAST CENTURY:

INTERESTING EXTRACTS FROM OLD RECORDS;

NOTICES OF THE NEIGHBOURING LOCALITIES OF HISTORICAL INTEREST;

TOPOGRAPHICAL SKETCH OF THE COUNTY;

BRIEF HISTORY OF PERTH, &c.

By GEORGE PENNY.

PERTH:
MESSRS DEWAR, SIDEY, MORISON, PEAT, AND DRUMMOND.

J. TAYLOR, PRINTER.

1836.

PUBLISHERS NOTE

The *Traditions of Perth* was originally in 1836 published in 'demy octavo.' This made the appendices in particular difficult to read because of the small size of print. This reprint has been produced in a larger size to ensure easier reading. The page notation of the first edition has been retained.

The original version contained no illustrations. This version contains fifteen illustrations relating to places, buildings or events referred to in the text and drawn from printed sources from the period 1789 to 1844. Nine illustrations are taken from Sir W. J. Hooker's *Perthshire Illustrated* published in 1844. The remaining illustrations are taken from the print collection of Perth Art Gallery and Museum and thanks are due to Mr J. Blair, Curator and Mr R. Rodger, Keeper of Art for their help and co-operation in choosing the illustrations and permitting reproduction.

Coupar Angus 1986.

ANTHONY J. COOKE

Anthony Cooke is a Lecturer in the Centre for Continuing Education, University of Dundee where he organises adult education programmes and teaches economic and social history. He has edited three research publications by Extra-Mural groups – *Stanley-Its History and Development, Baxter's of Dundee* and *A History of Redgorton Parish*. He has a particular interest in textile history and has published a number of articles in this field. He has lectured to a wide variety of archaeological and local history groups and has served as General Secretary of the Abertay Historical Society and as President of the Breadalbane Archaeological Society.

LIST OF ILLUSTRATIONS

ABBREVIATIONS

P.I.   Sir W. J. Hooker, *Perthshire Illustrated,* 1844

PMAG   Perth Museum and Art Gallery (Print Collection)

City of Perth from Tirsappie.

INTRODUCTION

Traditions of Perth is a classic local history. It shares the faults of too many other local histories – it tends to be vague on dates, is often unclear about its sources and the organisation of the material leaves much to be desired. There are no chapters and only a very sketchy index. Much of the book is written from personal recollection – either of George Penny himself after a lifetime as a weaver and working journalist or of his father who settled in Perth after the 1745 Rebellion.[1] As such, it is bound to contain errors of detail but it does give the book the great appeal of immediacy which makes this the most entertaining as well as one of the most valuable histories of Perth. If immediacy is one of the great strengths of the book, another is George Penny's voracious interest in all aspects of life in and around Perth. He writes knowledgeably and in detail about the unreformed Town Council – 'the Beautiful Order,' about births, weddings and funerals, about diet, dress and living conditions, about crime and punishment, about Perth's long military connections, about church life and schools, about Perth's old buildings and streets and about sports and pastimes.

Traditions of Perth is mainly concerned with the period from 1770 to 1830. This was a period of major upheaval in the social and economic life of Scotland and Penny's book is particularly valuable as a first-hand account by someone who had lived through the changes. The rapidity of change also explains Penny's interest in old customs and traditions which were being swept away and his desire to record them before it was too late.[2] Penny's father had been a weaver and he himself had followed that trade before turning to journalism. This makes his account of the growth of the textile industry in and around Perth one of the most authoritative for any Scottish town in this period, conveying the optimism and rapid expansion of the industry on the one hand and on the other the fragile credit system which led to 'knock-on' bankruptcies in times of depression. Penny also writes with particular authority about radical politics in Perth – he published the Whig *Perthshire Advertiser and Strathmore Journal* and had served as a spokesman for the Perth weavers in the depression year of 1819.[3]

George Penny was born in Perth on 30 October 1771. He was 'lawfully procreated' by George Penney, a weaver, and his wife, Ann Henderson. The child was baptised the following day by the Rev James Scott, the minister of the Town Churches in Perth and author of the first Statistical Account of Perth, so it appears that the family were in the mainstream of the Church of Scotland.[4] George Penny Senior had arrived in Perth after the 1745 Rebellion to follow the trade of a weaver. According to his son, George Penny Senior had introduced the manufacture of silesia linens into Perth about 1766 and in 1782 had introduced the cotton manufacture to the city. The *Traditions* also contains a story about the foundation of Stanley Mills, the cotton-spinning mills outside Perth. A meeting was arranged in the Kings Arms Inn, Perth between the Duke of Atholl, Richard Arkwright, the English cotton-spinner and William Sandeman of Luncarty bleachfield. George Penny Senior was introduced to Arkwright who was 'highly delighted' with the quality of muslin he was producing and gave the go-ahead for the building of the mills.[5]

George Penny seems to have followed his father's trade as a weaver. In 1819 he was chosen by the Perth weavers as their spokesman at a time of unrest during a depression in trade.[6] By 29 May 1834 he was named as the publisher of the *Perthshire Advertiser and Strathmore Journal* and continued as the responsible publisher up till 20 August 1840. This weekly newspaper had begun life as the *Strathmore Journal* in Coupar Angus in 1829 but moved into Perth and changed its name although it was still known colloquially as *De Trashmore*. Although claiming to be 'entirely independent' and to receive support 'from no political party' it became the spokesman of reform in opposition to the moderate Tory paper the *Perth Courier* founded in 1809. It campaigned for the unseating of the Tory MP, Sir George Murray, at the 1832 election, took up agricultural issues and rapidly overtook the *Courier* in circulation figures. By 1835-36 it was selling more copies than the combined sales of the *Courier* and the *Perth Constitutional,* a weekly journal of 'extreme Tory principals' founded in 1835.[7]

George Penny seems to have acted very much as a jack of all trades at the *Advertiser*. He canvassed for advertising, collected accounts and helped printers produce the papers. One account describes him as the 'scapegoat' for the newspaper. In appearance, he was a 'tall dark man (grey in his old age) of sallow complexion and good features.' He was married, possibly twice, as one account gives his wife's name as Barbara whereas she is named Margaret in the 1841 census. The couple had at least one child, a boy also named George. They were members of the East Church, one of the three churches that made up St John's Church, the parish church of Perth.[8]

By 1841, at the age of seventy, Penny was living with his seventy-five year old wife Margaret in Stormont Street, Perth, his occupation being described as a handloom weaver.[9] By this date, Penny had retired from the *Advertiser* and may have had to revert to his old trade to eke out a living. He continued to publish material in the local press including a letter on railways in the *Advertiser* on 14 January 1841 and a rhyme on Perth surnames in the *Dundee and Perth Journal* of 18 December 1841. In the same month, Perth Town Council paid him £2.00 for writing up a census of Perth based on the official survey. By 1846, Penny had moved to 'a two storeyed ochered house in Barnhill, facing the Dundee Road, where he died, possibly about 1850.'[10]

The *Traditions of Perth* was published in 1836. The printer was John Taylor, the printer of the *Perthshire Advertiser* and the publishers were the principal Perth booksellers – Dewar, Sidey, Morison, Peat and Drummond. C. G. Sidey, who had a shop on George Street, had a close association with the *Advertiser* and later became Lord Provost of Perth. P. R. Drummond (1802-1879) ran a library and bookshop in Perth and wrote *Perthshire in Bygone Days,* published in 1879, which is one of the main sources of information about George Penny. Sidey and Peat are more shadowy figures but Morison was almost certainly one of the well-known dynasty of Perth publishers and printers, possibly Robert Morison (1764-1853) the printer of the *Perth Courier.*[11] The book was published by subscription although there is no record of how many copies were produced.[12]

Traditions of Perth was reviewed in the *Perth Courier* on 26 May 1836. The reviewer singled out for particular criticism the book's 'fertility in personal anecdote of a kind which ought not to have survived the gossip of its day and of which the record can serve no good purpose.' Possibly he was offended by Penny's broad sense of humour, as in his story of the wedding feast where the guests were given purgatives by mistake.[13] The reviewer did however quote with approval Penny's account of the establishment of linen manufacturing in Perth as 'proof of the better spirit and tendency of the book.' Later commentators made similar points. R. S. Fittis criticised Penny for writing 'a very confused and imperfect account of the (meal) mobs of 1772-73 having evidently never consulted the authentic reports in the *Perth and Scots Magazines* – the only sources of information.'[14] In fact, Penny was writing in a rather different tradition and his accounts of these events are obviously handed down from his father, who was an eye-witness.[15]

A more sympathetic view of Penny is given by D. Crawford Smith in his book *The Historians of Perth.* He is critical of Penny's 'credulity' in repeating stories such as the digging of the four mile long King's Lade in one night by the military. More generally, he takes Penny to task for his fondness for 'racy stories,' absence of chapters in the book, flimsy index and general lack of organisation in his writing. Yet Smith is quick to see the merits of the book – its breadth of interest, its entertaining style and its birds-eye view of events and concludes 'notwithstanding all its drawbacks, Penny has given us a word picture of Perth in his own day and in his father's such as few towns possess.'[16]

For the modern reader, it is this 'word picture' of a Scottish town at a period of rapid change which is the main attraction of the book. Amongst a mass of stories and information about virtually every facet of life in Perth, Penny is perhaps strongest in three areas – his accounts of popular unrest, of old customs and of the growth of trade and industry.

Traditions of Perth describes popular unrest in the period from 1770 to 1830 when Britain was undergoing an Industrial Revolution at the same time as the French Revolution was taking place across the Channel. The resultant social and political upheavals were reflected in microcosm in a town like Perth from the meal mobs of the 1770's, through the Republican movements of the 1790's to the political agitation at the end of the Napoleonic Wars. Penny's father was an eye-witness of the meal mobs of the early 1770's and Penny himself was a young man at the outbreak of the French Revolution and an active participant in the events at the end of the Napoleonic Wars. Although a Radical, Penny was no revolutionary and was shocked by the irreligion and lack of 'moral restraints' of the Perth Friends of the People and United Scotsmen who were active in the 1790's.

Similarly in the depression year of 1819, Penny only accepted the chair at a general meeting of weavers in Perth 'on the express condition that no politics were to be introduced' and claimed to have exercised a calming influence on events.[13]

Penny's interest in recording old customs should be set against this background of rapid change. Some of his descriptions can be found in other literature such as his classification of the three different kinds of wedding – the free wedding, the dinner wedding and the penny wedding.[18] Others are more unusual, such as 'Riding the Steng,' when adulterers were made to ride on a pole through the streets before being pitched into the mill-lade. Alternatively an effigy of the offender was paraded through the streets, then burnt.[13]

An appendix to the book by Andrew Buist, Deacon of the Glover Incorporation includes an account of an even older custom – the semi-pagan Beltane or May Day ceremony of 'passing to the Dragon Hole,' a cave in Kinnoull Hill, which was suppressed by the Presbytery of Perth not long after the Reformation.[20] This appendix also includes an account of a 'sword dance' performed by the Glovers Incorporation at Gowrie House in front of Charles I in 1633.[21]

Perhaps the most valuable part of the book is the section headed 'The General Trade.' This begins with a description of traditional trades such as fishing, glove-making, shoe-making, dyeing, masons, etc. and goes on to describe the rise of printing in Perth. Then comes its most substantial section on the rise of the textile industry in and around Perth, perhaps the best contemporary account that exists for any Scottish town. Penny paints a vivid picture of a period when 'a manufacturing mania seemed to pervade society,' when 'not a herd boy could be found in the country; all flew to the loom' and when 'machinery and print shops rose like magic.'[22] He conveys equally well the miseries of the crash of 1810 which brought down some sixty small manufacturers in Perth, and after which things were never quite the same again in the town's textile industry.

The book ends with a topographical description of Perthshire taken from Chambers' *Gazetteer of Scotland* published in 1832. There is an appendix headed *Brief History of Perth* taken from the same source with the addition of a list of the first Reform Magistrates of Perth and a resolution from the Perth Friends of the People dated January 1793 protesting against the declaration of war on France.[23]

A second appendix consists of notes on the Glover Incorporation of Perth by Andrew Buist, the Deacon of the Incorporation. The Glovers were an important Incorporation in Perth and a letter from Robert Gray, a Perth glover, dated November 1794, features in the Old Statistical Account of Perth.[24]

Penny's book deserves to be better known. It is a vivid picture of a Scottish town, warts and all, during a period of major transition. It is popular history, which despite its faults of arrangements and occasional lapses from the strictly accurate, gives the reader a stronger impression than most books of what it was like to live through these times.

March 1986.   Anthony J. Cooke.

REFERENCES

1. George Penny, *Traditions of Perth* (Perth 1836) p.1 henceforth cited as *Traditions*.

2. This was true of writers in other parts of Britain. See E. P. Thompson, *The Making of the English Working-Class*, (London 1968), p.448.

3. *Traditions*, p.147.

4. Perth Register of Births. For Rev J. Scott (1733-1818) see D. Crawford Smith, *The Historians of Perth* (Perth 1906), p.68. Spelling was variable in this period – 'Penny' and 'Penney' being interchangeable.

5. *Traditions*, pp.250-251. For Stanley see A. J. Cooke(ed), *Stanley, Its History and Development* (Dundee 1977). For William Sandeman (1722-1790) and his bleachfields at Luncarty, see A. J. Cooke(ed), *A History of Redgorton Parish* (Dundee 1984).

6. *Traditions*, p.147.

7. R. M. Cowan, *The Newspaper in Scotland 1815-1860* (Glasgow 1946) pp.43-44, *Perthshire Advertiser Centenary Volume* 1929 and *Traditions*, p.248.

8. D. Crawford Smith, *The Historians of Perth* (Perth 1906) pp. 112-113, and P. R. Drummond, *Perthshire in Bygone Days* (London 1879), p.234.

9. General Register House, Census Enumerators' Returns 1841.

10. Smith, *op cit*, pp. 114-115. The census was published in 1842 as a 'Statistical Account of the City of Perth' (see Sandeman Library, Perth – Perth Pamphlets, Vol. 1).

11. Smith, *op cit*, pp.76, 150-152, *Perthshire Advertiser Centenary Volume* 1929, p.9 and R. M. Carnie, *Publishing in Perth* (Dundee 1960).

12. Adverts for *Traditions of Perth* in *Perth Courier,* 20 August and 15 October 1835.

13. *Traditions*, p.32.

14. R. S. Fittis, *Historical and Traditionary Gleanings concerning Perthshire* (Perth 1876), p.469. See also S. G. E. Lythe, 'The Tayside Meal Mobs,' *Scottish Historical Review,* Vol. XLVI, 1967.

15. *Traditions*, p.48.

16. Smith, *op cit*, pp.113-114.

17. *Traditions*, p.147.

18. *Traditions*, p.31.

19. *Traditions*, p.111. A similar tradition existed in parts of the North of England and was also called 'Riding the Steng.' E. P. Thompson, *The Making of the English Working-Class,* p.448.

20. *Traditions*, pp.320-321. For the origins of Beltane ceremonies see I. F. Grant, *Highland Folkways* (London 1975), p.65.

21. *Traditions*, p.327.

22. *Traditions*, pp.251, 253 and 256.

23. See R. & W. Chambers, *The Gazetteer of Scotland* (Edinburgh 1832) Vol. II, pp.848-862 and *Traditions*, p.315.

24. *(Old) Statistical Account* (1976 re-issue, Wakefield) Vol. XI p.499.

INDEX.

TRADITIONS OF PERTH.

THE City of Perth, to which the following observations refer, is so well known in the history of Scotland, for the many remarkable events which have taken place in it and the surrounding country, prior to the period here alluded to, that little need be said as an apology for bringing these sketches before the public. They refer to a period, during which there were, for many years, neither a local paper nor magazine to chronicle the passing events. They consist chiefly of the personal observations of the writer, and the accounts related to him by his father, who settled in Perth shortly after the memorable year 1745; and as the writer has spent his whole life time in it, and taken an active part in many of the events of the times, he trusts there are many little incidents, however trifling in themselves, that may prove interesting to the descendants of those who figured in the days to which these recollections refer. As the incidents related were written merely for his own amusement, at leisure hours, he trusts that the homely style in which the statements are given will not be despised.

EXTENT AND APPEARANCE OF THE CITY.

There is a tradition that, at a very early period, Perth, then called Bertha, stood at the junction of the Almond with the Tay; and some large beams have been found in the bed of the river near that spot. Be this as it may, we have records and charters, as far back as the eleventh century, to shew that, at that period, Perth, where it now stands, was a considerable town; but as I only mean to describe Perth as it was in the last century, I beg leave to refer to *Gall's Gabbions* for some very interesting particulars, referring to Perth in those early days.

A

About the year 1770, the City of Perth consisted of the High-street, from the river up to the port where St Paul's church now stands ; South-street, extending the same length in a parallel line : (this street was then and is still frequently termed the Shoegate ;) the Watergate still remains nearly as it was; as also the Skinnergate, the Horse-cross, the Castle-gable, and Curfew-row.   At the termination of the Castle-gable stood the North-port, situated at the south side of the gate now leading into Mr Condie's house, then Blackfriars' house, and the property of Mr Robertson of Tullybelton.   On the opposite side, a little old house, the porter's lodge, was long occupied as the house for collecting the customs of that port, then the principal entrance from the Highlands.   The Kirk-gate, which still retains much of its former appearance, was then one of the principal streets; the shops being occupied by many of the leading merchants in the grocery and the cloth lines.   The houses extended on the north side of the church to the same extent as at present, to St. John's-street, where they terminated in gardens.   On the east, stood a range of houses, between the two narrow vennels leading from the Wa-tergate ; from this there was a narrow vennel, called the Salt-vennel, leading to the South-street, in a straight line with the east end of the church.   The buildings in this vennel were very old wooden buildings, inhabited by the very lowest class of society, and here the beggars and vagrants generally lodged.   The School-vennel and the Flesh-vennel were just in their present state.   On the west of the church, the ground where the flesh market now stands, was the bowling-green.   In the year 1761, the present flesh and meal markets, and the academy above, were built.   The Meal-vennel has still much of its former appearance.   Mill-street was a dirty lane with only three houses in its whole extent, and one below the Glovers'-yard on the north side, occupied by the hang-man ; it was bounded on the south by garden walls, and on the north by the ancient city wall, which extended from where the new spinning-mill is built to the top of Methven-street; thence it turned south to the High-street, where the Port stood with gates and bars ; it then continued down Methven-street to the South-street, where the Shoegate-port stood with its gates ; thence it turned down Canal-street to the Speygate, which leads from the Watergate to the Greyfriars, where there was another port.   The course of the mill lade marks the position of the wall.   At that time the lade was uncovered all the way down Methven-street and Canal-street, to the Tay.

GOWRIE HOUSE.

At the foot of the South-street stood the ancient palace of Gowrie House, which extended from the Water-vennel to the line of Canal-street, bounded on the west by the line of the Speygate, and by the river on the east. The building formed three entire sides of a square, and half the fourth side, leaving the other half of the front open towards the South street, where the entrance into this ancient building was by an arched gateway. The gable end of the south side stood a little to the north of the gate of the new jail. This wing consisted of a range of lofty stone buildings, the lower part being bomb proof; the second storey was divided into two long and lofty halls; the upper one was divided in the same manner, but the apartments were not so high. On the east of these halls, in the angle of the buildings, was the grand stair-case which led to the south and east wings, with the little turrets at the top. The half of the eastern range was similar to the south, and divided in the same manner. The other half was a building of one storey, which appeared to have been occupied as shades or stables. The northern range consisted of buildings not so lofty as the southern, having only one flat above the bomb-proofs; and another above that, half garrets. On the west end of this range was the great kitchen, with a fire-place extending across the whole breadth of the house. The western range, north of the main gate, (forming part of the Watergate,) was similar to the south wing, consisting of halls in each flat, thus enclosing a spacious square. On the south of the building, to the line of Canal-street, was a garden, the city wall forming the western and southern enclosure. On the east of the building, a terrace ran along the river the whole length of the property. At the end of the terrace stood an oval tower, the interior of which was ornamented with drawings of the arms of noble families in Scotland. The tower was built in the angle of the eastern and southern walls, and was called the Spy tower, it is presumed, from its commanding situation, having a clear view to the west, south, and east. On the outside of this tower was a dock or basin, formed on the side of the bed of the lade, that still runs into the Tay below Canal-street, between the Old Shore and the Gowrie wall. Here the ship owners were wont to lay up their vessels for safety during the winter; the idea of exposing their property to the storms at this inclement season, never having entered the heads of the cautious merchants of those days. This tower, as well as the whole of Gowrie House, were reckoned amongst the greatest ornaments of Perth. The property fell into the possession of the City. When the Duke of Cumberland was here in the year 1745, with the King's army, the Magistrates presented him with the gift of Gowrie House, with all its gardens! which his Highness, immediately on his return to London, sold to the Board of Ordnance, who immediately converted it into an artillery barracks, making Perth head quarters.

The house in Spey-gate, fronting the jail, now occupied as a public-house by Mr M'Laren, stood opposite the window from which King

James the V. called for assistance in the alleged Gowrie Conspiracy, and was then the house of one of his nobles.

The palace of the Bishop of Dunkeld stood on the ground now occupied by the new buildings on the east side of St John Street. The public hall of this ancient building was long occupied as the linen stamp office. Another nobleman's house stood in what is now termed the Kirk Close, some parts of which still remain. The Parliament House was in the close which still bears its name, and was for many years used as an Episcopal chapel. About the year 1818, this building was pulled down, and a very elegant hall erected on its site, by the Royal Arch Mason Lodge, which is now much used for public sales. This hall was built with money, the bequest of Mr Murray, the founder of the Royal Lunatic Asylum.

Curfew-row, rendered famous by Sir Walter Scott's " *Fair Maid of Perth*," is still in existence ; but scarcely a vestige of the old houses remain, except one at the corner of Blackfriars'-wynd, where the curfew bell hung ; which used to ring every night at nine o'clock, to warn the lieges to put out their fires. Behind this house stood the Monastery of Blackfriars, where King James was murdered. On the same ground there is at present a house which was built for Lord John Murray, one of the Atholl family, and which was long considered the only genteel house in town. The Curfew-row was, from an early period, until a few years ago, occupied on both sides with malt barns, belonging to the brewers. The remains of these buildings are now occupied as a tannage.

The Watergate, at that time the only thoroughfare from the south, contained the only fashionable self-contained houses in the town. The writer can remember when five Provosts were all living in this street.

The Skinnergate was another principal street, and the only thoroughfare to the north by the Castle-gable and the North-port. The present line of Mill-street, Methven-street, and Canal-street, were then dirty, unpaved roads, without any buildings, save a number of malt barns and sheds, some of which are yet standing. Even limited as the extent of the town then was, many parts of the streets were unbuilt. The west side of the Meal-vennel, and the sides of the Shoegate above the Meal-vennel, were but partially built, and below the vennel there were many buildings lying in ruins, termed old walls. The only houses without the city walls, on the west, were the Glassite chapel ; and the Mill-wynd, which was built for a linen factory,

There was formerly a bridge across the Tay at the foot of the High-street, which was swept away by a "mighty inundation," as we learn from a grave-stone erected to the memory of Mr Mills, the builder. For a long period the only passage across the river was by ferry boats, similar to those now employed in bringing sand up the river. The boat house on the opposite side stood where the church of Kinnoull is now built; and the pier where they landed on that side was at the point that projected on Mr Patton's property, and was then called Gibraltar point. This pier projected a good way into the river, forming a deep bay below, which Mr Patton has filled up, and thus extended his grounds a considerable space into the bed of the river. On the Perth side the boat landed at the North-shore, through the arch below the west end of the Council-room.

There is an anecdote told of a regiment of Sutherland fencibles, during the war in the year 1756, who were on their march to the south. When they came to the Tay, they refused, to a man, to enter a boat, dreading that, if once on board, they would be shipped off to Germany. They therefore resolved to cross the river at a ford a little higher up, by wading; and the whole regiment, joining hand in hand, made their way through.

EXTENSION OF THE CITY.

About the year 1758, the east side of the New-row was partially built, by a company engaged in the linen manufacture, long known by the name of the New-row company. About this time, the proprietors of lands in the vicinity of Perth began to feu their property for building, and a desire for more commodious houses becoming general, the suburbs were rapidly extended. The Clayholes were taken in small lots, chiefly by weavers, who erected very humble dwellings, many of them of clay. Thimble-row was built shortly after. A row of houses of the same description was built up the south side of the Laigh Causeway, and turned round on the west side of the then Auchterarder road,—called Earl's-dykes. This row is now almost in ruins; and the old tenements on the west side of the Laigh Causeway have, within these few years, been replaced by good substantial houses.

The Glover Incorporation, who are the proprietors of the lands of the Leonards, feued out a great part of them. Leonard-street was speedily built; and Pomarium and the Cross-street filled up rapidly at the same time.

On the north side of the town, the building of the present bridge, which was finished about the year 1771, made way for vast improvements in that quarter. George-street was immediately formed, and an opening made to the High-street. About the year 1783, Charlotte-street was built, and immediately after that the lands of Blackfriars were laid out in streets. The first building was the house next Provost Marshall's, in Rose Terrace. At that period there was not a house to the west or north of the old tannage. Paul-street soon followed, and the street between it and the Mill-wynd.

The row of houses at the foot of Canal-street on the south side, were built about the year 1772, and the large building on the east end was added in 1780. Up the south side of Canal-street, there was a low, marshy piece of ground, extending from Prince's-street west to Shuttle-field-close, called the How Rig, which filled with water during the winter, and afforded excellent sport to the youngsters on the ice. The Star inn, Gaelic chapel, gas works, &c., are all built upon it.

The ground between this and the South Inch was all laid out in small gardens. To the westward, the Hospital Gardens; and on the north side of the city, the whole of the Blackfriars, and the lands of Drumhar, where the Barracks stand, were laid out in a similar manner—so that almost every family in Perth had a garden. The lands of Blackfriars were laid out in beautiful small plots, well stored with fruit trees and bushes, and intersected by green walks; forming an agreeable promenade in the summer season. These extended as far into the Inch as the railing.

CROMWELL FORT.

On the north end of the South Inch stood Cromwell Fort. This was a regular square fortitfication with four bastions. The north side extended along the Greyfriars to the Edinburgh road, and a considerable way to the westward where Marshall Place now stands. The east side extended from Graham's coal yard by the alley of trees, to a line with the chesnut tree that stands by itself, on the east side of the Inch. The whole was composed of the earth and sand dug out of the trenches, which were about 100 feet wide at the top, and had been originally very steep. About the year 1780, before the City began to fill them up, they were about ten feet deep, and used to contain a considerable number of pike. During the winter, they afforded excellent ice for skaiting. Sometimes boys were drowned here; and frequently they were the watery graves of new-born infants. Within the mound on the east side, a range of stables for dragoon horses was built, that would contain 200 horses, with a riding-house on the west end: these were pulled down when the present barracks were built; the rest of the space within the trenches was occupied as wood-yards. This fortification, of which not a vestige remains, measured about 266 yards on each side, the mounds were demolished gradually, by taking away the sand for paving the streets; and the trenches were filled up by rubbish carted from the town. The remains of the mounds were wheeled into the trenches to complete the filling up.

Monks Tower, Perth.

Gowrie House, Perth.

High Street, Perth.

Perth from East Shore.

During the digging, a seam of wheat was discovered about nine inches thick, which had been burned and reduced to charcoal; but every pickle was perfectly entire, and quite dry. A serjeant of the Guards, who was in Perth at the time, filled a tin cannister with it, and sent it up to London.

The streets were then paved with round bullets of stone, taken from the river, and formed a very rough road for carriages. About the year 1780, the system of paving with cut stones was introduced, first in the Watergate.

The water that supplied the City was conveyed from the mill lade, from a cistern above the mills, by wooden pipes. On relaying the streets, lead pipes were adopted in place of the wooden ones; but still the water, although plentiful, was not good; and at various periods attempts were made to introduce spring water. Frequent surveys were made of the springs throughout the neighbourhood; but the matter never went further, until the year 1829, when an act of Parliament was obtained for supplying the City with water, under a set of Commissioners, with power to assess the inhabitants in proportion to their rents. That act has since been carried into effect, and the inhabitants now enjoy the luxury of the purest water. This has obtained by digging a filtering well at the upper end of Moncrieff Island, from whence the water is conveyed below the bed of the river to the water-house, on the east point of the line of Marshall Place. This building is erected on an elegant plan, and is an ornament to the City. The whole of these operations were conducted under the direction of Dr Anderson of the Academy, with the most complete success. Trials have been made to ascertain how high the water would rise from the pipes on the streets, which is found to ascend to the roofs of the highest houses at the Cross.

It was during the time that Thomas Hay Marshall was a member of the Town Council, that the greater part of the improvements that have since taken place were projected. The North Inch was then only half its present size : it was bounded on the north by a wall, called the White Dyke, which was said to have been built by the fines levied from the brewers and bakers for fighting with the weavers; and was erected to prevent the encroachments of the Muirton farmers, who were in the habit of taking a few furrows, from time to time, from the common good. The dyke ran across from the river to Balhouse orchard, at the place where a few old trees are still standing, the remains of an alley that ran along the side of the dyke. About the year 1785, an excambion was made with the Earl of Kinnoull, by which the Muirton haugh was added to the Inch, for which the Town gave the greater part of the farm of Laigh Tullylumb, when the white dyke was pulled down, and a race-course

formed round the Inch. Provost Marshall became proprietor of the
Blackfriars, and exerted his interest with the county gentlemen to get the
line of road from Dunkeld and Crieff to come through these lands. About
the year 1760, the road to Dunkeld went from the High Street Port, in
almost the same line as at present. Shortly after that period, when the
bridge was built, it was altered and taken up through the North Inch,
and a row of trees planted on each side; one of these still remains to
mark the line. About the year 1788, it was again brought in a straight
line from the Bridge of Almond to the boundaries of the Blackfriars,
where it was twisted into angles to suit Marshall's plan of the streets.

The road to Crieff, which went from the High Street Port by Dovecotland and the Stone Cross, was altered to the present line which now
joins the Dunkeld road. The Stone Cross is yet standing to the west of
Goodly Burn. This was a large upright stone, raised on a pedestal, with
steps round it, originally having had the figure of a man on it. The arms
had long been broken off, the upright part alone remaining. An anecdote
is told of an English traveller who, on visiting the Cross, mounted to the
top and placed a crown piece there; many years afterwards, the same
gentleman was again in the country and paid the Cross a visit, and, to
his astonishment, found the crown piece exactly as he left it.

The ground on which Dovecotland is now built, was formerly the site
of a large establishment of friars. In digging these grounds, many old
coins have been found. About the year 1778, a plan for building this
place on an elegant scale was made out, but the want of water, and other
local circumstances caused the scheme to be abandoned; it was, therefore, feued out to any individuals to build to suit themselves. The
daughters of the first settler having established a notorious house, the
rough wits of the day bestowed a name upon the place which greatly
injured the sale of the rest of the property.

At the same time, an excambion was made between the Town and the
Blackfriars, by which the lade was straightened, a piece of ground was
given to the lands of Blackfriars, at the top of the Inch, and a piece of
ground at the foot of the Inch taken from these lands; by these arrangements, the Town became bound that no building should, at any
future period, be erected on the Inch to intercept the view from Blackfriars House and garden. About the year 1802, an excambion was made
with the proprietors of the gardens on the north of the South Inch, and,
on the west, with the Glover Incorporation, by which the marches were
lined off straight, and the ground of Marshall Place feued out. This
line was at first sold in seven lots for villas, but never was built. The
feus were given up, and the present plan adopted. In former times, the
road from Edinburgh came in by the Cloven Craigs, in a line with

Craigie and by the Leonards, where the road from Craigie, by Leonard-street, still passes. The Edinburgh road was altered about the year 1760, and brought in the present line through the South Inch, through Cromwell's mound, and the gardens where Prince's-street was formed.

Under Provost Marshall's superintendence, the Borough Muir was feued out, some of it in small lots of two and three acres, at a feu-duty of two bolls of wheat a-year. The whole of this extensive wood has been cleared, and the ground greatly improved, and is now studded with gentlemen's houses, and tradesmen's neat cottages. On some of these lands, which, forty years ago, was reckoned not worth a shilling an acre, wheat of the finest quality is now raised; frequently they have produced the heaviest wheat and barley in the county.

The houses in Perth were generally built on the plan of having arched door-ways and windows; but on the front wall there was erected a projection of wooden work, about six feet wide. On the ground floor these were open, and were termed Channels;—here the goods were displayed. Several of these houses are still to be seen, with the wooden fronts; but the channels are filled up and converted into shops. The Skinnergate, narrow as it is, was all the way finished in this manner; and so close did it bring the fronts of the houses to each other, that the inmates could hand their snuff mulls to those on the opposite side; which rendered the lower apartments sufficiently obscure. Many of the old houses were a foot or two below the level of the street, which added to their dismal appearance. Although the buildings were almost all confined within the boundary of the city wall, the streets and lanes were by no means built up. On the front of South-street, a considerable part was lined by garden walls, and the west side of the Meal-vennel was in the same state. Few of the shop windows had any glass in them—they had only a wooden grating.

Shortly after the Rebellion, a company started in the north of England under the firm of the York building company, who began their operations on a very extensive scale, and extended them to Perth. They bought the property east and west of the Skinnergate, and rebuilt the houses as they now stand; but their affairs fell into confusion, and the property was sold for their creditors. It would appear that their rights had not been sufficiently valid; for, about the year 1785, one Gregory, a tailor, having got possession of some old charters, he summoned the proprietors before the Court of Session, to surrender up the property. The whole of them, to save litigation, compromised the matter with him; by which he obtained a considerable sum of money. The flats of the old houses were extremely low, seldom above six feet between the floor and the roof, and the windows were very small. The roofs were covered with heavy thick slabs of stone, the weight of which often bilged the roofs, and presented a clumsy appearance. Several of these roofs are yet to be seen in the town.

The houses were uniformly divided, into separate flats, half-flats, or single rooms. The only self-contained houses were on the east side of the Watergate, between the street and the river. The 1st of these was possessed by John Richardson, Esq.—the 2d by Dr Wood—3d, Lady Stewart of Urrard—4th, Provost Caw—5th, Provost Alison—6th, the Sheriff-clerk's office, by Murray of Dollarie. On the north, Lord John Murray's, and Tullibelton's, now Mr Condie's. The rest of the good houses were let in flats to separate families, and generally consisted of a kitchen, a public room, (which served for parlour, dining room, and hall), with one or two bedrooms, and a closet. In most of the houses the entrance to the rooms was through the kitchen into the parlour, and from thence into the bed-room. Outside stairs to the first flat were very common, and had an awkward appearance on the street. A great part of the buildings in the closes were occupied by brewers, who kept public houses, and retailed their own ale. About the year 1780, there were upwards of sixty houses of this description. The principal inns then were the King's Arms, foot of High-street, now occupied by Mrs Slater; the second in the Thistle Close, first entry above the Skinnergate; the third, the Salutation, so called from John Burt, the landlord, having shook hands with Prince Charles. The King's Arms was considered the first; it enjoyed the patronage of the Duke of Atholl, and many of the first families in the county.

THE JAIL.

This old building was formerly a part of some religious house. At what period it had been converted into a prison, I am not enabled to state; but it was sufficiently gloomy for this purpose. On the ground floor there was one cell, 12 feet square, arched above. The window was raised about eight feet from the floor, and so thoroughly set with a triple grating that very little light entered the place. The door was composed of thick double oak planks; there was also an outside iron door. This was what was termed the condemned cell, or laigh iron house. Here the criminal was fastened to a chain in the floor; his bed a little straw on the damp stones, and a single blanket for a covering. Some years before it was given up, a cage was erected in this place, similar to those I shall describe above stairs, where there was only another cell for criminals and a small dark room for debtors. To these were added two garret rooms for debtors. The upper cells were about 16 feet by 12. In the lower one there were three cages; each about six feet long, and four wide, built up to the roof, and of double plank. The door into them was about four feet high, and eighteen inches wide, with a hole for handing in their bread, about 12 inches by nine, with iron gratings on it. Within were chains for locking the prisoners to the floor, a bundle of straw, and a blanket. Beside them was placed a wooden stoup, which was supplied with fresh water just twice a week, and their bucket with filth was only removed once a week. In the upper cell, which was usually alloted for women, there was only one cage, situated in the centre of the room. In these wretched places, with a scanty allowance of bread and water, were the poor wretches confined for months, some of them for years, without seeing the light of day, or enjoying a breath of fresh air. The common allowance was five halfpenny loaves a day, with water; until an old man, who was sentenced to twelve months' imprisonment, complained to the Court that he could not live on the allowance; when seven, instead of five, were ordered for the whole. Often were they in such a crowded state, that the smell, to a stranger, on entering, was intolerable, The debtors, likewise, had very wretched accommodation; sometimes three or four were huddled into one of these garrets, where there was just room for the bed, and a narrow passage between the door and the fire. place.

After an arduous struggle of nearly thirty years, the Duke of Atholl prevailed on the county gentlemen to erect the present jail and public buildings, which stand on the ground formerly occupied by Gowrie House; but even this structure, in point of accommodation, has been found quite inadequate for the purpose; and, at the present time, steps are being taken to get it enlarged, so as to admit of a classification of the prisoners. A chaplain has been appointed for the jail, who, every Sunday, holds worship with the prisoners, and gives instructions during the week, particularly to the young, in reading and religious knowledge; but the want of room, to admit of a proper separation of the criminals, prevents this salutary measure having proper effect.

The old Jail, which had lain useless since the erection of the new one, has been lately fitted up as a sort of penitentiary, under the management of the Police Establishment. The old debtors' room has been divided into cells, which are kept in good order, and properly ventilated; and the criminals' cells, with the three *cages*, have been cleaned out for the accommodation of the refractory. It, therefore, appears, that, under our modern police management, an individual, for the most trifling offence, is liable to be thrust into a den, which, half a century ago, was considered too horrible for even the most atrocious criminal.

In former times, when a person had the misfortune to be confined for debt, he had to remain until the first Town Court day before he could even make application to obtain an aliment; and had then to incur the expense of obtaining an order, and of serving an intimation on the creditor, that, at the expiry of ten days, he must allow him 6d. or 9d. a day. Here he had to lie for twelve or fourteen days before he could obtain any subsistence, and for this he had to pay 10s. 6d.; but his misery did not end with this, for the jailer charged jail fees,—for every night he was in custody, 3d., if a burgess; if not a burgess, 6d. For this sum, which frequently became heavy, the jailer indeed could not detain the prisoner; but if he had brought any bedding, this was arrested until the amount was paid. These jail fees have since been done away with, and the prisoner allowed to depart the moment his creditors permit.

BURGH COURT.

Many curious anecdotes might be told of this Court. A late worthy Trades' Bailie sat on the bench one day, on a case where he was himself the pursuer, and decided the case in his own favour, and decerned the defendant to pay all costs.

Bailie Allison was sitting judge, when a boy was brought before him for a practice, at the time very common, of getting up to the steeple from the roof of the church, by a window in the staircase leading to the steeple, the object being to swing by the bell-ropes. Sometimes they set the bells a-ringing, and alarmed the neighbours. This boy, the son of a poor widow, was caught in the act, and committed to prison until Court-day. When brought forward, the case was clear, and the Bailie sentenced him to two months' confinement. He was then ordered away to jail; but hesitating to leave the Court, "Take him away," was called out by the Bailie, rather in a pet at the culprit not obeying the order. In reply to which, the boy asserted that there were others present, equally implicated, and who ought, likewise, to be confined. " Tell me who they were," said the Bailie, " and they shall get the same fate." "I dinna like to tell," said the boy. " You must tell, or I'll double your time." " Sandy Allison was there." " Sandy Allison! what Sandy Allison?" " Your ain Sandy." The Bailie was dumfoundered. At last he said, " You may go home for this time; but if I catch you again, you may depend on being punished!"

Robie Aiken, the hangman at that time, lived in a bakehouse (having an oven in the end of it), near the north shore. Here the wretched creature kept a most infamous house, where many a row was kicked up by folks of all degrees, until one night, in a riot, poor Robie was kicked out of the world altogether. Amongst the magistrates at that time, there was a Bailie Duncan, *alias* Jamaica Pate, who was said to be very fond of the lasses, and had been in the habit of visiting Robie's; whether, as sitting magistrate, for the laudable purpose of keeping order, or otherwise, is not known. There was another worthy of the day, Perry Mitchell, well known in Perth for many dirty tricks. Perry was a daily visiter at Robie's. One night whilst he was there, a dreadful row commenced, in which broken heads abounded; some of the parties concerned were apprehended, amongst them Perry. When brought into Court, Jamaica Pate was on the bench. Perry had made his escape at the time of the row, but was apprehended shortly after, on the information of some of the others. He was asked from the Bench if he had been in Robie's on such a night? "Me there!—I was not: the last time I was in the house, ye was there yoursel' a' the time; an' ye ken if there was ony disturbance! Ye mind when somebody cam' to the door, that ye creepit into the oven; and when ye heard wha it was, ye came out again; and then we a' drank thegither. And whan Meg Bain thought you was dead drunk, I catch'd her hand in your pouch gaun to rob ye." The poor Bailie, unable to stop the body's loquacity, was glad to get him out of the Court on any terms. This Perry was long a nuisance about the town. He was frequently apprehended for petty offences. On one of these occasions, he was committed to prison; and when one of the Town Officers informed old Provost Marshall of it, he exclaimed "Filthy body, we are continually plagued with him; he deserves a good whipping." On this the officer went straight to the jailer, and told him that Provost Marshall had ordered Perry to be whipped. The hangman was brought, Perry stripped and bound, and led down stairs. By this time the thing had taken wind, and a crowd had assembled. Provost Marshall, whose shop was below the Skinnergate, seeing the multitude, asked the meaning. Some one replied, that Perry Mitchell was going to be whipped through the town. The astonished Provost instantly made his way through the multitude, and arrived just in time to rescue Perry from the hands of the hangman. This narrow escape, however, does not appear to have operated as a sufficient warning to induce him to mend his manners; for he was subsequently whipped by his friend Robie, and banished the county.

THE MAGISTRATES UNDER THE OLD SYSTEM.

It was formerly the case, that the office of City Treasurer was no sinecure. He kept the public purse, and had the duty of settling the whole public accounts.   One year, a certain baker, who could scarcely write his name, was elected to the office.   At this time the bakers were in the prac-tice of running accounts with their customers by the month.   Instead of a check book, each family had a thin stick hung by a string.   When the baker's man went round with the bread, he carried a bundle of these sticks with him, and the individual receiving a loaf cut a notch in his particular stick.   So thoroughly conversant was the Treasurer with this system of *Practical Arithmetic,* that he was thus enabled to keep a record of the whole income and disbursements of the City funds.   To the astonishment of his brethren in the Council, on delivering up his charge, instead of lay-ing before them the usual documents that his accounts might be audited, he brought in a whole basket full of nick sticks ; and, much to his honour, the accounts were all found to be correct ;—at least, no one presumed to challenge their accuracy.

Sometime afterwards, one of the Treasurers fell behind in his intro-missions, upon which the charge of the funds was transferred to the City Clerks, and the duty of the Treasurer became nominal.   For upwards of 30 years back a Chamberlain has been appointed, who now takes the charge of all the money matters,—the Clerk managing the rest of the busi-ness.   On the death of old Walter Miller, who, for a long period, had held this office, a keen canvass ensued for the situation.   One, Andrew David-son, offered £1200 for it ; but the Magistrates of the day had friends to serve, and Messrs Peddie and Stewart were appointed.   After the decease of Mr Stewart, Mr Peddie transacted the business till his death ; when Messrs Miller and Mackenzie obtained the office for life ; both of whom are esteemed able and upright men.

Notwithstanding the ample revenue of the city, the Magistrates of those days contrived to get the city involved pretty deeply in debt : to accom-plish this they had every opportunity, as they never rendered any account of their charge to the public.   Dinners and suppers were given on the most trifling occasions, and a reckless waste of the funds prevailed.   If a tradesman was employed about any little job, it was made the subject of one or more special visits by one or other of the Magistrates, accom-panied by a few of his acquaintances : the issue was an adjournment to a public house ; and if any of the party offered to pay their proportion of the reckoning, the offended Bailie would exclaim, with an air of offended dig-nity, " What, Sir, would you presume to pay in the presence of a Magis-trate !   Put it to the town's account !"   On every occasion of vindicating the law—in every case of pillory, whipping, or hanging—a magisterial dinner was held to be indispensible.

The delegation to the Royal Burgh Convention was an expensive job. One hundred pounds was the allowance for maintaining the proper dignity of the city representative at this assembly. About the year 1780, one of our worthy Provosts who was sent to the Convention, having fallen in with some light company, had the misfortune to have his pocket picked of his allowance and commission. As he could not appear at the Convention without the proper credentials, an express had to be sent over for another copy, which raised many unpleasant surmises at the Provost's expence.

About the year 1804, a spirit of economy began to obtain in the Council. The above allowance was not taken by the Provost, but merely a sum sufficient to cover his unavoidable outlay. The state of the funds was laid open to the inspection of the public; and all feasting at the expence of the city funds given up ; with the exception of the election dinner, which was considered but a very moderate recompense for the time and trouble bestowed upon the public business.

At a later period, Provost Morrison made a motion at the meeting of the Convention, to the effect, " That it should be dissolved for ever, as useless, expensive, and cumbersome ;" but he was not seconded.

THE OLD CROSS.

This structure stood on the High street, between the Kirkgate and the Skinnergate. It was about 12 feet high, with a balcony on the top, to which there was access by a flight of steps within the building. Proclamations were wont to be read from the balcony ; and here, on the King's birth-day, the usual loyal toasts were drank by the Magistrates. As each separate health was drank, the bottles and glasses were thrown among the crowd, and new ones procured for the succeeding toast. So much for the civic economy of the day.

About the year 1764, when carts and other carriages came to be introduced, this edifice, being found considerably to impede the carriage-way, was taken down. The city gates were removed about the same period.

MAGISTERIAL DIGNITY.

During the last generation, the magistrates were sufficiently impressed with a sense of their own importance, and were also resolved to exact a proper acknowlegment of it from the inhabitants. So atrocious an offence against all decorum was it held for a person to pass a bailie on the street without giving him a hat, that any one omitting the ceremony was generally ordered "up stairs"—that is, thrown into jail. About the year 1764, one of the bailies was such a rigid upholder of the civic dignity in this respect, that, " Put him up stairs, as Bailie Robert says," became a common bye-word.

BURGH ELECTION.—BEAUTIFUL ORDER.

This abominable system, calculated for the complete subversion of the liberties of the citizens, existed in all its splendour in the eighteenth century.   There was a particular junto that kept the civic honours among themselves.   The Provost was nominally elected every year ; but to hold office only one year, or, in the technical phrase, to be made an yearling, was held to be a disgrace.   He was, therefore, re-elected for the second year, when the former Provost was again appointed for other two years. The Dean of Guild was elected in much the same manner, from a leet sent down to the Council.   The Trades' Bailie was also chosen by the Council, from a leet sent by the Trade whose turn it was to have the Bailie.   The Treasurer was chosen alternately from the Guild and Trades' side of the Council.   The Magistrates were elected on the first Monday of October, and the Deacons of the Trades were elected on the Wednesday following.   The Trades which sent Deacons to the Council were the Hammermen, Glovers, Shoemakers, Fleshers, Wrights, and Tailors.   The Weavers, though a corporate body, had no seat at the Council board—they having at some period either neglected, or been defrauded of that privilege.   The Brewers and Dyers were incorporated with the Guildry.

In a few years the bustle incident to the ancient burgh elections will be forgotten, and after generations will learn with astonishment, that six weeks' painful canvass of the freemen was submitted to, and large sums sacrificed, in the remote prospect of obtaining the honour of Deaconship of one of these petty corporations.   Houses of rendezvous were opened by the contending parties, and suppers given, and morning drams in abundance.   Even to obtain the humble situation of Box-master, much *booing* often took place, and many curious manœuvres were resorted to, to remove obstinate members out of the way, in order that their vote might not be recorded.   Many a hard struggle was maintained for the office of Trades' Bailie.   To such an excess were these carried, that individuals in affluent circumstances, often brought themselves to poverty ; besides acquiring dissipated habits, and destroying their own health and family comfort.

The election of Deacons and Box-masters took place at nine o'clock on Wednesday morning ; but as early as five the different parties were at Athole brose, to restore the tone of their stomachs, after the fatigues of the table with the would-be Deacon on the previous evening.   After the election, the day was generally spent in tippling; and in the evening each Corporation dined together in their different halls; the expense of the entertainment being always defrayed from those funds which were understood to be set apart for the relief of the poor and infirm of their respective bodies.

On the following Thursday, the election of a Convener took place, after fortifying themselves with a public breakfast, invitations to which were given to the clergy, the magistrates, and those connected with the Convener's Court. The Convener's dinner concluded the festivities of the Michaelmas Elections. At this dinner, all those who at any time had held office as Deacon, Trades' Bailie, or Trades' Councillor, were entitled to attend during life, by payment of a guinea, on their entrance, to the funds of the Convener Court. This sumptuous entertainment was of course always well attended; and many of the ci-divant deacon bodies, that seldom allowed themselves the indulgence of a full meal, here threw away their cares and swelled the saturnalia. Friday was redolent with aching heads and qualming stomachs. Saturday was a day of repentance; and the Sabbath arrived as a blessed day to put an end to the debauch. But severe was the ordeal which many of the penitents had yet to undergo, before dissenting sessions, for drinking to excess, and swearing the Burgess' oath.

The dignity of the magistrates was supported by a small corps or body guard of town officers, five in number, being one for the Provost and each of the magistrates. At that time, only decayed burghers were appointed to the office, which then was no sinecure. Their regular salary was little more than three shillings a week; but they had a number of perquisites, arising principally from the business of the Town Court, which augmented their income. This court was held on Tuesday and Saturday. Since the appointment of the Justice of Peace Small Debt Court, and the establishment of the Police Court, the business of the Town Court has become almost nominal. It is now held on Tuesday, and the only business of importance brought before it, is serving heirs to property. Formerly, the powers of this court were both extensive and despotic. The sitting magistrate, without the sanction of a jury, had no hesitation in sentencing an offender to a public whipping. An instance of this occurred in the year 1776. A boy, belonging to some respectable family in the Watergate, was detected in some petty offence, and sentenced by the Bailie to be whipped through the streets by the hangman. The mother, when the boy was dragged past the door in this degraded state, fell on her knees, and imprecated a curse on the Bailie and his family—that none of his children might live to the age of her son: or if they did, that they might be brought to suffer the same disgraceful punishment. Whether

c

the idea of fatalism caused mental depression, and induced consequent
disease—or that the mother had invoked the more inscrutable workings of
Providence,—it was remarked, that every one of the Bailie's numerous
family died when they came to be about the age of her son.

MILLS.

Perth has long been famed for its mills.   To the west of the town, on
the King's lade, there are two flour mills, two meal mills, and a malt
mill.   The multure of these was formerly very heavy.   The Perth
bakers were bound to them, and had to pay the twentieth boll.   When
the flour mill of Balhousie was in separate hands from the town's mills,
the bakers, to escape the heavy multure, adopted the plan of selling their
wheat to the Balhousie mill, and buying back the flour.   Of late these
mills have all been in the hands of one company.   There was formerly a
waulk mill on the lade, above the flour mills, which was occupied by the
dyers ; it was subsequently used in wool-spinning.   At present the fall is
employed in driving machinery in the Perth Foundery.   At the foot of
Mill-street there was a barley mill, a malt mill, an oil mill, and a waulk
mill.   Some years ago these different structures were converted into a
wool-spinning mill and an oil mill, which have recently given place to a
flax-spinning mill in conjunction with the oil mill, under the management
of Mr Fleming, Bridgend.   Farther down the lade, on the site of Mr
Urquhart's shop in George-street, there was formerly an oil mill, which
was long occupied by John Richardson, who carried on an extensive trade
in that line.

On the Balhousie branch of the lade, at the foot of Charlotte-street,
there was a snuff mill ; and at the south west corner of the South Inch
there was another mill, which was latterly employed in spinning cotton.
The remains of this latter building are now entirely swept away.   From
various circumstances, it was surmised that this mill was wilfully set fire
to by the proprietor.   It was supposed to have been a very losing concern in his hand.

MILL LADE.

The lade by which these various mills are driven, is taken from the
River Almond, about four miles west from Perth.   It is said to have been
dug through the different proprietors' grounds in one night by the military, and has been hence styled the King's lade.   The admission of the
water from the Almond is regulated by a sluice, and an extensive em-
bankment of masonry called Low's work, and the whole is subject to the
inspection of the Magistrates.   The income of the city from the different
mills upon the lade has frequently been as high as £1000 a-year, and

forms a considerable portion of the city revenue. The oil mill, on the lowest fall on the lade, was removed to make room for George-street. The snuff mill, which had long been discontinued for that purpose, gave place to the very handsome building which forms the corner of Charlotte-street. In addition to the mills already mentioned, many extensive works are established on the different falls of the lade, before it reaches Perth. These we will notice when we come to speak of the manufactures.

THE BOOT OF BALHOUSIE.

This is a branch from the King's lade, which drives a flour and meal mill at Balhousie, and flows by the west side of the North Inch into the Tay. The history of this stream is rather curious. It is said that Oliphant, the Laird of Balhousie, preferred the apparently very modest request to the King to be permitted to take a bootful of water from the lade : which was at once granted. But the wylie laird interpreted the privilege in the way that suited himself, and immediately drew off as much water from the bottom of the lade as would flow through a pipe about eleven inches wide, the assumed width of the laird's boot top ! Such is the rapidity with which the water rushes through the pipe, that two or three of the laird's boots would have let off the entire water of the main stream. People troubled with sprains and rheumatisms are said to experience relief by bathing under the rush of water from the boot. In the recollection of the writer, the lades abounded with fine trout ; they were particularly plentiful in the different mill troughs ; while at present there is not one to be seen. The deleterious substances flowing from the different printfields and bleaching establishments, is generally understood to be the cause of this striking change. On one occasion, the writer, on passing along the lade, observed several fine trouts rise to the surface, turn over, and expire. On reaching the Tulloch, he found that some cf the vats had just been emptied, which at once accounted for the phenomena he witnessed. And yet this very water, which carried death in its course, was what the inhabitants of the town employed for family use.

The different branches of the lade go completely round the boundaries of the old town. The main stream flows down Mill-street, and joins the Tay at Deadland gardens. A branch turns off at Methven-street, and goes round by Canal-street, joining the river at the Coal Shore. From this a branch runs off above the Gas works, and flows round the west and south side of the South Inch, uniting with Craigie burn, and joining the Tay below the Depot.

It would appear that the ancient Monastery of Blackfrars, drew the supply of water from the lade which was required in the establishment,

as stone pipes have been discovered in digging the foundations of some of
the houses which have been erected on the grounds. Owing probably to
the absence of limestone in the district drained by the Almond, and the
numerous bleachfields on that river, and on the lade, the water is extremely soft, and is allowed to be unrivalled for the purposes of washing
and bleaching.

DRESS AND HABITS OF THE PEOPLE.

The dress of the working classes was wont to be of a very coarse
fabric, commonly hodden gray ; and the broad blue bonnet was universal.
The cut of a fashionable coat of former days differed considerably from
our ideas of elegance.   This important article of dress was made with a
very long waist, and gradually widened as it came down to the haunches ;
the tails were short, and spread round in front of the thighs ; the sleeves
were very wide, with immense cuffs folding back nearly to the elbows,
and were ornamented with a profusion of very large buttons.   Neither
coat nor waistcoat had any neck, and the shirt was merely secured at the
neck by a button ; very few, except on holidays, indulging in the extravagant luxury of wearing a neck-cloth.   The waistcoat was an important
and substantial article of dress, and, at pinch, might have stood in place
of a whole wardrobe.   It descended nearly to the knees, parting at the
top of the thighs into what was called flaps, each of which contained a
pocket so capacious, as might lead to the idea that the worthy owners
were in the habit of carrying their whole moveables about with them.
The breeches were very short, extending from the knee to the haunches,
upon which they hung, without the aid of braces.   The stockings were a
stout, and, generally, home-made article, produced by the females of the
family.   Many aged people, who had become incapable of more active employment, procured a living by knitting stockings.   The hair was worn
long, flowing over the shoulders.

The common every-day dress of the women consisted of coarse blue
plaiding petticoats, and a short-gown of the same.   The married women
wore a close mutch, which on Sundays they ornamented with some
showy ribbons.   Their Sunday dress was composed of linsey-woolsey,
which was chiefly spun in the family, and given out to weave.

The young unmarried women wore their hair tied round with a ribbon
or snood.   The plaid, brought over the head, served the purpose of a
bonnet.   In the matter of female dress, there existed, as at present, a
considerable diversity.

The dress of the more wealthy was fashioned as above described, but
of finer stuff ; to which was added a huge wig, decorated with numerous
rows of curls, and a large toupee in front ; the whole surmounted by

a magnificent cocked hat: so that when the respectables appeared abroad, with a long pike staff in their hand, reaching to about a foot above their head, or a gold-headed cane of similar length, their shoes and knees sparkling with immense silver buckles, they had a very consequential, though somewhat grotesque appearance.

The ladies and matrons were very particular about their dress. The gowns, which were of silk or brocade patterns, were very long in the waists, with long flowing trains, which were generally tucked up all round. High heeled shoes with silver buckles were the fashion. The hair was so dressed as to stand exceedingly high, if not upon end, and was covered with a fine lawn head-dress, with lappets and pinners, which hung down from the back of the head. About the year 1775, haunch hoops were greatly in vogue among the better classes; and the *haut ton* wore them round the skirts, of a diameter so great, that before a lady could enter a ball room, she had to raise the one side of her hoop as high as the head, and let the other come in towards her, to enable her to pass the doorway. Old men wore grammaches above their stockings, which were drawn up above the breeches to the middle of the thigh, and were fastened below by a flap coming forward on the foot, under the buckle of the shoe. The shoes or slippers of the beaux were made so low, that little more than their toes were protected by the instep; and this was completely covered by a plated buckle.

The lasses in those days, instead of being brought up to the piano, were taught the management of an instrument equally soothing, and generally much more agreeable to the head of the family—namely, the spinning wheel. As the whole of the household linen, as well as blankets, were home-made, a good supply of these articles was a matter of honest pride with the mother and daughters of a family.

HOUSEHOLD ARRANGEMENTS.

The furniture in the houses of the working classes was not only scanty, but of a very humble description. The bed was generally formed in a recess, with doors in front, and boarded round. Being often shut up, and difficult to clean, they were very unhealthy; and soon became the stronghold of such numerous colonies of intruders, that the only effectual expedient to get rid of those nocturnal visitants was to burn them out, by throwing the wood work to the street and making a bon-fire of it. There was another common sort of bed, with four short posts, and wooden bottom. This, though of a rude appearance, was a much more healthy couch than the former. Two chairs, and a couple of rude stools, a large buffet stool for a table, together with a spinning wheel, completed their leading

articles of furniture.   A heather besom was the usual implement for
cleaning their houses—washing them being seldom thought of.   The
greater part of the laigh houses had earthen floors ; and in wet weather,
or when water was accidentally spilt upon them, they were very disagree-
able.   The houses of the middling classes, although better furnished,
were still but mean.   Even the higher class of merchants had few of
those conveniences now so generally diffused among all ranks of society.
Carpets were a luxury known but to a few, and this only for the parlour.   There was always a bed in the kitchen, and often three beds in
one sleeping apartment.   The houses of common labourers and tradesmen
consisted of a single room, and as there was no cellar attached, they were
rendered more dirty and uncomfortable than they otherwise might have
been.   One room paid a rent of from 20s. to 25s. a year.   Two rooms
and a closet were let for about 50s. ; and the largest flat for about £8 or
£10.

From what has been already stated, it is not to be supposed that the
inhabitants were very cleanly, either in their household arrangements, in
their habits, or their dress.   Shoes were seldom cleaned but on Saturday
night, when it was necessary to soften them with oil or grease.   In some
country places brogues were made of undressed leather, secured with
thongs instead of thread.   These were by no means waterproof : but this
was of little consequence, as the wearer had frequently to steep his
brogues to keep them supple.

Furnished lodging were very scarce.   A single room in a family might
be had, but good accommodation was extremely scarce.   The only genteel lodgings were in a flat above Mr Porteous' shop, to the west of the
Guard-vennel.   These were kept by one Samuel Sampson, and were generally occupied by the commanding officer of the regiment stationed in
Perth for the time being, which imparted a military air to this part of the
town.   The drums beat up from this point ; the regimental parade was
frequently twice a day on the street ; and a couple of sentinels were here
continually on duty.

As the conduct of this Mr Samuel Sampson latterly made a considerable
noise in the town, a brief notice of the matter may not here be out of
place :—In the year 1765, he came down from London, and, assuming an
imposing style, with gold laced hat, and every thing corresponding, he
was looked upon as a man of superior fortune. He bought the flat already
mentioned, with one of the shops below, and vault beneath, and commenced business in the haberdashery line, in a style of great ostentation.   Every thing appeared to flourish.   The family lived high, dres-

sed well, and their house was furnished out in the first style of elegance ; but the certain fate awaited him of those who think all they have is their own. He stopped payment, and with the payment the business stopped likewise. He contrived, however, to retain the house and shop, as well as the furniture, and was thus enabled to let superior lodgings.

Sampson, after this change in his affairs, began to sell fishing tackle, and continued in this line several years, seldom appearing on the street ; and caused no little wonder among the gossips of the day, as to how he could maintain his family upon such slender means. This mystery was at last accidentally explained. One of the neighbouring merchants having met with a publican in Bridgend, they proposed taking their *eleven hours*, then a very common practice. Some black beer having been brought in, the landlord mentioned that he had got a capital bargain of it from Sampson. On the other expressing surprise at this, the publican said that he considered Sampson to be an extensive dealer, as he had frequently got bargains of different articles from him. It struck the merchant that all was not right, and immediately on his return he communicated to Mr Porteous what he had learned. A minute search was made by Mr Porteous, who had repeatedly missed articles which had been carried off from time to time. An opening was discovered in the brick partition wall, by which his cellar was entered from Sampson's vault ; and when the purpose was effected, the bricks were very accurately replaced. In this way had Sampson plundered his neighbour for years, and supported a family in idleness. He was apprehended, and lay in jail for nearly a year; when he was liberated on agreeing to leave the country.

DIET.

We frequently hear the "good old times" so highly praised, that one might be led to suppose that our ancestors lived at their ease, without labour or care, and fared sumptuously every day. The real state of the case, however, was very different. In the middle of the last century the labouring classes lived very poorly. The breakfast consisted of porridge or brose, with skimmed milk, or ale ; their dinner usually of water kail ; that is, green kail and other vegetables boiled with field pease and groats—barley not being then in use. Nettles were frequently used instead of greens. Pease bannocks were eaten with this mess to add nourishment to the meal. The supper consisted of sowens or brose. Occasionally a little flesh meat was procured for the Sabbath day. There is a local proverb, " As auld's the Muirton kail," the origin of which is now almost forgotten. It arose from some miserly farmer in this quarter being in the continual practice of adding the remains of the one day's

kail to the next day's pottage. A dispute arising on the subject between
him and his servants, it was proved in court that the kail were seven
years old. Brochan, or thick gruel, was rather a favourite supper, and
was also often taken to dinner.   During the salmon fishing season the
back bones of the fish, which were extracted in preparing them for the
London market, supplied a grateful addition to the dinner table of a
great portion of the inhabitants.   Although most families had a garden,
yet little else was cultivated than green kail.   These were in daily use,
and formed a principal ingredient in the celebrated Scottish dish of kail
brose.   This mess, was prepared by pouring a quantity of *kail* upon a
cog of oatmeal. It was truly a coarse repast; and might vie, in this respect,
with the celebrated Spartan black broth.   About the year 1750, the vegetables now in common use were so scarce, that when the Circuit Court
sat, the innkeepers had to get carrots and onions from Dundee.

The more wealthy breakfasted on porridge, dined on broth and meat,
and took porridge or sowans to supper.   There was generally an addition
of bread and cheese, or cold meat, to the morning meal.   One of the Provost's wives was such a rigid economist, that a servant lad played off a
practical joke one morning by way of revenge.   He poured a quantity of
water into the beds of the servants, and then asserted that it was in consequence of the watery diet upon which they were fed, that the beds were
in that state.   The story getting wind, the honest Provost was so affronted, that he ordered sowans to be for ever discarded from the supper table.

About the year 1760, bakers only heated their ovens twice a week ; as
loaf-bread was never used by the bulk of the people, their principal business lay in baking oat-cakes.   The practice being to return so many cakes
for each peck of meal brought in ; the surplus being a perquisite to the
bakers' men, who disposed of it to customers of their own.

It was then customary to lay in a mart ; or, flesh-meat sufficient for the
winter's supply. This was generally done by a number of families joining
for an ox, and dividing the carcase according to their wants. By this means,
it was procured rather cheaper, costing them about three-half-pence a
pound.   But the superior advantages which the regular dealer now affords
the public, of a fresh supply at all times, and a choice of quality and price,
has entirely done away with the old system.

At this time, white fish were very scarce. They were generally brought
from St. Andrews in creels, upon horseback ; but the distance of carriage,
and the state of the roads, raised the price far beyond the reach of the
labouring man. The fish cadgers only came occasionally ; when they frequently had a anker of gin concealed below the fish, by way of helping their

trade. In the spring, boats arrived at the north shore, with salted haddocks and codlings. The wives of the fishermen accompanied them, and hawked the fish from door to door.

It has been already stated, that there were about sixty brewers in town; each kept one or two men, who were boarded in the house. They were a set of stout jovial fellows, always ready for a row. Their most esteemed accomplishment, however, was their skill in brewing ale, which was greatly relished by all classes, and was sold at a *very fair price;*—a *pundie*, which contained nearly a choppin, was retailed out of the house at a halfpenny; and before tea became fashionable, was in high favour with the wives. Such was its efficacy, that a few applications to the pundie was apt to infringe the rules of decorum. In the house, this beverage cost a penny the bottle; and a more potent infusion was sold at twopence. To these halcyon days, when a company could enjoy themselves a whole evening at a penny a head, the octogenarian may look back with unavailing regret. Who that has visited the Turk's Head of an evening, and tasted Luckie Kettles' extra, and her salt herring and oat cakes, can ever forget the happiness and the devotion of the company in applying themselves to the business of the evening. Every body in Perth, whether soldier or civilian, knew Lucky Kettles; and her praises were sung, and her cheer extolled, by all who had ever the felicity of her acquaintance.

London porter became a favourite among the higher classes for their forenoon refreshment. It would appear that business was rather dry work in those days. It is said the old Red Lion alone sold a hogshead of porter every nine days. This trade began to fall off about the year 1790; the bottle was sold in the house for 3½d. After the business fell into the hands of small retailers, the article was generally adulterated with beer.

If it be true that an article becomes good and cheap in proportion to the demand, there must have been a great deal of spirits consumed. Highland whisky sold at a shilling the Scotch pint, and received especial patronage as a morning dram. This was a very general indulgence. The Indian was a moderate man who wished his throat were a mile long, that he might taste the rum all the way. Many of our worthies would have had no objections though the morning had lasted until night, if they could have drank whisky all the time. An old flesher, who was rather remarkable for his attachment to an early stimulant, always observed, as he drained the glass, " I have taken it off, as it is my *morning;*" he was often known to drink eight or ten before breakfast. The *morning,* was necessary to restore their nerves; a walk was taken, perhaps the length

D

of the Inch head, or Queen Mary's well, in order to qualify their morning ; when probably an additional dose would be taken to overcome the
fatigue of their walk.　Even many of the gudewives kept a private bottle ;
and as it was esteemed a specific for almost all the ills of life, it is little
wonder if they occasionally exceeded in their potations.　Some of these
dram drinkers were original characters.　One Patrick B——, a glazier,
had a houf in a merchant's back shop, where a knot of the same kidney
daily met for their morning tipple.　Patrick was never hindmost.　Either
from a matter of conscience, or in order to protract the pleasure, Patrick,
before taking his glass, always poured out a long discourse by way of
asking a blessing ; and then sat resolutely till breakfast time, when he
was generally as blind as an owl.　To such a length was the practice
carried in this shop, that the mistress, in the hope of getting rid of the
evil, induced her husband to give up the sale of spirits ; but this had little
effect ; the clique smuggled in the whisky, and persevered in their
habits till the end of the chapter.　Numbers of the rich and respectable
merchants thus tippled away their fortune and their lives ; and many who
might have lived in affluence, died in poverty and disease.

About the year 1765, tea began to be introduced ; and if it has promoted the change which has since taken place in the character, habits, and
social comforts of the people, we may hail it as one of the greatest blessings which commerce ever bestowed upon mankind.　At first it was
taken only by stealth.　The tea equipage was placed in the press, and
the goodwife, as she took the forbidden cup, stood with the door in her
hand, to be ready to shut it on the approach of any one.

It was long before the tea table assumed its present attractive elegance.
The first idea of making tea, appears to have been taken from a recipe
for preparing beat cabbage ; the *infusion* being thrown away, and the
boiled leaves retained for use, to be eaten with a slice of butter.　The
first tea dishes that appeared were an extremely coarse cream coloured
ware.　Indian china was excessively dear—the price of half a dozen cups
and saucers being from 20s to 30s ; the price of a tea-pot was half a guinea.
About 1774, Staffordshire ware appeared ; and the vast improvement
which skill and enterprise introduced into this manufacture, soon expelled
the Indian china from the market.

The writer recollects some amusing specimens of early tea drinking.　An
Ochil laird, who was in the habit of attending Perth market with butter
and cheese, breakfasted one morning in his father's house.　This laird
was quite a specimen of a class which has since become extinct, or
greatly modified ; and therefore merits a description.　His figure was tall
and gaunt ; his long grey hair flowed over his shoulders, and his rough

beard had been trimmed with a pair of shears; his dress was a suit of hodden grey, spun and dyed in the family; the shoes, of strong neat leather, were fastened with large brass buckles; the coat and waistcoat made in the fashion already described, exposed his long bare neck; with the shirt made of coarse tweeling, fastened with a button. John having been desired to help himself, commenced by cutting a lump of butter, which he proceeded to spread on a slice of bread, with his thumb, first taking the precaution to lubricate it well with spittle, to prevent the butter adhering to it; he then began to sup the tea with a spoon, in the manner of soup. A wag of a chapman who happened to be present, said, "Hout man, John, that's no the way to drink tea. Take the saucer to your head, and drink it as you see me do." John being thus corrected, conceived that the fashion was to drank the beverage after the manner of ale; and, accordingly, taking up the cup, drank their healths round; and an interchange of compliments was continued till they rose from the table. This worthy held a property in the Ochils that would now yield an income of £1000 a-year; and yet he came to Perth mounted on a galloway, with a straw saddle, and a pair of branks and hair tether for a bridle, and thus brought his butter and cheese to market. Having got breakfast, he generously invited those of the family who were of age, and the chapman, to drink his stable fee. Five individuals accordingly accompanied him, and John treated them to a bottle of ale, which cost him a penny; and this was all the recompense the public house received for stabling his horse.

About the year 1750, potatoes began to be cultivated in gardens, and were long esteemed a great rarity. As they became more plentiful they were eaten with the kail; partly as a substitute for the pease bannocks; and occasionally for supper. This, however, was only for a few months after harvest, as they were considered to be unfit for food after Candlemas. By the year 1770, potatoes were generally planted in gardens, in what was called lazybeds. Better modes of cultivation, and improved varieties, have since been gradually introduced, and the value of this important esculent vastly increased. The variety cultivated in this quarter for some years past, the celebrated Perthshire Reds, have never been surpassed, in their excellent qualities; and usually bring from five to ten shillings per ton more than any other potato in the London market.

THE TOWN'S MUIR.

The Town's Muir, near a mile west, was a large and beautiful wood, consisting of oak, elm, plane, birch, &c., and was intersected by fine avenues, which formed delightful walks for the citizens in the summer season.

There was a large park of full-grown Scots firs on the west side, from which the burghers were entitled to a cart load of trees for five shillings, on presenting a line from the Town Clerk to the wood-keeper. The last functionary kept a public-house, and was also fond of his glass. It was usual, when one went with a line, to have *three* carts instead of one in readiness, and while the purchaser was dozing the forester, and paying him the usual fee, the men got the carts loaded and driven away. One Sabbath morning, about the year 1800, one of the fir parks was discovered to be on fire. The writer, at that time, dwelt on the hill of Kinnoul, and observed the fire from the eminence. He immediately hastened to town and informed the Magistrates, who were proceeding to church. The clergyman intimated to the congregation what had taken place, and recommended all who could render assistance to hasten to the spot. The flames by this time were spreading with great rapidity, and presented a very magnificent spectacle. It was with great exertions the fire was got under. On the west side there was a large quarry, which was long wrought for the Perth buildings, but has of late been discontinued, from the stone being apt to moulder away with the weather. By the side of the quarry, there is a shaft which had been put down in search of coal, about 70 years ago. The workmen had succeeded in reaching a seam of coal, that, to all appearance, seemed well worth the working, when they all at once stopped short in their exertions ; and the report went at the time that they had been bribed by the Fife colliers, who did not at all relish the prospect of the citizens shaking off their ancient allegiance to them. Below this spot a little, there is an excellent spring, which used to be in great request with the good-wives of Perth, on account of its supposed superior properties in the making of tea. At the present time, the wood has almost entirely disappeared. The grounds were feued out at the beginning of this century, at a rate equivalent to the value of two bolls of wheat per acre ; and several handsome country seats have since been built upon them.

BIRTHS.

When the inlying approached, a notice was sent to all the gossips, requesting them to repair forthwith, and give their presence at the birth. The house, of course, was very soon crowded to excess, so that, in addition to the pangs of labour, the poor woman had to endure the noise and heat occasioned by such an assemblage. The child brought to light in health, was rolled up in bandages, as tight as a post, with the arms fastened down by the sides as carefully as if they were to be pinioned there for life. This accomplished, preparations were next made for *the merry meat.* A large pot was put on the fire, with plenty of butter, flour, bread, ale, and sugar, from which a strong pudding was made, and served up to the company. Then the pot was filled with ale, brandy, and sugar, with the addition of a small quantity of bread, and the beverage thus formed, termed *hot pint,* was served about, until the whole, both men and women, were tolerably elevated.

The baptism was also an important ceremony. A young woman carried the child, accompanied by a train of followers, provided with an abundant supply of oat cakes and cheese. A liberal allowance was given to the first person they met, and the rest was distributed, as far as it went, to all and sundry who came in the way. Much importance was attached to the person who chanced to be the *first foot,* his luck being supposed to influence in some mysterious manner, the prosperity of the child. At the return from the church, another feast took place; and to so great a pitch was this absurd practice carried, that numbers of the poor people were literally ruined by the expence it occasioned. The general introduction of tea drinking exploded the use of butter-saps and hot pints, and the presence of numbers were gradually and wisely dispensed with.

The baptism always took place in the church; the minister seldom inquired the name till he was about to confer it. On one occasion, a Highlandman had determined to call his child after Prince Ferdinand, a great warrior at the time. When asked for the name, he had either forgot it, or mispronounced it; for the clergyman, thinking that he meant to name his child after some of his Gaelic ancestors, christened it " F–rtin Andrew," by which mortifying appellation the young hero was ever after distinguished. To avoid mistakes of this nature, one clergyman never named the children he baptised. The plan of handing up the name written on a slip of paper obviated this difficulty; although in one instance it was productive of a somewhat ridiculous mistake : On the occasion of getting any new article of dress, it was customary for the drouthy cronies to exact a certain donum—on the payment of which the owner was exempt from farther annoyance : the article was then said to be *sealed.* An individual who had mustered an addition to his wardrobe, in order to improve his personal appearance at his child's christening, when the minister asked the name, he in mistake handed up a document certifying that his new coat had been duly *sealed* the previous evening. On another occasion, a man presented a merchant's account instead of the child's name. The clergyman being an eccentric character, read aloud the first item, " Twa ells and a half o' plaiding!" exclaiming, " wha ever heard o' such a name for a bairn ?"

In the country parishes, the invitations to the birth extended many miles—and for this purpose all the horses in the neighbourhood were put in requisition to fetch the howdie and other wives. Similar fare was here customary as in the town, only rather more substantial ; with a liberal allowance of butter saps, hot pints, and Highland whisky. As already observed, the introduction of tea has greatly abated these scenes of gormandizing.

MARRIAGES.

The celebration of the marriage rites among the lower orders in Perth, was much the same as the ceremonial which prevails in the country parishes to this day. The requisite supply of sheets and blankets having been spun and wove, the parties repaired to a public house, when an elder was sent for, to draw up the marriage contract. The parties were then proclaimed three separate Sabbath days ; and the wedding was usually deferred till the following Friday. On the Wednesday, the bride invited a party of her friends, and the bridegroom, accompanied by the best man, did the same. Thursday was occupied in sending home the bride's plenishing, which was done with as much pomp as possible. It usually consisted of a chest, containing sheets and blankets, and another containing body clothes ; an aumry, or large press, in two divisions ; a chest of drawers; a reel ; a spinning wheel, with a rock of lint decorated with ribbons ; and a quantity of meal, butter and cheese, with other articles according to their circumstances. In the evening, the young friends of the parties assembled at their respective houses to perform the ordeal of feet washing ; a ceremony which afforded ample scope for fun and frolic.

On the day appointed, when all was ready, the bridegroom set out for the residence of the bride, accompanied by his friends, who made a formal procession with him through the streets, preceded by an avant courier, designated " The Send," whose office was to herald their approach, and prepare the party of the bride for their reception. When both parties met, the whole company, men and women, sometimes to an incredible number, set off in regular procession to the minister's house, and returned in the same order, though they were often made to pay dear for all this idle pomp and parade, by enduring the bad usage which the blackguard urchins of the town never failed to inflict upon them, so often as a favourable opportunity occurred. Latterly, a party of this description might just as well have stood the pillory as walked the streets ; and the practice, by and bye, fell into disrepute. The festivities of the evening were conducted with a great deal of noisy hilarity.

There was three different kinds of weddings : First, what was called a *free wedding*, to which only a few select friends were invited, and where the guests were not allowed to be at any expence. The *dinner wedding*, where the dinner was provided by the marriage party; the company paying for the drink and the fiddler; and the *penny wedding*, which was of frequent occurrence, and often produced a tolerably round sum for the young couple. The bridegroom provided a great quantity of eatables and drinkables, and opened the door to all and sundry. Each guest gave a shilling for his dinner, and paid for his drink, at a rate sufficient to yield more than a reasonable profit; so that, where the company was numerous, there were frequent instances of persons who married without means, realising a sum from the festivities of the wedding, sufficient to furnish a house, or give them a fair commencement in trade.

The country weddings were celebrated in a manner similar to those in the towns; only the invitations were more numerous. Sometimes the whole parish were invited; and when the company had far to ride, the cavalcade had a very imposing appearance. Many of the farmers had their wives mounted behind them, and the lads their sweethearts.— The moment the bride started, all the old shoes about the house were thrown after her, fire arms were discharged, and the gridiron was rung with a thundering noise. There was a halt made at every public house on the way, and a quantity of spirits distributed; and the gridiron was again in requisition at their departure. But the most extravagant custom was that of riding the broose,—a practice replete with hazard, and often attended with serious accidents. When the returning party approached within a mile or two of the bridegroom's house, the more reckless and better mounted set off on a sort of steeple chase; the winner having the honour of welcoming the wedding party with a dram.

The writer was present at a scene of this kind at Fossaway. The bride's house was on one side of the Rumbling Bridge, and the bridegroom's on the other, so that the company had to pass it on their way home. At this time the bridge had no ledge, and was scarcely broad enough to admit the passage of a cart; and the danger was further increased by an abrupt turn of the road, close upon the bridge. The party being a little elevated, a number set off for the broose, before crossing this dangerous pass. It was truly terrifying to see the horses, even those which were double mounted, rushing across this awful chasm, which is upwards of two hundred feet in depth. There were two cripple dominies present, one of whom distinguished himself on the occasion. He was mounted on a strong horse, with his wife behind him. In rushing past a rival in the race, the wife unfortunately lost her hold. He was called on to stop and take up his wife, but he pushed on, crying out " Let the devil stop and take up his own." The dominie's horse,

like the post-boy's in John Gilpin, right glad to be relieved of so much of
its burden, sprang forward with increased speed, and succeeded in win-
ning the broose. Fortunately the wife had received little injury, and was
taken up behind one of the more sedate of the party.

After supper, dancing commenced in the barn. During the evening,
vast numbers from neighbouring places arrived to witness the dancing,
who had no connection with the marriage party ; but who, according to
custom, were always made welcome. On Saturday, there was a meeting
of the more intimate friends who had been present at the wedding, and
the day was usually devoted to festivity. On Sunday, a large party assembled to kirk the bride ; the bride's-maid carried a lap full of bread and
cheese, which was distributed to all whom they met. Those who had been
at the wedding, usually paid a visit to the young couple in the course of
a few days, bringing a present of some article to help the household
establishment.

At all wedding dinners, the leading article of the feast uniformly
consisted of a large dish of kail; the people of this county being
as much attached to this favourite mess as their neighbours, the re-
nowned kail suppers of Fife ; and the connoisseurs were lavish in their
praises of the cook, according to the quality of the broth. On one occasion, the damsel to whom the preparation of the kail was committed, unfortunately, instead of leeks, put into the pot a quantity of a strong
purgative plant, called horse gladdening, formerly used as a medicine
for cattle. The mistake was not noticed at the time ; but some hours
afterwards, when the guests had ridden a mile or two on their return
home, the dose began to operate as a brisk cathartic. Numbers had to
abandon their horses altogether, and, in order to be ready for any sudden onset, proceeded homeward with their inexpressibles across their
shoulders. But the parties who suffered most, was the unfortunate bride
and bridegroom, who, according to the established practice, had been
locked up in their bed-chamber for the night ; and who found escape alike
impossible, either from the confinement, or the unremitting attacks of the
enemy.

BURIALS.

When a person appeared to be dying, intimation was sent both to the
relatives and friends, and to all who had visited during the distress ; when
an immense turn-out flocked to be present at the separation between soul
and body, thus inflicting on the dying man, the additional sufferings arising from noise and a corrupted atmosphere. During the interval between
death and interment, the house was full of visiters from morning to night,

all of whom were regaled with bread, cheese, ale, and spirits, A few sat up and watched the corpse during the night. Funeral letters were not yet in use; but intimation of the decease, and time and place of inter- ment, was given in the fashion which, until a very recent period, was uni- versally prevalent in the Scottish Burghs. The bellman went round the town, ringing his bell, and occasionally halting to make some such an- nouncement as the following:—" Men and brethren, I let you to wot, that our brother, A. B., departed this life on Thursday last, and is to be interred on Sunday evening, at ——, when the company of all his bre- thren is expected."

Merchants and others, who had a death in their family, suspended all business from the time of the decease until after the funeral; and all workmen, whether employed on the premises or otherwise, were, during this period, thrown idle. About the year 1784, when Mr Robert Mor- rison the postmaster died, the post-office, in conformity to the above cus- tom, was shut. An honest Highlander, who had come a distance of several miles for his master's letters, finding how matters stood, anxiously en- quired if there were no other shops in town where they *sold* letters.

The majority of the funerals took place in the afternoon of Sunday; during the forenoon of which day, two men stood at each of the church doors, inviting all and sundry to attend. A company called mourners, too, went round the streets in a body on the day of the funeral, for what precise purpose, other than the love of show, it would be difficult to ex- plain. All this idle parade has long since disappeared, and no one can regret that the improved practice of later times has substituted a more pri- vate, and infinitely more becoming ceremonial in its place.

At country funerals, the company were invited a couple of hours before the time appointed for removing the corpse, which afforded time for re- freshment, and a few words of spiritual exhortation. Before proceeding with the service, some individual, who was understood to have the gift of prayer, was respectfully requested to ask a blessing. Diffidence was al- ways pleaded; but when some of these champions of the faith had once fairly begun and warmed on the subject, they would continue to hold forth for half an hour at a stretch, and unfold a complete body of divinity.

On the occasion of the funeral of an elderly lady, who had left consi- derable property to two sons, the glass went round till the company were a little ebrious; when some one hinted that it was time to proceed, as they had a considerable way to ride. Orders were accordingly given to get out the horses; the company mounted and set out, and proceeded a couple of miles towards the place of interment, before it was discovered that they had left the old lady behind.

Until a recent period, the bulk of the people attended funerals in their common clothes, if the funeral occurred on a week day. Many of the operatives attended just as they left the work-shop, without donning their coat, or doffing their night-cap ; or even staying to wash their face, or put off their apron ; exhibiting none of those external marks of respect for the deceased which now prevail ; and which tend, in some degree, to alleviate the sorrow of the mourning relatives.

RESURRECTIONISTS.

The trade of body-snatcher is not a new one in this quarter. The remains of those who died suddenly, or had committed suicide, were so eagerly sought after by the disturbers of the dead, that an idea very generally prevailed amongst the more simple of the natives, that the doctors employed the *fat* of these subjects in the preparation of those nauseous mixtures which the empirics pronounced to be infallible remedies for every thing but death. Hence, when any sudden decease occurred, it was customary to fill the coffin with quick lime, in order to accelerate the process of decomposition ; or otherwise to watch the grave for some weeks.

A young man had recently commenced business as a wright :—It having been surmised that he was connected with an attempt to steal a body from the Grey Friars, the fury of the inhabitants was so aroused, that he had to leave the town for some time ; the only thing which presented itself on which to wreak their vengeance, was the offender's new sign board, which was pulled down, and carried in triumph to the burying ground ; and hung up on a tree near the spot, to act, in the manner of a scar crow, as a warning to others.

On one occasion, a young bride drowned herself in the river Earn.— Shortly after interment, it was discovered that the body had been lifted. Her uncle, a stout old carle, came into Perth in quest of it. Several weavers receiving notice of his errand, a very numerous party was soon on the look-out, and succeeded in discovering the body in an old malt barn. The remains of the unfortunate girl were wrapped up in a plaid, and laid across the horse before the old man ; who was convoyed several miles on his way home by many hundreds of the inhabitants.

About the year 1784, a young man, the son of a widow, was out late one night, and got into a quarrel with a number of individuals, who so abused the youth, as to deprive him of life. It is not likely, however, that they were aware of the extent of the injury committed, as they were carrying him home to his mother's, when overtaken by a young man who had but recently come to town ; and who had, that night, been assisting a brother in some smuggling affair. When the party arrived at the door, the body was placed up against it ; and, having rapped, they ran off, leaving the stranger behind them, who had no idea that the deceased had been more than slightly injured, until the old woman opened the door, when the corpse fell at her feet. The mother's shrieks, and the noise of the fall, immediately alarmed the neighbours. The stranger, who was instantly secured, was absolutely confounded at what he saw, and could give no account of the transaction. He was committed to jail for the murder, and long confined in the laigh iron house ; but as no clue was ever obtained to the real murderers, and as nothing transpired to criminate the prisoner, he was at length permitted to enlist in the artillery where there is reason to fear he soon met with that fate from the bullet, which he so narrowly escaped from the gibbet. The body of the widow's son having been buried, the doctors' apprentices determined to obtain it. Spade, crow bar, and rope being provided, a hole was dug at the head of the grave, till they reached the coffin, the head of which they forced in, and were in the act of hauling up the corpse, when a number of the inhabitants burst in upon them, and put them to flight. On another occasion of body stealing, a scuffle ensued, in which one of the resurrectionists stabbed a man in the belly with a knife. The wound, though not immediately fatal, was the cause of the unfortunate man's death. The assassin, however, escaped, and was never after heard of.

Another instance occurred, where the corpse was detected after it had been removed to the street. The resurrectionists having placed it, as they imagined, beyond danger, left it doubled up on a barrow, under a covering at the side of the wall of Gowrie house, and adjourned to a notorious house at the foot of South-street. Their motions had, however, been observed by some boatmen who had just come up with the tide. They removed the body, and one of their number assumed its place. The violators of the grave having screwed up their courage by a hearty refreshment, were proceeding with the barrow, when one inquired if they would take up by the South-street? The boatman, beginning not altogether to relish his new position, at once got rid both of them and the difficulty, by roaring out, "No, by —! you'd better take the Watergate."

RELIGIOUS HABITS.

About eighty years ago, the manners of the people were extremely simple, as well as their dress and diet. Their religious sentiments were strong, and the sacred observance of the Sabbath was rigidly maintained. The attendance of the family at church was regular ; and in the evening, the whole family, servants and apprentices, assembled in the parlour, and engaged in reading the scriptures, gave notes of the sermons they had heard during the day, and were examined from the catechism ; and the evening was concluded with family worship. Every master held it a solemn duty to look to the moral conduct of his servant, and particularly as to his behaviour on the Sabbath. To stroll about the fields, or even to walk upon the inches, was looked upon as extremely sinful, and an intolerable violation of the fourth commandment. Parents would occasionally take their children the length of their gardens; and, after whiling away an hour amidst serious and profitable reflections, return with them; by this means keeping their family under their eye the whole day. This respect for the sanctity of the Sabbath was, if possible, even greater in the country, until the servants were expelled from the family hearth by the degrading bothy system. The intercourse of the clergyman with his flock was much more familiar, and the pastoral visitations more frequent; each minister making a point of calling upon his parishioners at least once a year, and examining them upon the state of their religious knowledge, and imparting, where necessary, consolation and advice. At the conclusion of these periodical visitations, a public examination of the parishioners took place in the church; or, in country parishes, at different houses, which were intimated from the pulpit. The shrewdness and extent of their acquirements in the knowledge of divine truth, exhibited on on these occasions, was remarkable.

There were numbers, both old and young, whose slender acquirements in the more abstract points of controversy, made them desirous of avoiding these examinations, and who, when caught, made but a sorry appearance. The country clergyman intimated one Sabbath from the pulpit, that on the following Tuesday there would be a diet of examination held in the house of John B——, and that all the cottars were expected to attend. At the time appointed, the parties assembled, and the minister considering it most respectful, began by examining the head of the family. John being rather an indifferent hand at these matters, and, of course, not much relishing close personal inquiry, replied, "Hout, sir, ye ken that yoursel' langsyne! I'm gaun awa to see if Janet has the kail ready." John accordingly made off, and took care to keep out of sight till the business was over. During the examination the minister asked a girl, "Who was the father of liars?" which she at once pronounced to be Pate Hallam the soutar. This worthy was famous in the district for his Munchasen exploits, and miraculous stories; one of which was, that he walked into Perth, one morning, a distance of eleven miles, in two hours, although the road was so covered with ice, that he slipped *two* steps backward for every *one* he went forward. He had a ready knack at saying graces; and such a gift of prayer, that at "weddings and draidgies" few could stand before him. Even the minister was not fond of meddling with Pate at the periodical meetings, as he had the tact to elude the questioning; and usually ended by putting Mess John himself through a pretty severe examination.

From numerous anecdotes, it would appear that the evening exercises were occasionally conducted with less ceremony than regularity. On one occasion, this gifted individual had started the psalm tune on a new key, when the colly dog, aroused by the unusual harmony, immediately joined chorus, pouring forth a volume of that peculiar sound emitted by the canine species, when excited by a sympathetic chord. Irritated beyond measure by this unseemly accompaniment, Pate made a vigorous stroke at the offender, exclaiming, " Od's curse ye for a devil!" but colly, who had more than one of his faculties employed, was too quick for him; and his knuckles came in contact with the temper pin of the spinning wheel, with a force that made the blood spring. Peter was occasionally so far overcome by carnal frailty as to fall into a state of obliviousness while in the midst of his devotions; but, on recovering himself, he would wrestle powerfully for these intromissions.

There was another worthy, a bachelor, a painter to profession, and an amateur in the fine arts, particularly in the art of cookery, to which the sleek plumpness of his person bore ample testimony. Having taken a country lad, named Andrew, for an apprentice—after the other parts of his duty were detailed, he was directed to a closet where he might retire in the evening, to supplicate for every good and perfect gift. One evening on entering the little sanctuary, Andrew's olifactories encountered the savoury steams of a roasted hen, which had been just prepared and laid by for his master's supper. It is probable that Andrew had also acquired a relish for the beautiful—he first admired, and then eat up the whole fowl. When his master returned, Andrew could not deny his agency in the annihilation of the hen. " What business had you in the closet at all, sir?" was sharply demanded. " I went there to pray," replied the humbled penitent. " To pray! Pray where you like, my man," replied the exasperated painter, " but I'll take care after this, that you'll never pray within reach of my supper."

Bailie Y——, of Perth, was also a very rigid observer of the Sabbath evening exercises, to a degree which rendered them rather irksome to the young people. There is generally a remedy to be found for every evil, when it becomes intolerable, from the insanity of " hereditary wisdom," down to the sanctimony of the bailie's exercises. One of his apprentices, afterwards distinguished by the title of the Black Prince, discovered rather an ingenious method of shortening the catechetical process : When the examination had proceeded a sufficient length, the young prince would start an objection to some point of the Bailie's doctrine ; when the worthy magistrate, being more passionate than powerful in argument, would suddenly put an end to the reading in the dumps.

In spite of these irregularities, the people, both old and young, were remarkable for their knowledge of the scriptures. At this period, the reading of the common people was limited to a few books of a religious character, such as the Bible, Confession of Faith, Shorter Catechism ; Boston's, Bunyan's, and Willison's works, and a few sermons. The lighter articles of literature were on a par with John Cheap and Leper the Tailor ; with a miscellaneous collection of ballads. There were no popular works on science, of a nature to amuse and instruct, within reach of the masses of the people ; or calculated to improve their social or intellectual condition.

KING'S BIRTH DAY.

George the Third's birth day was celebrated on the fourth of June.— This being the most pleasant season of the year, it was held by every body as a holiday. Steam-boats and railways being yet among the mysteries of futurity, those who were disposed to ruralize, proceeded to the country on foot, with their families, to get curds and cream. Delightful walks were also supplied by the Town's-muir, and Craigie-hill ; and the magnificent prospect from Kinnoul-hill, was open to the public, till the passing of the Reform Bill ; when, by a curious coincidence, this walk was shut up exactly at the time the elective franchise was thrown open to the people. Early in the morning of the royal nativity, the fronts of the houses were profusely decorated with boughs and flowers, the principal streets presenting the appearance of an avenue in a wood. At twelve o'clock, the bells were set a ringing ; the great guns fired a royal salute ; the military fired a *feu de joie* ; and the whole town turned out to see the sights, and give vent to their ardent feelings of loyalty. These were the days, when the people had not acquired the felicity of making themselves miserable ; when the cry for Reform and Retrenchment was not heard ; and when every sound politician judged of the prosperity of the state by the tension of his doublet.

In the afternoon, the Magistrates assembled in the Council Room, where the officers of the troops, the officers of customs, and a numerous company of strangers and gentry, were invited to join in drinking his Majesty's health. A band of music attended in the anti-room ; and a body of troops was stationed in the street, who fired a volley every toast. No cost was spared on wines and sweetmeats ; and each officer was presented with a burgess ticket.

By four o'clock, the High-street was completely filled with young men and boys, with their pockets well charged with squibs, crackers, and skyrockets; and an incessant discharge of fire-works and fire-arms, of every kind and calibre, was kept up for the remainder of the evening, to the inexpressible joy and delight of the inhabitants: even for many previous and succeeding evenings, the quantity of powder exploded on the streets was immense. By and bye, the splendour of these exhibitions, and the ardour of the people greatly abated. Democrats began to make their appearance; dead cats and basses were hurled about, and dirt thrown; and the birth day fell into great disrepute. These proved the fruitful source of bickerings and heart-burnings, till the authorities were often under the necessity of endeavouring to put a stop to the fire-works altogether. The inhabitants of Perth have been admirers of the wonders of hydraulics, from the introduction of the first force pump, down to the celebrated display under the patronage of the late Magistrates. When *fire-works* were interdicted on the birth day, the *water-works* were drawn in triumph through the streets; and every well dressed person that appeared at a window, was instantly overwhelmed with a torrent of water.

THE TOWN PIPER.

Down to the year 1800, in addition to a drummer, the town had an official under the above title; the last functionary was known by the appellation of Johnny Smout, and was famous for his skill in playing the Irish pipes. Johnny's official costume was a scarlet cloak, with wide sleeves and white cuffs; the sleeves hanging down loose by the side of his arms, and the pipes were carried under the cloak. The principal duty of Johnny Smout appeared to be, in conjunction with Geordie Munro, or, as he was called, the Rough Black Dog, to go round the town every morning at five o'clock, summer and winter, and disturb all and sundry with their ill-timed harmony. There was also an evening performance at seven o'clock, when these musicians were always accompanied by an immense number of idle women and children. After Munro's death, one Sandy Bell, a regular bred drummer, succeeded him, when the improved quality of the music created quite a sensation in the town, as they paraded the streets, playing Rosslyn Castle, and other old Scottish tunes. An officer, who had been in the Indian War against Hyder Alley, related the following anecdote in allusion to Johnny's pipes:—As the soldiers were ascending the Ghauts, a piper struck up an old Scottish air, when the officer heard one of the soldiers in his rear say to his neighbour, " L—d, man! does na' that mind you o' Johnny Smout in the Shoe-gate in the mornings?" The salary of the drummer and piper was three shillings a week each; in addition to which they realized a considerable sum by going through among the respectables with the drum and pipe on Handsel Monday.

NEW YEAR'S DAY

Has always been held in Scotland as a day of special hilarity. The festivities commenced on the evening of the last night of the old year. In addition to a sufficient supply of stimulants, each family provided a quantity of *carls*. These were oatmeal cakes of a triangular shape, prepared with treacle or other condiments. The whole circle of acquaintance visited for carls; and each individual had to sing for his supper, or at least for his cake. This practice has greatly fallen off; none but a rabble of children, called "Guisards," now maintain the custom. New Year's morning was ushered in by a dram from the gudewife's bottle. It was then the practice to wait up for what was called the cream of the well,—the fortunate damsel who succeeded in getting the first water of the year, being assured of a good husband before the end of it. The streets were crowded all night, by parties wishing to see what was going on, and by others on their way to call upon acquaintances. The ordinary restraints of society were thrown aside; and every man claimed the privilege of kissing any woman he chanced to meet. To this ancient and edifying practice, the whisky bottle came to be added, and the oblations of Bacchus were offered at the shrine of Venus. The changes which took place in trade about 1780, brought a great number of spinners and cloth printers to this neighbourhood, who introduced the custom of hot pints. On going to the houses of their friends, as first foot, they took with them a tea kettle full of a warm mixture of ale, whisky, and sugar; and as the visiter had also to do honour to the host's bottle, the parties, long before day-light, found they had taken rather more than enough.

Handsel Monday was the principal day with the working classes. By one in the morning the streets were in an uproar with young people, who appeared to consider themselves privileged to do whatever mischief they pleased. It was a constant practice to pull down sign boards, or any thing that came in the way, and make a large bonfire with them at the cross,—all being for the benefit of trade, and the support of the good old customs. Numbers of boys, belonging to the Glover Incorporation, were to be heard in every quarter selling small purses at a half-penny each; these were made of the parings of leather, and enabled the lads to gather something to hold Handsel Monday with. They were generally all sold off early in the morning. The tradesmen were all idle this day, and considered themselves entitled to handsel from their employers; and even from individuals in any way connected with the business. Thus the weavers, having received their handsel from the manufacturer, a deputation from the shop was sent to the wright who made their utensils; another to the reed-maker, and to the chandler who supplied them with candles; and a third to the company who boiled the yarn. The whole proceeds of these begging commissions were put together, and spent in the evening in a tavern.

Formerly, Christmas, as a period of festivity, was but little attended to, excepting among the Episcopalians. Latterly, as the above customs declined among the operatives, parties among the higher and middling classes, during the Christmas holidays, have rapidly increased.

PERTHSHIRE HUNT.

Horse racing and archery were formerly much practiced in this quarter. It is a well authenticated fact, that the affair of 1745 was concocted at Perth races, which, prior to that period, were attended by noblemen from all parts of the kingdom. The disastrous events of that year put a stop to these amusements, and scattered the Scottish gentry to different parts of the continent; the effects of which were felt for 30 years. About 1784, the exiled families began to return, and many of the forfeited estates being restored, a new impulse was given to the county. Many of the gentlemen formed themselves into a body, styled the Perthshire Hunt; and a pack of fox hounds was procured, and placed under the management of an experienced huntsman. Their meetings were held in October, and continued for a week, with balls and ordinaries every day. When the Caledonian Hunt held their meetings here, the assemblies continued for a fortnight. The present excellent race course was formed after the enlargement of the North Inch, and for a time the Perth Turf was among the best frequented in Scotland. Although races have continued to be held pretty regularly, they have lately greatly declined in point of attraction; seldom extending beyond two days, where they formerly occupied a week.

Many persons yet alive may recollect the stone at the foot of the South Inch, where the archers stood when they shot their arrows at the target on the scholars' knowe in front of Marshall Place. This ancient sport is now altogether unknown. The arrow, as a weapon of defence, by the altered practice of the age has long become useless; and as a game, it probably gave place to the discus and the golf; which, in their turn, have been doomed to give way to the more animated game of cricket, in which some of the Perth clubs have excelled.

RETRIBUTIVE JUSTICE.

During last century, several murders occurred in Perth, for which the perpetrators were not brought to account at an earthly tribunal; but which were followed by circumstances that might well lead to the conviction, that the commission of crime is visited by Divine retribution. During the unsettled period of the Rebellion, an English traveller on horseback, carrying a valise, arrived at a house in South-street, the second above the Meal-vennel. He was known to have entered the house; but man nor horse were ever seen afterwards. The landlord grew suddenly rich; and it was currently reported that the traveller had been murdered; but, owing to the troubled state of the country, the crime was never inquired into. Although human eye could not penetrate the mystery, the finger of Providence pointed to the deed. It was remarked, and acknowledged as a judgment, that the children of the family born after this event, were all insane; while those born previously were sound in body and mind. One of the daughters was afterwards well known in the town by the appellation of " Daft Lizzy Grant." Like the jewelled casket which was filled with worms and putrifying bones, Lizzy was remarkable for personal beauty; while of intellect she had little or none; and her moral faculties were so depraved, that she was incessantly committing petty thefts. After the old folks' death, the property passed into other hands. About the year 1808, the house was pulled down and rebuilt. In excavating the ground for vaults, a human skeleton was discovered under the spot occupied by the hearth-stone of the former kitchen.

About the year 1772, a son of Bailie Fife, (a very proud and arbitrary magistrate,) who had obtained a commission in the army, was on a visit to see him. Returning home with his gun one night, he encountered a man in one of the back passages leading to the Skinnergate. Some words having passed between them, young Fife, without the least hesitation, shot the man dead on the spot. When his trial came on, great exertions were made to get him off on the plea of insanity; and he was sentenced to confinement for life. He lay for some time in one of the Burgher rooms of the Jail, till his friends obtained a mitigation of the sentence, allowing him to be confined in his father's house. The public said, and firmly believed, that this was a judgment on the Bailie for his haughty cruel conduct on the bench. Be that as it may, his affairs did not prosper; and, after experiencing many difficulties, he died very poor.

A farmer of the name of Robertson, who had been in the habit of attending Perth markets, suddenly disappeared. He was last seen in life in the house of James Ross, brewer, in the Kirk-close. As it was known that he had that day received a considerable sum of money, it was believed that he had been robbed and murdered; and it was pretty generally surmised that Ross and his family were instrumental in his death. After some time the body was found in the river, but in a state which indicated that it had not lain in the water since the time of the decease. This circumstance was calculated to confirm suspicion; but although nothing more transpired to criminate Ross, his business declined every day. He became very poor; attempted to drown himself; and at length went mad; and was for years in a deplorable state, confined in a strait jacket, and tied down to his bed. His wife's sister, who lived in the house with them at the time Robertson went amissing, was seized with a strange distress, lost the ability of part of her body, and lay for years on the floor, a most deplorable object. On one occasion, when a clergyman was visiting Ross, he seemed inclined to unburthen his mind of something which appeared to lie heavy on his spirits. But the wife, observing this, stormed on the clergyman, for presuming to suppose her husband could have been guilty of any crime that required a confession. Another opportunity never occurred to get Ross to speak on the subject, and the wretched man went to his grave with his secret undisclosed;—the pangs of the parting hour being aggravated by the want of sympathy of his fellow men, and by the terrors of meeting an indignant God.

A publican in the Spey-gate having quarrelled with his wife, who had an infant in her arms at the time, aimed an angry blow at her, which struck and killed the child. He kept out of the way for some time, and escaped on board of a small vessel, about to proceed on her voyage. The vessel with all on board perished. A similar occurrence took place with a man of the name of Bell, who lived at the west end of the town. In a quarrel with his wife, he struck his infant a deadly blow. He fled to escape punishment, and joined the army on the continent; but that Power which can raise up a fly to execute his will, can never want an instrument of justice. One day, when the fugitive was leaning on his loaded gun, the piece went off, and blew out his brains.

MILITARY STATION.

Perth has been a military station since the Rebellion in 1745. Immediately after that period it was strongly garrisoned; and there was also an encampment of 5000 German troops formed upon the North Inch; the more effectually to overawe, and secure the submission of the country.— There are many persons still alive who may recollect the hollow parallel lines on the west side of the old Dunkeld road, which marked the ground of the encampment. As has been stated, when the Duke of Cumberland was here with the Royal army, the obsequious magistrates made him a present of Gowrie house, which, on his arrival in London, he sold to the Board of Ordnance for an artillery barracks. Thus the immediate effect of their conduct in giving away that which was not their own, was to circumscribe the liberties of the people. There were always one or two companies of artillery stationed here, from whence many hundreds of fine young men were sent up to the regiment. Some seasons they encamped on the South Inch, where they usually exercised, and frequently practised ball firing at a mark set up on the Friarton brae, where the Depot now stands.

During the German war, between 1750 and 1760, several regiments were embodied here, among which was a fine body of horse, called Keith's Light Dragoons. These troops were taught to leap high bars ; to swim the river ; and practised a great many clever manœuvres. The Rev. Mr Williamson of Auchtergaven, riding into town one review day, mounted on a *ci-divant* dragoon horse, entered the Inch at the White Dyke, as the kettle drum beat the charge ; the animal sprang forward, and when the line halted, the worthy minister was found in the front rank, with the loss of hat and wig.

At this period so little regard was paid to the liberty of the subject, that Provost Robertson of Tullibelton, secretly signed a warrant authorising the captain of the troops in town to seize upon, and impress the inhabitants for soldiers. The time chosen was that of a grand review on the north Inch. The day being particularly fine, and no one dreading danger, the concourse of people was very great. During this review one of the soldiers, who had omitted to return his ramrod to its place, shot a girl dead in her father's arms ; but the excitement produced by this accident was trifling, compared with what followed. When the review was nearly over, at an appointed signal, the soldiers sprang from their ranks, and each seized upon any man they could lay hold of. The guard houses and jail were immediately filled. Terror and dismay spread through the town, and the young men fled in every direction. It is probable that the burst of indignation produced throughout the country by this outrageous and tyrannical conduct, had led the ruling powers to question the *policy* of the business ; for when the captives came to be examined as to their fitness to carry arms, they were almost all let off on some plea or other. One or two good looking fellows whom they were loth to part with, were induced to enter the artillery. One of them, a weaver, of the name of Stewart, rose to be colonel commandant in the artillery. As it is seldom a private rises far from the ranks, it is probable the lustre of his advancement was intended to eclipse the disgrace of his impressment. During his mother's life, an annuity was remitted to her in proportion to his rise ; and he died during the late French war a lieutenant-general in the army. One hero being thought sufficient, others were discharged for unsoldier-like conduct.

The Provost, however, did not escape the just execrations of the inhabitants ; and he took the matter so much to heart, that he latterly became deranged in mind. His son, who proved to be even more insane than himself, made several attempts on his own life, and eventually succeeded.

During this war, the most unwarrantable means were adopted to fill up the army. Each parish was ordered to provide a certain number of men ; and these were selected, not by ballot, but by the arbitrary whim and caprice of the authorities. If any young man was accused of a natural child, or if any flaw could be found in his character, whether moral or political, he was instantly pitched upon and dragged away ; and, to prevent the possibility of escape, he was sent off immediately to the regiment abroad. This unnatural conscription rendered men callous to the yearnings of humanity : no appeal was listened to. The unfortunates were seized and sent off without a moment's notice ; although in many cases the heads of families, or the sole support of aged parents.

At the commencement of the late war, the artillery head quarters was removed to Leith fort. A detachment with four guns was still kept here, until government resolved to convert the old buildings into barracks for foot soldiers. The place was then new roofed and repaired, and the large halls were filled with beds. During the time the artillery lay here, the men were seldom changed, and they became in a manner associated with the place, and were much respected by the inhabitants. They messed together every day ; their broth was excellent, and many poor people were supplied with what was over. The large pot used for making their broth was hired at a penny a week, from an old man in the Watergate, who drew this sum for fifty years. One of their commanding-officers continued upwards of twelve years on the station.

About sixty years ago, an officer on duty here, of a witty but hasty disposition, employed Deacon Gibson to make a suit of clothes, to be ready for a dinner party. The deacon was reputed the first stitch in town, and was the most professional looking man imaginable. He wore, according to the custom of the trade at the time, a large cushion fastened on his sleeve, well stocked with the implements of the craft. His short snub nose stood sentry over a sharp chin ; his long slender neck was encased in a high white stock, and exhibited something of the appearance of a moulded candle. His legs had the true professional curve, and appeared as if fastened to his body like those of a Dutch doll ; and his spare visage was set off, surmounted by a full cut wig and cocked hat. The day and hour of dinner had arrived, and message after message had

been sent for the clothes, without obtaining any other satisfaction than an
assurance that they would be ready in a few minutes.   The captain,
fretting and fuming on account of the disappointment, had got
into a most uncontrollable rage, at the moment the deacon made his
his appearance with the suit.   Drawing his sword, he threatened instant destruction to the unfortunate fraction of humanity.   " Ay, ay,
sir," boldly replied the deacon, " would you draw upon an unarmed man ?
But I'm a dealer in sharps as well as yourself !   And if that's your cue,
here's at you !"   With that he whipt a needle from his sleeve, advanced
with a flourish upon the astonished officer, and fairly pinned him into a
corner.   The captain, perceiving the ludicrousness of his position, politely
begged pardon.   The story afforded a good laugh at the dinner table ;
and was a subject of lasting triumph to the deacon ; who declared, that
having defied all the *ghosts* in Perth, he was not to be daunted by mere
flesh and blood.

MEAL MOBS.

Between the years 1770 and 1777, there occurred a succession of bad
seasons and wet harvests ; and, as a natural consequence, provisions
were both dear and scarce, and of very inferior quality.   As yet little
advancement had been made in the knowledge of the advantages of commerce, and the interchange of commodities, which, by extending the
market, increases the production.   In consequence, the shipment of
grain was looked upon as most unwarrantable, and a direct infringement
of the rights of the population of the district.   Though a grain merchant might have imported fifty cargoes in the course of the season, if he
attempted to export one, he was marked out as an object of persecution.
On the first occurrence of scarcity, his effigy was paraded through the
town, and afterwards burnt before his door ; his windows broken ; and
sometimes the mob proceeded so far as to burst open the house, and
destroy every thing in it.   Even if a retailer was compelled to raise the
meal a penny per peck, he was liable to the same unpleasant distinction.
During Provost William Stewart's authority, Meal Mobs were frequent
and outrageous.   There were three worthies then alive who were particularly active in fomenting and heading these riots.   The masses, in
selecting their leaders, showed themselves above those little prejudices
connected with personal appearance, moral rectitude, or worldly circumstance.

The first, James Wilson, by trade a barber, was a tall, gaunt looking
personage, with a spare cadaverous visage ; knock-knee'd, and splay-foot-
ed ; he dressed in tawdry clothes, with tie-wig and cocked hat ; his shoes

often disencumbered of soles, and his stockings ornamented with needlework up to the knees. Wilson possessed that essential to every popular leader,—an unbounded stock of impudence ; he had also a good deal of satirical wit, and had made some appearance as a poet. In addition to his *barberous* performances, he carried on a considerable traffic in illegal marriages—saving the parties the expense of a journey to the famous Half-merk Kirk in Edinburgh ; or the no less notorious Whins of Falkland.

The second, Blair Flight, by trade a watchmaker, was an odd-looking figure. His countenance was of that description which indicates a mind capable of any mean action. Like Wilson, he had attained no little celebrity, for his facility in ratifying marriages ; and was at one time apprehended for this offence : but as many of the dissenting clergymen were in the habit of doing the same thing among their hearers, it was deemed imprudent to agitate the matter. Blair's exhortations on these occasions were somewhat original, and often tinctured with a strain of sarcasm. On one occasion, the writer's father witnessed the marriage ceremony of a couple who had come all the way from Cupar Fife. Blair assured them that marriage was no child's play ; but a thing that was to last for life. He continued—" You maun be good till her ; and she'll be kind to you. You maunna fight, nor kick up a dust like fools. Tak' her hand man. And to you, lassie, I wish a happy moment—an' that, I trew, it will not be lang till." Blair then received five shillings ; for which sum he thus made the girl an *honest* woman ; and her offspring was that night born within the pale of matrimony.

The third, Ned Keillor, like Tom Thumb, a little hero with a great soul. A weaver to trade, he stood, when his legs were out of the treddle hole, nearly five feet high. He wore a short round jacket, wide Dutch-fashioned breeches, a large broad blue bonnet, and leather apron. When excited, whether with liquor or otherwise, Ned had one of the most loquacious, unscraped tongues, that ever existed. Whenever he took a fancy for a jollyfication, he came down the town with a pipe in his cheek ; the circumstance of not having a farthing in his pocket never gave him a moment's difficulty. There were a number of gentlemen to whom he occasionally paid a visit ; and as these were not caring about casting out with him, Ned never left them without getting at least the price of a glass. In this way he would keep it up for days.

If at any time the price of meal advanced, these distinguised fountains of wisdom were sure to get up a mob. Notice was sent through the weavers' shops ; the men turned out in a body ; and came down the streets hallooing, and smashing the windows of the offenders ; and sometimes gutting the houses of every thing valuable. It does not appear to have then occurred to these politicians, who occupied themselves so much with other people's business to the neglect of their own, that they might have bettered their condition more, by seeking to raise their own prices, than by striving to depress those of others.

On one occasion, they resolved upon paying a visit to the farmer of Claypots. Being reputed to be rich, it was held as certain that he must have a great quantity of grain stored up beside him. Having got notice through the course of the day of the intended visit, the farmer got up a few friends to pass the evening with him, to persuade or control the multitude, if possible. The approach of the crowd was announced by the most outrageous yells. The writer's father, who was in the house at the time with the farmer, taking a candle in his hand, went out to them, and inquired what it was they wanted? " Corn, corn ! meal, meal !" was at once exclaimed by a hundred voices : " Auld Davie has plenty, and we are starving !" It was proposed to them, that if they would appoint five of their number, every key in the house would be delivered up, and they could thus satisfy themselves that there was no hoard of grain on the premises. Luckily the proposal was entertained ; and, after the most minute search, nothing more was found, than the necessary supply for the family, and a few bags of seed corn, which they had sense enough to see the propriety of the farmer retaining. When the delegates delivered their report, the people left the house with three cheers, in order to pursue the investigation elsewhere.

The party then proceeded in a body to Mr Donaldson's, at Elcho, who unfortunately did not escape so easily. Being disposed to resist these irresponsible inquisitors, a terrible scuffle ensued. The house was broken into, and the furniture destroyed. At this moment the house clock happening to strike twelve, a fellow who was swinging an axe, swore he would make it strike thirteen ; with that he dashed it in pieces at a blow. Much damage was done about the place, and some persons were severely hurt.

On another occasion, that same year, a mob assembled in great force in the town, and were proceeding to such extremities, that the magistrates were constrained to call out the military to their assistance. The artillery planted a couple of field pieces, charged with grape shot, in front of the Council-room ; and the cannoniers, with lighted lintstocks in their hands, awaited but for orders to sweep down the unthinking masses of living beings. The soldiers were drawn up in a compact body before the guns, and after suffering much from the incessant and unmerciful showers of stones from the multitude, they charged them up the High-street, and dispersed them ; but, getting into the Horse-cross by the Skinnergate, and the closes leading from the High-street, they rallied, and came round by the road now occupied by Charlotte-street and George-street, (which had been newly opened, and laid with channel from the river) and commenced a second attack with redoubled fury. Still the Provost, with a tenderness for human life, and regard for the welfare of the people under his care, which does immortal honour to his feelings as a man and a magistrate, would not permit the military to fire. The soldiers again charged the mob up towards the Inch, where they dispersed in all directions. The infatuated multitude rallied once more behind the White-dyke, and seemed determined not to yield ; when it was proposed that the Provost, accompanied by some individual, should go and endeavour to convince them of the folly of their conduct. The writer's father accompanied the Provost, and they were fortunately successful,—the people quietly dispersing on being assured that every means would be used to procure a supply of meal, if they would but allow it to be brought forward without molestation. No notice was taken of the offenders ; but such was the dread of future disturbance, that for a long period afterwards, a burgher guard was assembled every night in the Council-room.

Much to the credit of the magistracy, and to the military for their forbearance under these trying circumstances, no person was seriously injured. When similar riots occurred in Glasgow some years afterwards, in which nine lives were lost, the conduct of the Glasgow magistracy was strongly contrasted with the conduct of those of Perth. At that time, the public mind was so feverish in regard to the supply of meal, that if a merchant ventured to send a cargo round to Leith or Glasgow, his house was assailed ; and himself probably obliged to fly for his life.

THE HIGHLAND REGIMENTS.

We come now to a new era in military affairs. At the commencement of the first war with our American colonies, Perth became the centre of active operations for filling up the army for this ruinous contest.— The Highland Feudal Chiefs were at this time the instruments of giving the last and fatal blow to their own power, by sweeping the peasantry from the country. The Frazer Highlanders were levied in Perthshire, two of the battalions by officers, who procured their commissions by raising men. Almost all the officers were Highland lairds, who dragged out their tenants' sons to make up the appointed number. *Their* will was never consulted. They were compelled to submit, or their parents were instantly turned out of house and home. This is only an example of what took place all over the Highlands of Scotland. One Captain Frazer from the northern district, brought down a hundred of his clan, all of the name of Frazer. Few of them could understand a word of English; and the only distinct idea they had of all the mustering of forces which they saw around them, was that they were going to fight for King Frazer and George ta Three.

These hardy fellows were dressed in short black coats, and small bonnets, the natural colour of the wool. So many of one name had a strange effect. In calling over the roll, the sergeants, for the sake of distinction, had frequently to add a number to the name; as Donald Frazer the twenty-third; Donald Cameron the eighteenth.

When about 1600 had been assembled, they were marched off in a body to Greenock for embarkation. Immense numbers of their friends were present from all parts of the county, and the whole population of the town turned out with the most intense interest to witness their departure. So many young men dragged away from the bosom of their families, victims to the remorseless demon of war,—parents, sisters, and friends clinging to them in tears,—the wailing pipes pouring out plaintive farewell airs,—presented a scene which could not be witnessed without pain, or remembered with indifference.

On their way they were joined by different recruiting parties, and various bodies which had been collected in other quarters; by which means, when they reached Glasgow, their numbers were increased to about 2600. On reaching Greenock, the company who were raised specially for the service of King Frazer, found that their leader was amissing, and nothing would induce them to go on board without him. He was residing at Edinburgh at the time, and was far gone in a consumption. The state of his health was represented, but nothing would be listened to as an excuse; and it was found necessary to fetch the invalid from Edinburgh to embark with them. As might have been expected, he died before they were half-way across the Atlantic, his constitution proving unequal to the privations of a sea voyage in a crowded vessel. The men were equipped with their arms and accoutrements on their passage; and any little drill they received was on deck.

Immediately on landing, they suffered severely from an attack of a strong body of colonists. The Highlanders were armed with broadswords, in addition to the gun and bayonet, with the use of which they were not yet familiar. Being sorely galled, and seeing many of their comrades falling, they slung their guns upon their backs, drew their claymores, and rushed upon the enemy, crying "Hack 'em a'!" They however paid dear for their temerity.

This fine regiment was afterwards in much hard service, and behaved with distinguished bravery, until the surrender of Lord Cornwallis, when they became prisoners of war, and continued such till the peace; when the remains of the corps came home, and were disembodied at Perth. On account of their long imprisonment they had arrears of pay to draw, amounting to nearly £30 a-man, which many of them spent with that recklessness so characteristic of those who have lived a life of peril. To get a wife appeared to be the order of the day; and for several weeks two or three dozen couples were regularly proclaimed. This was quite a windfall to the girls; and as there were plenty in the market, they were easily picked up. No doubt, little enquiry as to character being previously made on either side, several of the matches turned out rather unpleasant. Such of the men as went up to London received a pension of 4½d per day; and some of the sergeants got the King's letter, which entitled them to one shilling a-day. An ensign's half-pay then only amounted to one shilling and nine pence.

SERJEANT MENZIES, *alias*, ROUGH RAB.

Amongst the serjeants who went up to London and obtained the King's letter, we must not omit to mention Serjeant Menzies, better known by the cognomen of Rough Rab, who lived many years amongst us.

This strange character joined the army at the age of fifteen during the French American War. He was born in Athole, and continued *a true Highlandman* to the day of his death. He was a stout, robust personage, about five feet ten inches, much pitted with the small pox. His appearance was uncouth, and, at first sight, stern and forbidding: but the moment a person got into conversation with him, he was captivated with his free, blunt manner. His various and lengthened services during both the American wars, rendered him a living chronicle of the leading events of that period. The regiment he first enlisted for was lying in Ireland, when he joined. Having observed in the neighbourhood a loch well stored with wild duck, the day he received his gun, he set off for it, without leave asked or given. By the time he returned, the regiment was drawn up on parade, in the street he had to pass through. As the colonel was coming along the line, Robert was passing in front of his own company, with a long string of ducks hanging over his shoulder, and his white trousers wet with mud up to the middle of his thigh. In this plight he was observed by his captain. One corporal was ordered to take him into confinement, whilst another eased him of his game. Fortunately for Rob, the colonel came up and inquired into the matter, when the captain gave in a formal complaint, that he had absented himself without leave, and had made an improper use of his arms. The colonel seeing such a string of fine ducks, and struck with the lad's open shrewd replies to some questions, ordered the captain to set him at liberty ; observing that he was certainly an excellent shot ; and desired Rob to call at his lodging, and he would give him a fowling piece that would answer him better. With the gun, he gave him permission to go to the loch at any time ; for which kindness the colonel's family were always well supplied with game. He was soon appointed serjeant, and went with the regiment to America, where he received a wound from a musket bullet in the thigh. Being eagerly engaged at the time, he was not sensible of the wound, until he happened to look down, and saw his white trousers covered with blood. He retired to the rear, got the wound tied up, and returned to the ranks determined to give as good as he had got. He was discharged from that regiment at the end of the war ; and when hostilities with the British Colonies broke out, he enlisted with the Frazer Highlanders, under Colonel Macdonald of Kinloch Moidart. Robert soon gained Colonel Macdonald's favour, and was appointed quarter-master-serjeant, then a pretty lucrative situation in a young corps. When they landed in America, their quarter-master was in a bad state of health. During his illness, Robert did the quarter-master's duty and his own, in such a manner as obtained the approbation of the General Officers, and also of the Commander-in-Chief. His blunt, open manner, led the officers to use a freedom with him seldom known in the army. Indeed, they took every opportunity of attacking him on some tender point, in order to draw from him that dry sarcastic wit in which he abounded. On these occasions, they were always sure to receive a hit ; but nothing he said was ever taken amiss.— One day, the quarter-masters of the different corps composing the army, were in attendance at the general store, to get the rations for each. They were all officers, excepting Robert, who was only serjeant. In his usual forward manner, he was pushing in for his share, when some one, considering him as intruding, ordered him to stand back till his betters were served. " And who are my betters ?—not any of you, I'm sure !" " Why so ?" returned a quarter-master. Robin, as his colonel called him, slapping his hand on his thigh, told them he was an honest man, and that was more than the best of them could say. The quarter-master-general from that moment took a fancy for him, and kept him almost constantly in the store, where he performed the duty of general quarter-master and serjeant. Much of the duty of collecting stores of cattle, and such other necessaries as could be procured, was entrusted to him ; as well as the distribution of the provisions. Every one had unbounded confidence in him, and the highest officer in the service was treated with just the same respect as any of the men. I shall quote one trifling anecdote, to shew what confidence was reposed in him :—He was in the habit of getting his own colonel to sign blank returns for stores and money, to be afterwards filled up when necessary. Being in want of returns one day, he bolted into the mess-room, where the general officers were assembled, and laid down a number of blank sheets of paper for his colonel to sign, which he instantly did. General Vaughan, who was present, seized Robert by the sleeve, and told him if he managed right, he might come and dine with him to-morrow. The colonel getting into a rage, told him to bring no more blanks to sign. Robert, however, continued the practice, but never afterwards offered them to him in public. At any spare time, the officers endeavoured to have a hit at him, but he generally had his revenge. On one occasion, a number of field officers were assembled in a wigwam they had got put together in a wood, and were enjoying themselves round a well furnished table. It occurred to Robin to play them a trick. In the vicinity there was a lake swarming with aligators ; observing some young ones basking themselves, he found means to get one entangled in a noose ; and pulling he creature up, he directed its head to the back of the wigwam. It so happened, that it made directly towards the hut : the ground was covered with dry leaves, which made a rustling noise, and attracted the attention of those inside ; when, to their consternation, they saw the head of the creature making its appearance through the branches. Instantly a rush was made for the door : table, bottles, glasses, men, and wigwam were overturned, and the disconcerted officers lay sprawling in an agony of fear in their endeavours to escape from the monster. Robin, who had been too eager to enjoy the sport, was discovered, and accused of sending the aligator amongst them ; but they found it impossible to be angry, their ludicrous exhibition rather inclining them to laugh at one another.

One night he took the duty of going round the outposts. The " Brig of Perth" was the watchword. On coming up to where a single sentinel was posted, one of his own Highlandmen, the man called out " Who comes ?" Robin answered, " A friend." " Be she friend, or no friend," returned the honest Celt, " gin she dinna bring ta ' Brig o' Perth' wi' her, she'll shoot." The consequence was, the sign had to be changed round the whole sentinels.

On the line of march one day, the troops had to struggle through some miles of morass : in many places the men sunk nearly to the middle, Not having any horses, Colonel Macdonald, who was a heavy man, had great difficulty in getting on. Robin kept beside him to help him ; but had to give so many pulls that he at last lost his temper. At one time the Colonel stuck fast, and called for help ; but Robin being mired himself, turned round, speaking gruffly, when he spied a large snake just about to dart on the Colonel. Drawing his sword, he cut the reptile in two; but the Colonel, not seeing the snake, cried out for mercy; thinking he had drawn his sword to dispatch him, in order to get rid of the trouble of helping him forward.

At one time the Colonel was without any money to pay the men. They had full rations of bread, beef, and rum, but still they had no money to tipple with. Being detached from the rest of the army, a general complaint was presented to Colonel Macdonald for their pay. He told them he had no money; but was willing to do every thing in his power to make them comfortable. Nothing would satisfy them. No pay, no service. Accordingly, their arms were piled up and belts hung upon them. During these proceedings, Robin had been out on a foraging excursion. On his return, he found the Colonel walking solus in front of the pile of arms. "What's all this?" exclaimed Robin in his usual manner: "Never mind," says the Colonel, "it's only a maggot of the men; they'll soon come to again." "Devil mak matter," says Rob, "this must not be;" and away he set to an old Stirling weaver, a character something like himself, who had fought his way up to the rank of Brigade-Major. The two contrived to lead a party from the next station into the wood near to where the unarmed and discontented men of the 71st were, and commenced a rapid bush firing. Apprehending it to be an onset of the enemy, every man rushed to his arms; and no more grumbling was heard about the pay.

Colonel Macdonald was the brother of the celebrated General Macdonald who was distinguished under Bonaparte. The General was then in the French service in America, a Lieutenant, and happened to be near where the Colonel was. The brothers had an interview by a flag of truce. The Colonel chose Robin to bear his flag, and the Lieutenant brought only a drum-boy with him. To this the Colonel objected; and ordered Robin to hold no communication with one so far below his rank. Accordingly, during the interview, the serjeant walked by himself, and the drum-boy did the same. The interview between the brothers lasted more than an hour, when they took a most affectionate leave of each other, and retired to their respective stations. On their return, the Colonel told Robin he was displeased with his brother for bringing only a drum-boy with him.

Robin used frequently to relate, that he had dined four of the first Generals in the British army on a piece of salt pork and biscuit; the ground for a table, and his pocket handkerchief for a cloth. He served them by cutting with his jockteleg a piece to each, and handing it round;

and gave them his canteen to apply to their mouths, for a drop of rum. Having finished their repast, they declared they had never enjoyed a better dinner.

Shortly after the regiment had landed in America, the whole tailors were collected at the general store to make clothing for the fresh troops that were sent over without either drill or regimentals. One day an alarm got up that a column of the enemy had made its appearance in a quarter whence no danger had been anticipated. It happened that the different divisions of the army were so posted that they could not be concentrated on that point, and there was no remedy but to bring the tailors off the shop-board. Accordingly, 900 of these knights were equipped in a few minutes. The only field officer who could take the command was the gallant Sir William Erskine, well known at that time as one of the bravest officers. The General, however, hesitated to take the command of such a battalion. Robin, with his usual forwardness, assured him that he had nothing to fear, for the 900 tailors would prove equal to 900 men. The result proved he was correct; the intrepid tailors completely routed the enemy, and captured a greater number of prisoners than the amount of their own body.

We must not omit the *coup de main* that obtained for him the appellation of " Rough Rob," by which he was afterwards known :—The division of the army to which he was attached, was at one time under the necessity of retreating and abandoning their baggage ; which was left in his charge, with orders to destroy it, to prevent it falling into the hands of the enemy. With the assistance of his own company of pioneers, and four light horsemen for carrying dispaches, he formed the resolution of bringing up the baggage. The British line had passed a river, and by the time Robin had commenced putting the baggage on board of boats, for the purpose of ferrying it across, the enemy had arrived on a neighbouring eminence. To keep them in check, he posted one of his dragoons at each end of a thick wood, that lay along the opposite side of the river, and the other two he kept riding express from one point to another, in such a bustling manner as led the enemy to imagine there was a strong force posted in the wood to receive them, should they attempt to descend to the river side. By this manœuvre, he succeeded in keeping them at bay until he got the whole over in safety ; then, burning the boats, he remained with his light horse until the waggons were considerably advanced. On joining the army, the general officers, astonished to find the baggage all safe, asked him if he knew that he had forfeited his life by his disobedience of orders ; to which he replied, in his usual independent style, " Deil mak matter—your baggage is safe. I can only die once ; and it'll be a' the same a hundred years hence."

When the army was on their way through the country, they came upon three Moravian villages, at about a mile distant from each other.— On their approach to the first, the commanding-officer, Lord Cornwallis, was addressed by a deputation of old men, with long grey beards, dressed in white gowns, girded round the middle with a broad belt ; with white rods in their hands. The conversation lasted for a short time, and then the old men retired, and the army again advanced. When the first division reached the village, the order was given to charge ; and each division as they advanced did the same, passing rapidly through the village.— They then halted, and moved on in line of march, until they reached the second and third villages, where the same orders were repeated. The whole army began to imagine that Cornwallis had gone mad ; amongst others, Rough Rob was wondering what the world he was " squinting at now." Lord Cornwallis being just at his back, overheard the allusion to his oblique vision; when Robin, discovering his blunder, began to make an apology ; but his Lordship took the joke in good part. It turned out that the Moravians had devised this plan to get the troops through their villages without offering any insult to their women ; who were all shut up in their houses, peeping through the windows.

One day, Robin led on a division to the field ; the weather was clear but calm, and the smoke rested on the spot, obscuring the parties from each other. Being supplied with gun and ammunition, he engaged pell-mell, and soon became so intent on the work, that he unwittingly got far a head of his division. A current of air clearing off the smoke, Robin found himself alone close in upon the enemy. Making a quick retreat, he fortunately regained his division in safety. The manœuvre of leaving Robin in a scrape was considered a good joke by the officers, and was often played off, for the sake of putting him on his high horse.

Robin had but small pretensions as a drill serjeant, although he occasionally got a squad to exercise. One day when thus employed, he gave the word of command, " Make ready—present —shoot !" The adjutant, who was at hand, told him to use the word " Fire ;" to which Robin replied, " If they shoot well, they'll mak' a good fire."

After the army surrendered, he maintained, by the force of his character, the same independent respectability among the men during the time they were prisoners.

During the time he was in America, there were some regiments raised there ; and Robin was offered a commission, but his colonel would not allow him to go, under the idea that there would be no half-pay, and that he would ensure him of a commission in the British army; but unfortunately the colonel died on the passage home, and Robin lost his commission, principally from his own carelessness. When he went up to London to pass the Board, he was met by General Vaughan, who desired him to call on him next day, and he would see what would be done for him; but Robin, happening to meet with some of his comrades, instead of waiting on the general, came off with them to Perth.

Robin was very successful as a recruiting serjeant. During the Nootka Sound alarm, when several independent companies were raised, he enlisted great numbers of young men. At the commencement of the French war, he was employed by the Earl of Breadalbane to procure men for the Fencibles; by Colonel Graham for the 90th; and by the Earl of Elgin for his Fencibles. When the Gentlemen Volunteers were embodied at Perth, he was appointed quarter master serjeant, with charge of the stores. He was much esteemed by this body, and held the situation until the corps was dismissed at the short peace.

Many of the officers who had served with him in America visited him during his residence in Perth; apparently happy to renew their acquaintance. One day, a gentleman called upon him, and talked familiarly; but Robin could not recollect him. The stranger at length asked if he remembered being at the taking of the Havannah? "I may remember that to the day of my death," said Robin, "for we lost our captain there, one of the best officers in the British army. I was close by his side when he received the fatal shot. There was a drum-boy near me, who burst into tears when he saw the captain fall; and just as he was raising his hand to wipe the tears from his eyes, another shot carried off the laddie's thumb?" The gentleman asked if he would know the drum-boy again; at same time pulling off his glove, presented his mutilated hand. It was the identical drum-boy; who had since been raised to the rank of major.

General Leslie inspected a young corps in Perth during the war; when the review was over, Robin stept up to the General and inquired how his Excellency did? The General was somewhat at a loss to know who addressed him, although he recollected the face and voice. "Indeed, your Excellency has seen and heard of me often," replied Robin, "for many a drop of rum I have given you from my canteen, in America." The General immediately recognized his old friend, and invited him to a bottle of wine in the evening; and, after fighting their battles over again, left him something substantial, as a token of his esteem.

After the regiment was reduced, his wife and family all died within a few weeks of each other. Being thus left solitary, the public house he had formerly kept to help him was given up, and not having been bred to any business in his youth, the shilling a day was but a straitened allowance for a man who had formerly been on the general's staff. With that commendable solicitude for others' welfare, which a man's friends are so apt to exhibit when it costs them nothing, some of his relations, conceiving that he would be lonely, at his time of life, without a helpmate, sent down a middle aged woman from the Highlands, with orders to wait on him and offer her services. When sitting by the fire one night with some of his cronies, relating his most perilous adventures, she made her appearance: Robin, turning round, bluntly asked what she wanted; and she as bluntly told him, that she was come to be his wife ! " The devil you are ! On my conscience you are a droll one !" " Your friends in Athole sent me." " Oh, ho ! that alters the case ; step in bye and sit down, and we'll talk over the business." She accordingly sat down ; the matter was settled in a few minutes ; and she became his married wife with all convenient speed. Age crept on with its frailties : amongst others, he became nearly blind. He died a few years ago, amongst the last of the pensioners of that era.

SERJEANT PHILIPS.

We may here mention another individual of a different stamp, who, for a considerable time, was a distinguished character. He was a native of Perth, and had entered the army during this war when a mere boy. On his return he entered the dragoon guards, and for some time was remarkably steady ; and was considered such an efficient duty man, that he was made pay-serjeant of the troop. He latterly fell into loose and dissipated habits ; until becoming embarrassed, he decamped with his horse and the company's pay. He sold the horse, but was shortly afterwards apprehended and sentenced to receive a thousand lashes, which torture the poor fellow underwent at two different instalments. He was discharged shortly afterwards, and returned to Perth, where he acted as porter about the shore. He was subsequently employed by General Graham of Gorthy, to recruit for the 19th regiment, then on foreign service. For some time he acted with great prudence and industry. He enlisted a great number of young men, and succeeded in obtaining the confidence of the colonel. It was at last discovered that he had fallen into the practice of making false returns, and drawing sums of money not due, which he squandered in low houses. For these acts of swindling and breach of trust, he was tried before the Circuit Court, and sentenced to be publicly whipped through the town by the hands of the common hangman, and thereafter transported beyond seas for life. Severe as this judgment was, Philips, who had ex-

pected sentence of death, thanked the judge for his lenity.   The sentence
was carried into effect in the most degrading manner, and the wretched
man, after lying long in Perth jail, during which time he made various
attempts to escape, was at length sent off to end his miserable life in bon-
dage and obscurity.

SERGEANT FORBES

Had been a drum boy in the 71st, and afterwards received an appointment to be recruiting sergeant in the 72d regiment.   This was the
corps which mutined at Edinburgh, and encamped on Arthur's Seat till
their grievances should be redressed.   Being cajoled out of this resolution, they were sent to India for a long period of years, as a punishment.
A recruiting party was stationed at Perth, and another at Inverness,
for keeping up their complement of men.   Forbes acted as sergeant-
major in Perth, and had one or two sergeants under him.   Great
numbers of boys were enlisted, or rather entrapped, and sent to India.
Forbes kept a public house ; and being always ready to give drink on
trust, or to lend them money, to be paid by a certain day, many young
fellows were thus inveigled.   When the day of payment came, they were
often more involved than ever, and took the bounty, as the only apparent
means of escape from their difficulties.   Forbes generally contrived
to get them to it spend about his house, instead of being laid out in
the purchase of their necessary equipments.   He was also occasionally
employed by officers to raise men for their commissions.   At the breaking
out of the French war, he was employed by Lord Lynedoch to raise men
for the 90th; and by various other officers.   On every agreement he received a new suit of clothes.   One officer presented him with a long full-
made scarlet coat, and cocked hat.   This he wore in conjunction with a
highland kilt and hose, exhibiting rather a ludicrous appearance, as he
swaggered along the streets, pursuing his vocation, on the market days.
On the raising of the Elgin Fencibles, he undertook to get a sufficient
number of men to obtain a lieutenancy for himself, and was so confident of
success, that he procured a suit of uniform, in anticipation, and became
one of the most consequential men imaginable.   This being no way
agreeable to his brother officers, who never liked him, they found means to
get rid of him, by withdrawing their assistance in completing his men ;
and he was thus thrown back to his former station.   The 72d having arrived from India, his services were no longer required.   He then went to
the west country, and became bellman or drummer in Glasgow ; and
afterwards got on the recruiting service at Inverness.   Had this man
acted with propriety or common prudence, he might have saved a great

deal of money during his stay in Perth; but his empty vulgar pride led him to be the dupe of those who knew how to take advantage of his weakness.

On one occasion, a recruit having decamped, Forbes stept into a neighbouring cooper's shop, and in his usual blustering manner related what had happened; regretting that he could not obtain a horse in all Perth to ride after the scoundrel. The cooper drily observed, that " he could not promise him a horse, but thought he knew where he could find a good staunch *mare !*" The serjeant jumped at the offer, and requested that she should be immediately got ready, while he prepared himself. He shortly returned, booted and spurred for the journey, and inquired if the mare was ready ? " Oh yes," replied the cooper, " my mare is always ready !" at same time pointing to the wooden tress on which he wrought. The rage of the man of war was ungovernable, and, in the charitable resolution of annhilating the individual who could presume to offer such an affront, he sent the cooper a challenge, defying him to mortal combat, as the only means of affording *satisfaction.* This was too important an affair for the serjeant to pass over in silence, so that by the appointed time a vast number of spectators had assembled at the White Dyke to witness the performance. Forbes was on the ground, parading in a very pompous manner, with a brace of pistols, affording no small amusement to the onlookers ; but the honest cooper, who saw nothing satisfactory in the idea of being converted into a target for ball practice, paid no attention to the generous invitation. The affair having reached the ears of the Procurator Fiscal, the sergeant had not been long on the ground before he was arrested, and constrained to find proper security for the preservation of the peace.

THE ATHOLE HIGHLANDERS.

Shortly after the departure of the 71st, the Duke of Athole, then a young man, undertook to raise a regiment for government, and vigorous measures were adopted for procuring men, which created the most harrowing feelings throughout his Highland estates, where the young men were torn from their families in the most tyrannical manner. The city Council of Perth voted him a certain number of men, and each of the Corporations agreed to procure two. The trades' deacons were converted into recruiting sergeants, and paraded the streets at night with flambeaux, offering high bounties, and the freedom of the trade to all who would come forward. Amongst these, the deacon of the Glovers was most conspicuous ; in his train the trades' officer, in the fantastic garb of a morris dancer, with jingling bells, performed a variety of antics. Besides these, innumerable low shifts were adopted by hired agents, to kidnap the unwary. The complement of 1000 men was thus soon obtained.

An anecdote is told, which illustrates the manner in which some of these men were procured :—An Englishman in a journey through Athole, one morning, observed a poor fellow running to the hills as for his life, closely pursued by half a dozen of human blood hounds. Turning to his guide, the gentleman anxiously inquired the meaning of what he saw ? " Ou," replied the imperturbable Celt, " It's only the Duke raising the royal Athole *volunteers*."

These men were enlisted for four years, or during the war. They were under orders for the East Indies, and were to be immediately embarked at Portsmouth, where they had arrived, together with some other regiments, under similar circumstances; when the news of the conclusion of the war was proclaimed. That moment the troops refused to a man to go on board, demanding their discharge, in accordance with the terms of their enlistment. Many attempts were made to circumvent them, which was the occasion of a serious mutiny, in which several lives were lost. Nothing could prevail on them to embark ; the officers lost all authority, and durst not be seen amongst them. Instead of being brought back and disbanded in Perth, the corps was broke up on the spot, and each man was left to find his way home the best way he could. From this circumstance, a dreadful outcry was raised against the Athole family, and a prejudice existed amongst the working classes for many years ; it being currently reported, that the regiment had been sold by the Duke to the East India Company.

RIOTS ON ACCOUNT OF CRUELTY TO AN IRISH REGIMENT.

After the Athole Highlanders, the 2d battalion of the Black Watch were filled up at Perth; and the Macdonald Highlanders, a fine body of newly raised men, 1000 strong, were trained here. They were succeeded by a body of Irish troops, called the White Boys, from being dressed in white jackets. This regiment was the cause of much disturbance in the place during their stay. It had been raised in haste, and at that time men of any description were eagerly taken into the army. Their officers were also of very indifferent character, and appeared to have little sympathy for the men. Those who know the army only in its present condition, can have but a faint idea of the privations and discomfort which the soldier had formerly to endure. Their daily pay was only 6d, which was subject to various weekly deductions for the doctor and chaplain ; they were also at considerable expense in cleaning their clothing, which was both scant and cold, and rendered still more uncomfortable by being continually daubed full of pipeclay. All their necessaries were obtained through the quarter-master and serjeants, at an extortionate rate, and of inferior value. There was no monthly settlement, and they were obliged to submit to exactions, which kept them in a continual state of misery. Those who had a wife and family were truly in a deplorable condition. A general muster took place only once in the year; and although a man died on the following day, his name was continued on the list till next inspection, the paymasters drawing the pay during the whole time. There was even instances of names being continued on the list for years after the parties were dead; substitutes representing the name being procured for the muster day from among the inhabitants.

There being no barracks, the soldiers were all billeted on the inhabitants, and in most cases were wretchedly lodged; often in open tiled garrets with an unglazed window, or in dismal vaults fit only for pigs.— Incredible as it may now appear, this regiment, when in Perth, were under stoppages, which left the men only 3½d a day. Their common breakfast was a half-penny roll, and a half-penny worth of Suffolk cheese; and those who sought to alleviate their sufferings by taking a glass of spirits, got no more food for twenty-four hours. The consequence was, that the men, from sheer necessity, were frequently driven to commit petty depredations; and as these, when discovered, were followed by punishments quite disproportionate to the offence, the North Inch became a scene of continual barbarity. It was no uncommon thing to see six, or even ten, of these unfortunate wretches suffer from 100 to 500 lashes each; and this was continued day after day, till sometimes the washerwomen interfered, and, partly by threats and partly by entreaty, succeeded in getting a few of them pardoned. At length a circumstance occurred which put an end to these *public* inhuman and disgusting exhibitions. A fine looking man, who had a wife and four children, driven by absolute want, entered a potato field in the vicinity, and pulled up a couple of shaws; nine potatoes were said to be the whole amount. Being detected in the act, he was complained of to the commanding officer, tried by a court martial, and sentenced to receive five hundred lashes. He was brought out to the Inch for punishment; but the peculiar circumstances of the case had created unusual sympathy in his behalf, and brought out a vast number of the inhabitants. On the way thither, the commanding officer was met by the wife, with an infant at her breast, and three at her side. She entreated him to have mercy on her husband; but he turned from her with contempt. She seized him by the sleeve, and implored, with tears in her eyes—but in vain; he thrust her from him with violence. These circumstances were soon communicated by those who had witnessed the interview, which inflamed the minds of the people still more against the commander. It so happened that seven men were brought out for punishment that evening, and several of them were tied up previous to this man. Some of them cried out terribly, which greatly roused the feelings of the multitude. When it came to his turn, he bore the first twenty-five lashes with considerable fortitude ; but the second twenty-five being inflicted by a left-handed drummer, had the effect of tearing up the skin and flesh at every lash ; and the unfortunate man was not able to endure the agony. His cries were piercing. His poor wife, who had lingered in the hope of getting some remission of his sentence, could restrain herself no longer. Setting down her child, she rushed through the ranks and held the drummer's arm, in the hope of arresting the punishment. She was seized, and dragged forth screaming ; and the punishment was resumed. This was the signal for the washerwomen, who, with their laps full of stones, and backed by the willing multitude, broke through the line, drove the officers from the circle, and liberated the prisoners. The soldiers had only their side arms with them, except the guard on the prisoners, and appeared more willing to assist, than to resist the people. The moment the prisoner was untied from the halberts, a general attack was made upon the officers. The adjutant was less fortunate than some of the others in escaping. He got a terrible mauling from the women ; who laid him down on his belly, in which position he was held by some scores of vigorous hands, till he had got a handsome flogging on the bare posteriors, in the presence of thousands—inflicted with an energy that would remain imprinted on his memory till the day of his death.

This put a stop to the flogging on the Inch ; but although the public were no longer shocked by these inhuman exhibitions, the practice was still continued in the orderly room above the guard house.

Shortly after this affair, another event occurred which created even a greater excitement, and which threatened to be attended with serious consequences. Among the broken-spirited men in this regiment, were three who were decrepit with age and rheumatic pains. At best, there was then little sympathy between the officers and men ; and these poor unfortunates experienced the full weight of official displeasure, from the adjutant down to the serjeant, who were in the practice of thrashing them continually with their canes, to make them stand erect ; the frailty of nature being held to be a proof of obstinate temper. The public may have heard of the use of dumb bells, and various athletic contrivances for straightening or strengthening the body, founded on erroneous principles ; but in this case a plan was devised, exhibiting profound ignorance of the delicate structure of the human frame, and outstripping everything that can well be conceived of deliberate cruelty. A wright of the name of Gardiner was employed to construct a machine or press, which, by a series of screws, was to force straight what nature, age, and ill usage had made crooked. A report that this machine was being constructed had spread through the town, but few believed that such a thing could be resorted to. The machine, however, was finished, and smuggled into the orderly room. One forenoon, the neighbourhood was alarmed by dreadful screams from this place of torture. The cry was instantly abroad that the screws were at work. Immediately a mob assembled, the guard was disarmed, and the door forced open. It was found that one poor creature had undergone the rack; another was fixed in the engine; and a third victim was awaiting his fate in agony. The multitude, rushing from all quarters, had, by this time, greatly increased; and, when they came to understand the extent of the cruelty, their rage knew no bounds. The commanding officer ordered the drum to beat to arms; and the officers, in attempting to rally the men, were attacked individually with sticks and stones, and handled very unmercifully. The soldiers, being probably cool in the cause, did not assemble. The prisoners were liberated, and the screws were brought out and burned at the Cross. Gardiner, who constructed the machine, being more in their power than the adjutant who ordered it to be made, the fury of the mob was turned against him: everything in his shop was destroyed, and he only escaped by getting out at a back window. Even the officers' lodgings were beset, and many of them had to obtain safety by flight.

The mob, however, were not indiscriminate in their fury. Among the officers, there was one who was known to be opposed to the disgraceful mode of discipline pursued, and who had frequently fainted when compelled to be an unwilling spectator of the punishment of the men. This gentleman was permitted to go about unmolested, when his brother-officers had to fly for safety. Provost Faichney attempted to quell the riot, but was altogether unequal to the task; and only got himself abused and insulted. The riot continued for several hours, but fortunately no lives were lost, neither was there any serious damage done, further than the destruction of the wrights' shop, and the windows of the orderly room. On the news reaching Edinburgh, an order was instantly transmitted from the commander-in-chief, for the removal of the corps. As might be expected, from the treatment above detailed, there were always numbers of the men in Hospital. The premises allotted for this purpose were the third flat above the guard house, and another room in the South-street. The first consisted of a single room about twenty feet square, which was crammed with invalids; and it was only when their discipline rendered this inadequate to the purpose, that the other was fitted up. When the regiment got the rout, they left their sick without any one to take charge of them; and a naked dead body was found at the head of the stair, for the town to bury. Besides the constant floggings, and the miseries of the guard house, this regiment, as an additional means of punishment, had the use of two dismal cells in Halkerstone's Tower, above the door of the West Church, where offenders were frequently confined for 24 hours, with their hands tied behind their back, and their mouths gagged with a drumstick.

The commander-in-chief, General Mackay, looking upon the treatment this regiment had received from the inhabitants in the light of an affront, resolved to send no more troops to Perth; which resolution he maintained during the time he was in command. This, however, was a crotchet for which the town had little cause to be sorry, for at that time the troops, however numerous, were billeted upon the inhabitants, who were obliged to find them lodgings, without any remuneration.

On the conclusion of the war with the Colonies, the 71st returned, and were disbanded in Perth. For some years there was little to disturb the equanimity of the town. The only troops lying here being a regiment of the line, and a company of artillery.

The next military hurry was on the occasion of a threatened war with Spain, about the Nootka Sound cat-skins. One hundred independent companies were ordered to be raised by officers in purchase of their commissions. Some of the Highland officers had again recourse to the old system of ordering out their tenants' sons; among these, the most distinguished was the Marquis of Huntly, then a stripling. He marched through the town at the head of a hundred young men. The streets of Perth were filled day and night with parties recruiting for the various officers, who had flocked here to procure men. The affair, however, was made up; and the best of the troops were drafted into regiments in India, and other foreign stations.

REFORMERS AND FRIENDS OF THE PEOPLE.

Shortly after the conclusion of the war with the American States, the country began to direct attention to political grievances, and the cry for Reform became the order of the day. By the most unprincipled stretch of power, the kingdom of Poland had been dismembered and divided between the three leading despotisms of Europe. A strong feeling of commiseration for the sufferings of that brave but unfortunate people prevailed in this country, which was expressed in resolutions passed at numerous public meetings. In this neighbourhood, John Richardson,

Esq. took a prominent part.   Sums were also collected for their aid; but
these efforts were unavailing before the overwhelming tide of oppression,
or were only useful in assuring the unfortunate Poles that there were
some portions of their fellow men who sympathised with them in their
sufferings.   In these demonstrations Perth was distinguished.   Among
the numerous eloquent speakers which the occasion called forth, a young
man of the name of George Mellis was remarkable for his vigorous and
impassioned eloquerce.

After the excitement regarding Poland had subsided, the subject of
Burgh Reform was taken up, and numerous meetings were held on the
subject.   A considerable portion of the Guildry were warm advocates in
the cause.   Mr David M'Leish, dyer, headed this party; he was a man
of unbending principle, true to whatever he took in hand; and although
not distinguished as an orator, he was endowed with an ample fund of
common sense, and advocated the cause against all the sophistry which
was brought against him.   He continued, through good and bad report,
all the days of his long life, a staunch friend of Reform.   Mr Mellis also
exerted himself in this cause; and when petitions were sent up to the
House of Commons, he was called upon to give evidence.   He was small
in stature, and of youthful appearance, and displayed such powers of
oratory, that he was termed "the Scots Boy."   Mr David Johnston,
manufacturer, and Mr James Wylie, merchant, also exerted themselves
on this subject.   Year after year they brought it forward in the Guildry,
but the *Beautiful Order* prevailed, and effectually resisted every attempt
at improvement.

Finding their efforts in this quarter unavailing, the public began to
direct attention to Reform on a broader scale, and to agitate for *Reform
in Parliament*.   Public meetings were held, speeches delivered, and resolutions passed, but all with little prospect of success.   A fair representation in Parliament, upon pretty rational principles, was the basis
they set out upon : but the more this was resisted, the more was public
opinion driven upon extreme measures, till at length a large party in the
country began to think of Revolution instead of Reform; and Annual
Parliaments and Universal Suffrage became the demand of the day.—
About this time the French Revolution engrossed attention; revolutionary doctrines began to be publicly lectured on; Paine's Rights of Man
and Common Sense were read with avidity, and Political Societies were
formed in every town and village in the kingdom.

At a meeting of the Perth Society for Parliamentary Reform, Messrs
James Craigdallie and John Burgess appeared as a deputation from the
weavers; with a proposition to unite their Societies, and thus form one

on a broader scale. The proffered union was rejected; and the deputies, taking this amiss, adjourned to a public house, and drew up a set of resolutions for the formation of a new Society, to be styled the " Friends of the People." This Society became so popular, that, like Pharoah's lean kine, it swallowed up the other. Similar Societies were established all over the kingdom, and corresponding deputies appointed. So complete were their ramifications, that the smallest matter of importance was speedily known throughout the kingdom. These Societies soon became very bold in their proceedings, and appeared to imagine they could set all law at defiance. Strong resolutions and handbills were continually issuing. At a meeting in the Guild Hall, a delegation from the Friends presented a set of resolutions which threw the assembly in an uproar. One of them was to the effect, " That as Providence had given every man his calling, he had a right to exercise it to the best advantage, independent of exclusive privileges." No sooner had this portentious sentence been enounced, than Deacon Martin, cordwainer, and quondam Methodist preacher, who was said to have been deposed from the latter office, owing to his habit when at prayer of directing his rolling eyes towards the plate, the moment he heard the clink of a copper :—this man, who was always somewhat furious in word and gesture, started up in wrath, and swinging one arm round him, and thumping the table with the other, bellowed out in a voice of thunder, that "having hitherto maintained their exclusive privileges, they would defend them still with the last drop of their blood!" So much for reformation when it comes to a man's own door.

The wild doctrines which agitated France began to spread here, and these societies rapidly increased for a time; but when the rational and moderate part of the members, who started with them for the purpose of obtaining Parliamentary Reform, saw the extreme lengths to which the deluded votaries of anarchy were disposed to go, they withdrew, and left them to become the dupes of the violent men who took the lead, and used every art to inflame the people against the Government. In this attempt a portion of the press lent its aid. Newspapers in London and in Edinburgh were printed, full of inflammatory speeches delivered at public meetings. Pamphlets, in which Monarchy and the Aristocracy were denounced, and the majesty of the People exalted, were circulated with incredible rapidity; and the community became divided into two parties, the Aristocrats and the Democrats. A large hall, which stood in the High-street, on the ground now occupied by the head of St John-street, was fitted up as a coffee room by the democratic party in Perth. Peter Watson (notorious for Republican principles) was appointed keeper

In this room, the party newspapers and pamphlets were read with extraordinary avidity. Several young merchants attended so closely to read to the mobility, to the neglect of their business, that their affairs went to ruin.

A new Society was now formed, called the *United Scotsmen.* The members were bound by secret oaths; and its ramifications extended into the army, as well as among civilians. This society was started in Perth by a stranger from Glasgow, who was introduced to Robert Sands, the Secretary to the Friends of the People. Their ostensible object was Universal Suffrage, and Annual Parliaments; but their ulterior aim was purely Republican. This man administered the oath to Sands, who in his turn was very successful in his exertions to increase the number of partizans. Vast numbers were sworn in, among whom was James Thomson, one of the town officers. By one of the clauses of his oath, he was bound to pay particular attention to what was going on amongst the constituted authorities; and on the least symptom of any thing occurring likely to affect the members of the Society, he was to give the earliest notice. Another part of the oath bound the members to stand true to the cause, and to one another; and in the event of any of their number being apprehended, none were to give information or evidence on trial. This Society soon assumed a formidable attitude. They became exceedingly bold in their declarations, which were daily issued; and their speeches at public meetings were of the most inflammatory nature. The Society, which spread over the whole of Scotland, was divided into sections, and each section appointed delegates to meet with others, and to visit the different parts of the kingdom. When the general meeting of delegates was held in Edinburgh, two weavers were appointed from Perth. At their election, Dr Bisset, who took a lead in these transactions, said, he had no doubt that the two citizens whom they had now elected, would form an influential portion of the first National Convention! At this meeting, which was held in the Relief church, the King was denounced; and Pitt and Dundas, and several others, were declared to be wicked men and traitors to the People, and ought therefore to be immediately brought to the block.

Liberty and equality became such cant words, that ignorant and deluded people were encouraged in the belief that equality of property was their grand aim, and that a speedy division was to take place;—that the banks were to be plundered, and the spoil divided;—that the taxes were to be abolished, and that the exciseman would cease from troubling;— that all invidious titles of distinction were to be annulled, and the only terms by which men were henceforth to be known, was that of citizen.

Extravagant as were these political nostrums, they were innocent compared with the flood of immorality, profligacy, blasphemy, and infidelity, which rapidly spread to the most deplorable extent. Heads of families renounced the Christian religion, and adopted Paine's infidel notions as the standard of their creed. The Bible was declared to be a silly fable; and some of the deluded wretches actually burnt the sacred scriptures at their profane meetings. The Sabbath was their chief day for holding committee meetings, when numerous parties wandered the fields, reading political pamphlets, and singing songs of shocking profanity, of which they had abundance. To such a length did Infidelity advance, that a party one Sabbath held a mock sacrament on the Town's Muir, applying the bounties of Providence to the derision of the ordinances of religion. Nature they looked upon as their only God—death as an eternal sleep—and heaven and hell as mere bugbears to frighten children. To such dreadful length did these infatuated men carry their views, that it appeared as if society was about to be overwhelmed in anarchy.

Many of these misguided men persevered in these courses till they had reduced their families to misery and want. Their work was neglected, and much of their time occupied during the day with political pamphlets and discussion, and in the evenings their earnings were squandered at club meetings. The weavers and shoemakers, the trades which chiefly distinguished themselves in these matters, had good wages at the time, and were enabled to sport away for a time, particularly the weavers, who, in addition to high prices for their labour, had their time in a great measure at their command. But these habits soon involved them in debt, to an extent which constrained many to leave the town, and to abandon their families to the utmost distress; thus demonstrating, that no species of tyranny is so pernicious as the want of self government.

It is but justice to state that these doctrines were not those of the Reformers, nearly the whole of whom withdrew themselves when they observed a set of individuals struggling for political supremacy, who would be satisfied with no measure of rational reform, and who appeared bent upon throwing the country into confusion.

From this violence of political opinion, it became evident that the peace of the country would soon be endangered, if vigorous measures were not speedily adopted to prevent such a catastrophe. Public meetings had become general throughout the country, and the resolutions adopted were truly alarming; but extreme as were the opinions of many, few were prepared to follow the suggestions of Robert Watt, the spy. This heartless wretch (who was afterwards executed in Edinburgh, having fallen in the snare himself to which he had endeavoured to decoy others) came over to Perth to persuade the democrats to join in the manufacture of *pikes;* but no argument could prevail upon them to take any hand in the matter. This man was the natural son of a Highland gentleman, who had been pretty liberal in giving him education in Perth. He was well known here; and during a residence of some years after the completion of his education, was much esteemed, and considered a young man of amiable disposition, and remarkable for religious habits. Perhaps it was on this account that he was selected as the most fit person to be sent on such a mission.

As has been already observed, the public meetings became frequent, and the language employed on these occasions so bold, that the existing Government became alarmed for their consequences; and the motions of the party were therefore narrowly watched.

At a meeting in the Relief Church, several of the Dissenting clergy took a prominent part. In the course of the business, an individual happening incidentally to use the word Reform, the *cap-out* minister exclaimed— "Reform! Reform, indeed; public opinion was a hundred miles before Reform! That was like pursuing a hare when it was behind. A revolution, and nothing but a revolution, would now satisfy the country, and they were determined to bring it about!" Some of these clerical gentry declaimed strongly against the Government from the pulpit. One of them, of whom better things might have been expected, had constant recurrence to the subject, holding up the career of the French as an example of public virtue and patriotism. Hostilities having commenced between France and Austria, it was a constant note in his prayer for the success of the former, and that they might drink the blood of their enemies—a metaphor at least sufficiently horrible. A precognition having been taken before the Sheriff, as to the ministerial exhibitions of some of these worthies, a damper was put upon their zeal. They still, however, continued warm in the cause in private.

The Perth Hunt, then newly instituted, having assembled at the races, the Friends of the People took the opportunity of displaying their sentiments in a way which could not be mistaken. The assemblies were then held in the Glover's Hall, and the ordinaries in the George Inn. At the time appointed for the meeting of the assembly, a numerous body of the Friends ranged themselves in two compact lines, forming a lane betwixt the inn and the hall, along which the gentry had to pass, exposed to that searching species of criticism which consists in finding faults. Every individual who was supposed to be a friend to the rotten constitution, had a severe ordeal to undergo; even the best of them had to walk, hat in hand, and make obesience to the *Majesty of the*

People. When the Duke of Athole appeared, a terrible clamour was produced. The cry arose, "There comes citizen Murray, Black Jock who sold the Highlanders. To the guillotine with him, that he may receive his deserts." Mr Dundas also received especial notice. Many of the nobility came in chairs, but this did not save them; the occupant was examined: and even ladies were compelled to endure the insults of the rabble.

A significant display of their power and sentiments, in the burning of Mr Dundas in effigy, was on one of these evenings resolved upon. The necessary habiliments having been procured and stuffed, the figure was taken to a barber's shop to get his wig dressed. During the performance of this operation, the two worthies who had it in charge entered into a political discussion, and in the ardour of debate so far lost sight of their immediate duty, that they let poor Harry fall on the floor, when the intrepid shaver gave him a kick on the part which has been described as the lower end of the back, exclaiming, "Ye'll fall soon enough, ye b——r; ye might have sat till I had done with you!"—When all was nearly ready, the Friends down the town, who had been apprised of what was about to take place, shut up their shops with all convenient speed, to the astonishment of their more ignorant neighbours. These were not, however, kept long in suspense. In a short time, the street was in an uproar, and the effigy made its appearance, mounted on a long pole, while the air rung with the shouts of delighted thousands. After parading the town, the crowd halted in front of the George Inn, that the nobility present might have an opportunity of witnessing the exhibition. An inflammatory harangue having been delivered by one of the leaders, fire was set to the effigy: the belly of which being filled with combustibles, and the head with gunpowder, poor Harry, in the face of his enemies, ended his career in a luminous manner, and with a good report.

The Friends became so numerous, and the excitement so great, that it was determined to hold a public meeting on the North Inch; and immense numbers turned out to witness the proceedings. Walter Miller had just commenced an harangue from the top of the White Dyke, when Sheriff Chalmers, with a number of assistants, came up in order to disperse the meeting. Miller was ordered down, and obeyed; but intimated that another meeting would be held in a few minutes, at a different part of the Inch, to which the whole mass immediately repaired, hurraing as they went. The orations had scarcely been recommenced, when the Sheriff dispersed this meeting also; but after following the multitude from one part of the Inch to another, as fast as his short legs and obesity would permit, he at length gave up the attempt as being hopeless, without the assistance of a stronger force than he could muster. The agitators being thus left masters of the field, the affair was looked upon in the light of a victory, and strong resolutions were passed, to the effect that they would not submit to be crushed by the hand of power. The manifestations of the party in short, became so bold, that the well disposed portion of the community trembled for the consequences. Numerous plots were hatched against the peace of the State; and so swift and secret was their intercourse, that the general rising of the Friends in Dublin, which was only discovered by the authorities there twenty-four hours prior to the appointed rising, was known in all its details among the Friends in Perth, six weeks previously.

When hostilities commenced between the French and Austrians, the former gained some advantages in the field. The news was hailed with the greatest joy by the Friends, who ordered a general illumination; and the houses of their party were soon lighted up. No sooner had they obtained the power than they manifested the will to become despotic, and in the first moment of exultation, with the aspirations of freedom on their tongues, they began to enact the part of tyrants, by breaking the windows, and destroying the property of those who had not their houses lighted up. The steeple was forcibly taken possession of, and the bells were rung during the whole night. In emulation of the French, a fir tree was brought from the wood and planted at the cross, every branch of which was stuck full of lighted candles; so that the tree of liberty, though somewhat out of its element, shone very bright for one night. At a short distance from this fiery emblem of liberty, a large bonfire was kindled; and tar barrels, and every species of combustible property that could be got hold of, was sacrificed as a burnt offering at the altar of freedom; while surrounding multitudes rent the air with shouts for Liberty and Equality, and for the downfall of the King and Aristocracy.

Old Provost Caw was then in office, and although a very amiable man, had not sufficient nerve to take the lead under such trying circumstances. When the alarm was given, the Magistrates appeared to have been terror-struck, and no measures were taken to check these proceedings. The Magistrates, indeed, had little in their power, for there was no military in the town at the time, to support them, and there were but few constables to call out. It was, therefore, resolved not to disturb the rabble, so long as they kept within the bounds of moderation. Fortunately, the night passed over with little injury; but to prevent further mischief, from the bold attitude they had assumed, a couple of troops of the 4th Dragoons was immediately procured from Kilmarnock.

Conversation and Evening Walk on the North Inch, Perth 1794.
See overleaf for reference numbers.

1   Provost Caw.
2   Doctor Robertson.
3   Mr And. Davidson, Writer.
4   Lord and Lady Breadalbane.
5   Major Dalton.
6   Major Hooper.

7   Mr A. Watt, Haberdasher (or Beau Watt).
8   Miss McIntyre, Milliner.
9   Mr John Stewart, commonly called Cotton Jack.
10   Mr John Skene, Merchant, called Long Skane.
11   Mr McGregor, French Teacher.
12   Miss Robertson of Tullybelton.

By this time the civil power began to use vigorous measures for suppressing the Republican spirit which was everywhere spreading. Several of the citizens were apprehended : Watt and Downie, the leaders and instigators of these perilous doctrines, were tried and condemned at Edinburgh. Watt was hanged and beheaded. Downie, having become insane in prison, was not brought to execution.

Mr Fysche Palmer, the Unitarian clergyman in Dundee, was tried before the Circuit Court at Perth for sedition. But owing probably to an apprehension for the effects which might be produced by his able defence, more than to any crime with which he could be directly implicated, he was sentenced to banishment for life. He lay nearly a twelvemonth in Perth jail after his trial, where one of the Burgher rooms was fitted up for his accommodation, and where his acquaintance were allowed to visit him. Mr Palmer had begun to entertain the hope that his sentence would be commuted to a period of imprisonment, when a chaise one day drew up to the jail, and he was ordered instantly to get into it, being scarcely allowed time to pack up his clothes. Mr Muir, advocate, was tried in Edinburgh about the same time, and received a similar sentence.

Among the Friends of the People, or the *extreme left,* as it is now called, Messrs James Craigdaillie, John Burgess, and Robert Sands, had been principal movers. The former was the individual first sought after. He narrowly escaped, and owed his safety to the fidelity of one of the party, who had discovered that a warrant was being made out for his apprehension. Craigdaillie lost no time in destroying any documents which might tend to inculpate himself or others, and had only proceeded a few yards from his father's house, when he met the Sheriff and a party of military on their way to apprehend them. It being dark, he fortunately escaped unobserved among the crowd which the military had attracted. For several months he was incessantly hunted through the country ; although conveyed from place to place, and sedulously concealed, by the Friends. He afterwards went up to Manchester, under the assumed name of John Brown, where he was received with open arms by his party. Not feeling safe even here, and fearing that he might be the means of bringing others into trouble on his account, he at length embraced the only means of escape from pursuit which presented itself—that of entering the army. He accordingly enlisted into the Clan Alpine Fencibles, and was thus constrained to swallow the bitter pill of swearing allegiance to that King and Government which he had used his most strenuous endeavour to overthrow.

The indictment made out against Mr Craigdaillie (which had been left at his father's house,) charged him with the crime of sedition; with

K

being a member of the United Scotsmen; and conspiring to bring about a revolution, annual Parliaments, and universal suffrage. A few years ago, on the National Jubilee, held in commemoration of the passing of the Reform Bill, when every one was striving with his neighbour in the ardent expression of their feelings, Mr Craigdaillie carried in the procession a copy of the Scotch Reform Bill, stitched to his indictment : the Reform Bill forming, in his opinion, a strong commentary on its injustice.

Of the other leaders, sixteen were apprehended. John Burgess, their clerk, was taken up at Kirkaldy, where he was confined some time previous to being brought to Perth. Every effort was made whilst he lay in Perth jail to draw information from him ; but neither threats nor promises could induce him to compromise his friends. He was at length liberated, without being brought to trial. He never afterwards settled to his trade, but wandered about the country singing ballads. Robert Sands, the secretary, was not so honourable. Although he was the first man that took the oath in this quarter, and was very instrumental in inveigling others, when he was apprehended he gave information against Mr Mealmaker, which sent him to Botany Bay. Sands got clear off without a trial, and afterwards enlisted into the 70th regiment, where he acted many years as schoolmaster.

Walter Miller, hardware merchant in the High-street, and principal orator and leader of the revolutionary party, was also taken into custody. One morning before breakfast, a chaise, accompanied by a party of dragoons, drew up to his door, where an officer had been in waiting to seize him at the moment the chaise came in sight. Miller being instantly thrust into it, was on his way to London before even his family became aware of what had taken place. He was confined in the Tower for many months, but was afterwards liberated without being brought to trial. Notice having reached Perth that Miller would return on a certain day, his friends determined on giving him a public welcome. For this purpose they assembled at the Cloven Craigs in great numbers, and when the coach arrived, they took out the horses, and drew him in triumph into town. Whether it was only the more inflexible Reformers who were tried and banished,—or whether Mr Miller had acquired *solid* reasons for altering his opinions, certain it is, that shortly after his return, he published a large volume in defence of the King and Government, which produced no small astonishment among the public, who had hitherto looked upon him as a staunch Republican. He also experienced a sudden conversion in his religious creed ; and from being a notorious infidel, assumed the walk and conversation of religious restraint.

These proceedings greatly quashed the Republican spirit which had got abroad. The party, however, still continued to meet and to carry on correspondence, but not so openly. Emissaries were sent into the army to subvert the allegiance of the soldiers; but such was the vigilance of government, that every attempt was detected. There was plenty of money among them, but there were always some of their needy members ready to take it, and betray their secrets.

When the Irish State prisoners passed through Perth, it was currently reported, that an attempt would be made by the friends here in their favour. A great multitude turned out on the day of their arrival; but the military were in such force, that even if such an intention had existed, it would have been madness to attempt it. The prisoners arrived in six carriages, guarded by four troops of dragoons. Instead of being placed in the jail, they were lodged for the night in the large room of the George inn, where beds were placed on the floor for them. A number of sentinels were posted in the room, as well as without; and the rest of the military were in readiness at a moment's warning.

Many individuals who had taken an active part in these commotions, afterwards came to see their folly, and acknowledged that they had attempted to drive matters too far; whilst others who persisted in their courses, and had thrown off all moral restraints, gave themselves up to idleness and dissipation, and reduced their families to a state of utter misery. Of those who had made a scoff of religion, many died in the most awful and deplorable condition.

It has been stated that immediately after the planting of the Tree of Liberty, a couple of troops of the fourth dragoons were brought to Perth. In a short time the whole regiment arrived, and continued here. On hostilities commencing with France, this regiment was augmented from six troops of 50 men, to ten troops, each 100 strong. The stables in Cromwell's mound accommodated 200 horses, and the remainder were billeted throughout the town. Fresh horses and recruits arriving daily, an excellent market was created for corn and hay. The riding-house on the South Inch having been down many years, a new one was erected in Canal-street for training the young troops. This building was latterly converted into a coach-work. It having occurred to Government that the billeting of the soldiers throughout the town, when so many of the inhabitants were supposed to be disaffected, was exposing them to the influence of disloyal opinions,—a barrack, calculated to accommodate six troop of dragoons, was erected on the grounds known by the name of Drumhar Gardens. As no estimates were taken for this erection, it proved an excellent job for the tradesmen employed on it.

MILITARY—COMMENCEMENT OF THE FRENCH WAR.

There was now an extraordinary demand for men for both army and navy. The Town of Perth undertook to raise a body of men for Admiral Keith Elphinston, then a captain. Every day the streets were paraded by a party, bearing a large ship flag, and beating drums, recruiting for seamen; and numerous parties, employed by various officers, who were eager to fill up their companies. The Earl of Breadalbane obtained a warrant to raise two batallions of Fencibles. Three hundred of his tenants' sons marched into Perth in a body, and exhibited the finest specimens of men that could anywhere be found. These troops having been only raised as Scotch Fencibles, when disturbances broke out in Ireland, no argument could induce them to serve in that country. Lady Breadalbane, who had taken great interest in these proceedings, was so incensed at their obstinacy, that she is reported to have declared, that she would raise a regiment that would march to the d——l if she desired it. A third regiment was accordingly embodied to serve in Ireland. By this time the new doctrines of the Rights of Man had been extensively spread through the country, and produced an important change in the public mind. The officers who had formerly been in the service, now found it a different business to deal with the men. They had acquired a knowledge of what was their due, and courage to demand it. One of the buttalions of Breadalbane Fencibles, had not received their arrears of pay and bounty: on the morning on which they were to march, the regiment was drawn up in front of the George inn; when ordered to shoulder arms, each man stood immovable! The order was repeated, but still not a man stirred. Upon enquiring into the cause of this extraordinary conduct, the officer in command was informed, that not having received their arrears, the men were determined not to leave the place till these were settled. This was a dilemma as great as it was unexpected. The paymaster had no funds at his disposal, and the Earl of Breadalbane was not at hand. After much argument and entreaty, they were prevailed upon to march to Kinross; the officer pledging himself that every thing would be settled there on the return of an express from the Earl. A mutiny broke out some time afterwards in the first battalion; in consequence of which two of the men were shot, by order of a general court martial.

The present venerable Lord Lynedoch, the gallant self-taught general, was at this time in the south of France. When hostilities commenced, he took an active part at Toulon, as a volunteer. At the seige of Mantua, when the garrison was reduced to the utmost distress, he escaped from that fortress through the French lines, with dispatches to the Austrians.

At this time he was plain Thomas Graham of Balgowan, of fox-hunting notoriety.   He was distinguished for his reckless daring, had perform- ed many incredible feats of horsemansip, and was considered the first horseman in the country ; but his true genius had not yet been developed. The news of his active and distinguished services were therefore received with surprise in this country.   The next information respecting him was his arrival in Perth, with a warrant to raise and embody a regiment (the 90th).   Recruiting parties were established in all directions ; the jails of the metropolis and the provinces delivered up their inmates, and in a few weeks the ragged regiment mustered in the Inch 1,500 strong, exhibiting as motely a crew as ever stemmed a bullet.   Broken-down lawyers, ci-divant preachers, play-actors and pickpockets—English, Irish, and Scotch.   Amongst the squad, one fellow, who had been a clergyman, was very conspicuous.   On the Sabbath day he might be seen preaching with zeal and solemnity to a serious multitude ; and in a few minutes after- wards, be engaged in a lark, or stripped to the skin at a boxing match. The whisky at this time being little more than a penny a gill, was a source of exquisite delight to the Irishmen and Cockneys.   The former became so notorious for desertion, that few officers would take them into their regiments, when raising men for their commissions, in conse- quence of the heavy loss thus frequently entailed upon them.   Pat, how- ever, soon became sly enough to disguise his brogue, and continued to pocket the bounty, till an officer here invented an appropriate shibboleth. The Irish were always caught with " *Whisky*." But to return to the " Grey Breeks," as they were called, the desertion became so great, that to pre- vent their escape, troops were stationed at the different roads ; at the Bridge of Earn, the Bridge of Almond, Forteviot, &c., and on every pass from the town.   To keep them in humour, they were frequently regaled with public dinners on the Inch.   Entire oxen were roasted, and London porter distributed in hogsheads ; the whole corps being seated on the grass in fifties, a plentiful supply of meat and drink was served to each. The first battalion was marched to Leith before receiving any dis- cipline, and shipped for foreign service, where the gallant 90th soon ac- quired a name by their intrepid bravery.   General Graham, during his presence with the army at Toulon, had observed the merits of a Captain Moncrieff, a gentleman belonging to an ancient and respectable family in the neighbourhood.   This gentleman he made his Lieutenant Colonel ; and had no cause to regret the appointment, as Moncrieff proved to be one of the most able officers in the army.   The second battalion went up to England, and was shortly afterwards drafted into other regiments.

Bodies of cavalry were raised by the different counties about this time. Perthshire raised two troops of Fencibles, to be under the command of Moray of Abercairney. During the time they were embodying here, a mutiny broke out, which at first wore a serious aspect. The men when enlisted, were told their pay was to be a shilling a day ; without any reference being made to other items of allowance. One evening at parade, Graham of Inchbrakie read a statement of their pay : sixpence a day, with the Queen's bounty, grass money, and some other small allowances, amounting in whole to one shilling. This unexpected intimation was received with bitter disappointment. The men had considered themselves entitled by their agreement, to a shilling a day, in addition to these allowances. One of them boldly told the captain that they were attempting a gross deception, and that he, for one, would not submit to it; adding something more offensive. The enraged captain ordered two corporals to take the offender into custody, but the moment the corporals seized him, the men rushed from the ranks and rescued him. The captain and quarter-master were the only officers present. With some difficulty the men were again formed into line, and the quarter-master kept them occupied in marching up and down the Inch. In the meantime, the captain hastened into town, and brought out a body of the 4th Dragoons, and took the whole of his corps prisoners. The most active of the leaders were put into confinement, and the rest dismissed for the night. Marshall, the individual who replied to the officer, when he saw the Dragoons approaching, sprung from the ranks, and escaped ; but gave himself up next day. An express having been immediately sent to Abercairney and the other officers,—on their arrival the prisoners were tried for mutiny. Marshall was sentenced to receive seven hundred lashes ; but was afterwards respited.

These different bodies of Fencible cavalry formed altogether a large and very expensive force. They were superseded by the Militia and Yeomanry. When the Fencibles were disbanded, the adjutants and quarter-masters were pensioned for life. Some of the quarter-masters are yet alive, and drawing their pensions of £40 a-year.

THE GENTLEMEN VOLUNTEERS.

This body, although not mentioned first, were embodied at the commencement of hostilities with France. The corps at first consisted of three companies of sixty men each, with a major commandant, three captains, six lieutenants, an adjutant, surgeon, and chaplain. Captain Sharp of Kincarrathy was appointed major; this old veteran had been thirty years in the service, in the East and West Indies, and in America

Mr John Young of Bellwood was captain of the right company, Mr Charles Archer of the left, and Mr Patton, sheriff-clerk, of the centre. A fourth company was afterwards raised, under the command of Mr Robert Ross. This corps agreed originally to serve without pay, and to clothe themselves; each member to pay a guinea and a half of entry money: but the demand for men to fill up the numerous corps of volunteers then raised being great, and the duty becoming more than a counterpoise for the glory, the Government thought proper to allow two days' pay weekly, for which they received two days' exercise. This pay, although regularly drawn, was all put into a general fund, from which was defrayed the expense of clothing and other outlay. Under the instructions of the drill serjeant, the corps rapidly assumed a warlike attitude. Their costume was somewhat parti-coloured and picturesque: consisting of a long superfine *blue* coat, the skirts turned up with *white*, *red* neck and cuffs, and gold laced button-holes at the neck and sleeves; *white* cassimere vest and breeches, long *black* gaiters; a round hat, and *white feather*. Their undress was a short blue coat with gold loop on the neck, buff pantaloons, and short gaiters. When the fourth company was added, Major Sharp became colonel commandant, and Mr Patton was promoted to the rank of major. Their band consisted at first of only four drums and fifes; but one was afterwards established on a scale of magnificence which made them pay for their whistle; the equipments and other expenses amounting to 3000 guineas. Mr Vogell, a French count, and eminent musician, was engaged to instruct the band at 15s. a day. A German musician, who had been band-master to the Breadalbane Fencibles, then newly disbanded, was afterwards engaged at £150 a-year. Shortly afterwards, an English regiment of fencible cavalry lying here, offered him a higher salary, on which he sent in his resignation, assigning as a reason that the air of Perth was so moist that it filled him with rheumatic pains. He had not been many months in this new situation, when the regiment was disbanded. He would then have gladly returned to the Perth volunteers, but they could not allow him to expose himself to rheumatic pains on their account—the more especially as they were now able to dispense with his services.

During the time the volunteers were embodied, they were frequently called upon to quell riots. During the early part of the war, the price of grain was frequently very high, sometimes owing to bad harvests, and sometimes to obstructions in the communication between the different parts of the country, and the impediments which the war threw in the way of commerce. The first occasion on which the volunteers were called into active service arose out of the following trifling circumstance:

A gentleman of rather timid character, who was a speculator in grain, and dealer in yarn and other commodities, inquired one day at a manufacturer with whom he had been transacting business, what the weavers were saying about the scarcity of meal?—to which it was jocularly replied, that they were threatening to have a riot to turn out the grain which they conceived the dealers had in store. This information threw the grain dealer into the utmost consternation. He instantly repaired to the Magistrates, and succeeded in imparting to them a portion of the fear which distracted himself; the result of which was an order for a captain's guard of 40 men to meet in the Council Room that night. This intelligence soon spread to the west end of the town; and the general belief of the weavers being that the volunteers would never stand opposition, a *row* was of course determined on, that they might have an opportunity of at once and for ever putting them down. The guard had assembled, and were making themselves extremely comfortable over the good things which had been provided for the occasion, when information was received that a large body of people were on their way to the Magdalens, then tenanted by Mr Laurence Buchan. A party of twenty men was instantly dispatched, under the command of Captain Archer. Taking a near cut through the Inch, they pushed on with all haste—but as many of the corps were more distinguished for rotundity than speed of foot, these were sadly distressed by the time the hill was ascended. They arrived at last, when the work of destruction was at its height.— Mr Buchan had been considerably hurt in endeavouring to protect his property, and his wife and daughter had retired to the garret; the windows were demolishing, and the furniture was beginning to share the same fate. Upon the appearance of the *white feathers*, however, the whole decamped with such precipitation, that only one individual, a wright lad, who appeared to have been a mere spectator, was seized near Craigie Bridge in the retreat; the Perth burghers being traditionally celebrated for their success in accomplishing the retrograde movement! One individual, who was remarkable for boasting of his courage, was seized with such a panic, that he never looked behind till he reached the woods of Dupplin, where he lay concealed for some days, till the pangs of hunger compelled him to venture back to town. On their return from Buchan's, the volunteers were somewhat roughly handled by the democrats, in their way down Leonard-street, where piles of stones had been prepared for the purpose; however, by their firmness and forbearance, no serious accident occurred. The prisoner was examined next day, by a summary process before the sheriff-depute, Mr Campbell of Clathi, and ordered to be sent to the navy, which sentence was instantly put in force. By this time notice of what was going on had got abroad, and a multitude assembled with the intention of effecting a rescue. Some disturbances occurred between the volunteers and the crowd ; and the moment the chaise started with the prisoner, the dragoons which guarded it were assailed with a shower of stones ; and carts and hogsheads were hurled across the street to impede their progress. The annoyance was kept up as far as the Cloven Craigs, when the mob, seeing their numbers greatly diminished, gave up the cause as hopeless. In a few days thirty pounds was raised by subscription, to obtain the prisoner's liberation. A lawyer was employed to negociate the business, who got the cash into his possession ; but the lad was never afterwards heard of. Thus ended the first campaign of the Gentlemen Volunteers.

Shortly after this affair, a vessel having taken in a load of grain for Leith, it was resolved in the councils of the West-end that it should not be permitted to sail with the cargo ; and a crowd assembled one evening accordingly to unship the grain. Upon notice of these proceedings reaching the Magistrates, the volunteers were hastily mustered ; and as the affair wore rather a serious aspect, they were ordered to load with ball cartridge. In performing this operation, however, it was asserted by the wags, that some of the corps were so excited by the ardour of the moment, that they spilt the powder upon the ground, being unable to find the muzzle of their guns. It was dark when they passed down the Speygate, where a party of artillery, with lighted matches, were bringing out some field pieces, which gave things an alarming appearance. By this time the mob had commenced the work of destruction about the vessel, The volunteers having been drawn up at the Grey Friars' gate, the chief magistrate, Provost Caw, stepped into the midst of the destructives, and by using his influence, and endeavouring to convince them of the folly and injustice of their proceeding, induced them to disperse ; at the same time assuring them, that the Magistrates would make every effort to provide a sufficient supply of meal, if they would, by respecting the rights of private property, but give confidence to the holders of grain to bring it freely to market. Thus by the judicious conduct of the Provost, this affair was happily quashed, which, by a different course, might have been attended by unpleasant consequences ; and the second exploit of the Gentleman Volunteers was concluded without bloodshed.

A second battalion of the Volunteers was afterwards raised, consisting of four companies. This division was filled up by tradesmen, who also received two days' pay weekly. Their dress resembled that of horsemen, consisting of a short red coat and tight pantaloons, with a helmet and red feather. Their commander Provost Fechney, a man far advanced in years, and ignorant of military tactics, was but ill qualified to take the command of a battalion in the field. Besides, being somewhat corpulent he made rather a grotesque appearance in the dress. On the occasion of one of the quarterly inspections, the field-officer ordered the colonel to put the battalion through their exercise, on which the colonel expressed considerable diffidence in his abilities to go through the business in a proper manner. The field-officer replied in terms not very polite, that in that case he was of no use to the service. This induced the worthy Provost instantly to resign the command, to which Major Hay Marshall succeeded.

The volunteers were afterwards frequently called out to quell meal mobs. A serious riot having occurred one night, a party was ordered to clear the streets, which they at length accomplished at the expense of some broken heads and shins; but as these mishaps were received in the service, they were met with becoming intrepidity. Pathetic stories were told of parting scenes, when the dear goodman took up his musket to go forth to battle—the tender embrace—the last kiss. Perhaps to return with broken bones, a mutilated victim; or perhaps a corpse!—weeping, and the last farewell! All fudge;—when in full dress they were men of valour, and could parade the streets with as much ostentation, and pompous demeanour, as ever an Irish giant strutted in a caravan. In the gentleman corps, the rule of choosing the man of one height and size was but little attended to. Mr Spittal, the left-hand man of the grenadier company, was upwards of six feet three inches, and as fine a figure of a man as could be found in Scotland. Fiscal Rutherford, the right-hand man of the rear rank of the next company, was only four feet nine inches. It thus frequently happened, when the battalion was told off, that Fiscal Rutherford, four feet nine, had to *cover* a hero of six feet three.

The Yeomanry cavalry had by this time been embodied under the command of the Earl of Kinnoul. They were chiefly composed of farmers, and a number of gentlemen about town who kept horses. When their colours were presented to them, the corps assembled at Dupplin; there was a troop from the Carse, one from Strathmore, and another from Strathearn. Colonel Macfarlane of the 72d, then in quarters here, was to be on the ground as inspecting field officer; and a captain's guard of the Gentleman Volunteers, consisting of 60 men, marched out in full

dress in the morning to keep the ground, and fire a *feu de joie* at the conclusion of the ceremony. It was intended that the whole company should
dine in a body on the lawn, but the morning proving very rainy, this arrangement had to be altered. On the arrival of the Volunteers in the
morning, they were shown into the hall, where there was a plentiful supply of bread and cheese, with large cans full of double-strong whisky,
which gave much satisfaction to some of the Perth bon-vivants. By
twelve o'clock there was assembled a vast number of nobility and gentry,
admirals, post-captains, generals, and commanders of corps, with their
ladies, the whole forming one of the gayest spectacles ever seen in the
county. The Yeomanry were drawn up on the lawn in front of the
house; the Volunteers were in line on the side of the court between the
gate of the house and the Yeomanry, their fine band being at the door.
When all the arrangements were completed, the Countess made her appearance, bearing a standard in each hand, and after a salute from the
Volunteers and the Yeomanry, the band advanced, playing the Highland
March, followed by the Countess, with about forty ladies, by
twos, all dressed in white muslins. These were followed by a great
number of gentlemen in different uniforms, in the same order. On their
arrival on the lawn in front of the Yeomanry, they filed off from the
right of the corps, the Countess and her train following, and the Volunteers bringing up the rear. The whole then marched round to a park,
where there was a platform erected in front of an arbour; on this the
ladies and gentlemen took their station; the Yeomanry in front, and the
Volunteers in the rear. After the consecration of the colours by the
Rev. Mr Beatson, chaplain of the corps, the standards were presented to
the officers in fine style by the Countess, with a suitable address. The
Volunteers then fired three vollies, which concluded the ceremony; when
the whole marched off the ground to another park, where the corps
were met by Colonel Macfarlane, and received the approbation of that
distinguished officer. Now came the tug of war for dinner: The
alteration of the original arrangement had put every thing in confusion.
The Earl, with the ladies and gentlemen, were provided for in the castle;
but the Volunteers and the Yeomanry were divided in outhouses,
wherever room could be found. Some companies were done with dinner
before others had begun; some whole companies were without knives;
in lieu of which the Yeomanry cut up the meat with their sabres,
and if the fleshing of their swords did not inflict bloody wounds, they
were at least effectual; every one hacking away at whatever he could lay
his fingers on. By the time the dinner was devoured, the trumpet sound-
ed for a turn-out. It had been part of the original plan that the whole

were to assemble in a body, to receive thanks from the Earl for their conduct on the occasion ; but his Lordship had made himself so happy with
his company, who by this time were far in the mist, that the thing
was given up. Just as they were drawn up here, some hogsheads of ale
were started on the lawn, and the servants carried out large baskets full
of bread and meat, and flung them on the grass to the crowd, leaving
the stoutest fellow to share best. When the Volunteers reached home,
many of their heads were lighter than their heels.

The Militia Act was the cause of much disturbance in the country,
when it came into operation. The parish schoolmasters were attacked in
various quarters ; attempts were made to burn the session books, some of
which were destroyed. Two troops of the Ayrshire Cavalry were lying here
at the time ; and every day expresses arrived from different quarters for
troops to keep down riots and quell disorders. The Gentlemen Volunteers
were ordered to wear their side arms when they went out, and a captain's
guard was mounted every day in the Council Room. This was glorious
work for the gourmonds ; an abundant supply of pies and porter, bread
and cheese, &c., being daily provided. The bill for meat and drink
in the guard house, for ten days, amounted to upwards of a hundred and
sixty pounds ! Whilst these doings were going on in this quarter, some
parishes in the Highlands had become extremely outrageous : they became organized into regular bands, under the guidance of one Cameron,
and opposed the cavalry. The Auchtergaven company of volunteers
had been marched up to Blair Castle, and a troop of light horse went up
express above Dunkeld, their great object was to seize Cameron, who
had hitherto baffled all attempts to secure him. Rumours went abroad
that the Highlanders were up in arms, and that they had defeated the
troops sent against them. The numbers of the disaffected were wonderfully magnified. One day during the prevalence of these reports, Mr
Campbell, the sheriff, and Mr Patton, his clerk, were walking up the
High-street, conversing together, when they met a person whom Mr Patton
knew to belong to the volunteers ; he told him to repair instantly to the
alarm post with his arms, and to tell any of the corps he knew to do the
same ; but by no means to let it be known to others. In a few minutes
volunteers were seen hurrying down the street from all quarters. The
mystery of the affair created an intense interest. In a moment a thousand reports were afloat. The Castle of Blair was burnt to the ground ;
the Duke's house at Dunkeld, the whole Highlands, were in a blaze ; and
thousands of the Highlanders were on their march for the low country,
to sweep every thing before them. Many of the volunteers' ladies naturally demurred sadly at allowing their spouses to depart on such a

desperate expedition as this was represented to be. At this juncture there were many sad adieus, in the sincere belief that cold steel was to end the business. Both battalions, however, were soon on the ground; and each man was supplied with ten rounds of ball cartridge: when all was ready, they moved off in double quick time up George-street.— It was instantly surmised that Dunkeld was their place of destination; and the worst alarms were confirmed. A laughable incident occurred during the march down Charlotte-street; Mr Glass, a tailor by trade, and a member of the corps, had turned out amongst the rest: Mrs Glass, however, had become somewhat jealous of this feasting and marching, as tending to weaken the tailor's allegiance to her authority; pushing her way through the crowd, she succeeded, after some unavailing efforts on his part to escape, in seizing him by the cuff of the neck. Taking the gun from him, she dragged him from the ranks, and bestowing some hearty proofs of her sincerity, fairly drove him home before her.

The march of the two corps was continued up by the Barracks, beyond which they were ordered to halt for a few minutes. A party of dragoons was seen coming down the road, surrounding a carriage and four. They were allowed to pass, and the volunteers wheeled round and brought up the rear. The carriage drew up at the Jail, and two prisoners were safely lodged; a strong guard was mounted in the Council Room; four sentinels were posted at the jail door, and four at the back of the prison; and at night four were posted on the bridge, and four at the foot of Charlotte-street. The secret was now out. Cameron and his confederate had been apprehended, after a stout resistance by the highlanders, who followed the party of dragoons with the prisoners to the Boat of Inver, attempting to rescue them. The sheriff had been on the spot, and posted down to have a sufficient force in readiness to meet any contingencies.— During the night the most alarming rumours were afloat;—the highlanders were to be down in great force; the guards were doubled, and patrols went round every half hour; but no enemy appeared. Next day the prisoners were taken from the jail, to be examined in the Council Room; when crossing the head of the Council Room stairs, Cameron bolted down the stairs, and gave his keepers the slip; he ran, and they ran, and every one ran, until he got down a back entry, and into a house in the Castle-gable. He was traced to the house, which was diligently searched, and the very chest removed in which he was shut up and almost suffocated. He remained concealed about the house until night, when, disguised as much as possible, he set out for Edinburgh. By the time he arrived there, notice had been received of his escape, and messengers were in quest of him. He took a seat in the Glasgow coach;

one of his fellow passengers was a Mr Williamson, a messenger, proceeding to Glasgow in search of him. Cameron, however, was fortunate enough to escape detection.

During the time the Gentlemen Volunteers were embodied, there were various changes made in the system; amongst others, quarterly inspections were ordered before they could draw their pay. On these occasions the officers at first treated the inspecting officer with a dinner at their own private expense: but this being found to be an intolerable burden, it was resolved to take the expense from the funds of the corps. This led to grumbling among the beef-eaters, and those who could not bear the idea of so many good things going past them. To put an end to which, at a general meeting, the Colonel proposed that the whole corps should have a public dinner on these occasions, at the expence of the funds. This was hailed with universal satisfaction; and it was resolved that each company should dine in a house of its own choosing.

These dinners gave rise to many curious circumstances, that might fill a volume. Let some small specimens be offered, to show how some of these worthies conducted themselves: In one company, three notable knights of the trencher were seated together; they had taken good care to help themselves to the choicest bits; and those seated near them, aware of their eating propensities, took very good care to help them liberally. Their plates were no sooner loaded, than the contents disappeared, as if by magic; their knives and forks went like a drummer's sticks, when beating double-quick time; roast beef, veal, lamb, pies, came all alike, and vanished alike quickly. Some of the wags found means to get an infusion of jallop into the last pudding set before them. Each of them had a pint of wine and two bottles of toddy, which they found no difficulty in dispatching. In a short time, besides, one of them cabbaged a bottle of wine from the waiters. This, too, with a considerable quantity of toddy from some of their neighbours, all went with inconceivable rapidity. But lo, and behold the effects of the jallop! One of them was sent for to serve some ladies in his shop with goods. Alas, alas! the poor volunteer became a voluntary, or rather an in-voluntary, in more ways than one. He was obliged to take flight, and leave the ladies to choose their goods at their pleasure. He was advised by some of his friends, who had been watching for the sport, to get into the Tay, as the only means of being purified. He accordingly jumped into the river, to the great amusement of the bye-standers. The other two were not so fortunate. They could not reach the door; they, however, reached the floor, where they lay in their glory. One of them was carried home in a barrow; the other lay until late, in the midst of every thing filthy. One gentleman, remarkable for his amiable temper when sober, stripped to fight with any body or every body, and required two men to hold him. Some were singing without any body to listen to them; others who had no voice, were drumming with their hands and feet.

In another company in the Salutation inn, universal uproar reigned. A stout brawny son of Vulcan had quarrelled with a celebrated auctioneer, who had a very high opinion of his fine person. To avoid being knocked down below value, by the thundering fist of this notable son of Vulcan, he made his exit by the window of the second storey—no bad leap. Here was no room for observation; besides, there was an imminent risk of being involved in a quarrel.

In the Council Room many of the company had retired before madness had become universal. Of those who remained, one party was gathered round a gentleman, who at that time ranked high among our respectables. He was amusing the company by singing inflammatory, immoral songs; the more surprising, as he was a man advanced in years, and was the father of a numerous family. The other party were at the lower end of the table, and much of their procedure was in pantomime. One young gentleman was conveyed away by a party; having found a gig on the street on their way home, they put him into it, and after parading the streets with him, hurled him to the door of Robie Aitkin, the hangman, where they left him fast asleep, and where he was found in the morning in the same situation.

In the George inn confusion was twice confused. The toddy and other liquids were running out below the room door. In one corner of the room a Gentleman Volunteer was lying on the floor, quite mute; in the bight of his arm lay the supper he had just eaten. On some chairs there was stretched another, laid out as if for the grave, wrapped in a table cloth. The captain was in the act of making a speech, but he might as well have addressed the winds. All were speaking; and the noise resembled that of a school taught in the old fashion, where all the children were reading and bawling aloud. Determined, however, to make himself heard, he got upon the top of the table, and flourishing his drawn sword, bawled out at the top of his lungs for silence; but, alas! he was now a captain without command; and he found himself under the necessity of delivering his fine oration, without having even the pleasure of hearing himself. Like the companies in the other rooms, there was a great deal of mute manœuvres, for all the noise that was made. Some of them were far beyond speaking. Dancing and singing were carried on in dumb show in a most ridiculous manner. Some of them attempted to treat the visitors to a glass, but the bottles were corked, although they could not discover so ; others, although they got the bottle, could not see the glass. However poorly the drill was attended on common occasions, the inspection was sure to command a grand turn-out. All the beef-eaters were there, although not present between the feasts.

This corps, during the period they were embodied, drew from Government about L.2,200 a year. It had been often proposed to form a fund for the relief of decayed members and their widows, which, if they had done, might have amounted before they were reduced, to above L.30,000 ; but this was uniformly opposed by a set of tippling gentlemen and needy tradesmen, who, for the sake of the belly, sacrificed every thing ; and what was rather singular, a great number of these creatures were so reduced before the corps was paid off, as to petition the committee of management for a few guineas in charity. Their funds were sported away in a most shameful manner. A young man coming to be a shopkeeper or a clerk, was admitted a member, and had a full suit of clothing, which cost the corps about six guineas, and perhaps was off in a few months. Any person that did a job for them charged an enormous price. Each of these dinners cost the companies about L.25 a piece ; and what with band, and dinners, and pipe allowance, would amount to L.250 every three months. Of all the money drawn, when they came to be reduced there was only about £700 left, which was devoted to the building of the Seminaries. Of this corps, which was composed of fine young men in general, very few are at this time alive. Of all the officers there are only two. There is no doubt that the Volunteers came forward with a good intention, but it proved to have a very bad moral effect. Their frequent meetings to drill was the cause of much tippling. When they met for drill, gills were drank before they assembled ; when the long roll was beat for falling in, they were to be seen issuing from the various public houses in the vicinity of the parade ; and when they returned from drill, all those who liked a glass adjourned to a tavern, where they spent the evening ; and in the morning they required a *cauker* to put them to rights.

The Gentlemen Yeomanry felt the effects of this most severely. Their field-days were always on the Fridays, and Lord Kinnoull frequently gave them a dinner ; but this did not end the day. When once on the fuddle there was no bounds to their folly, which often led to much unhappy family discord. Many laughable circumstances took place with these gentlemen farmers. On one occasion a big jolly farmer went into a house in the Skinnergate, at the sign of " Six bottles,"—well known for a certain description of character. Here he became so glorious, that in going home, he was found mounted on his horse, with his face looking towards the tail ; his helmet the back end before, with a bunch of ribbons. In this plight he was led along the bridge, and through Bridgend, with a gay assemblage.

When the volunteers were paid off, and the arms and stores sent to London, the arms of a whole company, amounting to sixty stand, and upwards of forty barrels of gunpowder, were smuggled away, of which Government never got account.

On the commencement of hostilities the second time, a corp of volunteers was again raised, under Colonel Marshall, of young tradesmen, who drew pay. They had two drills a week—but they had each season fourteen days permanent drill, frequently at Stirling or elsewhere, where the officers and many of the men had droll manœuvres ; but these volunteers were superseded by the Local Militia. Perthshire had four of these corps, consisting of 1200 men each, besides a vast number enrolled throughout the county as pikemen, pioneers, and drivers of cattle. The corps of the eastern district was commanded by Colonel Hay of Seggieden ; the central, by Sir A. Muir Mackenzie ; the Highland district, by Colonel Butter of Fascally ; and the western, by Sir Patrick Murray of Ochtertyre. A company of artillery was embodied in Perth, under Captain Young of Bellwood, consisting of 80 men, with a complement of officers for four guns ; two of these guns were got from Government, and two six pounders were cast at St John's foundry, from a number of small guns got at Dunkeld. This company was styled the " Kinnoull Rock Artillery," and frequently " Captain Young's Christian Horse," from their dragging the guns. At a dinner given by the captain, they were entertained by songs, composed for the occasion by some members of the corps. To shew the spirit of the times, the following song is given, composed and sung by Lieutenant M'Vicar, to the tune of " Johnny Cope :"—

THE PERTH VOLUNTEERS

Hey, Volunteers, are ye waken yet ?
Ho, jolly lads, are ye ready yet ?
Are ye up, are ye drest ?—will you all do your best,
    To fight Bonaparte in the morning ?

Now, brave Volunteers, be it day, be it night,
When the signal is given that the French are in sight,
You must haste with your brethren in arms to unite,
    To fight Bonaparte in the morning.

Then our brave Captain Young shall foremost be seen,
To lead on the corps and to fight for renown ;
To protect all that's dear, from the cot to the crown,
    And we'll beat Bonaparte in the morning.

M

Hey, Johnny Smith, are ye waken yet ?
Ho, Davie Fife, are ye ready yet ?*
Your knapsacks fill—gie your canteens a gill,
    And we'll beat Bonaparte in the morning.

And should the usurper in truth reach our shore,
We quickly shall march, and our cannon shall roar ;
And we'll soon let him see we have grape shot in store,
    To salute Bonaparte in the morning.

And when by the favour of heaven on our arms,
We have conquered our foes, and are freed from alarms,
With joy we'll return to our wives and our bairns,
    When we've beat Bonaparte in the morning.

Then each jolly lad shall be met by his lass,
With a smile on her cheek, and a joyful caress ;
And then shall the corps drink a full flowing glass,
    In remembrance of that glorious morning.

And now when we've met let us drink to our King,
May his life be prolonged, may he happily reign,
May he always command an artillery train,
    Fit to guard all our rights night and morning.

Let us drink to his Grace,† the patron of our train,
And to Fenwick,‡ from whom all our knowledge we gain,
To his men who assist and take so much pains
    To instruct us at drill in the morning.

This corps was drilled by the captain of the artillery stationed here, and his men, and soon became wonderfully expert in working the guns. They made a splendid appearance on general field days, when the different battalions were assembled on permanent duty. One season, the Edinburgh volunteer artillery, consisting of eight guns, came over to join the different corps assembled here ; and these, with the regular artillery, and the Kinnoull Rock company united, made a splendid appearance.

Besides these different corps, there was a company of sharpshooters enrolled under Provost Caw ; but as they never made their appearance, they were styled " Captain Caw's Invisible Riflemen." The four battalions of local militia, with the regular and supplementary militia, upwards of 1200 strong, and yeomanry and artillery, formed altogether a very strong force. The ballot for the militia came to be a very heavy burden upon young men, to which was added a ballot for the army of reserve, which made an intolerable burden. Bounties rose amazingly high ; so much as L.70 in some instances being paid for a substitute, and many poor men

* Two serjeants in the corps.—† The Duke of Athole.
    ‡ Captain of Artillery in Perth.

were forced to sell the blankets from their beds to pay for protection from the ballot. Perth being found such an excellent military station, it was resolved to fit up Gowrie-house as a barracks for foot soldiers, as the horse barracks only held the same number of men above, as horses below. Gowrie-house was taken from the Board of Ordnance, and a new roof put upon the building. The different halls were filled with beds, and all things put in readiness for the troops, when it was discovered that the building was insecure and dangerous. Means were found to get it condemned as unsafe; the commanding officer of the regiment then here declared that he would not risk his men in it. But the plain truth was, the building had stood for centuries, and would have stood for ages to come. The only deficiency that could be found was in the lintel of the main entrance, which was broken at one end, and could have been replaced in four hours' time : beside this, there was neither crack nor flaw about the whole building ; this fine piece of antiquity was thus sacrificed to serve a particular purpose. The whole transaction was one of the most shameful ever done in Perth. It had been for many years in agitation to build a new Jail and a County hall ; and it being considered that the ground on which Gowrie-house stood would be the only fit situation for that purpose, terms were entered into for the purchase : the result was, that the town of Perth purchased the ground on which the Depot now stands, from the Moncrieff family, and gave it to Government for Gowrie-house. We have now a paltry thing of a jail, unworthy of the County, instead of the old venerable pile, which formed one of the principal ornaments of Perth.

THE DEPOT.

About the year 1810, it was resolved to build the Depot for French prisoners. As a numerous garrison would be required here, the horse barracks were fitted up for infantry; the stables were converted into rooms ; and the whole were filled with double beds, one above the other, in a very crowded state—which rendered it unhealthy, and filled the place with bugs and fleas to such an extent that they were uninhabitable. The Depot was pushed forward at an immense expense. Extensive as it appears above, there is little less workmanship under ground. It was commenced in the fall of the year, and carried on during a severe winter in spite of every obstacle ; fires were used to thaw the lime, and large coverings of straw to preserve the hewn stones from the frost.— Stone quarries were opened in several quarters, and roads made from them at a vast expense : upwards of 1500 hands were employed about the work, besides an immense number of horses and carts. By the month of August next year, a part of the building was ready for the reception of prisoners. The first division that arrived, consisting of 400 men, were landed from a frigate in the Tay at Dundee, and marched up through the Carse. Never was there such a turn out in Perth, as there was to witness this novel sight. On their way from Dundee, they were lodged for the night in the church of Inchture. During the night they found means to extract the brass nails, and to purloin the green cloth from the pulpit and seats, with every other thing they could lay their hands on. This division were in pretty good condition, and had some women with them ; but, in the course of the winter, great numbers arrived after the battle of Salamanca ; these were landed in the Frith of Forth, and marched through Fife ; the weather was dreadfully wet, and the roads bad. The poor creatures, many of them half naked, were in a miserable plight ; many of them gave up on the way, and were flung into carts one above the other ; and when the carts were capable of holding no more, others were tied to the back of the carts with ropes, and dragged along. The building was calculated to hold 7000, besides an hospital. One of the wards was allotted to officers who had broke their parole. This establishment, when full, was a very novel sight. There was a governor, with clerks, and a number of turnkeys ; the whole walls were planted with lamps, and sentries posted at short distances on the tops of stairs, now taken down. From these a view was commanded of the areas within. It was apprehended by many, that such an increase to the population as seven thousand prisoners, and four regiments, would greatly raise the price of provisions, but this apprehension was found to be groundless. The moment the demand for these articles was known, fat cattle, grain, and in fact every thing required, were brought from a distance, and purchased on moderate terms. Cattle heads, feet, and offal, were sold to the poor on very low terms. The prisoners were allowed four hours of a market every day, at which great quantities of potatoes, cabbages, and all sorts of vegetables, were taken in and sold. In this way a number of poor individuals made a living, by selling small wares. Among other things it may be observed in passing, that this was the origin of the potato trade for the London market. Many acres had been planted in the neighbourhood for the supply of the Depot, and when the peace came, they were disappointed of a market by the release of the prisoners. Some of the farmers thought of trying the London market, with a view of getting quit of them, and found that the advanced price there obtained, more than covered the expense of freight.

To the daily market of the prisoners all were admitted, provided they carried no contraband articles. Potatoes, vegetables of all kinds, bread, soap, tobacco, firewood, &c., were all admitted. Vast multitudes went daily to view the market, and buy from the prisoners their toys, of which they had a great variety—many of them made from the bones of their beef.— They had stands set out all round the railing of the yards, on which their wares were placed, and a great number of purchases was made every day by the numerous visitors, for which they paid high prices. The scene was altogether a novel one. Whilst a part of them were busied in selling their wares, others were engaged in the purchase of provisions and other necessaries ; some of them were traversing the wards, bawling out "relie o," which signified boiled potatoes ; others were playing on the fiddle, flute, and other instruments, for halfpence ; Punch's opera, and other puppet shows were got up in fine style. Though many of them were gaining a little money by their industry, there was another class who gambled away every thing, even the clothes from their bodies ; and some of them were to be seen wandering about with a bit of a blanket round them, without any other covering. Many cut their clothes into small stripes, and made them into shoes for sale ; but this was one of the branches of traffic that was prohibited, and for which the purchaser, if detected by the turnkeys when searched, was made liable in a penalty. Straw plait, a manufacture then in its infancy in the country, was another article prohibited. As much straw plait as made a bonnet was sold for four shillings, and being exceedingly neat, it was much inquired after. In this trade many one got a bite ; for the straw was all made up in parcels, and smuggled into their pockets for fear of detection. The following is an instance of the manner in which they practised their deceptions : An unsuspecting man having been induced by his wife to purchase a quantity of straw plait for a bonnet, he attended the market and soon found a merchant. He paid the money, but, lest he should be observed, he turned about his back to the seller and got the thing slipped into his hand, and then into his pocket. Away he went with his parcel, well pleased that he had escaped detection. On his way he thought he would examine his purchase, when to his astonishment he found, instead of straw plait, a bundle of shavings very neatly tied up. The man instantly returned and charged the prisoners with the deception, and insisted on getting back his money ; but the man could not be seen from whom the purchase was made. Whilst hanging on to catch a glimpse of him, he was told that if he did not get away they would inform the turnkey, and get him fined for buying the article. Seeing there was no chance of getting amends, he was retiring, when one came forward, and said he would find the man and make him take the shavings back, and get the money. Pretending deep commiseration, he said he had no change, but if he would give him sixteen shillings, he would give him a note, and take his chance of the man. The dupe was simple enough to give the money and take the note, thinking himself well off to get quit of his purchase—but to his mortification he found the note to be a well executed forgery on the Perth Bank. Enraged at his own simplicity, he again returned in the hope of finding the fellow who deceived him, but in vain. He was advised to apply to the governor, who, when any mis-behaved, shut up the market of that ward for a certain time, as a punish-ment—but the dread of being informed on for buying plait prevented him, and he lost both money and straw. When this establishment was full, and the four regiments in the garrison, a large sum of money was put into circulation,—not less than L 400 a day. Great expense had been incurred to get a supply of water for the place : pipes were laid through Magdalene farm, and the hill above, and the water collected into a reser-voir, and thence conducted into a cistern within the buildings ; but the supply being found inadequate to the demand, pipes were laid across the Cow Inch to the Tay, and an engine erected on the lade which raised the water into the Depot.

After the prisoners went away, it was intended to have a general mili-tary store here. The whole prison was filled with clothing and various ar-ticles for the army. A great number of women and boys were employed in brushing and cleaning them. To such an extent were they employed, that the value of the articles would soon have been paid for by their keeping. This scheme was therefore given up, and the stores sent back to London.

The prison has since been either empty, or let for granaries, for which it is admirably adapted ; but it might be far better occupied as a national bridewell—where convicted felons, instead of being sent out of the coun-try at so great an expence, could be employed in labour to maintain themselves. The governor, clerks, and turnkeys were all discharged after the peace, and a new governor, at a small salary, and three keepers, were appointed ; two of these men have since been discharged—and the present establishment consists of the governor and one man. In such a place as this, prisoners could be properly classified ; the males kept from the females ; and the old hardened offender separated from the young in crime. Here they might be employed, with men of respectable character distributed amongst them, to take charge and work along with them. This would have a better effect than a hundred task masters with the whip over them. Besides, supported by their labour, they might be in-structed, and come out at the expiry of their terms with a small sum to set them a going again in the world, better men than when they went in.

PERTH SHERIFF COURT.

Since about the middle of the last century, the office of sheriff-substitute has been filled by men of great ability. First in order is Mr Mercer, who built Potterhill; his successors were, Mr Richardson, Mr Duncan, Mr Chalmers, Mr Husband, and, at present, Mr Barclay.— These gentlemen were deservedly respected, both in private, and in their official capacity. Mr Richardson was for some years blind, which unfitted him for business. Mr Chalmers, too, was long incapacitated by bodily infirmity. The late Mr Husband sat on the bench for a long period; and to his honour, extremely few of his decisions were reversed by the superior courts—a strong proof of the correctness of his judgment. Mr Barclay, the present sheriff substitute, has exhibited proofs of ability, which will bear comparison with any of his predecessors. From the year 1770 to 1780, there were just eight gentlemen practising before the Perth bar; viz. Messrs John Rutherford; James Ross, procurator fiscal for the county; Andrew Davidson; David Black: William Small; Peter Duncan, jun.; James Miller, the city fiscal, and his brother John. Mr Patrick Miller, the father of the two last-named gentlemen, held the office of town clerk for many years, and was highly respected. Nor must we forget to mention our late worthy sheriff-clerk, Mr James Patton, who for a long period filled that office, and was highly esteemed by all classes of the community, not only as a public man, but as a private individual of the most amiable disposition. We need only refer to the marble tablet in the sheriff court room, for a confirmation of what is here stated. He has been succeeded by his son, Mr J. M. Patton, who is also held in general esteem.

Previous to the institution of the small Debt Court before the Justices of the Peace, an immense number of small cases and petty quarrels were brought before the Sheriff and Burgh Courts, in which men of business were employed, which now come before the Police Court. When the Justices took up these cases, hearing the parties personally, the Procurators suffered severely; and more so since this business has been transferred to the Sheriff Court. Yet, in spite of all these discouragements, the faculty have greatly increased. At present, instead of eight practitioners for the town, there are upwards of fifty; and above twenty more for the country districts.

The shire has not been less fortunate in its sheriff-deputes. Towards the close of the last century, Lord Swinton, Lord Dunsinane, Lord Nairne, and Lord Methven, were all on the bench at the same time, who from being sheriff deputes of the county of Perth, had been removed to the Justiciary bench. Lord Alva, in the Court of Session; the Lord Advocate, Campbell of Clathie, who afterwards was appointed Lord Chief Registrar, under the name of Sir John Colquhoun of Killermont; and Lord Medwyn, at present one of the Lords of Justiciary, were also connected with the Perth Court.

However much we may boast of the respectability of sheriffs and sheriff-clerks, we can say but little for the sheriff officers. Until of late years, their limited incomes and dissipated habits rendered their office more disreputable than it might otherwise have been.

Upon the death of Mr James Ross, procurator fiscal, he was succeeded in that office by his son William, an active young man, who was universally esteemed. Unfortunately, he fell into a rapid consumption, which carried him off in a few months. To Mr Ross succeeded the late Mr John Rutherford, who was esteemed one of the first orators at the bar. For some years he filled the office with great credit to himself and satisfaction to the public. His sudden death was much regretted by his numerous friends and acquaintances. To him succeeded Mr Thomas Duncan, the present talented procurator fiscal. He has wrought a wonderful improvement in the condition of his officers.

The procurators, both in town and county, are now formed into a kind of corporation, with president, treasurer, and secretary. They have a considerable and rapidly extending library, consisting chiefly of books on law. Their office-bearers are chosen annually; after which the members dine together.

Perth being the seat of the Circuit Court for the three counties, the prisoners are all brought here for trial. Formerly the punishments to which they were sentenced were also inflicted here. Perth was at that time very frequently the scene of whippings and executions; but of late years the criminals have been sent to their respective counties, which has rendered such punishments rare in Perth.

THE PILLORY.

Amongst the corporeal punishments formerly in use, the pillory was frequently resorted to. This machine was erected near the foot of the High-street, the pillar being fixed in a stone in the centre of the street, and surrounded by a flight of steps. On the top of these steps stood the culprit, with his arms fettered with ropes, from which hung a halter, by which the hangman led him. An iron hoop, which was fixed on the

top of the pillar, was then fastened round his neck, and there he stood
for an hour bare-headed, with a label on his breast in large characters,
stating the crime he was convicted of.   On some occasions men and women were exhibited tied up together, to the gaze of the public; and if
it was the popular opinion that they merited the punishment, by anything
cruel or singular in the crime, they were sure to receive a most severe
punishment; every kind of missile—rotten eggs, dead cats, &c., being
thrown at them.   On one occasion, Sandy Dowie, the hangman, after
tying up his own daughter on the pillory, turned round to the multitude
and told them she was a base b—h; that he was clean affronted with her!
The pillory has not been resorted to for nearly fifty years; and is now
generally obsolete as a punishment in Scotland.

<h3 style="text-align:center">PUBLIC WHIPPING.</h3>

Whipping through the streets was a punishment very frequently inflicted by order of the supreme court; and also by order of the sheriff
and magistrates.   When it occurred in the case of a female, it
was truly disgusting to see her led through the streets bare-headed, and
her back bared to the lash, which was applied at every place where the
town drummer stopped to cry his advertisements.   They usually went by
the Watergate, up South-street, through the Meal-vennel, and down the
High-street.   On some occasions there were dreadful riots at public
whippings, in which broken heads were the consequence, often followed
by trials for mobbing, and severe punishment.   Between the year 1780
and 1784, two instances of this kind occurred, which created a great
sensation at the time.   The first was the case of three men and two women, who were tried before the circuit for being engaged in a meal mob
at Kirriemuir, who were sentenced to be publicly whipped; but the
populace, being dreadfully enraged at such a sentence, openly avowed
their intention to rescue them.   The 3d dragoons, then in Perth, were
ordered under arms on the South Inch, where their stables then were—
and a troop was brought to the jail door to escort the magistrates and
criminals.   An immense multitude assembled the moment the culprits
were brought out, and a tremendous assault with stones was made on the
dragoons—but, in spite of every opposition, the cavalcade advanced.—
At the end of the Watergate, the attack was renewed.   Still, although
the horses became restive from the shower of stones, the men kept their
temper wonderfully.   Through the Watergate the opposition was not so
great, from want of room—but by the time they arrived at the south end,
the multitude was immense, and the street completely wedged in.   Here
again the dragoons had to force their way through an immense shower of

stones ; and up South-street a serjeant and two men, acting as rear guard, were very roughly handled. Through the Meal-vennel there was no room to act, but at the High-street a desperate effort was made by the mob ; and during their progress down the street, the rear guard was partly beaten off. The whole troop were forced to wheel about and charge up the street, when a scene commenced that beggars description. The poor criminals, with the hangman, were left wallowing in the mud, and the troop galloped up at full speed, smashing away from right to left. Those who could find shelter in shops and closes were fortunate ; numbers were trampled down by the horses ; but, what was singular, not an individual was cut. Several of the rioters were apprehended and committed to prison.

In the other case, a man and a woman who kept a house of bad fame in Dunfermline, were tried for the murder of some person in their house ; when the jury, instead of a verdict for murder, brought in one for culpable homicide ; and the sentence was, that they should be publicly whipped and banished. The public, conceiving that they ought to have been hanged, showed strong symptoms of discontent. A guard of 100 burgesses was summoned to attend the execution of the sentence. They were rudely treated by the mob ; but succeeded in repelling the assault aimed against the prisoners.

CAPITAL PUNISHMENTS.

Amongst the capital punishments which have been inflicted since the year 1745, some of them have been attended by circumstances which render them worthy of notice. A drummer belonging to a regiment lying in Perth, had been in a public house in Scone, where several partisans of the Pretender were among the company. In the course of drinking, the health of the Prince had been proposed, when, unfortunately for the drummer, he was prevailed on to join in the toast. The mistress of the house having given information against him, he was tried by a court-martial, found guilty, and sentenced to be shot. He was led to the top of the North Inch, where he was shot, and buried near the spot. A stone was placed on the grave, with a drum-boy beating his drum carved on it ; which remained till the year 1793. The boy's mother went with her son's bloody shirt to Scone, and smote the door posts of the house with it, imprecating divine vengeance on their heads. It has since been remarked, that the family, who were then numerous and affluent, have dwindled away, and fallen into poor circumstances.

When the place where the fire-engines were kept, in the north aisle of the Middle Church, was cleaned out, there was found amongst the lumber a large heavy gibbet. The history of the execution on this gibbet is rather remarkable, as being the last which took place without a regular indictment. The house on the south end of the Kirkgate, still known by the name of the Cross-keys, was at that time very much resorted to by the best company. A dancing-master who lodged there, and taught his classes in the large hall, had a ball one evening.— An officer of a regiment then in town lodged in the same house, and, on the night of the ball, he, with some others who had been drinking together, forced their way into the room, and began to use freedoms with some of the girls, which the master interfered to check. Not paying attention to this, he was ordered to the door, and actually put out.— Nothing occurred that night; but next morning, while the dancing-master was washing himself at a pump-well in the close, the officer came behind him and run him through the body with his sword. The alarm was instantly given, and the neighbours who collected together, filled with rage at the bloody deed, seized the officer and dragged him before the court which happened to be sitting in town at the time. He was instantly convicted, and hung upon this gibbet at the cross, within six hours after the murder was perpetrated. The sword with which the deed was committed is still in the family of the then town clerk.

The common place of execution was in the Burgh Muir, where there was a permanent gallows. After the rebellion, two young men were sentenced to death, who belonged to respectable families. Their offence had been of a political nature, and great interest was made for them, but in vain. On their way to the place of execution, the hangman was seized with sudden illness, and, having called for a drink at Welshill, his body swelled rapidly, and, before he reached the place of execution, he died in great agony. It was thought nobody would be got to do the business before the hour limited by the sentence had expired, and that the lives of the condemned would thus be saved; but an express being sent into town to endeavour to find another executioner, the office was accepted by a man in the jail who had been committed for a capital offence, on the assurance that his own liberty would be granted. He was brought forward with all speed, and the young men suffered. It was discovered that the hangman had got poison, supposed to have been given him by the friends of the culprits, to prevent the execution. The poor wretch who accepted the job was disappointed; for it was adjudged that the magistrate had no right to offer the terms which induced him to to act as hangman.

The next that followed worthy of notice was the celebrated Serjeant More, the Highland robber. This man had long been the terror of the country ; besides robbing individuals when he found an opportunity, with his band he levied blackmail over the country. In the midst of all his depredations, he did many generous actions. On one occasion, a young officer belong to the King's army, on his way with money to pay the troops, having lost his road, fell in with Serjeant More, who led him to his cave, gave his horse room and provender ; and a good supper and a bed of clean heather was provided for himself. During the evening many of the gang arrived at the cave, and the night was spent with great glee, over a good supper and plenty of whisky, which was served out in wooden caps. On retiring to rest, the Serjeant requested his guest to entrust his valise to him—pledging himself for its safety. In the morning, a hearty breakfast was set before him ; and afterwards his horse was brought forth, and his valise, with its contents, delivered to him. Being mounted, the Serjeant conveyed him a considerable distance; and, at parting, told him who he was, and hoped he would not betray him ; adding, if ever he heard of Serjeant More coming to an untimely end, he would say that he had found him capable of doing a generous action. More, with his gang, was at Crieff market, when a dealer from Perth purchased a lot of cattle. Finding that More and his gang were in the market, the dealer; becoming alarmed lest he should not get the cattle home in safety, sought out the Serjeant and had a glass with him. They soon became the best of fellows ; and a party of the gang were ordered to escort the drove some miles on the way. This cattle dealer kept the public house now in ruins opposite the end of Paul-street, where he sometimes killed a fat beast and sold it ; after this event the supply of beef was large and steady ; but although the carcase appeared in the morning, there never was either hide or horn seen ; and the impression was that Serjeant More's black mail were brought there and sold. More was at length apprehended, and sentenced to be hanged, and his body hung in chains.

On the same gibbet, M'Ewan was hung in chains for murder. The discovery of this horrid deed was very singular. The parties resided near Muthil. A young woman whom M'Ewan had seduced, having become pregnant, he trysted her to meet him at a certain hour in a neighbouring wood. At the time appointed she went with a boy led in her hand : the villain was there waiting—and had a grave ready dug. In cold blood he murdered the unsuspecting young woman, and the boy she had along with her, and flung the bodies into one grave. The young woman was immediately missed, but no trace of her could be found. During the harvest, some shearers in the vicinity of the wood, whilst seated at dinner, were horrified at their master's dog coming among them bearing the arm of a child in his mouth. Suspicion as to the victims immediately flashed upon them, but where to find the bodies was the question. By the advice of the clergyman, the dog was tied up for twenty-four hours, and then let loose and watched, when, as was expected, he ran straight to the grave, where the bodies were deposited. M'Ewan was apprehended, tried, and condemned to have his right hand cut off at the place of execution, and, after being hanged, his body to be hung in chains, and the hand stuck on the top of the gibbet. When M'Ewan was thrown off, the rope broke, and he alighted on his feet : he cried out that his life was saved ; but the youngest Bailie (who always took charge of the punishments) replied "not if another rope can be found in Perth." A second cord was speedily adjusted, when he was again thrown off. Amongst the multitude assembled to witness the execution, was a tradesman's wife, in a state of pregnancy, who, in due time, was delivered of a stout healthy boy ; but, singular as it may appear, he wanted the hand just by the same place where the murderer's hand had been amputated. The boy was bred a teacher, and for a long period acted as parish schoolmaster in the neighbourhood. He died a few years ago.

On another gibbet were hung the bodies of two soldiers, Chapel and Campbell, for the murder of a farmer. They had observed him getting a sum of money in the market, and watched him through the day. On his way home in the evening they attacked him in the South Inch. One of them sprung on the horse behind him and held his arms, while the other stabbed him to the heart with his bayonet—which, in the hurry to be off, they left behind ; and proved the means of their detection. After all, they missed the money they expected, and found only twopence-half-penny on the farmer. It is remarkable that the regiment to which Chapel and Campbell belonged, was the same to which the officer was attached who stabbed the dancing-master. Also, that during the third time this regiment lay in Perth, some years afterwards, the Master of the band was executed for robbing the commanding officer's desk of a sum of money, in Samuel Simpson's lodgings ; and that this Samuel Simpson had to leave the town for a systematic course of plunder which he had carried on against his neighbour.

One poor creature was driven to the place of execution, who, on the fatal morning, had found means to cut his throat ; before life had become extinct he was discovered, and the wound sewed up. When the time arrived he was carried out of the jail, and laid on the scaffold on a truss of straw, and drawn to the gallows. By the time he arrived at the place of execution, he was able to sit up and speak a little to those near him. He was, however, shoved off with very little difficulty. The ancient practice was by means of a treble ladder which was set up against the gallows ; the criminal mounted on one side and the executioner the other, and when the fatal signal was given, the hangman pushed the culprit off the ladder. It was afterwards the custom, as an improvement, to drive the cart from under the criminal, and let them swing. One poor creature, who could speak little English, was condemned for stealing cattle, which, he asserted, he had been hired by a stranger to drive along the road. The cattle were however found in his custody, and not being able to give any account of them, he was found guilty, and sentenced to be hanged. The day of his execution proved very cold and stormy ; the culprit was dressed in the county criminal uniform, a white linen jacket, and white trousers. He complained that " She was vera cold ; Oh ! she was vera cold." The prisoner then called out if Donald M'Glashan was in the crowd. Donald made answer that he was there. This person had come with a cart to convey the body of the prisoner home to his friends in the Highlands. The criminal told Donald to drive the cart with his body as hard as he could until he came to the Bridge of Buchanty, and there he would get a bottle of whisky. A party having formed to carry off the body on the road, Donald found good reason to drive hard.— Some of the assaulting party found means to get one of the wheels taken from off the cart ; but one of the friends took hold of the axle-tree, and kept up that side while running, until the hostile party were completely beaten off.

The last criminal who suffered on the Moor was a fine looking young woman for stealing clothes from a washing house, about the year 1776— the only instance of the execution of a female that had occurred in the county for a long period before ; neither has there been one since.

The day of an execution was at that time the occasion of extreme excitement and bustle in the town, So early as ten o'clock the dead drum was beat through the street, again in a short time, and at twelve for the third time, which set all the town in motion. There was a guard of an hundred burghers, with a captain and two lieutenants called out, who made but a very motley appearance; some being armed with flowling pieces, some with rusty broad swords, and many with pikes. A lofty scaffold was erected on a cart, with a seat on the top of it for the criminal. The cart was drawn by two horses, and the carters claimed as many new ropes as they could stow away about the horses. They were to be seen literally covered with ropes. An immense multitude joined in the procession, the muffled drum beating all the while. When the body was to be hung in chains, a revolting operation took place on the spot. The corpse being cut down it was laid on the scaffold, and the hangman proceeded to rip it up, and take out the bowels in presence of the multitude, which were buried at the foot of the gibbet. After the scene was over, the carters who owned the horses took themselves out of the way as quickly as possible, leaving the hangman to bring the horses into town. This was the time for commencing a row. Stones and sticks, and every thing that came in the way, were pelted at him.— The return presented a very odd scene : the stones flying from all directions ; the hangman whipping away at the horses; the guard running brandishing their weapons ; the roaring of the mob, and the appearance of bloody wounds on many of the guard, formed a strange contrast to the solemn march to the place of execution. The guard were paid with a sixpence each, then the daily pay of the army. The Magistrates concluded the day with a hearty dinner, and the town-serjeants got five shillings each, and the hangman a guinea as his perquisite. At that time, besides his wages, he had the largest piece of coal from every vessel that came to the shore, a fish from every boat, and one from every creel; but this was done away with, and a fixed salary given him. Of late years Perth has dispensed with this functionary. Formerly this official made his appearance in the Court behind the bar at the trials, and when any one was condemned, he laid his hand on the prisoner's head three times, each time calling out, " Dead ! dead ! dead ! by the law you are dead !" Hence the origin of the word doomster, or demster, as he was called."

The place of execution was changed to the foot of the High-street, where a door was broke out from the Sheriff Court-room, and a scaffold erected on the street, with a drop beneath a beam set out through the wall.

Among the culprits who suffered here, was the noted Charlie Graham. Charlie belonged to a gang of tinkers, who had for a long time travelled through the country, whose head quarters were at Lochgelly, in Fife. They were to be found at all markets, selling their horn spoons, which was their ostensible occupation. But there was a great deal of business done in the pick-pocket line, and other branches of the thieving art. About Charlie there was some remarkable traits of generosity. In the midst of all the crimes he committed, he was never known to hurt a poor man, but often out of his plunder helped those in a strait. His father was in the same line, and was long at the head of the gang; but being afterwards imprisoned for theft, housebreaking, &c., he was banished the county, banished Scotland, and publicly whipped. On one occasion he was banished, with certification that if he returned, he was to be publicly whipped the first market day, and thereafter to be banished. Old Charlie was not long away when he returned, and was apprehended and conveyed to Perth jail. A vacancy having occured in the office of executioner, the first market day was allowed to pass without inflicting the sentence, upon which Charlie entered a protest, and was liberated. In various ways he eluded justice, sometimes by breaking the prison, and sometimes for want of evidence. The last time he was brought in, he was met by an old acquaintance, who asked, " What is the matter now ?" to which Charlie replied, " O ! just the auld thing, and nae proof ;"—which saying has since become a common proverb. But this time they did find proof; and he was again publicly whipped, and sent out of the country. One of his daughters, Meg Graham, who had been bred from her infancy in the same line, was every now and then apprehended for some petty theft. Indeed, she was so often in the jail, that she got twenty-eight dinners from old John Rutherford the writer, who gave the prisoners in the jail a dinner every Christmas. Meg in her young days was reckoned one of the first beauties of the time; but she was a wild one. She had been whipped and pilloried, but still the root of the matter remained. Young Charlie was a man of uncommon strength and size, being about six feet high, and stout in proportion. His wrist was as thick as that of two ordinary men; he had long been the terror of the country, and attended all markets, at the head of his gang, where they were sure to kick up a row among themselves. Two of their women would commence a battle-royal in the midst of the throng, scratch and tear one another's caps, until a mob was assembled, when the rest were very busy in picking pockets. In this way they were frequently very successful. At a market to the west of Crieff, a farmer got his pocket-book taken from him : it being ascertained that Charlie Graham and his gang were in the market—who were well known to several of the respectable farmers, who frequently lodged them on their way through the country—it was proposed to get Charlie and give him a glass, and tell him the story. Charlie accepted the invitation ; and, during the circulation of the glass, one of the company introduced the subject, lamenting the poor man's loss in such a feeling way, that the right chord was struck, and Charlie's generosity roused. An appeal was made to him to lend the poor man such a sum, as his credit was at stake. Charlie said they had done nothing that day, but if anything cast up, he would see what could be done. During this conversation another company came into the room; amongst whom was a man with a greatcoat, a Highland bonnet, and a large drover whip. After being seated this personage was recognised as belonging to the gang, and they were invited to drink with them, whilst the story of the robbery was repeated. On this Charlie asked his friend if he could lend him forty pounds to give the poor man, and he would repay him in a few days. The man replied that he had forty pounds which he was going to pay away; but if it was to favour a friend, he would put off his business and help him; when, to their astonishment, the identical notes which the man had lost were tossed to him; and Charlie said that that would relieve him in the mean time, and he could repay him when convenient. It was evident that Charlie smelt a rat, and took this method to get off honourably. Of course the forty pounds were never sought after.

Charlie was one day lodged with a poor widow, who had a few acres of ground, and kept a public house. She complained to him that she was unable to raise her rent; that the factor was coming that night for payment, and that she was considerably deficient. Charlie gave her what made it up, and in the evening went out of the way, after learning at what time the factor would be there. The factor came, received payment, and returned home; but on the way was met by Charlie, who eased him of his cash, and returned the rent to the poor widow. The Rev. Mr Graham of Fossoway came one day to Perth, to discount some bills in the Bank of Scotland; having got his bills cashed, his spirits rose to blood heat; and a hearty glass was given to two friends, until the parson got a little muddy. His friends, loath to leave him in that state, hired a horse each, to convey him home. It was dark and late when they set out, and by the time they reached Damhead, where they put up their horses, it was morning. The house was re-building at the time; and the family living in the barn, when the parson and his friends were introduced. Here they found Charlie and some of his friends over a bowl, of which the minister was cordially invited to partake. His companions also joined, and kept it up with great glee for some time—the minister singing his song, and Charlie getting very big. One of the friends, knowing how the land lay, was very anxious to be off, for fear of the minister's money, and ordered out the horses; but to this Charlie would by no means consent. This alarmed the friends still more; as for the minister, he was now beyond all fear: however, in a short time a number of men came in and called for drink; and then Charlie, after the glass had gone round, said he thought it was time for the minister to get home, and went out to see them on their horses; when he told them he had detained them till the return of these men, who, if they had met them, might have proved dangerous neighbours; but now they could go home in safety. He was one day on his way to Auchterarder market, when he met a farmer going from home, in whose barn he had frequently lodged, when Charlie told him he was to lodge with him that night. The farmer said he could not take strangers into his barn in its present state, as his summer's cheese, and many other things, were lodged there. " D—n your cheese," replied Charlie, " do you think, old boy, I would lay down my honesty for your trash of cheese." They parted, and Charlie got possession from the gudewife for himself, as there were no others with him. The farmer came home late, and knew not that Charlie was there. In the morning when he went into the barn, he was astonished to find it all in an uproar. Upwards of twenty individuals, men, women, and children, were lying among the straw. The wife was called upon to see what state the barn was in; and the old man, in no very soft voice, railed at her for admitting such a band. She replied, she would send them away quietly: and this she did by giving them as much brose and milk as they could take. On their departure, Charlie told him he was a d—d old crab, and that his wife was worth a hundred of him. However he kept his word as to the cheese, and nothing was touched. In the market next day, a good deal of business was done in his way; several pockets were picked, and a number of petty thefts committed. Charlie being in the habit of dealing with a respectable merchant for horn spoons, he was one day in the shop getting payment for a parcel : the money was counted down, but during the time his wife was taking it up, the merchant turned to speak to some one in the shop; the wife on taking up the money said she wanted five shillings; the merchant said he was positive he laid down the whole. She still insisted that she wanted five shillings, and the merchant was determined to resist; on which Charlie interfered saying " Come, come, ye limmer, down with the money; none of your tricks here." At one time he took it into his head to enlist for a regiment in India, with a party here; he did very well until they were ordered to join the regiment. All the recruits being assembled but Charlie, he at last was found drinking in a public house, but would not stir a foot. The officer was got, and the party attempted, after fair means had failed, to take him by force. They only got him the length of the street, when he drew a short bludgeon from an inside pocket, and laid about him from right to left, in such a way that the whole were soon sprawling on the street, and he escaped. The officer, seeing what kind of a character he was, desired the serjeant not to look after him, as he would have nothing to do with him. At all the fairs, he was present with his gang : if any row commenced he was sure to take a lead—and whichever party he joined were generally left masters of the field. One Midsummer market here, a dreadful row got up between the weavers and the farmer lads, hundreds of whom attended the market at that time. Charlie and his friends joined the weavers; the streets were soon in a perfect uproar; the chapmen's stands were upset, and themselves tumbled in the midst of their goods; sweeties and gingerbread were scattered in all directions by the pressure of the contending parties; and broken heads and faces were to be seen in abundance. The whole fair was thrown into a dreadful state of confusion, until a party of military were brought out, who at length succeeded in restoring order;—but Charlie and his friends were not to be found. Many individuals lost their hats, &c., and got bruised bones and torn coats; it was also discovered that many pockets had been picked during the affray. Charlie had often been convicted of theft, imprisoned, and banished the county.— He not unfrequently made his escape by breaking out of prison; but was at length apprehended for horse stealing; and, during his confinement, was put in irons, in one of the strong cages in the old jail. During his imprisonment he was very cheerful, often declaring they could have no proof against him—but a short time convinced him of his folly. He was tried, found guilty, and sentenced to be hanged. When brought out to execution, he was attended to the scaffold by four artillerymen, for fear of resistance. He recognized many of his old acquaintances in the multitude—particularly the merchant with whom he dealt in spoons, and gave him a bow and a wave of his hand. When the fatal hour approached, he appeared quite subdued, and submitted to his fate with calm resignation. After his body was cut down, it was conveyed to the grave by an immense multitude; the coffin was opened and filled with quicklime, to render it useless for the surgeon. Charlie's death was a severe loss to the gang; immediately after this Charlie Brown, his brother-in-law, became leader. This fellow, although not so large a man, was stout, firm built, of great activity, and, like Charlie, had been frequently in the hands of the law, and made shift to get clear, until at last the fiscal was determined to have him. It being ascertained that he was in the neighbourhood, a party of light dragoons was sent out with the officers, who traced him to Auchtergaven. When he saw the party he set off through the fields, until fairly run down by two of the horsemen, and brought to Perth. This desperate character had on him about eighty guineas; he was charged with several crimes, convicted, and sent to Botany-bay for life. After this the gang, who had for a long period invested the country, dispersed, and was seldom heard of.

Some years before Graham suffered, a man of the name of Marshall, from Auchtermuchty, was convicted of poisoning his wife. He had formed an intimacy with a woman in Perth, and adopted this method to get rid of his wife. About the time of her death, some suspicions had been entertained of foul play, but it lay over until the body was ten weeks in the grave, when several circumstances occurred which convinced the public that all had not been right. The body was raised, and the stomach examined, in which arsenic was found in considerable quantity. The evidence was so clear and conclusive, that the jury unanimously found him guilty; after Marshall was condemned, he acknowledged his guilt. It was a little singular that Lord Dunsinane passed the sentence; and that Katharine Nairne, his lordship's sister, had been convicted of a similar crime, but had evaded the law by getting out of prison by a trick. It was observed that the passing of this sentence was extremely painful to him.

Two Irishmen were also condemned for highway robbery: one of them suffered on the day appointed, the other was respited for a fortnight. The first behaved as become his situation; the other, when brought out, behaved in every respect like a play-actor. He refused the service of a clergyman; gave out a psalm and sung it himself, none of the assemblage joining him, so struck were they at such conduct. He then prayed kneeling; but such a prayer was never heard before: he thanked God he was going to a country where there was no rascally judges who would condemn a man for his country. Indeed, the whole he uttered was little other than blasphemy. He then made a spring up on the drop, threw off his neckcloth and shoes, and put the halter over his head, telling the populace, in a jocular way, he would shew them the Irish way of dying; and then, before the executioner was aware, flung himself off from the drop. The whole scene appeared so strange, that little sympathy was felt for him.

About the same period an exciseman from Comrie was convicted of murder. He had quarrelled with a baker there, about a bird cage which the baker had lent him. At the time, the baker was sitting before his door, with a child on his knee, when the exciseman lifted a large oak kaber from a load of peeled wood, and beat out the man's brains with it. The jury brought in a verdict finding him guilty, at four o'clock in the afternoon. In the interval one of the excisemen in Perth remarked, that some of the jurymen appeared very young: an enquiry was set on foot instantly; and the result was that two from Montrose were below twenty-three years, and one from Perth was only nineteen. Haggart of Cairnmuir, the counsel for the panel, craved an arrest of judgment, on the ground that, by the law of Scotland, no man can serve on a jury until he be twenty-five years of age. The court did not sustain the objection, but as the case was singular, remitted the whole to the High Court of Justiciary, who sustained the objection; and also found they could not try him again for the same crime. He was, therefore, liberated on condition of banishing himself from Scotland for life. Some years afterwards he was in Perth as a recruiting serjeant.

At that same circuit, a strange character was tried before the court for theft. When brought in he had a piece of bread in his hand ; his eyes were rolling in a strange manner, and his arms shaking as if he had the palsy. When put to the bar he flung pieces of bread to the judges, telling them it would keep the witches from them. The court sat some time mute, beholding him, and then dismissed him simpliciter from the bar. The very next circuit he was brought forward, charged with four separate acts of cattle stealing. His counsel pled insanity, and that he was not a fit object to go to trial. A jury was impanelled to try the issue, and many witnesses were examined : among the rest, the jailor. He had at different times been 180 days under his charge. Among the first questions put to him was—What did he know of the panel at the bar? He replied that he knew many things of him ; amongst others, that he bullied his judges, and got clear off ! " What do you say, sir ?" exclaimed the judge (Braxfield), " do you recollect you are on oath ?" " I do, my lord ; and I repeat it on oath, that he ' bullied his judges and got clear !' " " How do you come to that conclusion ?" " On various grounds : among others, he came into my house after he got out, and, over half a mutchkin, boasted that he had played his part so well." At length, after much cross examination, he was asked to give his opinion of the prisoner, when he said " My lord, I think he's just one that we say wants a cast, but more rogue than fool." He was then found fit to go trial, and proved guilty ; but in passing sentence, the court restricted the punishment to transportation, on account that, though he was not insane, still they considered there was something silly about him. A short time after he was sentenced, he found means to cut through the bars, and get into the lobby of the laigh iron house ; and was found behind the outer door, with an iron bar in his hand, with which he intended to knock down the jailor.— He was secured at that time ; but afterwards made his escape.

About the year 1796, a man of the name of M'Craw, a weaver, was hung for the murder of his wife. The cause of quarrel was her taking an ounce of tea in a shop on credit—for the payment of which the merchant had craved him. M'Craw went home, and butchered his wife in a cruel manner.

The only native of Perth who suffered capital punishment here, at least for the last century, was John Larg. He was executed in company with one Mitchell, for hamesucken, committed at the Friarton toll, about the year 1815.

In the year 1806, Donald M'Craw was hanged for the murder of a

young girl, almost an infant, by abusing her in an unseemly manner.—
This man was upwards of seventy years of age. He had been at one
time in the Black Watch, had a pension of one shilling a day, kept a
respectable shop in the Kirkgate, and had a good business. This man
was for many years serjeant of the town-guard,—attended all the executions,—and paraded in great pomp at the foot of the gallows; little
dreaming that he was one day to suffer on the spot.

During the late war, a Danish sailor, belonging to a vessel then lying
at Burntisland, was brought up to the Circuit Court, and tried for rape.
Several circumstances in this man's case created much sympathy—
being a foreigner, with little or no English; unacquainted with the
laws of the country ; and last, though not least, the woman was
known to be of a worthless character. Much influence was used in his
behalf; but in vain. At that time, the number of prisoners of war in
the country was great ; many had made their escape, and were
prowling through the country; and it was currently reported that government meant to make an example. When it was known that there was no
prospect of a remit, public feeling became so much excited in his favour,
that the authorities deemed it prudent to send an express to Dundee
for military aid. Half a regiment arrived on the day appointed, and
took up their ground at the place of execution, right across the High-
street, a little below the Watergate, a few minutes before the criminal
was brought out. Nothing, however, occurred, and the poor fellow was
thrown off without the least symptoms of any disturbance.

We have already stated, that when the place of execution was changed,
a scaffold, with a drop, was introduced ; but in this instance, a new method was adopted. A scaffold was erected in front of the centre window
of the Council-room ; over which a beam was fixed, on the side of the
window, with the same length of beam within as without. To the end of
the beam within, a rope was attached, and a hole was cut in the floor,
through which a rope descended into the weigh-house, where a heavy
weight was fastened, about 3 feet from the ground. When the signal was
given, this weight descended, and the beam rose on the outside, raising
the body from the scaffold. The troops that had come up from Dundee
returned next day.

Of late, executions have been exceeding rare. The last who suffered
was John Chisholm, an old man upwards of sixty, for murdering his
wife in a beastly manner, similar to M'Craw. He denied the crime to
the last, although the evidence was clear against him. Chisholm was
long a merchant in the South-street, and held a rather respectable status
in society.

Formerly, various summary punishments were inflicted without either judge or jury. If a lecherous wight was found in correspondence with another man's wife, or any similar crime, the neighbours assembled, seized the culprit, and he, or she, were made to *ride the stang.* A large pole was provided, on which the party was mounted ; men at each end bearing it on their shoulders. The delinquent was retained in his unpleasant seat, by people holding by his legs. In this manner they were marched through the streets ; and the ceremony was concluded by sousing the offender into the Mill-lade. Another popular method of expressing disapprobation was by burning the obnoxious individual in effigy, after having paraded it through the streets.

THEATRICALS.

It is said that Shakespeare performed in Perth ; but we have no account of a theatre or players until the reign of Charles II., when a play was performed on a platform on the river, before the King and his nobles, who were seated on the terrace of Gowrie House. Religious prejudices were so high against theatricals after the Reformation, that players had but very poor encouragement ; and, among the Dissenters, a person who was known to visit the theatre, was deprived of Church privileges. Even so late as 1780, several individuals were taken before the session for going to see a play. At that time, a small company made their appearance in a flat of one of these houses a little below the North Secession Meeting-house, where they played three nights in the week to very poor houses, perhaps 30 to 40 shillings a-night. Their personal appearance was the shabby genteel, in the true sense of the word, and their moral conduct ranked very low. Since that period we have had repeated visits from companies in the Guild-hall ; but they were of the same tag-rag description, until the Edinburgh company came over for a few weeks, with some of the first-rate actors of the day with them. They met with pretty good encouragement. By this time, the Glovers'-hall was built (now the coffee-room), and fitted up in a temporary way as a theatre, with a pit and gallery, but no boxes. Some excellent companies paid us visits, and drew full houses. During one season of Sutherland's company in the Glovers'-hall, the gallery broke down : the play was Macbeth, and the house crowded to excess. Macbeth was on the stage, looking at his hands, and exclaiming, " This is a sorry sight !" when, in an instant, the supports of the gallery gave way, and the whole came down with a dreadful crash on the floor, from a height of from ten to twelve feet, with upwards of 300 people in it. The scene that ensued baffles description ; the appearance of the house was frightful, and in some instances ludicrous.

Men and women were crawling out from amongst the broken rafters, with torn clothes; women wanting bonnets, with bleeding faces ; and many, who were seriously hurt, were unable to extricate themselves.— On the alarm many of the ladies in the pit, unable to get to the door, had sprung upon the stage, where ghosts, witches, kings and queens, ladies and gentlemen, mingled together, made a motley appearance.   The news of the accident soon spread through the town, and the people flocked from every quarter, every one anxious for their friends, it being rumoured that a great number were killed.   The stairs became so crowded with these wanting in and others endeavouring to get out, that an alarm that the stair was giving way, created a dreadful confusion.   It was reported through the town that the players had been representing the Day of Judgment, and that the fall of the gallery was a judgment on them ;   hence some of the Dissenting clergy took occasion to denounce theatricals as the works of the devil.   Several persons got severe wounds and bruises : some had their arms, and one man, a painter, his thigh-bone, broken.   This man had a large family, and the manager gave him his wages during his stay in Perth ;   and, after he left, sent supplies from Dumfries, until he was able to follow his business.   When the Seminaries were built in Rose Terrace in 1806, the old Grammar-school was taken for a theatre, and occupied by Mr Henry Siddons and the Edinburgh com-pany, and by Mr Ryder.   It was here that Rob Roy was introduced to the public by Ryder.   This piece drew amazing houses for many nights, and induced many individuals to go to see it that never were within the walls of a theatre before.   Even religious prejudices were given up, such was the fame of this piece, and of those who played the principal parts.

About the year 1821, the theatre was built in Athole-street, and fitted up in an elegant manner with a range of boxes round the house.   The theatre was built by a joint stock company ;   but has never paid.— From the direction that new buildings have taken, a great proportion of the genteel population are now removed to the south side of the town, at a great distance from the theatre.   Indeed, the taste for theatricals has de-clined so much, that even the first talent has failed to draw a good house. It has been remarked, that ever since boxes were fitted up, the attendance has fallen off rapidly.   When there was only pit and gallery, the gentry got into the pit—the ladies without being in full dress; and the price was so much lower, that it was easier for a family to go to the play ;   but now, many who would have gone to the pit when there was no boxes, do not choose to go there, and will not pay for the boxes, but rather stay at home altogether.   During the seasons the theatre has been open of late years, we have seen almost all the London Stars on our boards—Kean, Macready, Young, Mrs H. Siddons, Paganini, Emeliani, Wilson, Miss Inverarity, and almost all the eminent performers and vocalists of the age. Of late the officers of the 71st and 92d regiments, have performed in the theatre for the benefit of public charities, when considerable sums were collected.

STREET IMPROVEMENTS.

From the year 1750 to 1780, the streets were exceedingly ill lighted, and ill paved. The shop windows, too, were extremely small, and emitted very little light, from the small cruise that burned on the counter. The street lamps were very clumsy things, of a square shape, and the cruise within ill calculated to throw light on the street. In fact, a person a few yards distant appeared just the same as if seen through a mist ; and if any rubbish was thrown out, or stones laid down for building, people ran the risk of getting their bones broken, as there was no protection provided against such accidents. The lamp-lighters were just as clumsy as the lamps ; and were to be seen in the evenings moving about at a very slow pace, bearing on their shoulders a huge ladder, like a trap up to a hay loft, with a lanthorn and candle slung to their sides by a belt. By the time they got their ladders fixed, the candle taken from the lanthorn and again replaced, any one may judge what a time was consumed in lighting a single lamp. Besides the dreary appearance of the streets during the fore part of the night, by eleven o'clock they were frequently in total darkness.

At that time the streets were infested with gangs of thieves, who prowled about, entering shops, lifting shop windows, and picking up every thing they could lay their hands upon. Amongst these there was one gang headed by Gibby Gray, a resolute fellow, who boldly committed street robberies, and soon became a terror to the inhabitants. Parties of his gang would station themselves in closes, and pounce upon any person who happened to be passing by. They had a lump of lead with a hole in it, by which one end of a cord was fastened, and the other end made fast to the wrist ; this proved a dangerous weapon when flung with force at a person's forehead. By this means their victims were knocked down before they could see who assailed them. For years the streets were infested with this gang, and some others, and much mischief was done ; Gibbie was at length apprehended, tried, and convicted, and after a very long confinement in irons in the laigh iron house, sent out of the country. Another leader of a gang, who had long committed many depredations, by breaking into houses and laying hands on whatever he could find, besides attacking people on the street, was at

length apprehended.   This fellow was known by the appellation of Pirnie
Peter.   After being convicted, he lay a long time in the laigh iron house
before he was transported; whence he has returned within these five
years.   He died of the cholera at the time it was raging in Perth.

At a former period, numbers of boys were employed by pye-bakers,
who went through the streets with boxes containing halfpenny pies,
each of them larger than a penny one at present.   In this way one lad
would sometimes sell a half-dozen of dozens in an evening, by calling at
public houses; but this system was the means of making many of them
arrant thieves, by traversing the streets, and going into people's houses,
and carrying off whatever came in their way.

Shortly after the year 1782, the old system of lamp-lighting was given
up, crystal globes were substituted for the clumsy lamps, and nearly
double the number lighted.   The bridge, too, at this time was lighted up,
A Mr Bell, an Englishman, contracted for supplying the lamps with oil,
and lighting them; the unweildy ladder and lanthorn were thrown aside,
and he was to be seen with the light ladder and torch, flying about in
double quick time.   This system continued until the globes were superseded by the elegant gas lamps which at the present day shine with so
much splendour.   At the period above stated, although the lights were a
little improved, there still was no police, and frequently it was found
necessary to mount a strong guard of inhabitants in the Council-room
every night, who sent out parties each half-hour to patrol the streets.
At these guards many laughable circumstances occurred: numbers
occasionally got supremely drunk, and made themselves very ridiculous.

Besides the inconveniences arising from want of light at night, the
streets during the day were in a most deplorable plight with filth.—
At all hours the contents of dunghills, &c., were wheeled out on the
streets, and there left, perhaps until next day, waiting the convenience of
the farmers to drive them away.   Every housewife emptied her soil-
buckets whenever she took a fancy, so that the streets exhibited a
most unseemly appearance.   From morning to night the celebrated
metropolitan custom of "Gar-de-loo" was universally practised: hence
it was no uncommon thing for a person to be overwhelmed with a deluge
of this abomination.   The streets got a kind of a sweep by a few worn-
out old men, who were quite incapable of performing their duty with
effect.   A load of street or ash-pit dung was sold for sixpence, and cow
or horse manure, at eightpence; so litte was dung in request, that the town
manure in the South-inch, which was then the depot for it, lay sometimes
for years unsold.   This system continued until the year 1819, when the
streets were let to a number of contractors.   From the year 1803, when

the dearth produced such an alteration in agricultural operations, the rise in the price of dung was immense. Some years the tacksmen sold a dunghill as high as six guineas, and occasionally even much higher. Some of the farmers who had good horses, would have driven away one of these dunghills at sixteen loads. Much of this dung was driven ten miles, and a couple of tolls paid, which made the price very high. Even private ash-pits were sold in loads to the farmers at five shillings per load, and byre manure at six; but the introduction of bone dust, and the bringing down of byre refuse from London, in the ships that went up with potatoes, has reduced the dung-hill produce from 30s o 40s each. Since the establishment of the police, all dung-hills must be removed, and all filth and ashes laid out under certain regulations—which has put an end to the abominable custom of laying out filth on the Sabbath mornings, which formerly rendered the streets a disgusting sight throughout the Sabbath day.

DIVERSIONS.

Foot-ball was frequently played on the Inch, the matches at which generally were the married against the single men, for a small bet or prize. The foot-ball at Scone was so famous for the reckless character of the sport, that it became a common proverb, " A's fair at the ba' o' Scone." At this game many legs and arms were broken ; and, it is asserted, that during the sport, the opportunity was often taken to avenge old quarrels.

The Shinty or *Club*, used to be played in all weathers on the Inch ; and frequently on the streets, by large assemblies of stout apprentices and boys. This game was also played on the ice by large parties, particularly by skaiters, when there was usually a keen contest.

Archery appears to have been a very ancient game ; but was nearly worn out by the middle of the last century. Many still alive will remember the bow butt on the lower end of the South Inch, which stood a little north from the circle of trees in the south alley. The shot was between this stone and the scholars' knoll, situated a little in front of Marshall Place.

The Golf is likewise a very ancient game, and has long been practised here, by the merchants and men of business. After the close of last century, this game fell off considerably ; but, within these few years, it has been revived, and is now become highly fashionable. A society was recently constituted by royal charter, under the denomination of " The Royal Perth Golfing Society," with president, vice-president, and other office-bearers, annually elected. On the day of election, the society dine together ; and as it is now joined by many of the most influential of the county gentlemen, there is generally a good turn-out. Two prizes are played for in the spring and autumn—the one a silver club, the other a gold medal.

Curling used to be much played during the winter. For this game they had frequently excellent ice on the Tay, but almost constantly, whilst the frost lasted, at the back of the Muirton, before the mound was thrown across the bog; as well as at Balhousie orchard; and on the pools in the South Inch ; but these places are either filled up, or the fishers lay hold of the ice the moment it is formed : this has driven the game to the country. Some good matches are still played at Scone, Methven, and other places.

Quoits were a game much esteemed by the merchants here at one time. In the evening, parties were to be seen, in various quarters, play- ing at the quoits, for a small sum, which was uniformly expended in hila- rity. This game is now rarely to be seen.

The Ball and Nine Holes was another game frequently played. Nine holes were formed ; the one in the centre counted nine when the ball was put into it; each of the others counted as they were numbered, from one to eight ; the party won who first gained the number fixed on.

The Hand-ball was much played, for which there were some very fine situations. One of them between Dr Hossack's house and the Lady's Pend. At that time the ground was so low at that place, that there was a descent into the Inch by a flight of at least twelve steps. Here parties were engaged from morning till night at this game ; and there was often a struggle to get possession of the ground. But the best place was the south side of the square of Gowrie-house. In that wing the windows faced the south, whilst on the north side, they were all built up. There was then a spacious square, with a wall about 40 feet high. The artillery, who had but little duty to perform, frequently took a game at the ball, and always allowed any respectable party to join them. In fact, the company of artillery were so seldom changed, that they became quite do- mesticated, and were much respected by the inhabitants. Another station for the game was the porch of the West Church door, then open. This was chiefly occupied by the youths and young tradesmen ; here the game was played by doubling the ball on both sides.

The Ball Paces was formerly much played; but is now almost extinct. In this game a square was formed ; and each angle was a station where one of the party having the innings was posted. A hole was dug in the ground, sufficient to hold the ball, which was placed on a bit of wood, rising about six inches above the ball. The person at the hole struck the point of this with a bat, when the ball rose ; and in its descent was struck with the bat to as great a distance as possible. Before the ball was caught and thrown into the batman's station, each man at the four angles ran from one point to another; and every point counted one in the game.

Leap Frog was sometimes played, and frequently afforded much sport, particularly to the juvenile portion of the population.

Cricket was never much practised in Scotland, though much esteemed by the English. It was lately introduced here; several cricket clubs established; and is now becoming popular.

For in-door amusements, various games were resorted to. A billiard-table was some time ago set up here, but only resorted to by a few of the first class of society. Balls and assemblies during the winter months were frequent. The first class of society had monthly assemblies, to which the ladies turned out in the richest dresses. The teachers of dancing had balls every month, and a practising every fortnight, to which the parents usually went; and before the ball was over the old folks joined in reels and country dances. Card parties and evening card assemblies were very frequent.

Music was formerly at a great discount in Perth. A great many of our old Scotch songs were sung, chiefly picked up by the ear from the maids at the wheel; but there was scarcely such a thing as teaching singing, until about the year 1780, when some teachers came round for a few months, and introduced this branch. Mr Smith, who was appointed precentor for the East Church, opened a school for singing. He also published a large volume of the best of our Scotch songs, set to music, which was very much admired. Pianos began to be introduced, instead of the spinnets, which were played by a very few ladies; and teachers for the piano became numerous. Backgammon was much played by private parties; and in the Coffee-room, which was then in a wooden house where Mr Myles' shop now is. So much was this game the rage with the merchants in their back shops, and even on the counter, that many of them hurt their business by it;—customers declining to enter those shops which were continually full of loungers engaged in this game.

Tod and Lamb Board was another game here, which was played on a board formed by four intersected squares of lines, three rows of holes in each square, in all 32 holes—for which there were 15 small pins placed on one side, and in the centre a large one, the tod; the small ones were the lambs. Between the holes diagonal lines were drawn which the lambs were allowed to traverse; the tod at same time moving in a similar direction, the object was to hem in the tod.

Cards were played by parties of tradesmen at home, and in public houses over a bottle of ale ; as the game was uniformly catch the
ten, and played merely for pastime, the thing was allowed by respectable houses, and thought quite innocent.   By times the drinking of gills
superseded the good old custom of a bottle of ale, and persons of very
loose morals took the opportunity of introducing various games at cards,
and the dice, for gain, which frequently ended in quarrels.   The keepers
of respectable taverns began to see that allowing such games to be played
in their houses, laid them open to the admission of the very worst of
company, and wisely prohibited this species of gambling.   At the present
time few respectable innkeepers will allow any thing of the kind.

Another in-door amusement during the winter evenings was the telling
of stories, which were chiefly of the horrible kind.   About fifty years
ago, " Satan's Invisible World Discovered," a book consisting entirely
of relations of ghosts of murdered persons, witches, warlocks, and fairies,
was in universal circulation.   This book was read in the presence of
children, and followed up by tales of the same description, until the
youngsters were afraid to turn round for fear of being grasped by the Old
One ! So strong was the impression, that even grown up people would not
have ventured through fear into another room, or down a stair, after
nightfall.

The Ghaist of Mause was a favourite story of this class, combining,
as it did, the requisites of horrible, superstitious, and romantic.   The
tradition went, that a traveller had been robbed and cruelly murdered,
and the body concealed in a wood at Rochallie.   The misfortune of being
robbed and murdered might have been submitted to in pious resignation,
but to be excluded from Christian burial was what no ghost of proper
feeling could endure.   The ghost accordingly, after waiting till its patience
was exhausted, informed a devout elder of the kirk of what had occurred ;
entreating that the bones might be removed to consecrated ground.—
The fear of ridicule deterred the elder from immediately complying with
the injunction, but the nightly appearance of his supernatural visitant
soon operated so powerfully that he was constrained to lay the case before
the session for advice ; when it was agreed to comply with the solemn
request ; but in performing the ceremony, having omitted to remove the
skull, the whole process had to be gone over again before the unhappy
ghost could find rest in its grave.   This story, which for years horrified
the younger section of the community in that quarter, had its rise in a
very simple affair, of which the following is an account, extracted from
Perthshire Advertiser of 3d February 1831 :—

" When a boy, I herded cows in the wood of Rochallie, and often have I trembled to pass the spot where it is said the celebrated ghost directed the bones to be lifted. One night in particular, being obliged to pass by the place on my way home, I got a sad fright. The darkness was scarcely penetrated, by here and there a wreath of snow that had not yet yielded to the thaw in the first of March. The wind was up ; and the wood of Rochallie moaning to the passing gale, conspired to heighten the terror of the time. This is a dreary place, said I to myself, and oh ! this is a dismal night ; should the ghost appear to me, I am sure I would die on the spot. Just as I uttered these words, a rustling among some wither-ed branches behind me, made my head crouch down between my shoulders, and my hair stand on end ; and as I ventured a glance towards the place, oh ! horrible ! a thing like a dog was just ready to leap upon my back. I screamed aloud, Mercy ! mercy ! and fled with the utmost precipitation ; but the object of my terror still kept close at my heels, until I reached my father's house,—where the innocent prattle of my sister's, " Eh, Geordy, whar did ye get Colly, for he's been awa a' day," scarcely prevented me from fainting, while it half convinced me that what I had been so much afraid of was nothing more than my father's old dog, which had gone into the wood that day after a hare. " Where's my father ?" enquired I, ra-ther hastily. " Ben the house wi' a stranger man," was the reply. Ac-cordingly, I went ben, when my father seeing me so much agitated, ask-ed what was the matter, and very Scotsman-like answered his own ques-tion, by saying, " Ho, ho, you've been fear'd coming through the wood." " What made you afraid, my man," said the stranger. " Naething," said I, sheepishly. " O, he's been fear'd for the ghaist," said my father. " What ghaist ?" said the stranger, " O, by the bye, the Ghaist of Mause ; I recollect now ; weel that was a well played game ; is that story still be-lieved real ?" " Real !" said my father, " aye as real as I believe you to be Charlie M'Intosh ; and, although I'm no fear'd for it mysel', I do be-lieve it to be true." " It was just as much a ghaist as I'm ane," said Charlie, giving proof that he was no spirit, by swallowing a glass of ' mountain dew,' that graced the table, in company with a wooden trencher, well replenished with bannocks and cheese. " I'll tell you the true story, (continued he, setting down his glass,)—The old Laird of Rochallie was a merry fellow, as you well know, and one of the servant girls had a bairn to him, of which he was very fond, and was also anxious to have it chris-tened ; and although it was a bastard, he was so intimate with the minis-ter, (Mr L.)—for many a glass they had together—that he thought there would be little danger of sorting things, as he called it ; but to his confu-sion and disappointment, a Wm. Soutar, who was a staunch member of the Church, withstood his claim, and vowed he would make the case known to the Presbytery if it was done. This so operated upon the Minister and the Session, that the laird was told that unless he made satisfaction, the child could not be baptised; and as the Minister carried the voice of the Session to him, he at the same time told him that it was Soutar that had knocked the thing on the head. This intelligence so enraged the laird (who a short time before had come between Soutar and ruin, by taking him by the hand when his creditors were just going to roup him to the door) that from that time forward he determined to vex him. The laird had a man who was fou o' tricks, to whom he told the story, and proposed to give Soutar a fright. So next time Soutar was in Blairgowrie attending the Session, the laird's man waylaid him at a lone place above the Bridge of Lornty, and having fitted two or three sheeps' skins to his body, and got upon all fours, appeared somewhat like a dog; and by barking and howling, he succeeded in frightening poor Soutar almost out of his wits. Next day it was spread through the whole country side, that Wm. Soutar the elder had seen a ghaist, in the shape of a big dog, which had barked at him, and spoken to him, and threatened to appear to him again. Prayer-meetings were set up in Soutar's house, and every means tried that could be thought upon, to lay the spirit; but the man continued to visit him in the same way; till at length getting wearied of so many nightly excursions, he said to his master that it would be necessary to bring the business to an end,—and as he recollected a spot where a dead calf had been buried many years before, after having cut off its head, in order to terrify an old woman with it, he proposed to make Soutar believe its bones to be that of a murdered man, and to cause him to lift and bury them in the kirk-yard. The laird approved of this plan, and the fellow again appeared to Soutar, and told him that he was the ghost of a man that had murdered another man, and that he must come along with him, and he would show him where he had buried the body, and that if he would lift the bones and bury them in consecrated ground, he would trouble him no more. Soutar at first refused, but after the ghost had made several appearances, and threatenings of vengeance, he at last suffered himself to be led at the dead hour of midnight to the calf's grave,—where the ghaist, after again renewing his charge anent the lifting of the bones, vanished with a hideous howl into a hazel bush, while poor Soutar groped his way back from his horrible situation, the best way he could.

" Next day the minister, the elders, and nearly the whole country side, turned out to the lifting of the bones, and both the laird and his man were present, and heard what passed. All the bones except the shanks were decayed, having been buried upwards of thirty years. The minister said, "he had been a strong man;" and added, "but the strongest may be overcome." "I wonder," said one of the elders, "how the skull is not to be seen, for I have known the skull to be quite whole when no other bone was to the fore; surely his head has been made away with." "No," said William Soutar, "for the ghaist told me that he was brought down by help of a dog, and then murdered with a stick." The murmurings for want of a skull, raised in the minds of the laird and his man a fear lest the whole should be discovered; and to prevent this, they procured from the nearest kirk-yard a skull, which they flung down near the place whence the bones of the calf had been lifted, and the ghaist again appeared to Soutar that night, and told him that he had left a bone which he must go back and find, or else he would get no peace, Accordingly, the next day the skull was found; and after it and the shank bones had been waked, (which was done with all due solemnity,) they were conveyed to the church-yard of Blairgowrie, where almost the whole parish assembled to witness and perform the funeral obsequies of a *calf*."

"When Charlie had finished, my father exclaimed, "Weel than, if that be true, there's mony ane been frightened for naething," "There's nae fear of it being true," said Charlie, "for Sandy Rory, the laird's own man, told it to my uncle, who told it to me before I went to Germany with the 42d; and where could ye hear it better than from the ghost himself?"

"Such is the account which honest Charlie Macintosh gave of the matter. On talking over the story with him some time since, he told me that his uncle had likewise spoke to him of a drover, who, failing in the world, gathered in what gear he could, and set off, nobody knew where, and was never heard tell of after, and that this was the person who was generally supposed to have been murdered. Be this as it may, I can vouch for Charlie's veracity, that he would not have eked a single sentence to what he had heard; and the whole country-side, through which he occasionally directed his wanderings, can testify that he was a modest old pensioner, and one who was a *stickler for truth*."

THE BRIDGEND GHOST likewise created an awful panic among the single-minded folks of Perth, by making an incessant racket in an old tenement in Bridgend. By night and by day the mysterious presence was thus manifested to crowds of gaping petrified listeners, who did not fail to magnify its terrors, till its fame rivalled even that of Mause.— The Bridgend Ghost was singular in this respect, that it never deigned to make itself visible, or condescended to reveal the cause of its displeasure. The panic, however, was no way diminished on that account; and some of the more learned and zealous ministers of the place tried, though unsuccessfully, their skill in exorcising it ; but the ceremony was more creditable to their piety and faith, than their knowledge of accoustics, for the ghost was neither laid, nor the cause of the noise explained. A similar case occurred lately at Manchester—and it is probable that the explanation of the one may throw some light on the nature of the other. The good folks of Manchester being thrown into a state of perturbation by a variety of inexplicable sounds, which proceeded from a vacant house, a number of unbelievers instituted a minute investigation, when it was discovered that the flooring of a large room in an adjoining public house was continued through the wall, and thus transmitted, with increased intensity, into the haunted room, every sound which was made on the floor of the public house.

The absurd practice of mothers and nurses threatening children with the appearance of bogles, was almost universal. This had such an effect on the young mind, that it required a strong effort of reason in after life to throw off these impressions. We have known several instances where individuals have been rendered idiots for life by this absurd practice.

SHOWS AND SPECTACLES.

In the early part of the last century, it was common for bullies to come round and challenge any individual to fight in the town, offering to forfeit such a sum as he named, to the individual who would take him up and beat him. The last instance of this description was before the year 1740. One of these individuals, after advertising himself, erected his stage on a Friday in the High-street, when an immense crowd assembled. The usual mode of procedure was to beat a drum, and challenge any person to come and break the head of it, which was considered accepting the challenge. This ceremony having been performed, the bully had not waited long when a stout fellow ascended the scaffold, and kicked in the head of the drum. The battle commenced with great fury, and continued for a considerable time. The odds soon appeared against the bully, who at last received a blow which put an end to the battle and the fellow's life. This was the last instance of this barbarous spectacle heard of in Scotland. The hero's name was John Burt.— His son, John Burt, was for more than half a century a teacher in Perth, and died only a few years ago.

Stage doctors frequently paid us a visit, and were much followed after. They always exhibited on the Fridays, on a stage erected in the

High-street. Operations commenced by twelve o'clock ; and they would have kept the multitude together until six or seven o'clock in the evening. The one of greatest note in the country was a Doctor Green, whose grandfather and father had been long known in the country in the same line, and were all highly respected for their skill in surgery. This gentleman kept his carriage and a couple of servants. He had a few prizes, the head one a large silver cup. Each individual threw up a shilling, for which, besides the chance of the prize, he got a packet of medicine, and a small bottle of British oil, famous for burns. The Doctor was accompanied by a merryman with an infinite fund of humour : besides a tumbler, and sometimes a rope-dancer. On one occasion the rope-dancer announced that next day he would walk on a rope across the street from a chimney head to a garret window, when a very great multitude assembled to witness this daring feat. He walked from the window to the chimney top in perfect safety, but on returning to the window lost his balance and fell. Fortunately an Irish soldier happened to be near the spot, who seeing him in his descent, had the presence of mind to rush forward, and give him a violent push aside, which broke the force of the fall, and thus saved his life. Green was the last of these stage doctors who appeared here, in the least respectable. He died at Newcastle during the time his company were last performing in Perth, which then broke up.

The people used to be very fond of shows and processions ; of these we had a number, and they were sure to attract much attention. In the month of July the Gardeners made a splendid turn out, and walked through the streets, when everything the gardens could furnish was displayed. The Weavers followed in August. There were three societies, each having a beautiful flag, with a loom, and other insignia of the trade. Besides, they had a very ancient flag of beautiful needlework, done by the unfortunate Queen Mary, and presented to the Corporation of Weavers in Perth. Crispin's day, the 25th October, was at a rare time honoured by a splendid and numerous procession of King Crispin and his court. The first turn out they had in our remembrance, was graced by the presence of the whole of the company of artillery, which greatly enlivened the scene. In the month of October, the Brewers, then a numerous body, had servants to the amount of seventy or eighty, who had a procession at Michaelmas in the evening with torches ; and a supper and ball in the Guild Hall. In the month of December, the different Mason Lodges had processions. The Royal Arch in the evening, with a brilliant display of flambeaux.

A great number of shows came round, exhibiting ground and lofty tumbling, and legerdemain, with many optical illusions, which received much attention; these exhibitions were generally in a room engaged for the purpose. Caravans were not known at that time.

There is a certain clergyman in Perth among the Dissenters who has outlived many of his prejudices. In early life he denounced plays and shows as the works of the Devil, and threatened those of his flock who frequented such sights with an appearance before the session. Happening to be on a visit in a house in the High-street, at the time Mr Punch was performing his gambols with his wife Judy, within sight of the window, but not so near as to allow the clergyman to get a proper view of the *show*, the servant was sent out to the showman to request him to come below the windows of her master's house, that the clergyman and his wife might enjoy the sight. This was accordingly complied with; and Mr Punch appeared in all his glory, in presence of the clergyman, who enjoyed the fun exceedingly. The session, however, got word of what had occurred; in consequence of which the reverend gentleman was severely censured.

Another species of amusement, or rather superstition, was resorting to fortune-tellers. It is almost inconceivable the extent to which this credulity prevailed. Numbers of young women resorted to persons of this description to get their fortunes read; and if any article was stolen, these gentry were applied to for information. Of this tribe Black Jean, who resided in the Meal-vennel, was for many years the most conspicuous; and astonishing confidence was placed in her. Incredible as it may appear, the writer has known young women travel the distance of thirty miles, to get this old hag's opinion about the choice of a husband.

DISEASES.

The Plague.—A couple of centuries ago, this pestilence raged in Perth, sweeping whole families away with the most fearful rapidity. It was observed that individuals who had recovered from the disease, were exempt from farther attack; and on these was devolved the duty of attending the sick, and burying the dead. The latter melancholy duty was performed by a cart going round at certain hours with a bell, and wherever there was a dead body it was brought out by the cleansers, till the cart was full, when it was driven to the Grey Friars, where the dead were buried in a mass. During the prevalence of the plague, business was totall arrested, and the town had the appearance of being completely deserted. When a family died out, the cleansers claimed whatever had belonged to it; and in this way they became possessed of much property, which many of their descendants hold to this day.

Ague.—Prior to the year 1780, when the farmers began to drain and improve the land, agues were frequent and severe. This malady prevailed every season, and when an individual was once affected, every recurrence was of greater severity. Although seldom fatal in itself, those attacked rarely recovered their former health. It was also the means of inducing other diseases of a more virulent character, such as bloody fluxes, having much of the malignant character of cholera, and nearly as infectious. The improved condition of the land, by draining and cultivation—and habits of cleanliness, and more comfortable style of living among the people—have now almost extirpated these dreadful disorders.

Consumption.—During last century, this insidious enemy of our race made dreadful havoc among the young of both sexes, more especially between the ages of 18 and 30. In every street—in almost every dwelling, this vampire seized upon its prey; the sinking victims, while sufficient life remained to drag along their enfeebled limbs, still flattering themselves they were daily getting better. At that period, numerous friendly societies were formed in Perth, which were all ruined by the overwhelming number of sick members. It had been feared in the commencement of these institutions, that they would sink under the weight of their aged members; but it never entered into the calculations, that they were to be swallowed up by the young; and the evil was only discovered when it was too late to apply a remedy. Owing, probably, to the increased comforts of life, one case of consumption does not at present exist for twenty which occurred 50 years ago.

Small-pox.—This remorseless scourge was extremely fatal, and remarkably infectious; and the virulence of the disease was greatly aggravated by the unskilful manner of treating it. Overpowering dozes of spirits were administered to set the eruption " out from the heart;" and while in a consequent state of fever and distress, the utmost care was taken to exclude every breath of cool and uncorrupted air. When mortification ensued, the reprehensible custom of allowing the sick room to be filled with visitors, and the practice of *waking* the corpse, was an infallible method of spreading the disease.   Between 1770 and 1780, innoculation was introduced, but met with violent opposition, especially among the lower orders, and a set of fanatics, who denounced it as an impious temptation of the Almighty to bring on distress, which they sagaciously observed, "came soon enough of will." Many of the clergy endeavoured to impress their hearers with the advantages of innoculation; the fatalists, however, maintained that the duration of the life of each individual was already decreed; and, therefore, neither innoculation, nor any other means, could prevent the fulfilment of that which had been ordained to come to pass.   To this

it was replied, that even admitting this to be the case, still innoculation was a benefit, as it evidently alleviated the severity of this fearful
malady, in which the head of the agonised patient was occasionally
swelled to twice the natural size,—the skin became black as soot, and
the whole body one disgusting putrifying mass. The admonitions of the
clergy were seconded by example in the innoculation of their families ;
but, although a milder form of the disease was thus induced, the artificial
method made but little progress till the discovery of the *Cow-pox*,
by the celebrated Dr Jenner ; after which, innoculation was rapidly
adopted, and proved almost universally successful. A few cases of small-
pox having occurred after innoculation for the cow-pox, has led to the
opinion, that in order to render the latter an effectual protection against
the former disease, frequent recurrence ought to be had to the cow, for a
renewal of the virus ; and a more rigid attention given to the state of
those children from whom others are innoculated.

Measles frequently followed the small-pox, carrying off many whom
the latter disease had spared ; even when not fatal, they often undermined
the constitution, and laid the foundation of much future distress.

Chincough was also much more prevalent than at present, and many
children sank under this disease, after a lingering illness.

Worms in the Stomach, were very prevalent amongst children, often
inducing nervous disorders, and occasionally proving fatal. As the disorder is not now half so prevalent as formerly, the change may possibly
be greatly owing to the alteration in the system of diet, now adopted.—
Much may also be attributed to the custom, then universal among the
children, of eating quantities of brambles, and other wild fruit which
abounded in the neighbouring woods and waste lands ; the young having
then more time to ramble in quest of these things, not being set to any
employment until 14 or 15 years of age.

Broken-out Heads.—This disgusting disease also chiefly selected its
victims among the young, and occurred to a fearful extent. In any
school of a hundred scholars, ten or twelve children might be found affected with the eruption, which was both painful to the sufferer, and loath-
some to the person who had to dress the parts. This obdurate malady
has now also given way before the increasing knowledge and cleanliness
of the day.

The Scotch Fiddle.—It is said to have been a sage London maxim,
when a Scotsman entered a house there, to put a stick and a knife into his
hands, to afford him occupation. Whether this had any connection with
the opinion of the Highlandman that all luxuries were merely comparative, and, in this point of view, that nothing was equal to a seasonable

scratch,—certain it is, about fifty years ago, the fiddle was in such general repute, that few allowed themselves to be absolutely idle,—the fiddlers
devoting all their spare moments to this agreeable pastime.   It is only
those who have come through the trying ordeal and searching purifica-
tions necessary to overcome this insidious disease, that can fully appre-
ciate the advancement which society has since made, and emphatically
thank God their hands are clean.

Cruels, or *King's Evil* was at one time awfully prevalent.   We are
told in Sacred Writ, that the sins of the parents are visited on the children.   As this hereditary and incurable disease is fast disappearing, or become greatly modified in its character, it may be held as evidence of a
more virtuous and higher moral condition of the people.

Iliac Passion and *violent Cholics* were also very frequent; and carried
many suddenly off.   The quantity of greens and watery diet consumed
by the common people, and the too free indulgence in new made ale,
was by many ascribed as an exciting cause of this complaint.

Palsy and *Apoplexy.*—While we may congratulate ourselves on deliverance from many of the evils which afflicted our forefathers, there are
others which have increased upon us.   Palsy and apoplexy now occur
much more frequently than formerly.

Fevers.—This scourge also holds its sway ; but now generally assumes a milder form, and is not characterized by the sweeping contagion
which formerly marked its progress.   Much of the evil still arises from
the imprudent practice of acquaintances crowding into the chambers of
the sick, and the pernicious custom of sitting in the same apartment with
the corpse prior to interment.

Insanity.—This most distressing and hopeless of all the evils of Pandora's
box, formerly prevailed to a great extent.   Objects of mental weakness or
derangement, were continually to be seen : some of them silly, harmless,
wandering creatures, covered with rags, filth, and vermin : others, who on
the least provocation, were rendered dangerous, or furiously mad.   Happily the arrangements now made for keeping these wretched beings in
safety and comfort, have at least removed this sad spectacle from the
public streets.

Cholera.—In the year 1832, when this awful scourge was making
dreadful havoc in the country, the leading inhabitants of Perth bestirred
themselves to ward off the disease, or to modify its virulence.   A thorough inspection of every cranny in the town took place, followed by
rigid purification, wherever lodgments of soil were discovered or suspected.   Pigstyes were demolished, and the inmates doomed to slaughter,
or banished to the country.   Dunghills were detected in cellars, and in

dwellings, where for years the fever had constantly prevailed; but which, after a thorough cleansing, became immediately as healthy as other houses. A soup kitchen was also established, where the poorer portion of the inhabitants received daily a good substantial meal; and every exertion was made to promote personal cleanliness. The salutary effects of these endeavours were demonstrated by the fact, that during the prevalence of the cholera in Perth, the gross mortality was less than during ordinary seasons! Of those who were attacked, its first victims were selected from among those whose constitutions might be supposed to be shattered by dissipation, or enfeebled by meagre living; but as the disease advanced, it became more indiscriminate in its attacks. On the whole, however, Perth escaped wonderfully, compared with other places; which certainly must have been greatly owing to the excellent preventive measures adopted. A cholera hospital was fitted up, but, unfortunately, the rapid course of the disease afforded little ground of hope of relief from this measure; and in point of fact, it is questionable if a single recovery from the true disease occurred in it. Of course, it soon became unpopular; patients expressed an unwillingness to be removed from their own houses—and the institution became inoperative.

Obesity.—It may be a matter of doubt with some whether the sturdy subjects of this complexion ought to be placed upon the sick list; or whether the tun-bellied knights ought not rather to be considered as high specimens of health, indicating an originally sound and vigorous constitution. Owing to some difference in the animal health, or to superior mental energy—the collision of intellect, and activity of mind of the inhabitants of the present day, keeping the body in abeyance— there is now hardly a remnant of this once numerous class of worthies. Dr Wolcott says, " fat ties ideas by the legs and wings;" and certainly to observe a couple of these substantial burghers moving off to take their *eleven hours*, with double chin resting on their breast, a paunch hanging down to their thighs, and faces radiant with expectation, it was evident they were untroubled by care, except it might be for the untoward encounter of a cart in a narrow street—an evil they had no way of avoiding, except by turning back, or wedging themselves into an entry till the cart moved past. Every thing is liable to change, and there is now scarcely a *presence* remaining; there is not half a dozen men in Perth but can see their feet and tie their shoes! In extreme cases it might be questioned whether the belly belonged to the man, or the man to the belly; if size determined the point, the belly was the man! This state of lusty life was not peculiar to the gentlemen, many of the fair sex even outrivalled their husbands. Two sisters who resided in the Kirkgate, each weighing 24 stone, having occasion to visit Glasgow, no coach could be got to convey them, and they were constrained to go by the carrier, who charged them so much the hundred weight.

At the period alluded to, 1780, the town enjoyed the services of two doctors and one surgeon. Doctor Wood, or old Rob Wood, as he was usually styled, had his shop in the Watergate, and Dr Robertson had his in the north end of the School-vennel. Matthew Davidson, surgeon, had his shop at the Parliament-close, and Dr Johnston, the apothecary, had a very fine one first door east below the Guild-hall. There was a laboratory, chiefly for the sale of herbs, kept in the premises now occupied by Messrs R. & J. Greig, by a person of the name of Steedman, who was not regularly bred to the profession. These gentlemen had the assistance of Dr Nisbet, who was for upwards of forty years stationed here with the artillery. This gentleman's services were always ready to the poor gratis; he also often gave away medicine. At this Mrs Nisbet would grumble; and to prevent her complaints, he would slip a piece of money into their hands, that they might make a pretence of paying for what they got. When any poor convalescent whom he had attended came to ask his charge, he would tell them in a serious tone that the bill would be very heavy, and that they must go home and work hard, for it would be long before they would be able to make it up: and thus the bill was paid. This generous friend to the poor died about the year 1803, in a good old age, universally regretted. At his funeral there was an immense assemblage; and the Gentlemen Volunteers, then embodied, attended to pay all the respect to his memory in their power, and buried him with military honours. Dr Wood was esteemed a man of much skill, but of a rough and forward disposition. Dr Robertson was quite the reverse, being of a quiet reserved character. Dr Davidson was a good natured man, something akin to Dr Nisbet: he attended chiefly to the disorders of children. Medical charges were extremely moderate at this period At the conclusion of the American war, the medical fraternity was considerably extended.; since which period the increase of their numbers has kept pace with the augmentation of their fees.

Some time ago, Dr Brown, an aged native of the city, bequeathed £500 towards building a Fever Ward. This has been followed up by a general subscription for building an Infirmary. The sum of £6,000, required before proceeding with the building, is at present filled up, so that the work will likely be soon commenced.

R

GLENCOE CLUB.

For many years a club flourished in Perth, under this denomination. What was its origin is now difficult to ascertain ; but so far as can be learned, it appears to have arisen with the natives of the Highlands, residing in Perth, who, in some manner, were related with the *Massacre of Glencoe.* For the last twenty years the club has been nearly extinct, and the name rarely mentioned, but by a few people familiar with their meetings. Their original object appears to have been of a commemorative nature, as they had no funds, neither was any advantage reaped by being a member. They had an annual meeting, and then dined together in an inn within their own district, which they reckoned to be between the Meal-vennel, and the High-street-port. At this meeting they elected their office-bearers, viz., a provost, dean of guild, bailies, treasurer, and councillors. The members were chiefly confined to men in business in that district, and when any of their number committed a breach of the rules, they were brought before the council ; and although they were punished with neither bonds nor imprisonment, they were *bled* pretty freely in the purse, which was spent in the rendezvous. The last provost of any notoriety, was Mr David Peter, a spirit-dealer. Before his reign the chair was filled by Mr Wright (uncle to Provost Wright), whose happy humour qualified him to take the lead in any festival. During his reign the society attained the zenith of its glory; he was succeeded by King Davie, a nailer, who kept the public-house still known by the name of the *Glencoe Tavern.* After the deaths of these worthy citizens, the club greatly declined,—but since the Parliamentary Reform, it appears to have emerged from obscurity. When the Church of St Paul was built, one of the members of Glencoe, a home-spun poet, presented a petition to the Lord Provost and Council of Perth, for a bell on St Paul's Church, which was granted ; and shows that Glencoe, at that time, was influential. The bell is rung every morning at a quarter before six; besides answering religious purposes. In that district there was another club kept up, with an annual feast, termed the *Willie Club.* This club was originally confined to individuals of the name of William ; but, some years ago, it died a natural death. Many persons were admitted to it, whose only business was to chat over the days of langsyne, and keep up a personal kindly feeling for each other. Their dinner was held in Gunny Christie's Hammermen's inn, at that time famous for being a good house for travellers ; but, as the old members died, the club failed entirely. Since the passing of the Reform bill, the fourth ward of the Burgh of Perth have again assumed the title of Glencoe. Among themselves they hold several convivial meetings. At all the elections of councillors for the burgh, they have returned Reformers; and so linked are they, that no Tory need pretend to serve them, in burgh politics. They seem so connected together, as to form, although a part of the city, a community entirely disjoined from the other three-fourths of it, by habits and manners of thinking peculiarly their own.

TURNPIKE ROADS.

Before the introduction of the turnpike act, the roads in the county were in a miserable state—indeed, inferior to the worst of our present statute labour roads. Many were mere hilly tracts, on which carriages could not venture, and totally unfit for foot passengers. From this cause business was necessarily retarded, and could only be carried on generally by pack horses. When a farmer sold his grain to a baker or a brewer in town, all his neighbour's horses were put in requisition, a sack with a boll of victual laid across each, and away they marched in troops to town. To have met a party of farmers, on their way home, after selling their stock, and getting a liberal allowance of ale, flying furiously along the narrow rugged road, where it was difficult to get out of the way, was extremely dangerous. Where carts could be used, two bolls of barley was a load, or four bolls of meal, and their progress only averaged about a mile and a half an hour. Generally the roads did not admit two carts to pass but at particular places; and so deep were the ruts that, it was impossible to get on without occasional assistance. In the winter season the mode of conveyance was doubly hazardous.— Horsemen fared little better. In the Carse of Gowrie, now so much famed, farmers rode with great caution, and selected their paths with much care. About 40 years ago, a proprietor near Errol who had recently come to Scotland, was riding quickly along the road then in use, which led to Perth, when he met a tenant of his own, and Mr Thomas Baird, sen., now of Bridgend, mounted, but walking slowly, whom he accosted thus, " Well, Clashbenie, you and your friend Baird seem afraid to ride ;— but look at me, I'm not so." They answered, " You do not know our roads yet, sir." The laird, in an air of defiance rode briskly off; but presently they heard a cry, which, on turning round, proved to be the laird and his horse stuck fast in the centre of the road. Assistance was procured, the laird was dragged out in a well mudded uniform, and then his horse by means of ropes. Several of the old farmers in the county will, on the recital of this single incident, recall many similar. The mercantile gentlemen travelled on horseback; saddle horses were very numerous, gigs were not known; there were a few post chaises, but their progress was very slow. After the year 1775, a chaise with two horses was set

a-going between Perth and Edinburgh, styled the *Fly*. This conveyance set off from Perth the one day at seven in the morning, and reached
Edinburgh at nine at night—and the day following started and returned
at the same hours. This *Fly* to Edinburgh three times a week was considered not only very expeditious, but of great utility to the inhabitants,
and the proprietor was loudly praised for his noble enterprise. At present,
the Aberdeen Defiance reaches Perth from Edinburgh in four hours, just
ten hours less time. Any repair the roads underwent was by statute
labour, each farmer giving a certain number of men for so many days,
who perhaps would have to travel ten miles to the place. The day's
labour consisted in throwing bullets of unbroken stones gathered from the
fields into the holes in the roads, and where stones could not be found,
they were filled with earth out of the ditches, so that travelling even in
a carriage was dreadfully fatiguing, from the jolting over the stones so care-
lessly laid, and sinking into holes. The line of the roads seem generally to
have been little regarded, for the nearest cut was selected, however inconvenient; and we still see many of the old roads up one brae and down another. The old road to the Queensferry, and the Auchterarder road,
are beautiful specimens of this kind. The mail, at the time we speak of,
was a very simple machine. It consisted of a board above the axle of a
pair of wheels, drawn by a single horse; the driver having the whole
responsibility of the letters. The royal vehicle came from Edinburgh
at first twice a week, then it came and went each alternate day. The
letters were delivered by a woman, who went through the lieges at her
own leisure on the second and third day after their arrival. The letters
beyond Perth were subject to delay and insecurity. The carriers, on
whom a great part of the business of the town devolved, were much respected, and many of them made large sums of money. Those between
Edinburgh and Perth took a fortnight to go and return; and the charges
for goods was in proportion to the accidents of the journey. Cases occured where carriers were capsized several times before they reached
their destination, often sustaining the loss of a horse, besides damaging
the goods.

Parties to the country, to spend a day as now enjoyed, was in those
times never dreamed of. Instead of a visit in a drosky, no family ever
thought of leaving town, unless in cases of a domestic calamity. The
mode of travelling was, for the most part, for the guidman and wife to
ride together on horseback, and the family, if young, were placed into
creels slung over another horse, whose halter occupied the hand of their
mother, while the father managed the first.

Wednesday and Friday are the ordinary weekly market days. Tho *butter market* was anciently held on the pavement on the south side of the High street, above the Kirk-gate, but the merchants found it to be a nuisance, which shut up their doors. On a complaint from them about thirty years ago, it was confined to the High-street, below the Watergate; but since that time a convenient market at the west-end of the Flesh-market has been erected, with stalls and benches for the use of the country people and retailers, where it is now held. A great number of carriers come from all quarters on the Tuesdays, Wednesdays, and Fridays.

The first fair in the year held at Perth, is the first *Friday before Old Handsel Monday.* This fair used to be termed the "leg and the loaf day," and the "hen and the hesp day," which arose from the circumstance of the wives of many of the small farmers and cottars bringing in their yarn and hens for sale, and purchasing a leg of mutton and a large loaf to celebrate Handsel Monday with. The bakers had always very large loaves provided for this day's sale. A man could always find a loaf suitable to his family, however large it might be. Peck loaves, and two peck loaves, butcher meat, &c., were carried home for Monday's feast, although for the next twelve months not a bit of flesh was seen by their families. Strange as this may appear, it was in many instances the case: they had their bit of land, which yielded meal and lint; their cow kept them in milk; and with the produce of their garden, they made a shift to get through the year without the luxury of butcher meat. Since the cottars and small farmers have decreased in the conntry, the market has fallen off, and their small cans of butter, cheeses, &c., have been converted into large kits and substantial cheeses, which come to St. John's-day market.

The First of Luke market, or, as some will have it, "the first hail ouke of March," was held on the 10th of March. If it happened on a Saturday or Sunday, it was held on the first succeeding Tuesday; but it is now held on the first Friday, and is frequented by dealers from all quarters. In this market horses are to be found, from the small Shetland pony to the heaviest draught, or the finest riding horse: there is also a good cattle market, at which a fine show is usually on the ground.— About the middle of last century the cattle markets were held in the Gallows Park on the Burgh Muir. A guard of the burgesses armed with Lochaber axes, under a captain, were marched out to keep the peace ; but the distance having been found inconvenient for transacting other business in Perth, the market was shifted to the North Inch. Of late years, all the cattle markets are held on that part of the South Inch where Cromwell's fort stood. This fair still retains the same features it was wont to have. The horse market is now held in the South-street of Perth—and the show generally extends on both sides of it, from the Jail up to Methven-street.

The Sand market for cattle were held on the Shore every Friday in May, old style ; but in lieu of these markets, a weekly cattle market has been established throughout the year on the Inch.

Midsummer market, the greatest of all the fairs, in ancient times continued for a fortnight. It was long held on the 5th of July, or the first Tuesday after, but it is now held on the first Friday of the month. It has a great horse and cattle market. Before hand labour was superseded by the thrashing machine, the farmers had more men and women about them than at present, all of whom claimed Midsummer fair and Old Handsel Monday as their own peculiar holidays, which is still conceded to them. This fair was anciently the feeing time ; but fee or not fee, they make a point of attending it, and do so in such numbers that it is a complete squeeze to get along the streets. The country, fifty years ago, was full of chapmen, who travelled on horseback with large packs and lodged at farm-houses. They were generally well received and lodged for their packet of news, which they always had ready to vend with their wares. It was no uncommon thing for orphan boys to be set adrift in the country with a small box of needles, pins, laces, &c., and a few ballads, and afterwards succeeding in acquiring a horse, as well as a good and valuable pack. Midsummer fair was for these persons a central point, where they annually assembled. As a body, they were not only intelligent but wealthy—and formed themselves into an association, directed by a preses, who was styled "my lord." It was by this class of men that the cloth shops in Perth used to be occupied ; the summit of their ambition was to fill a shop ; and many of the fortunes of our most respectable merchants originated in the profits of the pack. They appeared in such numbers at the fairs, as literally to fill the High-street from the Kirkgate to the Guard-vennel, with a double row of stalls, covered with blankets. An awning extended in front about four feet, and the back of the stalls was furnished with shelves for their goods. Towards the afternoon the lasses collected in parties on the street, or ranged themselves in front of the chapmen's booths, waiting anxiously the arrival of their joes, to give them their fairing. Towards evening they again made their appearance, and not unfrequently battles between the country and town lads was the consequence ; when a general uproar was the result ; to the benefit of pickpockets and such like gentry, the non-conservators of peace and justice. On the following day, which was kept as a part of the fair, the packmen held their meeting for the election of their preses and other office-bearers. On this occasion they had races on the South Inch of a singular description. A gallows was erected, with a ring placed on the cross-beam, through which each rode at full speed with a rod in his hand ; and the man who could carry off the ring on his rod gained the prize. Afterwards a small barrel inclosing a cat and a quantity of soot, was hung up. Again they rode through, giving the barrel a stroke ; and the man that broke the barrel and let out the cat (by which he received a plentiful shower of soot about his ears,) gained the prize. The poor cat was then tossed about amongst the mob, which put an end to its future usefulness. Its remains afforded rude sport to the youths ; and whoever happened to be present at this period of the amusement, met with rough usage. Among the last of these meetings, a respectable citizen's wife was present, whose offspring bears a very legible testimony of the existance of this old usage. She happened to be at the time *enciente*, and was struck on the side with the cat ; the child bears to this day, a vivid mark of the cat on her side.

St John's Day, formerly the 9th, is now kept on the 1st Friday of September. It consists of a horse and cattle market. In the horse market frequently 1000 horses are for sale ; the cattle market presents also a great show. Formerly, a great plaiding market was held the day previous ; when the fair happened on Tuesday, the plaiding market was held on Monday morning. On such occasions, the Sabbath evening presented numerous bands from the Highlands, with their small ponies loaded with plaiding and blankets, coming into town. Great quantities of wool were also brought in. St John's market is regarded among the inhabitants principally for butter and cheese, the sale of which has so increased within the last forty years, that the carts now occupy the High-street below the Watergate. George-street, on both sides, as far as the bridge, and part of Charlotte-street. There has of late been upwards of 240 carts of dairy produce sold on one day. A good deal of business was done at one time in bleached linen ; the spinning and weaving of which afforded occupation to many families in the country. By these sales a great part of their rents were paid. Another article was oak spokes, from the Highlands, for cart wheels ; these generally met a ready sale. At this market, the streets and inches were long pestered with slight-of-hand gentry. De'el boxes, wheels of fortune, clubs and garters, pins and thimbles, ginger-bread, pins, and swindlers of that stamp ; but, some years ago, when Robert Ross, Esq. of Oakbank, held the office of Lord Provost, he declared war against all these unamiable-looking gentry. Wherever he met them, he upset their tables, kicked away their pins, and persevered until they became afraid of his magisterial authority. Now, few of these public pests are to be seen at the fair. At this market, sheep were annually bargained for—being near to the season when flocks were brought from the Highlands, and bought up by the Perth butchers, who kept them on the inches until they were required. Since feeding with turnips has been introduced by graziers, another system of purchasing sheep has been adopted. These Highland sheep were much smaller in size than they now are ; 8lb. the quarter was thought very large; they generally averaged barely 6lb. a quarter. The meat of the Highland sheep was remarkably sweet, and sold here from a shilling to eighteen-pence a quarter.

Little Dunning market, held on the 20th of October, is now kept on the 3d Friday of that month. It is also a great butter and cheese market ; frequently, there is as much of these articles at this, as at St John's Fair. In 1834, there was 230 carts in the market. This fair is now established for hiring or feeing farm-servants, instead of Mid-summer ; which brings a great attendance of men and women, who assemble principally between the Watergate and the Skinnergate, where they are fee'd. Of late years, several young men have fee'd to several masters, with no intention to enter their services,—spending their aerls, in dissipation. This unprincipled procedure has, in a number of instances, proved hurtful to the farmers ; a stop has however been put to it by Sheriff Barclay, and farmers are now more on their guard. Formerly, great quantities of flax were brought to this market. Farmers were then in the practice of keeping a number of maids, principally with a view to spinning—the produce of their labour forming the chief source from whence the rent was made up : a farmer's kitchen exhibiting in the long winter evenings much of the bustle of a little manufactory : three or four maids spinning ; the mistress of the house reeling their yarn; and the master, men-servants, and herd boys, assiduously employing their vacant time in knitting mits and hose, or occupied in repairing the horse gear,—while the whole party were edified by the interesting horrors of a ghost story. Owing to great changes in the management on rural affairs, and the unwearying efforts of the giant steam having banished the cheery thrifty wheel from the ingle side, little flax is now raised in the country. Little Dunning cattle market is well attended. This fair, and some others in the country round, was frequented by people to buy their winter marts, a practice that long prevailed here. Many who were not able to purchase entirely, joined togeher, to have one amongst them. This so raised prices, that little fresh beef was to be had through the winters, except that of milk cows, fed by the cow-feeders in town, which were very poorly kept. Since the stall-feeding of cattle has become general, the salting of winter beef has fallen into disuse. Numerous flocks of goats were formerly brought from the Highlands to this market; their flesh was much esteemed for hams, but since planting has become so general, they have been banished from many quarters: their skins were at one time much used for soldiers' knapsacks, dressed with the hair on.

Andersmass Horse and Cattle market, held on the 11th of December, is always well attended. There is generally also a good supply of butter, cheese, &c. Formerly large droves of small Highland swine were driven to this fair; but this small kind have entirely disappeared. The day after this fair, and the day after Mid-summer, are the terms on which the house rents in Perth are paid. At Andersmass, the houses are given up or are taken by tenants, for another year. The term for removing is Whitsunday.

Palmsunday-eve market is held the first Friday of April. The chief business done at this fair is in barley, and grass seeds. Formerly a great deal was done in lintseed. It is also a cattle, but not a horse, market.

At these fairs, and on the weekly markets, the coopers bring out their different articles, and expose them on the High-street, between the council-house and George-street. This branch of business has, however, declined since the introduction of tinplate articles. The cap market has also declined from the earthenware being so reasonable in price.— There is still, however, one or two stands with wooden dishes and riddles, situated on the north side of the High-street, between George-street and the Skinnergate. A great number of nailers used to come to the fairs from Pathhead, with cart-loads of nails; these, however, have entirely disappeared. A great number of country shoemakers used to attend the shoe market, in the South-street. There are, however, very few who do now attend it.

Wool Market.—Last year, 1835, the Magistrates of Perth established a market for wool. The samples, which were single fleeces, were exposed in the council-room, and the sales were extensive and satisfactory to the sellers. At four o'clock, the wool-staplers and sellers dined in the Salutation inn, where a great deal of business was done. This market in future is to be held a week after the Inverness wool market, which takes place in the month of July each year. The samples of wool in future,

s

are not to be confined to one fleece of each kind merely, but to three
fleeces of wool. Although the notice announcing this market was limited,
a great number of wealthy wool-staplers attended, and every support has
been provided, to establish it successfully. The establishment of this
market is due to John Richardson, Esq. of Pitfour, a young gentleman,
who, for several years back, has exerted himself to promote the prosperity
of the City of Perth.

BAD SEASONS.

Perth is generally esteemed a healthy place. From the improved state
of the country around, as well as from the excellent police of the town,
much has been added to the health and comfort of the inhabitants. There
is nothing more conspicuous than the change that has taken place since
the country has been relieved of heavy woods, for well drained lands.—
The winters have been nothing in severity or duration to what they were
formerly. The ravages of the Tay on the breaking up of an intense frost,
are now but seldom heard of ; nor are the labours of the poor retarded by storms. This change is most gratifying ; and still more so when
contrasted with years of famine that have gone by, during which the industrious poor suffered so severely.

The year 1740 was long memorable for the length of its severe winter,
and still more severe dearth, or famine. Its severity I shall represent by
reference to cases, from which the reader may estimate the extent of the
calamity in this, as well as succeeding years which I shall notice.

An old man in Perth who had a family, gave a pitiful description of
the state of the inhabitants in Perthshire. The frost set in with the
greatest severity very early in the season, binding the earth to a great
depth, which happened to be very wet at the time. A strong north-east
wind then set in, with a heavy fall of snow, which continued for four
successive days. The river Tay was frozen almost to the bottom ; horses
and carts passed over it freely, without creating a crack ; and an ox was
roasted on the river which was sold for one shilling per pound. The
spring came on, but no thaw. The snow gradually gave way ; but still the
season advanced without heat to relieve the ground. The frozen clods were
ploughed down, and the seed committed to the ground in this state. The
summer continued cold and bleak in the extreme, with little sunshine.
The harvest passed in the same cheerless way ; the little of the seed
which sprung up was very poor both in grain and straw. The supply of
food for man and beast became extremely scarce, and sold at extravagant
prices. The importation of grain from foreign quarters was then unknown
to the general body of the people, and the national feelings at this time

prevented measures from being concerted to alleviate the common distress. In England distress was partially felt. In Perthshire there was no potatoes, and little or no wheat; butcher meat could be had, but so poor as to be little better than carrion. To this food in many places not a bit of bread could be obtained. In some districts in the Highlands, families lived for months on the flesh of their sheep, without tasting bread or meal. The distress was not confined to man alone. The beasts in the field were driven by destitution to the nearest dwelling houses; their natures were subdued into tameness, and many died from starvation— which the poor assiduously searched for in the mornings. The same old man who described the horrors of this year, gave an instance of brute suffering which occurred in his house, then infested with rats, although not before that year. He had a loom in the one end of his house, at which he constantly wrought. When his wife dished up the kail to cool in the cogue, they were set on the lid of a chest beside him, (for they had neither table nor plates to sup from,) and he had to keep his ellwand at hand to drive away the rats. The continuance of the severe weather increased their boldness; and latterly they became so familiar with him as to wait for a portion of his cheer. When the season became friendly, to use the old man's words, " the brutes flitted frae me !"

The succeeding severe winter laid aside almost every description of labour. Spring brought again the same bleak chilly easterly weather. During its continuance, the frozen clods formerly ploughed down were now turned up in the same state: any seed they had preserved was of such a doubtful quality, that little hope was entertained that it would spring at all. It was, however, sown; and when it did spring, the description my informant gave of it was, " that he could lie down in a field and not hurt a stalk of it." About the beginning of June, a thorough thaw commenced; the wind came round to the west; the sun shone forth in all his splendour; the weather became all at once exceedingly warm, with genial showers, which made the seed to spring up, as if by miracle, which yielded a crop more favourable than the farmers anticipated, from the previous general appearance of the thin corn fields.

Since 1740, we have been frequently visited with bad harvests by which the poor suffered most severely. The year 1782 was remarkable for the " snawie" harvest, which prevented the corn from ripening. The meal was dear and scarce, besides being of a very bad quality. Potatoes were then raised to some extent, but the growers had not the method of preserving them through the winter. Indeed, they were deemed unfit for use after the new year. During the succeeding spring and summer, meal was hardly to be got for money. When a small supply came to

Perth, the people assembled in multitudes, which rendered it dangerous for old or weakly people to attempt to get any of it. When meal could not be procured, Provost Ramsay obtained from England a number of cargoes of white pease, which he made into meal. This at the time was a great blessing to many families.

The harvest of 1791 was extremely wet, attended with direful consequences. After harvest was commenced, a constant rain set in ; for three weeks the shearers never attempted to cut a stalk : as they were at that time all hired for the harvest, they became a heavy burden on the farmers. The grain was got lodged ; part of it rotten, and part was put in the stack damp which heated. To have seen the corn-yards, one would have thought they were on fire, from the great smoke they sent forth. To have seen them from a hill, they resembled so many smothered fires here and there. The meal this season was very bad in quality ; it was red as iron rust—with so little substance that, however full the stomach was after a meal, a person in the course of an hour became as hungry as if he had fasted for a whole day. This was not all, it introduced severe fluxes and fevers, which spread extensively, especially among the poor, who suffered severely. The horses and cattle, from the great scarcity of food, became weak. In the spring, many of the horses had to be lifted up in the mornings ; so general was this, that the small farmers went from farm to farm to help their neighbours to perform this office.

Of the seasons that have been remarkable for dearths and consequent distress, " the dear years," as they are significantly termed, exceeded them all. They pressed heavily on all classes of society ; and while they are painful to reflect on, they were no less remarkable for the revolution they brought about in the whole system of agriculture, as well as the immense rise in the price of every article necessary for existence. After the breaking out of the French Revolution, Mr Pitt, then Prime Minister of this country, formed the idea of starving the French nation into his terms. In this, however, he failed ; a policy which, in course of time, reverted upon our own heads ; for the whole of the ports on the Continent came to be under the controul of the French, who caused them in turn to be shut against us, so that no supply could be had from that quarter, even had they been able to give it.

In 1800, the spring set in with a cold easterly wind ; the usual seed time continued cold and wet throughout, strong frosts at night with a bleak and barren sky, accompanied with frequent snow blasts through the day, created general alarm. The summer continued cold and barren ; and when the harvest came round it was found that corn, wheat, barley, pease and beans, and potatoes, were each deficient in quantity and quality, to an great extent; when the grain came to be thrashed, the worst fears were realized. The produce was small; what was of it was little better than dust, without nourishment either for man or beast. Out of sixteen bolls of corn sent to the mill, only two bolls of meal of the proper quality was got, A general and unprecedented rise in price took place in grain, butter, cheese, milk, hay, and straw; this was aggravated by a heavy reduction in the wages of the manufacturing classes, along with a very great difficulty of finding work at mere nominal wages. When the labouring classes did procure money, a difficulty arose as to what provisions for their family could be had for the amount. The condition of the poor at this time was heart-rending : many of whom existed on diets of the humblest kind ; which merely sustained life.

The spring of next year set in still more inauspicious, with a cold barren drought, accompanied by furious gales from the north and north-east, that raised the soil from the fields in clouds of dust: vegetation was completly checked. The summer came with great heat and drought, which withered every blade of grass, garden stuffs, &c. The seed that had been sown in the spring was of such poor quality, that little of it germinated, and that little was completely scorched. The general distress now became extreme. Even the Continental States felt its horrors. From America little supply could be obtained. Indian corn meal was the only thing that could be procured: at first it was very ill relished, but dire necessity reconciled people to it. As this supply was soon exhausted, nothing was to be had but flour bread—which in turn was also limited. The diets of a family were measured out to each individual, in quantities which only provoked the appetite it was meant to appease. Even where there were no children to provide for, food and flour were hoarded with the most rigid care, and in many cases refused to the most needy families. At this time the penny loaf weighed $2\frac{1}{2}$ ounces; the quartern loaf sold for twenty-pence—sometimes it could not be had for money. It was quite common for the bakers to shut their shops by noon, when their bread was sold, to avoid the distressing importunity of the poor. Besides the difficulty of procuring grain, there was a great scarcity of water generally felt. Almost all the country mills were dried up ; even the mills in Perth were inactive, and with difficulty the water wheel could be made to revolve: the millers' exertions were utterly insufficient to meet the loud demands. Carts were arriving daily from Dunkeld, Crieff, Auchterarder, and other towns in the county, to get a small supply of bread or meal of any kind. Even on Sabbaths their arrivals were frequent, and their case so urgent, that bread had to be baked for them in violation of the Fourth Commandment. It was often with great reluctance that these carts were allowed to depart. To obtain food, many of the labouring classes had to sell their furniture; and the poorer of them were reduced to the necessity of disposing of their bedding and blankets, and many articles of use, to keep their families in existence. Poor old men and women were often seen searching the dunghills, picking out bones and remnants of vegetables, to boil into soup. During the calamity, a number of people at the west-end of the town, on hearing that a cow-feeder had lost a cow by some disorder, the carcase of which, after being skinned, was thrown into the Clayholes, assembled in bodies, and with creepers dragged out the carcase, on which they fell with all the eagerness of cannibals; tearing it to pieces, each struggling for a bit, as if it had been the finest of food.

Farmers and cow-feeders at this period were reduced to the greatest difficulty in keeping their cattle alive. Fields of whins were let as high as £12 an acre, and readily taken. The cutting and thrashing them gave temporary employment to many poor villagers, which afforded them and their families some little relief.

From the great pressure on all classes of the community, and painful cries of want and distress, the Legislature was induced to pass an act prohibiting the making of any flour finer than just taking the coarse bran from it. In all genteel families it urged each person to be restricted to a loaf per week. This act was complied with; and the baking of pastry, confectionaries, &c. entirely given up. So strictly was this observed among the nobility, that I may just give an anecdote in proof of it. The Hero of Camperdown, with his daughter, happened to stop at the George Inn of Perth at this time. At dinner, some pastry was brought forward, to which his daughter asked permission to help him. The Earl smartly lifted it from before her, in presence of the waiter, saying, "it was shameful to indulge in any dish of the kind, whilst thousands could not procure a morsel." His daughter, like a woman of sense, begged forgiveness for the unintentional offence, as it arose from no motive of selfishness.

Liberal subscriptions were made to procure grain, for sale, at reduced prices to the poor. In this quarter they were attended with the happiest results. Besides these, a public kitchen was established, which provided to applicants one meal a day, made from cattle's heads, houghs, and pieces of beef, boiled down with plenty of barley and pease. Every day the making of the broth was superintended by a part of the committee of management. It was not uncommon to see the Lord Provost, or a reverend gentleman, standing over the boilers and handing out the broth to the numerous attendants. Their number was very great, and embraced many worthy people who had seen better days. As they generally assembled before the time for distributing the soup, each as they arrived stood in succession and formed a line which extended from the centre of John-street, where the kitchen was, as far up as the Meal-vennel, advancing in single file with their flaggons. With the soup each got a small loaf at a reduced price. Notwithstanding this benevolent measure, there were many industrious families, who from false delicacy, declined coming forward to share in it. Many of them were days without breaking their fast; sometimes they had but one meal a day, such as it was. Many instances occurred of labourers in the fields who fell into the furrows they were digging, through weakness from want of food; and were only protected from premature death, by the anxious attentions of their families, who watched their hours for return.

Of the many instances of family suffering, a record of one will suffice :—There was a decent citizen in the west-end of the town, with a large family; the little he could procure by labour went but a short way amongst them. He had struggled industriously day after day, and asked credit in every quarter, in the hope that times would shortly come round when he could discharge it. Here he was disappointed : those who had anything to sell saw the utter impossibility of getting payment : and thus every door was closed. Distress entered the family; the whole of them, with the exception of himself, were confined to bed. From hard labour in the day, and the want of rest at night, he also became unfit for much exertion. One Saturday morning, the last morsel he could command was consumed by the members of this sick family. Every exertion through the day to get a supply failed; at night he became mentally distressed, for Sabbath was approaching, without a morsel for their sick pillows. Wearied thinking on every shift, he resolved to commit himself to Providence, who alone could relieve them—conscious that he had done all he could honestly do. In this frame of mind he went to the bedsides of his family, and prayed fervently for them all. On the Sabbath morning he was aroused by a rapping at the door, which on opening he found to be a sister of his wife's, a farm servant, who had come ten miles with a supply of meal, meat, butter, and cheese, which her mistress had given her for their use. This happy relief was acknowledged by prayer. It appeared that, on the Saturday evening, a poor woman from Perth called at the farm-house, who, in the course of conversation, gave an account of the state of the family, which caused her mistress to dispatch the welcome messenger early in the morning to relieve their necessities.

In the midst of all this calamity, his Grace John Duke of Athole, with his usual kindness and attention to the county, bought up a magazine of corn which the goverment had laid up in London, for some intended expedition that did not take place. This supply he bought at 45 shillings per boll, which amounted to £30,000. His Grace caused it to be forwarded with all speed, with orders to give every parish a portion corresponding to its extent, at PRIME COST, after allotting a quantity for seed. This proved a signal blessing in both ways, as the farmers had very little grain fit for seed. When this seed was sown it was easily distinguished from any other species of the same grain. Much though his Grace did, ignorant people raised a cry against him, because he did not sell the corn far *below prime cost*. They openly alleged that he was enriching himself at the expense of the people. Many other injurious statements were made against him, which only established his Grace's character for benevolence among the intelligent part of the community.

The harvest of 1802 proved disastrous in the extreme. The failure of the crops had again been general all over the Continent, and the political feeling of the warlike Powers towards Britain, rendered it impossible to procure any supplies from that quarter. Oatmeal in Perth, when it could be had at all, sold from 3s. 4d., to 3s. 6d. per peck; even at that price the inhabitants had to undergo a squeeze for an hour or two, before half-a-peck could be got from the dealers, who were prohibited from selling more to one family. Frequently the quality was so bad, that nothing but dire necessity caused it to be used. Many families were reduced, through the winter, to the necessity of steeping the coarsest bran and barley, and made the pourings into a kind of sowans In spring, their situation became deplorable. Subscriptions were raised to supply the poor with meal at reduced prices, which did much good. As labour was difficult to be had, money of course was not much in circulation among the poor, who felt this season the more acutely, from their clothes being reduced by wear, and having no funds to replace them. In addition to hunger, they had to endure cold. They conducted themselves, however, with great fortitude under their severe privations.

The spring of the year 1803 set in with the same dreary aspect; again the cold and barren north and east winds continued to blow in heavy gales, that withered every green blade. The prospect was appalling in the early part of the summer : there was neither dew nor rain.— The heavens had become as bright as brass, and the earth as hard as iron. Gloom filled every countenance, and the only topic of conversation was the appearance of the crops, and probable change of weather. What had briared in the fields was sickly, and gave no promise.   The Mid-summer market of that year set in fair and clear.   Towards noon a small cloud appeared, which soon spread into extreme darkness,   In a few minutes lightning flashed with astonishing rapidity in one quarter of the heavens ; and in another, balls of fire were seen rolling along, zig, zag, like forked lightning, which, darting through the darkness, produced a terrifically grand effect.   This was succeeded by tremendous peals of thunder ; and rain fell in torrents.   In a moment, the crowded scenery of the fair vanished as if by magic ; the streets that had, a few moments before, been impassable by crowds, were left without a single individual.   Never did any person witness such a torrent ; its continuance, general extent, and vivifying effect, produced what was most anxiously looked for.   This was succeeded by general warmth, which produced a most luxuriant crop.   Past miseries were forgotten, amidst the anticipation of abundance.   The change of weather was the theme of joy everywhere, which was enhanced by the sudden and unexpected news of peace with our enemies abroad.   However high provisions were before this, the prices experienced a sudden change : meal fell from 3s. 6d., to 2s. 4d. a peck, and other provisions in a corresponding ratio.   Families that had money ran and bought up a year's supply, at the current price, thinking that past experience justified such prudential conduct.   In a few weeks thereafter, meal sold at a shilling a peck.

These " dear years" produced a wonderful revolution in the agricultural and mercantile world, entirely changing the state of society.   Before this period, the rent of land was very low, and an industrious farmer had no difficulty in making money ; land afterwards, however, rose in value.   Various theories were advanced at the time, for this change ; but the one most currently believed in, was, that entails imposed many restrictions upon land proprietors in Scotland, as well as in England. To secure their consent to measures then going on in Parliament, for meeting an expensive war, a proposal was made, that no corn should be introduced into Britain under a specific price.   This policy forced the waste lands into cultivation, and enhanced the rentals throughout Britain. It also provided the means of sustenance to our kingdom, should the world declare war against us, as it had done before.   Whether this is the correct theory or not, it was generally believed, and met with a great many supporters.   It may, however, be stated, that land in this county, rose in value nearly one hundred per cent. ; but while land was thus fictitiously raised, a like fictitious value was not added to all our other industrial branches of wealth.

T

The uncommon circumstances in which the country was placed, by the breaking out of the war again, tended to keep up, rather than diminish the rent of land. Every salary under government was augmented ; the pay of the army was doubled ; high bounties were offered mechanics in most of the branches of trade for home consumption. They got wages in proportion to the rise in the price of provisions ; whilst many other branches in the manufacturing line suffered a heavy reduction, which placed the workmen in a miserable situation. Speculations in land and in farming were, however, carried to an unprecedented extent; rents were increased three fold. Farms were let by public auction, and so high did the bidders go on these occasions, that one gentleman, astonished at the advance offered for a farm he was letting in this way, called out to the company to remember he was only letting the land, not selling it !— Merchants and others, who had saved a little money, became farmers. When the new leases of the farms in the Muirton were drawn out, there was a clause in the lease, that if the lands around the North Inch should be feued out, the tenant was to have a reduction of L.5 an acre, for what was taken from him. To the proprietor's astonishment, the bidding went about L.3 an acre above that rate ; these farms were formerly let on an old lease below L.1 an acre. The pendiclers speedily disappeared in every quarter. Farm was added to farm, until, in many parts of the county, whole parishes were in a few hands, and the population thrown into the towns and villages.

The farm servants, who formerly resided in the house with their master, and formed part of the family, were now turned into comfortless sheds or bothies, where they slept, and prepared their humble diet : the extensive wealthy farmer not brooking the idea of living in the same house with his servants. The family meals were commuted for a certain allowance of meal and milk, and upon this food, with the occasional luxury of potatoes, on which the Scottish peasant may be now said almost exclusively to live. It was formerly the pride of Scotland, that her peasantry were the most independent and intelligent in the world ; but the degrading bothie system, with its concomitants of severe labour, mean living, and promiscuous intercourse, has operated with terrible effect in prostrating those feelings of independence, and even in subverting their intellectual superiority. This system also deeply affected the servants in their matrimonial alliances. For as farmers in these parts had cot houses, a servant had generally to retire, when he got married, to the nearest village, or become a labourer at the outskirts of some populous town.

In 1810, the effects of the war proved highly disastrous to the Perth manufacturers. The town also suffered during the calamities of 1819, arising principally from a number of speculators of no capital, who carried on for a time with great success. To keep moving, many had to sell by means of agents on commission, thus forcing off goods in every state of the market. These gentry, the moment they had a lot of their fabrics ready, sent them off to their agents, and drew to a certain extent, at three months' date. By the time it came due, the agent took care to have the goods disposed of at any rate, to honour his acceptance; in this way the funds of the needy manufacturer, or rather of his creditors, melted with a rapidity inconceivable to those unacquainted with this accommodation system. In a short time many of these manufacturers had to compound their debts with one shilling per pound. At this time the whole kingdom was involved in the deepest distress; heavy failures were daily taking place in every quarter, to an enormous amount; every post brought the news of some insolvent or bankrupt house, by which one or other of the Perth citizens were involved. The banks drew in their discounts, and confidence seemed to be at an end. Manufacturers reduced the wages of the weaver, again and again, so very low, that it was impossible for a man, with the utmost diligence, to procure even the coarsest fare for his family; and eventually employment, even at a nominal rate, could not be had.

In the West country, the distress had become so heavy and general, that dissatisfaction against the government became almost universal. Although the legislature could not controul commercial transactions, yet the weavers believed that it was entirely to blame; open resistance took place, which ended with the loss of lives, and other serious consequences to those concerned. Fortunately, in Perth a different course was pursued: a general meeting of the weavers was called, at which George Penny, now of the Strathmore Journal office, was chosen preses. He accepted of the chair, on the express condition that no politics were to be introduced; if they were, he was invested with power to dissolve the meeting. This was adopted, and rigidly observed through all their subsequent proceedings. This prudential step was a dreadful disappointment to a party who had come prepared with a set of resolutions, which they intended should be set forth. Instead of these, a respectful memorial was drawn up, one of which was sent to the Lord Lieutenant of the county, the other to the Lord Provost of Perth, both stating their situation, and praying that means might be devised for finding employment to hundreds of families, entirely destitute. It is but justice to the memory of his Grace John Duke of Athole, to state, that he instantly laid the memorial before Provost Morrison, both of whom gave instant attention to the subject. A general meeting was convened of the county gentlemen, in which A. M. H. Belshes, Esq. of Invermay took an active hand, and got a subscription commenced. The Duke put down L.100 ; the City of Perth L.100 ; the Earl of Kinnoull L.100.— Many of the other noblemen and gentlemen belonging to the county, and the city, came liberally forward. A fund of upwards of L.2000 was soon placed under the management of a committee, to find out-door employment. Under this committee there were soon about a thousand persons employed. In the Muirhall quarry, which Mr Richardson of Pitfour kindly gave for the time, some were engaged breaking stones ; others trenching ground, in the neighbourhood. Another difficulty started,—the men being turned off the loom, hundreds of women, who subsisted by winding yarn, and draw-boys, became also destitute. The women were directed to turn their attention to spinning ; but here they had another obstacle to encounter, the spinning-wheels had all been converted into winding ones, and the committee found themselves under the necessity of repairing them. This cost L.160. The price given for spinning was so much reduced, that the committee added 3d. to each spindle. In no instance, except in desperate cases, was any relief given without labour. This system of compelling all to work was an excellent preventive of disaffected meetings, then spreading fast in the west.

The winter of this year set in very early ; the labourers' situation in consequence was truly deplorable. Any little clothing they had was ill suited to stand the winter blast, particularly those who had been accustomed to labour within doors. Besides weavers, relieved by this subscription, many other classes applied to the committee for work during the winter. The clothing of the majority of the labourers was deplorable : frequently were the poor men seen at Muirhall, on the top of the hill, standing with hardly the vestige of a sole on their shoes, amongst the snow, exposed to the keen north wind ; with only a few cold potatoes and a little salt to their breakfast, which sustained them until they went home at night. The weather at last became so severe, that all labour was at a stand. In one week, L.160 in money, and about 30 bolls of meal, was given for their support. This state of things, more or less distressing, continued from August to April, when the funds were exhausted. During this severe privation, the individuals submitted with uncommon resignation. Whilst other towns were running riot, with insurrectionary movements, all was quiet and orderly here. Twice a week, a small supply of meal was issued, according to the numbers in the family ; and to shew the general dread that was in the country, of insurrection, one trifling circumstance may be here related. When the meal was to be given out to them, the men all assembled at Penny's house, (who had been appointed to superintend its distribution,) to receive tickets and directions to go in squads to certain dealers, to receive their allowances. One evening after dark, as the whole bodies were moving from his house to their respective places, they were met on the way by some gentlemen from the country, who were not aware of their object, and became extremely alarmed. They set off to the Procurator Fiscal, whom they found dining out. On entering the room where he was, they exclaimed, " The Radicals are up in immense bodies, and there will certainly be mischief to-night in town." The Fiscal asked in what direction they were going? On being told, he laughed heartily, and replied, " They are Penny's Radicals; as fine a body as ever was in Perth, and too well drill'd to create alarm." The gentlemen seemed not quite satisfied. The Fiscal then stated, " that the *bodies* they saw were too grateful to be dissatisfied, and it was beyond his province to prevent them from going to their meal girnals."

Notwithstanding the general good behaviour of these men, on this, as well as on other occasions, there were a few idle, discontented, and worthless people always eager to stir up mischief. Of these a few were formerly leaders of political movements, who endeavoured to assume an ascendancy over the rest. They formed a secret committee among themselves, with a view to controul the whole, and regulate the hours and price of labour. One day, when Penny went out to Lethendy, where the whole body was then employed, he was met by this party, with one of the overseers on their shoulders, on their way to heave him into a deep pond, because he would not concede to their views. Next day, when on the way out, he found about two hundred of them on their way again to intercept him. For this purpose, they formed into a body across the public road, and would have him to read a communication which they had induced some gentlemen to sign, directed to their committee; to which he replied, he could not recognize any gentlemen but the committee under whom he acted, and then forced his way through them. On this they moved away past him, but they formed again in a more determined manner, without offering any violence, when he again broke through them. He had not, however, gone far, when one of their leaders came up in front of him, with a stone in each of his hands, and in a menacing and brutal manner, ordered him to stop or he would knock his brains out. Without a moment's hesitation, he replied, that " no man would stop him on the King's highway;" and on this gave the bold intruder a push backward, that made him stumble and fall. Penny then walked on, and left the crowd a little astonished, and the majority heartily ashamed of their conduct. These unruly spirits were immediately removed from the rest, and perfect order restored. Had efficient means not been used at this first bursting out of their insubordinate plans, the labours of the committee of management would have been rendered useless, and the well disposed molested in their honest endeavours in behalf of their families.

Since the year 1819, there has been some other seasons of severe pressure in the mercantile world, in which Perth suffered severely. Among these, we may class the memorable Joint Stock Companies, or Bubbles, as they were called, which produced many heavy failures.

Before concluding this chapter, it is proper to state, that the distresses of 1740 obliged the Town Council of Perth to commission 600 quarters of pease and 200 quarters of oats from England. L.800 was borrowed from the old Bank to pay the same. They also commissioned from London L150 sterling of halfpence, and L.50 sterling of farthings ;— specie being then very scarce.

PERTH BRIDGES.

The City of Perth, it is well known, was for long the seat of Government of this part of the now United Kingdom. Placed nearly in the centre of Scotland,—strongly walled and fortified,—the key to some of the principal passes to the Grampians, by which, alone, the arm of the law could keep under subjection, the powerful and turbulent spirit of the northern clans,—Perth was thus esteemed a place of no small importance ; interposing a powerful barrier betwixt the northern and mountainous districts of the kingdom, and the more fertile and civilized plains of the south ; taking a principal share in the (then) foreign commerce of the country ; and, above all, affording, by means of its bridge, a safe and commodious medium of intercourse between the most distant parts of the kingdom.

The river Tay has its source on the borders of Argyleshire, but takes that name only upon its issuing from Loch Tay, a fresh-water lake, of about sixteen miles in length, and situated about 500 feet above the level of the sea ; running thence eastward, between two of the ranges of the Grampians, and from them augmented by a number of rapid mountain streams, it assumes a southerly direction, in passing Perth ; and again runs eastward, until it falls into the German Ocean ; the length of its course being upwards of seventy miles. From the mountainous country, where it takes its rise, and through which it passes, collecting so

James Stewart

Perth Bridge, North Inch from Rose Bank.

Joseph Swan

many tributary streams, it frequently swells to a magnitude, not to be anticipated from its general appearance, and acquires a velocity and impetus, the power of which would be difficult to calculate. Indeed, at all times the Tay pours more water into the ocean than any other river in the United Kingdom.

On a river of this magnitude and nature, forming so considerable a line of separation betwixt a great part of the north and south of Scotland ; and which, during the time of its land floods and severe frosts of winter, presented such obstacles to the free intercourse of the country ; it is no matter of surprise, that the erection of a bridge should have been early attempted, and when effected, should be duly valued. Accordingly, although the period of the first erection of a bridge over the Tay at Perth is not ascertained, it must have been very early, for that correct chronicler, Fordun, in his account of the great inundation which took place in Perth in the year 1210, says that it swept away not only houses, but *the bridge*, and an anciently founded chapel, which stood near to it. Of the subsequently erected bridges, it is not necessary to enter into any particular enquiry, farther than to mention, that the existence of one during the reign of Robert the Bruce, is proved by a charter granted by him to the town, on 29th June 1317. During the reign of King Robert the III., he, by charter, on 10th April 1395, bestowed the fines and amerciaments of the Justice Ayres, to the repairing and upholding of the bridge over the Tay at Perth ; and by another charter, dated the 31st January 1405, granted £11 sterling, of the Burrow mails (duties payable to the crown), for the same purpose. King James the IV. confirmed the said grant on 18th June 1494 ; and King James the VI., by a charter, 15th November 1600, confirmed these grants, and added considerably thereto. The view taken at this latter period, of the importance of this bridge, cannot be more forcibly expressed, than in the words of the last-mentioned charter,—they are given from a translation made in 1653 : " And because the bridge of our said Royal Burgh of Perth, which is called the bridge of Tay, is a most *precious jewel* of our kingdom, and a work not only profitable and prymely necessary to our whole kingdom and dominion ; and for the suppression of rebels and such as are viciously affected ; most commodious, and also keeping the one-half thereof, in faith, obedience, and duty of office towards us, their King, in our kingdom and dominion." And amongst other reasons for granting the privileges conferred, adds—" But also, the said bridge, as a public and common work, is edified and builded upon the common tribute and expenses of all the people and subjects of our kingdom and dominion." This bridge, so highly and justly prized, was swept away by a land flood ; the loss of which was severely felt. A public sub-

scription was immediately opened for rebuilding it. King James the VI.
subscribed 100,000 merks, Prince Charles 10,000 merks, and the nobility
and gentry of the kingdom followed the example. But the death of King
James, and the difficulty of raising sufficient funds, left the country for
more than a century, destitute of the advantage of a bridge over the Tay
at Perth. After it fell, the communication on both sides of the river was
kept up by boats, which the nature of the Tay not unfrequently impeded,
for days: and in winter, for weeks together.

As the population and the commercial and political intercourse of the
country increased, the want of this bridge came to be more and more felt,
and at various periods attempts were made to effect the erection of a new
bridge ; but the want of public spirit, combined with the poverty of the
country, rendered every effort abortive, until shortly after the middle of
last century, when, by the strenuous exertions of that truly patriotic nobleman, Thomas, Eighth Earl of Kinnoull, the public attention was sensibly
awakened to the subject. A subscription of new was set on foot, to which
the principal nobility of Scotland, and others, liberally contributed.   The
community of Perth, and individual citizens, were not behind in their
exertions, both personal and pecuniary ; and such a sum was subscribed,
as to induce an application for an act of Parliament, which was obtained
in 1765, for erecting the present bridge. Still, however, the sum raised
by subscription would have been totally inadequate to the purpose, had
not government, strongly impressed with the utility and importance of
the undertaking, come forward and granted *more than the one-half* of the
expense of the erection.

The present bridge, under the direction of that eminent engineer, the
late Mr John Smeaton, was commenced upon the 13th day of October
1766 ; and completed and opened to the public upon the 31st day of
October 1771, at an expense of L.26,631, 12s. 5$\frac{3}{4}$d. ; of this sum L.7290
was raised by subscription, L.5533, 12s. 5d. borrowed on the credit of
the tolls, and repaid by the pontage, and the remaining L.13,800 given
by Government. So large a sum, granted by government, in voluntary
donation, demonstrates their view of the bridge as a national advantage,
Considering the state of the country, the value and scarcity of money, at
that period, the raising of L.7000, by voluntary subscription, is no less
a proof of the opinion of the public. The pontage, continued from 1771
to 1788, which, at an average, produced L.750 per annum.

By the act of Parliament, the Bridge Commissioners were directed to
raise a sum of L.1,500, the interest of which was annually to go for the
future upholding of the bridge. This sum was accordingly raised and
lodged in the hands of the Town of Perth ; the interest thereof and

L.20 of yearly rent of what was formerly the pontage of the bridge. The sum expended for repairs during the first twenty years after its completion, from 1775 to 1794 inclusive, was L.528 14s, which, on a yearly average, is L.26 8s 8d annually. The sum laid out for the twenty years ending 1827, was L.1246 8s, or L.62 6s 5d yearly. Some years ago repairs were reported necessary to the extent of L.1000, of which L.700 was ordered. The fund for future provisions to this edifice has therefore, from necessities not provided for by the Act, become nearly if not altogether exhausted.

The only defect now found with the bridge, is its extreme narrowness for the present thoroughfare ; and several plans have been suggested, at different periods, for widening it, by adding projected paths, which would give ten feet of additional width. A plan was some years ago procured from Mr Stevenson, civil engineer, with a state of the expense, which he then estimated at L.8000. On this it was proposed to apply for a new Act of Parliament to carry it into effect, but the proposal was opposed by many in the town and county. It is now generally believed, that a new act will be requisite, as the provisions and powers of the existing one is not now suited to the yearly wants of our good old bridge.

The bridge has hitherto been lighted at the joint expense of the Commissioners and the Magistrates. This, however, is optional on the part of the town, and hitherto been done solely to aid the bridge funds.

INUNDATIONS.

About two years after the bridge was finished, the strength of the building was put to the most severe test. In December 1773, a severe frost came on, followed by a heavy fall of snow during the month of January. On the 10th of that month, the Tay was frozen across to such a degree, that the spring tides had no influence in breaking the ice.— There was no thaw until the 11th of February succeeding, when the spring tides commenced. The thaw continued until the 16th, when the tide raised the ice about four feet, which loosed it at the sides ; but when the tide fell back, the ice again fell down unbroken. Whilst the Tay remained in this condition, the other small rivers rose considerably, bringing down huge masses of ice, which began to make an impression on the river a little above the bridge. Fears were naturally entertained for its safety, particularly should the melting snow from the mountains swell the river, before the ice gave way below the bridge. At the time the river from below the mouth of Earn, up to above Luncarty, was one continued sheet of ice. The snow, however, swelled the river, as was dreaded, and tore the ice to pieces above the bridge. About mid-day the water, denied a passage through the bridge, soon spread over the North Inch, broke down the wall at the head of it, lodging immense blocks of ice on the green, it tore up the trees along the Dunkeld road, which was rendered impassable ; the town appeared to be situated on an island, as the water now ran furiously through the Castle-gable and north end of the Skinnergate, laying the houses completely under water. Many sick and infirm people had to be removed by boats. The water from the Inch now took its course through the Blackfriars ground, driving down a stone wall that ran through the middle of the grounds. It then directed its course up by the Mill-wynd, and in a few minutes laid the houses in that quarter upwards of six feet under water. In the New-row, the houses were inaccessible; the Hospital and the Spey Gardens were under water ; and the tenants obliged to fly to the tops of their houses.

The first relief to the anxious inhabitants, was their observing the water, with the immense blocks of ice, breaking the stone walls of the Deadlands below the bridge ; fortunately, the trees there prevented the pressure of the ice from sweeping the houses on the Deadlands into the river. By this time, the immense masses of floating ice were in tremendous motion towards that place, where it found a vent. This had an instant effect on the water above the bridge. Fortunately, a little after this, the ice at the back of the Barracks broke right across, which gave immediate relief to that quarter of the town ; from three in the afternoon until nine at night, the confusion and alarm was extreme. At the latter hour, the ice above the bridge began to give way, with a terrible noise ; the water rose some feet above the piers, carrying down immense blocks of ice. The parapet walls at the North Shore were broken down ; the water rushed through the arches below the Council-house, and lodged large blocks of ice as far up the High-street as the first shop above the Skinnergate ; many of the garden walls behind the houses in the Watergate were torn down.

In the year 1794, the Tay was frozen over for many weeks. Early in the spring the ice broke, but closed up again ; the blocks of ice piling on one another, presented a very rough surface ; in which state it continued till the middle of March. This rigorous season was severely felt by tradesmen, many of whom were prevented by the coldness of the weather from working. Masons and wrights were idle. The ground-stove, now in general use in weaving shops, was not then introduced, so that weavers were obliged to give up work. The dressing, when put on the brushes, froze instantly ; and when they did succeed on getting it on the yarn, it became hard as wire, and perfectly unmanageable ;—thus many poor families suffered greatly during this long and severe winter. When the thaw set in, the melting snow and ice rushed down from the hills in an immense flood, presenting a formidable spectacle when viewed from the bridge. The principal damage done by the flood was amongst the vessels lying in the river, some of which had their bows cut by the vast floating masses of ice.

In 1814, the river was again frozen for some weeks. At the close of the storm, the mild weather set in very gradually; the low country being nearly clear of ice before the hills were affected; the consequence was, that although the ice broke up, there was not a sufficient current of water to carry it off. Below the bridge, the ice remained entire; whilst above, it broke and closed up the arches of the bridge. In this state it remained for some time; the thaw having at length commenced in the hills, the water suddenly rose to a great height, bringing down immense masses of ice, which were piled up at the bridge, and all passage for the water was entirely shut up. About twelve o'clock at night, the whole water in the Tay directed its course across the North Inch, flooding Rose Terrace and the street behind, the Castle-gable, the Skinnergate, the foot of the High-street, and Prince's-street. The Edinburgh road, through the South Inch, was so much under water, that the mail had to be conveyed by the Leonards and Craigie, to the Upper Friarton. On the west side of the town, the Newrow and Hospital gardens were completely inundated. One family living in a gardener's house behind Marshall Place, had to take refuge from the swelling flood on the top of the house, until relieved in the morning. In Rose Terrace, a supper party were enjoying themselves, when their mirth was unexpectedly interrupted. An old gentleman was in the act of digesting his supper, and refreshing his juvenile recollections by the performance of *Shantruse,* when the water burst in upon them. The party immediately endeavoured to escape by the back door, but here they were met by an equally strong current; and it was with difficulty they got up stairs. The water continued to rise through the night; in the morning it was sufficiently high to float boats along the Terrace. Many families, in the general alarm, removed from their houses; even several who occupied the upper flats of the Terrace. To those who remained, supplies were brought by boats. In this state the water continued to flow during the whole day. After midnight the ice at the first arch of the bridge began to give way, when the whole current of the river rushed through with an impetuosity which caused the entire fabric of the bridge to tremble, hurling down in its fury the immense blocks of ice which had impeded its course. Goods which were lodged in low lying warehouses and cellars, were greatly damaged or entirely destroyed ; five vessels were also thrown out of the river upon the Coal Shore, which had to be relaunched. When the flood subsided, the North Inch was left covered with masses of ice to the depth of six feet. From the quantity of ice, it was feared the summer pasturage would be worth little or nothing ; but under the genial influence of the spring sun and western breeze, the ice rapidly disappeared, and a finer crop of grass has not since been on the Inches.

Owing to the extent of the mountain rages, of whose waters it is the common outlet, the Tay is very subject to sudden overflowings. Occasionally the river has been known to rise 15 feet perpendicular height above the ordinary level of the stream, on which occasions the Inches and the lower streets of the town are under water, exhibiting, as viewed from the bridge, a majestic stream, though not affording a very comfortable subject of contemplation.

FIRES.

Whether the calamity by fire has been spared to Perth, from a want of fuel, or from the general attention of its inhabitants, is not easy to determine. This, however, is true, that on comparison with other places, it will be found that the city, considering its crowded buildings and population, has been singularly fortunate.

About the year 1765, a fire broke out on the south side of the High-street, a little below the Meal-vennel, which consumed the whole line of the street, between the Meal and the Guard-vennels. The loss of movable property was great, in addition to the loss of lives. The day following nine bodies were dug out of the ruins black as jet, and shockingly scorched ; presenting an appalling sight. Their remains were very properly hid from their female friends, but sufficiently identified by neighbours. In the course of the afternoon, the bodies were placed in a large coffin, and attended to the grave by hundreds of the inhabitants. At the time this fire broke out, an old man named Thomas Saddler, a wright, who lived on the opposite side of the street, was confined to bed in the height of a fever. On the alarm of fire, all the attendants ran out, and left the sick man, delirious as he was, under the charge of his wife. Understanding there was a fire, he got up in spite of her exertions, and rushed out. To her astonishment, the next sight she got of him was on the top of the chimney of one of the burning houses ; and every attempt to get him down was unsuccessful. When the fire was subdued, he returned ; when to their joy, they discovered that, although exceedingly weak, the fever had left him.

Instances of fever having been subdued by strange and sometimes simple means, have frequently occurred. One of these, although unconnected with the subject of fires, may here be mentioned, as it occurred in the same close with the above. At a later period, the employer of the above-mentioned individual was attacked by fever, and rendered delirious to such a degree as to require considerable exertion to keep him in bed. During one of these violent fits, Dr Wood happened to visit him, when the patient called out, " Oh man, do you sell any porter here ; I would give a shilling for a bottle of good porter." On this subject he raved for a considerable time, when the Doctor ordered him a bottle, which he emptied at a draught, declaring it to be the best he ever drank in his life. He immediately afterwards fell into a sound sleep, which continued some hours. When he awoke, to the joyful surprise of his family he appeared quite composed, without any symptom of fever, but very weak.

Shortly after the above fire, another took place in the inn that stood on the piece of ground, now called County Place, kept by one Luckie Waterston, frequented by all travellers, and jolly fellows of the town. In these days smuggling was carried on to a great extent, in which Luckie, like her neighbours, joined. A vessel from Holland had arrived, and she, with the aid of a trust worthy character, smuggled up quantities of gin and brandy, which were placed into her cellar. In the course of the afternoon, this precious store was inspected by the light of a candle, which was incautiously placed on the side of a bottle rack, and left to guide the bearers of the succeeding burden of contraband. Luckie and her servant had left the inn for the harbour, where the vessel was lying ; but, during their absence, the candle kindled the rack, which soon communicated to the spirits, and blew up with a tremendous explosion. The furniture was scattered, and several persons barely escaped with life.

About the year 1777, a fire also broke out in Leonard-street during the night, which consumed six houses. One old man, who was in bed, was so severely burnt, that he died within a few hours afterwards. The whole of the families escaped with life, but lost all their property, for whose relief collections were made at all the church doors on the ensuing Sunday, which yielded the greatest sum at that time known.— About the year 1786, a large house in a garden, now part of the Salutation inn, was consumed, and an old lady's maid burnt to death. Soon after that, one of the houses in Canal-street, then occupied as a lodging-house, was burnt down. About the year 1788, a house in Bridgend was discovered by a debtor from the jail window, to be on fire; but before assistance could be rendered, the whole was consumed, with the loss of seven lives. Some of the bodies presented a shocking spectacle. About the year 1794, that house occupied by Mr George Gray, at the foot of South-street, was discovered to be on fire early one morning : the walls were left standing, but no lives lost.

During the late war, whilst the yeomanry were embodied, that range of stables belonging to the Salutation Inn, on the north side of Canal Street, was discovered to be on fire. The premises were employed at the time as a store for grain : in the upper part of them were lodged the yeomanry stores ; part of these consisted of barrels of blank cartridges, barrels of ball cartridges, and a few barrels of gunpowder. The fire soon made rapid progress, and was fast approaching the critical spot where the powder was lodged. A general panic seized the people, who became alarmed lest the whole should explode, to the injury of life and the neighbouring properties ; no one was inclined to hazard his life in the perilous task of attempting to remove the cause of danger ; which in a few minutes would have proved disastrous. In this dilemma, a butcher, named Robert Fenton, boldly rushed forward through the fire, and, by extraordinary exertions, succeeded in throwing the whole combustible materials out at a window, which happily relieved the public mind from intense anxiety ; and saved much property from certain destruction.— Fenton was not rewarded. His conduct at least justified some verbal acknowledgment ; but cheap as this was, it was not even given.

In 1816, the George Inn stables were burnt down, and twelve fine horses destroyed. One of the hostlers who slept in a room immediately above the entry to the stables, was buried in such a profound sleep, that all the noise and confusion created by the fire, the rattling of the engines, and the noise and shouts of the people, never once disturbed him ; and it was with no small amazement he beheld, when he awoke in the morning, the fearful changes which had occurred during the night. This outdoes the case of the man who fell asleep in the inside of a steam-boiler, while his fellow workmen were ringing on it with sledge hammers, rivetting the plates.

In 1823, the old Grammar-school in School-vennel, was burned down. In 1831, a wright's shop in the Kirk-close was destroyed. A young woman died shortly after, from over-exertion in carrying water to extinguish the fire. In 1834, an old property at the foot of the High-street was discovered on fire about midnight ; the whole tenement was consumed, and still lies in ruins. Fortunately no lives were lost. This was succeeded by one at County-place, early one afternoon ; which suddenly broke out, and burnt with such fury, that besides loss of property, it recorded the death of an old respectable citizen, the father of Mr Menzies, County-place. His remains were some days after attended to the grave by a numerous body of gentlemen. During the night of 12th January 1836, a building in Parliament-close, occupied as a bakehouse and tinsmith's shop, was burned down. Fortunately no lives were endangered; and the night being calm, the fire was confined to the building in which it originated.

Besides the destruction of buildings above recorded, much loss of life has occurred, especially of children, by their clothes taking fire, from the light and combustible nature of their dress; and it cannot be too much deplored that the effects of fashion are so strong as to overcome the dictates of prudence and maternal solicitude. An upper garment of any of the countless varieties of woollen fabrics, or of its combinations with other materials, would afford complete security against this most distressing calamity. A lamentable case occurred some years ago, which throws some interesting light upon the nature of our physiology. A woman, whose clothes had taken fire, was so severely scorched, that the skin of her entire body was blackened and destroyed; yet the unfortunate woman survived about thirty-six hours, without experiencing any acute pain; her sensations indicating no more than a slight degree of uneasiness. It is thus evident, that the beneficent Author of our being has bestowed on his creatures no more of the sensation of pain than is necessary for self preservation, or to excite a curative re-action, in the case of partial injuries.

After giving an account of the fires, it may not be improper to insert the *Regulations for the Fire Engine Establishment.* The master of the engines has the entire management of them, and it is his duty to see that every thing about them is in proper working order. He has to enter into a book every fire that the engines are called to, to whom the property belongs, with whom it is insured, what time was occupied in extinguishing, the expense incurred, and the number of extra men employed. He has also to enter the names of the men who have conducted themselves meritoriously at the fire. It is his duty to call out the men to quarterly drills, and intimate to the Magistrates when and where the same is to take place. The superintendent of police, with as many men as he can spare, has to attend all fires, to preserve order and protect the property. On a fire breaking out or an alarm being given, the watchman in whose district it happens, must communicate the intelligence to the Police Office in the quickest possible way; he must alarm the firemen in his vicinity, and proceed to the office to receive the instructions of the superintendent. Those engaged as firemen are required to give in their name and place of abode to the Police Office, that their address may be known to the police officers. They must be punctual in attendance on drills, and prompt in turning out to fires, but on no account to turn out without their badge on their hat or cap. Firemen's wages are—first hour, 3s; for each succeeding hour, 1s.; for false alarm, if given by watchmen, and the firemen arrive at the engine house fifteen minutes after it is given, they shall receive 1s. Extra or supernumerary men, for first and second hour, 1s; each succeeding hour, 6d. Those firemen only, who arrive at the fire within the first half hour from the time the engine leaves the house, are paid for the first hour; those who arrive within the second half hour, will only be paid 1s 6d. Any of the firemen who absent themselves altogether from a fire, without being able to give a satisfactory excuse, or come in a state of intoxication, or be disobedient to orders, are liable to a fine of 1s; and on a third offence are dismissed from the service. Those who distingush themselves by prompt and meritorious conduct at the fires, on the recommendation of the engine master and superintendent of police, receive a gratuity from Magistrates over and above their pay.

CHURCHES.

St. John's Church is a Gothic building of considerable extent and antiquity. It originally extended to the west of the present Flesh-market; and was one of the few edifices that escaped the fury of the Reformation. No certain date is given when it was erected, but from writings extant, it was built before the tenth century. It is said to have belonged to the Monastic brethren of Dunfermline, and intended for the purposes of education. By the writings, assigning the patronage of this church, it appears to have been surrounded with a good extent of ground, or yard. The grant was made in 1604, by Queen Anne, with consent of her husband, King James, who conveyed to the Burgh of Perth, the great College-yard, with the right of advocation, donation, and patronage of the parish of Perth, with the rector and vicarage teinds of the same. This was subsequently confirmed to the town by King James, in 1616.

The church, before its division, was one long building. The pulpit stood on one of the pillers that supports the steeple; the Magistrates' seat was round a pillar at the south-west, and the King's pew was at the north-west side. It was only partially and rudely fitted up. Whilst in this state it was no uncommon thing for soldiers to be playing at pitch and toss at the east end of the building during worship; and here and there, at the extremities of the church, committees of men held conversation on the topics of the day. For a right of sepulture in the church, the family of Mercer of Aldie disponed to the community of Perth the

St. John's Church, Perth.

grounds forming the North and South Inches. The place allotted to them for this valuable gift, was on the north side of the church, below the north gallery of the Middle Church, and immediately under the pews of the cordwainers, which require to be lifted when an interment takes place. This burial vault has descended to the Baroness Keith.

Early in the seventeenth century, St. John's was divided into three churches, each of which took its name from its local position. The west end was first fitted up ; hence its name, the West Church. Shortly afterwards an arch was built up, which divided the other section of the edifice into the Middle and East Churches. In these churches parts were allotted to the different Incorporations of the city of Perth, for the use of their members, which are still retained by them, and for which they draw rent when not used by the members themselves. This partition of churches was general in Scotland, and intended to secure stability to the Protestant religion, in towns throughout the kingdom.

In the West Church was placed the pulpit from which the great Reformer, John Knox, preached. The Rev. Mr Scott, who was the father of the Antiquarian Society here, strongly recommended its preservation as a relic, but the *local powers* that were, removed it without ceremony to give room for a more modernized one. This relic was afterwards broken to pieces.

In the Middle Church was placed the King's seat, which was occupied by the lawyers of the city when Royalty was absent. It was also used by the Judges on the Circuit, who were anciently obliged to remain one Sunday in town. The Magistrates also sat in the south gallery of the church, opposite the Royal seat.

In the East Church was placed the cutty or repenting stool, or rather the seat of the unvirtuous, on which many unfortunates were forced to mount in sackcloth, besides paying the stool dues. There were in the last century many instances of *married persons* being obliged to sit there for a whole year, during public worship.

In one parish in the neighbourhood of Perth, the session resolved to double the stool dues, from the increase of unfortunates; which made the dues fall off, the delinquents preferring to go to other cutty-stools, where they could sit at a cheaper rate; but on the remonstrance of the beadle, who was alone interested, it was resolved to let them down to the old rate. The beadle, therefore, on the first Sunday after, proclaimed most lustily, that " They were a' welcome back again, for the auld rate o' four punds."

The East Church was at first partially fitted up. The only gallery in it was occupied by the Wright Incorporation ; the Earl of Kinnoull

W

occupied a pew near the pulpit, which was placed on a pillar on the south side, near to the centre of the church. The congregation were exclusively confined to a small space near the west-end. To the east the space was occupied by the fire-engines, the wood used as the scaffold, the hurdle, or machine for driving condemned prisoners to the place of execution, the gallows ladder, &c. There was no pavement in the church but the ancient tombstones laid flat, many of them of a kind of blue marble stone. One of them has lately been lifted and placed in the east wall, having two human figures engraven thereon, supposed to be one of our ancient Kings and his Queen.

On the north side of the East Church stood the sacristy, which in latter times was used as the session house, and for keeping the church records. This part of the building projected so far out as to leave only a narrow entrance from the Kirkgate to the east end of the church. It was a dismal looking place, with small windows strongly grated with iron bars. The benches and chests within were made of oak, and bound in the same heavy manner. The entrance was by a small arched door from the inside of the church. This relict of ancient days was pulled down when the street improvements commenced; for accommodating the session, the south-west porch of the West Church was pulled down, and a lofty house of four storeys built. This house had been put up in so slight a manner, that a few years ago it became necessary to pull it down; at the present day not a vestige of the ancient porch is to be seen. Within these few years Halkerstone Tower, already noticed, has been taken town. This tower, which was a beautiful piece of groined arch-work, was erected above the north porch of the West Church. It consisted of two dismal cells, one above the other; in the one, culprits were confined; and in the other, such dead bodies as were found were laid out until claimed by relations, or buried by the public.

From time to time the ground or square around the churches was encroached upon by adjoining proprietors. This and other local improvements, however, have now reduced the size of it. In all the alterations that have been made on the churches and around them, immense numbers of human bones have been dug up. Indeed, they have been found in such a way as to lead to the supposition, that they had been deposited in cartsfull; but it is accounted for by the fact that the ground round the church was at one time used as a burial yard.

About the year 1780, the Magistrates resolved to reseat the East Church in a handsome manner: estimates were ordered, and a Mr Francis Buchan from North Berwick, much esteemed in Haddingtonshire for his professional taste and ability, was selected to plan and fit it up. His offer amounted to £800, a fair specimen of what material and wages were at that period. When the church was finished, many influential families became sitters, principally from the comfort of its interior accommodation. The Royal seat was at this time removed with that of the Magistrates from the Middle to the East Church, where they have remained ever since. The Royal seat now goes under the name of the Writer's seat, and is yielded to the Circuit Judges when detained in town. In front of this seat is the figure of Justice. The other public bodies who have seats, have them ornamented with the emblems of their calling.

The Middle and West Churches were shortly after repaired, and their comfort as places of worship much increased. In the Middle Church, the Dean of Guild has a seat, with several of the Incorporations; other of these bodies, again, sit in the West Church. In the latter, a gallery was erected called the cock loft, which was set apart for the soldiery; but when their chaplain performed service, they had a right to the rest of the church. The last service performed there was by the chaplain of the Scotch fusileers. The soldiers now go to *St Paul's Church*, which in 1799, was built at the head of the High Street. The service is now performed to them between the hours of one and two o'clock, by the Established clergyman, who has a small allowance from Government in addition to his stipend.

There is only one incident worth noticing regarding the erection of St Paul's Church, which is, that when the labourers were digging out its foundation, they found, 12 feet under the surface of the ground, a stone wall of fine ashlar work strongly united, having iron rings. This singular discovery led to the belief that it one time formed part of a pier for landing vessels. This supposition was not ill-judged, considering the local situation of the town, and the tendency of great rivers to change their beds. As one branch of the Mill lade still runs close by the spot, it is possible that this stream may at one time have been sufficiently deep to admit small vessels. This supposition is farther strengthened by the fact, that one of the *fish markets* is still held near this place.

After the erection of St Paul's, the Magistrates established annual visits to the four churches, which is still strictly adhered to. In March 1807, the parish of Perth was, for ecclesiastical purposes, divided in four separate parishes; by the decreet of erection and disjunction of that date, they were thenceforth called the East, Middle, West, and St Paul's churches. The right of presentation is in the Magistrates and Council, who hitherto have always paid great attention to public opinion in appointing a clergyman. On the 3d December 1832, the Magistrates, after a full discussion, resolved, " That this Council, deeply convinced of the evils arising to the Church of Scotland, from the law of patronage, as it presently stands, and is frequently exercised ; and anxious that an effectual reform should be made in that law, are unanimously of opinion, that, should a vacancy occur in any of the four parishes of Perth, the patronage of which is vested in the Council, no candidate ought to be appointed who has not the majority of votes of male members in full communion with that particular congregation ; but that, should there be two or more candidates having an equal number of votes, the Council should have the power of selecting either of these candidates.'

A few years ago, the Town Council resolved that the West Church should be pulled down, and an elegant building erected ; for which plans were drawn out, and other arrangements made. The building was to extend across the street between the present church and the Mealmarket, which was to be taken down, and a new street opened between the High-street and South-street, in a line with the Flesh-vennel. So firmly was it believed that this would be carried into effect, that when the Middle Church was repaired, some of the ornaments, which now appear on the west side of the steeple, were built on the understanding that they would form part of the plan to be adopted for the new church. This excellent arrangement, however, was laid aside ; and the old church from time to time temporarily repaired, so as to render it pretty comfortable ; but still this church is in bad condition, and out of keeping with the other section of the building.

The walls of the whole edifice were lately cleaned, repaired, and ornamented : those of the East and Middle Churches being surmounted with a neat stone railing, which has greatly improved the general appearance. The large eastern window has also been replaced by one of stained glass, which, throwing in a flood of "dim religious light," produces a rich and pleasing effect, as seen from the interior. Each of the churches require ventilators, but more especially the West Church, owing to its high upper gallery, and low and irregular roof. They are also very cold and damp during the winter season. Sensible of this discomfort, Mr Esdaile has recently exerted himself to promote a subscription among the sitters in the East Church, to get this part of the building properly warmed and ventilated.

The belfry, which is ascended by a very narrow flight of steps, formerly contained a set of very superior bells ; but of late years several have been destroyed. The best and largest, usually termed the fire bell, was struck by a fellow with a large hammer, which cracked it, and destroyed its sound. There is a mystery and waywardness in the constitution of bells, as well as other musical instruments, which set scrutiny at defiance. Although the pride of St. Johnstone was recast, with the same materials, and of the same size and shape—starting like a phœnix into new life from the ashes of its predecessor—yet the new bell, which is now tolled at ten o'clock at night, bears no resemblance in sound to the fine mellow tones of the old one. Another of the bells was removed to St Paul's Church; and a third, though small one, was removed from the steeple to regulate the attendance of the workmen at the erection of the Depot. This bell, in a cracked condition, is now suspended at the late Stock-market.

Before the set was broken by damage and removal, the whole bells were in such perfect unison, that Mr Peter Trosach, who fitted up the small music bells, offered also to fit up the large ones to perform tunes.

An excellent view of the town and neighbourhood is commanded from the bartizan of the steeple. The spire was formerly constructed of immense oak beams, cut from the hill of Kinnoull; these were covered with numerous plates of lead. There is an account of a dreadful whirlwind which tore off the lead from the spire, rolled it into various forms, and hurled it into the Fountain-close, foot of the South-street. To some this may appear incredible; but is not more so than the following fact, which occurred comparatively recently. On a Christmas day, a violent hurricane tore the lead from the flat roofs of Rose Terrace, and carried it over into the lade in a large sheet which required twenty men to lift it.

About the year 1765, the wood of the spire being found much decayed, was reconstructed. The names of the magistrates and council, and of the architect and plumber, engraved upon the lead, record the period when this took place.

List of the Established Ministers of Perth.—Since the Reformation, Perth has been celebrated for ministers eminent for piety and literary attainment. Since that period their number has amounted to thirty-nine. The first, Mr John Row, was appointed minister at Perth, July 17th, 1560, and died at Perth, October 1580. He had been several years at Rome as commissioner from the Popish church of Scotland. He returned to his own country about the year 1555, with instructions from the Pope for opposing the progress of the Reformation: but having heard the discourses of John Knox, and acquired some knowledge of the principles of the Reformation, he became a convert from Popery; and at Mr Knox's earnest desire, entered into the ministry among the Reformers.

2. Mr Patrick Galloway, called to be minister at Perth, November 14th, 1580. He fled into England, May 1584; having fallen under the displeasure of the King and the party which then prevailed, because of the attachment he had expressed to William Earl of Gowrie.

3. Mr John Howyson, minister of Cumbuslang, appointed minister at Perth, *pro tempore*, November 1584.

2. Mr Patrick Galloway, having regained the King's favour, returned to his charge at Perth, November 1585. The General Assembly, June 1589, appointed him to leave his charge at Perth, and wait upon the King. In June 1607, he was appointed one of the ministers of Edinburgh.

4. Mr John Malcom, formerly one of the regents, and afterwards principal of St. Leonard's College in St. Andrews, was ordained minister at Perth, November 4th, 1591; and died at Perth, October 3d, 1634.

5. Mr William Cowper, formerly minister at Bothkenner, in the Presbytery of Stirling, having for some time preached at Perth, was admitted minister at Perth, with Mr John Malcom, June 23d, 1595. Made bishop of Galloway, July 31st, 1614; resigned his charge at Perth, October 22d, 1615. Afterwards made dean of the chapel royal at Edinburgh; and died at Edinburgh, February 15th, 1619.

6. Mr John Guthry, ordained minister at Perth, with Mr John Malcom, February 20th, 1617; translated to Edinburgh, June 11th, 1621; made bishop of Murray, November 20th, 1623; deprived of his bishopric at the re-establishment of Presbyterian government in 1638.

7. Mr John Robertson, ordained minister at Perth, with Mr John Malcom, March 3d, 1621; deposed by the General Assembly, May 28th, 1645, for his having conversed at Perth with the Marquis of Montrose, an excommunicated person. He was restored to the ministry, by the Synod of Perth and Stirling, October 11th, 1654. But an act of Assembly having been made, that no deposed minister should be restored to the parish in which he had formerly served, Mr Robertson, though he continued to live in Perth, never again exercised his ministry there.

8. Mr Joseph Laurie, formerly minister at Stirling, admitted minister at Perth, with Mr John Robertson, February 1635; and died at Perth, July 1640.

9. Mr Robert Laurie, son to Mr Joseph Laurie, ordained minister at Perth, with Mr John Robertson, August 4th, 1641: translated to Edinburgh, March 1644. Made dean of Edinburgh after the restoration of Charles the Second; and afterwards bishop of Brechin; died at Edinburgh in 1677.

10. Mr George Halyburton, formerly minister at Menmuir in the Presbytery of Brechin, admitted minister at Perth, with Mr John Robertson, August 4th, 1644; made bishop of Dunkeld, January 18th, 1662; resigned his charge at Perth, October 1664; died, February 1665.

11. Mr Alexander Rollock, formerly minister at Dunkeld, admitted minister at Perth, with Mr George Halyburton, September 25th, 1645; died at Perth, October 1652.

12. Mr William Colvill, formerly minister at Edinburgh, admitted minister at Perth, with Mr George Halyburton, February 1st, 1655; died at Perth, September 1662. When minister at Edinburgh, he had been deposed by the General Assembly, July 1648, for favouring what was called "the unlawful engagement," or the levy for war, which the Scotch Parliament had enjoined for the re-establishment of King Charles the First, when prisoner in the Isle of Wight; more especially for his having refused to intimate a fast which had been appointed for the purpose of defeating that levy. He was restored to the ministry by the Synod of Lothian, November 8th, 1654. Henry Guthry, in his Memoirs of Scotland, says of him that "for his eminence in learning, diligence in his calling, and strictness in his conversation, he was an ornament to the Church of Scotland." Also the Presbytery of Perth, April 8th, 1657, in their answer to a scurrilous paper, give him the like attestation; and observe that "his ministry had been remarkably blessed since he came to Perth."

13. Mr Henry Auchinleck, formerly minister at Mains, in the Presbytery of Dundee, admitted minister at Perth, with George Halyburton, bishop of Dunkeld, December 23d, 1662: died at Perth, March 1667.

14. Mr Mungo Law, ordained minister at Perth, with Mr Henry Auchinleck, June 1st, 1665; died, July 1671.

15. Mr William Lindsay, formerly minister at Auchterderran, in the Presbytery of Kirkaldy, admitted minister at Perth with Mr Mungo Law, April 9th, 1668; made bishop of Dunkeld, May 7th, 1677; resigned his charge at Perth, October 1678; died 1679.

16. Mr Alexander Ross, ordained minister at Perth, with Mr William Lindsay, November 14th, 1672; resigned his charge at Perth, May 7th, 1683, on being appointed professor of divinity in the College of Glasgow. In 1686, he was appointed principal of St Mary's College in St Andrews; and the same year was made bishop of Murray. Made bishop of Edinburgh, 1687, but was deprived of his bishopric by the Act of Parliament abolishing prelacy, July 22d, 1689; died at Edinburgh, March 20th, 1720.

17. Mr Alexander Skeen, formerly professor of philosophy in the

University of St Andrews, ordained minister at Perth, with Mr Alex. Ross, June 26th, 1679 ; resigned his charge at Perth, May 31st, 1680.

18. Mr David Anderson, having first been professor of humanity in St Leonard's College in St Andrews, and afterwards minister of Dunbarney in the Presbytery of Perth, was admitted minister at Perth, with Mr Alexander Ross, October 27th, 1680 ; he was deprived at the Revolution.

19. Mr William Hay, formerly minister at Kilconquhar, in the Presbytery of St Andrews, admitted minister at Perth, with Mr David Anderson, March 1684 ; resigned his charge at Perth on being made bishop of Murray, February 4th, 1638 ; was deprived of his bishopric at the Revolution ; died at the house of his son-in-law, at Castlehill, near Inverness, March 17th, 1707.

20. Mr Adam Barclay, formerly minister at Keig, in the Presbytery of Alford, in the shire of Aberdeen, admitted minister at Perth, with Mr David Anderson, May 1688 ; deprived at the Revolution.

21. Mr John Anderson, formerly minister at Auchtergaven, in the Presbytery of Dunkeld, but now conforming to Presbyterian government, was appointed, by an act of the Synod of Perth and Stirling, minister at Perth *pro tempore*, after the deprivation of Mr David Anderson and Mr Adam Barclay. Though never actually acknowledged as minister by the Town Council, he continued to exercise his ministry at Perth, until Mr Robert Anderson was admitted ; and then was translated to Edinburgh.

22. Mr Robert Anderson, formerly minister at Leuchars, in the Presbytery of St Andrews, admitted minister at Perth, June 4th, 1691 ; died at Perth, July 26th, 1704.

23. Mr Thomas Black, formerly at Strathmiglo, in the Presbytery of Coupar, and afterwards minister at Weems, in the Presbytery of Kirkaldy, admitted minister at Perth, with Mr Robert Anderson, April 3d, 1698. Appointed professor of divinity in the University of St Andrews, in 1707 ; but was retained in his charge at Perth by the pressing importunity of his parishioners. Died at Perth, October 25th, 1739.

24. Mr George Blair, formerly minister at St Madoes, in the Presbytery of Perth, admitted minister at Perth, with Mr Thomas Black, October 23d, 1705 ; died at Perth, May 14th, 1712.

25. Mr John Fleming, formerly minister at the Castle of Edinburgh, admitted minister at Perth, with Mr Thomas Black, February 24th, 1713 ; and died at Perth, April 12th, 1719.

26. Mr William Wilson, probationer in the Presbytery of Dunblane, ordained minister at Perth, with Mr Thomas Black and Mr John Flem-

ing, November 1st, 1716 ; deposed, together with seven other ministers, by an Act of Assembly, May 15th, 1740, for following a divisive course, and for declining the judicatories of the Church ; died at Perth in 1741.

27. Mr William Stewart, formerly minister at Blairgowrie, in the Presbytery of Meigle, admitted minister at Perth, with Mr Thomas Black and Mr William Wilson, July 4th, 1737 ; died at Perth, May 22d, 1771.

28. Mr David Black, son of Mr Thomas Black, ordained minister at Perth with Mr Thomas Black and Mr William Wilson, June 14th, 1737; died at Perth, May 22d, 1745.

29. Mr Henry Lindsay, formerly minister at Bothkenner, in the Presbytery of Stirling, admitted minister at Perth, with Mr David Black, October 15th, 1741 ; died at Perth, May 2d, 1745.

30. Mr John Warden, formerly minister at Campsey, in the Presbytery of Glasgow, admitted minister at Perth, with Mr David Black, March 16th, 1747 ; translated to the Canongate of Edinburgh, November 6th, 1755 ; died there.

31. Mr John Bonar, formerly minister at Cockpen, in the Presbytery of Dalkeith, admitted minister at Perth, with Mr David Black, July 29th, 1756 : died at Perth, December 21st, 1761.

32. Mr James Scott, from Kinfauns, was admitted, with Mr David Black, in 1762. Mr Scott was much esteemed in Perth for many years ; he was active and zealous in the discharge of the several duties he was called to perform, particularly among the young men and boys. Of these he had classes that attended him in his own house in the evenings : always giving each a volume of a book home with them, and on their next visit he examined them on the subject they had been reading. His public sermons were in the first style of composition ; delivered in an earnest and impressive manner, which fixed the attention of his hearers. Unfortunately his voice was soft and low, and it was with difficulty that he could be heard in the distant corners of the churches, particularly in the Middle and East Churches. Towards the close of the last century, he was prevailed on to accept the assistance of a helper, to whom the Town Council agreed to pay L.50 a-year. The first individual appointed to fill this situation was Mr Murray, who had been ordained to a small Chapel of Ease in the south country. For some time his sermons were admired by the people, but he fell into habits that lowered him in the estimation of the public. He had a custom which his slender income might palliate, but not justify—that of inviting himself to family parties. At the house of a certain Bailie his visits had become so frequent and burdensome, that the servant-maid was fully aware how little respect

x

was paid to him in the family. On admitting him one morning, she was accosted by him, when dishing up the children's porridge, in the following manner :—" Well, Mary, have you got the porridge made ?" " Yes,' returned Mary, " but I did'nt know of your coming, and, therefore, your share was not put in the pot !" Mr Murray had also acquired a taste for card playing, and as much liking for the bottle as rendered him ridiculous. Having got into debt, and being straitened in circumstances, he disappeared from Perth. The only accounts that were received of him was, that he had entered the navy ; been taken prisoner by the French ; and kept long in confinement. He was afterwards seen in London, by some Perth people, in a very destitute condition.

Mr Thomas filled the situation for some time. He was afterwards appointed minister at Newburgh, where he continued until his death. Mr Miller, who was afterwards ordained in Abdy, near Newburgh, was for some years helper ; also Mr Dempster, now in Denny, and Mr Burns, now in Paisley, and were each much respected. After the beginning of the present century, Mr Scott, imagining he would be well enough heard in the West Church, continued to preach some time there.

33. Mr James Moodie, from Mousewald, in the Presbytery of Lochmaben, was admitted, with Mr Scott, in 1772. Mr Moodie, to an elegant personal appearance added an excellent style of delivery : his discourses were of the best composition, but he appeared to have but a small stock of sermons, as he frequently delivered the same discourse more than once. At this time the ministers were not confined to a particular church, but went over the three in rotation—so that one sermon could serve for three weeks.

34. After Mr Moodie's settlement, Mr John Duff was ordained assistant. This gentleman was the very reverse of Mr Moodie in his public appearance ; his sermons, however, were much esteemed, but they were delivered in a stiff monotonous manner that greatly injured their effect. In the latter part of their ministry, both Mr Moodie and Mr Duff employed assistants at their own expense.

About the year 1806, after the building of St Paul's Church, a proposal was made by the Town Council, that Mr Scott and Mr Duff should retire on a stated allowance. These gentlemen accepting the proposal, and Mr Moodie at same time giving up his charge, there occurred a vacancy for four ministers. The Council, with Provost John Caw at their head, having resolved to lay aside private interest and party spirit, and to exert themselves with the sole view of obtaining clergymen of piety and talent, sent deputations through the country to hear certain gentlemen of whom a good report had been received. When the election came on, the Rev. Andrew Thomson was appointed minister of the East Church, the Rev. William Aird Thomson to the Middle Church, the Rev. John Findlay to St Paul's Church, and the Rev. Donald M'Kenzie to the West Church. These gentlemen met with a most cordial reception, and were inducted into their respective charges during the year 1807.

Mr Andrew Thomson was not long settled here when he accepted a call to St George's Church, Edinburgh. He was succeeded by the Rev. James Esdaile from Montrose, the present incumbent, who was likewise cordially received, and who still continues to enjoy the esteem of his congregation. Besides attending to his clerical duties, he has ever been the steady and zealous friend of the poor and the distressed.

Mr M'Kenzie, in his early days, acted as helper to Mr Kemp, minister of Gask : this old gentleman was subject to fits of a distressing nature. One Sabbath morning he was attacked whilst in the act of prayer ; Mr M'Kenzie, who was beside him in the pulpit, was so much affected, that he was seized with a nervous disorder, which for some years disabled him for the performance of his clerical duty. On his recovering from this mental disorder, he was engaged by Mr Moodie as assistant. For some years after his settlement in the West Church, he appeared to be perfectly free of any symptoms of his malady; but unfortunately the disorder returned with such increased violence as to render it necessary to keep a man in waiting night and day. One Sabbath morning he seemed much better, and advised his attendant to go home and shift himself. Unfortunately the person complied : and on his return discovered to his horror that the unfortunate gentleman, in a state of mental darkness, had passed from time into eternity. Mr M'Kenzie being universally esteemed, this event created a deep feeling of sorrow amongst all classes, Dissenters as well as Churchmen. He was succeeded by Mr Keay from Edinburgh, a man eminently distinguished as a zealous and eloquent preacher. Being of a weakly constitution, he did not long enjoy the situation ; a rapid decline soon carried him off.

The Rev. Mr Kennedy, son of Mr Kennedy minister of St Madoes, was, at the unanimous desire of the congregation, next inducted to the charge, in the year 1820. During fifteen years he continued to endear himself more and more in the affections of the people. He died on the 30th December 1835, after a few days' illness. His disease was supposed to have been caught whilst engaged in the pastoral duty of visiting the sick, in the house of one of his parishioners, where three of the children were ill of scarlet fever. His funeral was attended by the Magistrates and Town Council, the Presbytery, and Elders of the four parishes, who walked in procession before the pall-bearers, followed by the members of his congregation, with many of the respectable inhabitants of Perth, the whole forming a most impressive spectacle.

The clergymen in Perth formerly visited and examined at stated periods, the members of their congregations, the same as in country parishes; but this practice has latterly fallen much into disuse, particularly the diets of public examination, which are now entirely given up. In the above duties each clergyman took a separate district of the town, going over the whole by rotation; thus each became acquainted with the whole. Before the division of the town into parishes, there was only one session, composed of the ministers, elders, and deacons; each district of the town had an elder and a deacon to superintend their morals, and the distribution of charity to the poor. Each church has now its separate session: and the whole meet as a general session once a month.

In 1834, a number of respectable individuals, taking into consideration the want of accommodation in the Establishment, resolved on building a Chapel of Ease, for the express purpose of providing cheap accommodation for poor families. The requisite funds having been obtained, a neat place of worship has been erected in King-street. Since it was begun, the General Assembly have admitted the pastors of Chapels of Ease to the same status and privileges as ministers of the Establishment; it thus turns out that a locality must be assigned to it as a parish, and that the inhabitants of that locality are to be entitled to the first offer of the seats. The ostensible reason for erecting this chapel,—to provide cheap accommodation for the poor,—is thus frustrated, unless seat rents are lowered in the churches generally. A constitution for the chapel has been obtained, by which the original subscribers to the building are empowered to elect the first minister; and in all time coming the election to be by a majority of communicants. On this subject considerable difference arose among the parties interested, the seat-holders being almost unanimous in their support of Mr Currer, and the proprietors supporting Mr Miller, chaplain of the jail. The Presbytery, on the plea of adhering to the constitution of the chapel, overruled the petition of the congregation, and the latter gentleman was declared duly elected.

Besides the Established Churches, there were two Episcopal Chapels, one Conformists, the other Non-conformists. The first had their place of worship in the Parliament-close, on the spot where the Royal Arch Mason Lodge now stands. This congregation was long under the ministry of Mr Peebles, a man who was universally esteemed. The Rev. Mr Scott, at a meeting of the Antiquarian Society, in speaking of Mr

Peebles, pronounced him to be as free of faults as it was possible for human nature to attain. The Non-conformists, usually termed Jacobites, were but a small body, who met in the Wright's Hall, under Mr Walker. Political changes having brought about a general conformity, this congregation merged into the other. The Parliament House falling into decay, and becoming unsafe, an elegant chapel was built, in the year 1796, in Prince's-street, which is attended by many of the nobility and gentry in the county. It is furnished with a very good organ, now considered indispensible in the Church of England service.

At the time the Secession took place, Mr Wilson was one of the ministers who was deposed by the General Assembly for following divisive courses. He went to the East Church to preach one Sabbath morning as usual, but finding the doors shut against him, he shook the dust from his feet as a witness. Some of his elders and congregation who adhered to him, proposed to adjourn to the Glover's-yard, where they could receive the benefit of his discourse. On their way thither, one of his elders observing that Mr Wilson hesitated and cast an anxious look behind, pulled him by the sleeve, and dauntlessly told him to remember Lot's wife. The Dissenters soon formed themselves into a body, and the church on the south side of the High-street, long known as the Burgher Church, was built for them. Since the union of the Burghers and Seceders, it is called the South Secession Church. A difference arising among the original Seceders concerning the Burgess oath, another division took place. A separation was the consequence; and the Seceders who would not allow the Burgess oath, built a meeting-house nearly on the opposite side of the street. This structure was but a mean looking edifice, but for many years was exceedingly crowded: a new church was afterwards built. Mr Troup, their first minister, was beloved by all denominations. It was remarked on his death, that his funeral was attended by the largest assemblage ever witnessed in Perth. He was succeeded by Mr Brown, a very worthy man; who was succeeded by Doctor Pringle, who has now been nearly sixty years their pastor.

The congregation that remained with the Burghers was numerous and respectable; indeed many of the most influential inhabitants were members. Mr Jarvie, long their pastor, was a man of amiable disposition, and much beloved by his people: his sermons were in a very primitive style. He was for many years much troubled with the gout, and had, whilst preaching, to sit on a high stool. About the year 1780, they provided an assistant, or rather a colleague, who preached half the day for him.

About the same time Mr Black was appointed along with Mr Pringle.

In a few years after Mr Aikman was appointed : a difference arose amongst the Burghers about the 26th chapter of the Confession of Faith, on the subject of the civil magistrate. This dispute partook much of a political nature, and was carried on with great acrimony on each side. Old Mr Jarvie was a staunch aristocrat, and Mr Aikman as staunch a democrat, as they were then styled. Mr Jarvie's party was but small in number, but stood high for respectability and intelligence ; but Mr Aikman's were much more numerous. Matters went on for some time, each maintaining their opinions with great rancour, until it was at length resolved on by Mr Aikman's party, that Mr Jarvie should be ejected from the church, and a general muster was summoned for the ensuing Sunday, to keep him out of the pulpit. This resolution having taken air, Mr Jarvie's friends also came to the church prepared to force their way to the pulpit. When they reached the door leading to the pulpit, they found a strong party of Mr Aikman's friends determined to keep him out. Although no blows were actually struck, dreadful confusion ensued. After a severe struggle, Mr Jarvie's party were forced to retire to the Guild-hall, where the old man, in a painful state of agitation, commenced worship. An application was made to the Sheriff, who appointed that the Church should be occupied by each party alternately, one in the forenoon and the other in the afternoon, until their respective claims could be adjusted. A short time after this, Mr Jarvie dropped down dead on the street whilst attending a funeral : he was much and justly regretted. His supporters were styled the Old Light Burghers, and Mr Aikman's the New Light. They continued to preach alternately in the church, while a pending law-suit was sapping its foundations ; exhibiting a practical illustration of the text, that a house divided against itself cannot stand. Meantime the Old Light gave a call to Mr W. Taylor, from the West country, which was accepted. For a considerable time he attracted crowded audiences, but the extra demands for collections ever sounding in their ears, was the means of causing numbers to withdraw, until the congregation dwindled to a very small number. For upwards of twenty years the law-suit was delayed between the Court of Session and the House of Lords; it was at length decided in Mr Aikman's favour, with the enormous sum of upwards of L.2,000 expenses to each. Mr Taylor's party built a small chapel in Kinnoul-street, where he continued to preach until lately. Mr Aikman continued for many years with the New Light, until bodily infirmity compelled him to resign his charge. He was succeeded by Mr Newlands, their present gifted and intelligent pastor.

During the progress of these disputes among the Burghers, a similar spirit spread among the Seceders, and a separation ensued. Mr Black adhered, with a small portion of the congregation, to the Old Light, who built a chapel in South-street. Some years ago Mr Black resigned his charge, and was succeeded by Mr Manson, who is esteemed a good preacher; but this body has not increased. The Seceders, who continued with Mr Pringle, some years ago obtained the assistance of Mr Young.

When this party first separated from the Establishment, they were extremely rigid in their discipline, and cherished strange prejudices against all other denominations of christians. None of their members durst attend sermon in another church, without being deprived of church privileges, or submitting to a public rebuke. A remarkable instance of this occurred about forty years ago: A very respectable man had a son receiving education for the ministry, but during the progress of his studies, conceiving the Establishment afforded a better field for his talents, he changed his plans accordingly, and obtained a license. His father very naturally went to hear him: for this offence he was called before the session, and, not being disposed to submit to a public rebuke, he was expelled. On the introduction of fanners for clearing corn, their effect was ascribed to agency of the devil, and declared unlawful. So far did they carry their prejudices, that they would not even join in prayer with persons of any other sect. Their old clergymen were in the habit of singing over their sermons with a long monotonous drone, which had rather a ludicrous effect on strangers, although much relished by the old worthies among themselves. Tent preachings in the country parishes, and with the secession in Perth, were universal at the sacraments. The assemblage in town from a distance was so great, that two tents were employed on the Sabbath day, one on the green beside the church, and another on a piece of ground near the Mills called Maggie's Park, which was usually crowded with people of all denominations. On sacramental occasions, numbers of their own denomination attended from Glasgow, Edinburgh, Dunfermline, Kirkaldy, and Stirling. When the sacrament was held at Kinkell or Abernethy, and other country places, vast numbers attended from the surrounding districts, and even from Perth. On one occasion at Kinkell, in the year 1786, during the time their place of worship was rebuilding, the tempestuous state of the weather rendered tent preaching, to say the least of it, exceedingly uncomfortable, when some one proposed that they should take the benefit of the old parish church, which was at that time unoccupied. After some scruples of conscience on the subject, Mr Muckersie, the pastor of the congregation, complied, and the forenoon's service was becomingly performed under the protection of the "auld kirk." The matter was viewed, however, in a more severe light by the austere portion of the congregation; and in the interval of service, the minister was waited upon by a deputation of elders, who signified that if he did not come out of that den of pollution, the corrupt prelatic church, they would immediately withdraw. The afternoon service was accordingly performed in the open air, the party enjoying the consolation of worshipping according to their conscience, while the rain fell in torrents sufficient to wash out the sin of the forenoon's intromission.

When the congregation of the North Secession Church resolved on having a second minister, a majority were in favour of Mr Aitken, a very able and popular preacher, and would gladly have received him as their pastor; but unfortunately he was the son of a cottar. A rich farmer and influential member of the congregation, could not brook the idea of bending to his cottar's son as his minister, and the interest and influence of this gentleman and his friends was exerted against the unfortunate Mr Aitken. Having received at the same time a call from Kirriemuir, it was referred to the Presbytery, which of the two calls Mr Aitken should accept. Mr Muckersie, the father of the Presbytery, being asked his opinion, replied as follows :—" Reverend fathers, —I think it would be more for the glory of God and the good of men's souls, to send him to Kirriemuir, where Satan has his seat!" Poor Mr Aitken was accordingly sent to Kirriemuir, to contend with Satan, on a slender income, regardless of the earnest desire of the Perth congregation.

The tent preachings were well frequented by traders in spirits and ales; and vast numbers attended for the sake of a ramble or drunken frolic, although on the Sabbath. A ludicrous scene occurred one day, with an empty coxcomb of a barber, styled by way of eminence, " Beau Peddie," who sallied forth on the occasion, dressed in the very pink of fashion. Although much attention had been bestowed on the outward man, he had not neglected to make suitable provision for supporting the earthly tabernacle. Accordingly, having stuffed his outside coat pocket with a roasted fowl, he set out; but the day being warm and the distance great, notwithstanding the *spiritual* assistance with which he sought to invigorate himself by the way, he was so overcome when he reached the conventicle, that he speedily fell asleep. Unfortunately the legs of the fowl were observed peering out of the pocket, which somewhat disturbed the gravity of the younger section of the congregation, who observed the circumstance. Impelled by another faculty, a number of the farmers' collies made a simultaneous discovery, and a general battle presently arose among the canine attendants for possession of the booty. The astonished and discomfited barber was thus suddenly involved in a contest from which he could neither extricate himself nor guess its cause, and the tumult became so great that the minister had to stop the service till the beadle cleared the ground of the dogs.

These tent sermons attracted such numbers of drunken and disorderly characters, that serious people were scandalized for attending, and the interests of religion injured. Parties of tipsy people were frequently seen retiring thence, quarrelling and fighting. Farm houses by the way-side were entered and pilfered of ought that came to hand. Whatever may be said by commentators on the growing depravity of the race, there has been an evident amendment here; the good sense and purer standard of morality now prevailing, having put an end to these unseemly interruptions of divine worship; while much of the prejudice which formerly actuated different sects, has of late years disappeared; Churchmen and Dissenters now co-operating in support of benevolent institutions, and mingling together in acts of devotion.

The *Glassites*, or, as they are styled in some places, Sandemanians, (although Glass was the founder of the sect,) have a small chapel a little to the west of the High-street port. During the latter part of the last century, they were a very flourishing body; and many influential families in town were members. They had no fixed minister with a stipend; but an individual elected from amongst the congregation led the services of the day. They assembled at nine in the morning, that being considered by them the scripture hour of prayer. The leader called on one of the members by name, who stood up and prayed; a portion of a hymn was then sung, and afterwards another member was called upon, and devotional exercises continued during the first hour, when the reader, another office filled by election, commenced, and went over portions of scripture from the Old and New Testaments; after which the leader delivered a discourse by way of exhortation. Each Sabbath afternoon the sacrament was dispensed, and worship was concluded by singing a hymn; after which the members retired to their hall, where a comfortable dinner of broth and beef was provided, styled a "love feast." All the joined members, male and female, were entitled to sit down to the dinner; although any impropriety in their conduct excluded them from this privilege, until suitable contrition had been expressed. They had a collection of hymns of their own, which were usually sung to old Scottish airs. The bulk of their members being good singers, this part of their service had a very pleasing effect.

Y

This sect were remarkably kind to their poor. If a brother fell into distress, the interest of the whole church was exerted in his behalf, and with so many influential men amongst them, some situation of emolument was generally procured for him.

At the beginning of the present century, the spirit of division got among them; a party broke off, who held their meetings in a room in the High-street. This section consisted of the poorer part of the original body; and for economy they were content with a love feast of bread and cheese. Both parties have greatly fallen off. Many of the old influential members of the original body have now died out, whose children have joined the Establishment. Their chapel has been divided by a wall, and a school is kept in one end of it. Besides Sabbath worship, they hold evening meetings twice a week.

Another small body of Independents, called Balchristies, after the name of their founder, have been established for half a century. Their mode of worship is somewhat similar to that of the Glassites.

Gaelic Chapel.—About 56 years ago, a Gaelic Chapel was erected in Canal-street, to accommodate the numbers of Highland people who but imperfectly understood English. The Rev. Duncan M'Farlane was appointed minister. This gentleman gave much satisfaction as a preacher; but unfortunately, having but a small stipend, he thought to better his income by entering into a farming speculation, which completely failed, and for years involved him in great difficulty. He had formed an opinion that by adopting a new system of agricultural operations, he would make a fortune. One of his projects was sowing a number of acres of onions; but alas, he was soon overwhelmed in the evils of an overstocked market, with a perishable commodity on hand. Having got involved with the managers of the chapel, to relieve themselves they detained his stipend until they were paid up. Fortunately, the Sutherland fencibles, who were stationed here for a considerable period at the time, attended the chapel in the evenings, and were very liberal to him. Some years afterwards his brother bequeathed him a sum of money, that enabled him to surmount his difficulties: but new troubles arose between him and the managers about money matters, until at length he took possession of the books and papers, and assumed the management; letting the seats and drawing the rents, and proceeding so far as to deprive members of church privileges, until their seat rents were paid up. Matters could not rest long in this state, and the managers, to get rid of him, offered him seventy pounds a year during life, if he would retire and allow them to find another pastor. To this he at one time agreed, but becoming unreasonable in his demands, he objected to the security offered for his stipend, and refused to deliver up the keys of the chapel, the books, and other documents. The Presbytery having been applied to for advice, Mr M'Farlane became, if possible, still more refractory, and would listen to no terms ; until at length the Presbytery, wearied with his stubbornness, deposed him for contumacy and contempt of their authority. Mr M'Farlane is still a hale old man, although ninety-two years of age; and is as determined to pursue what he considers his right, as if he were only twenty.

About the year 1784, a want of accommodation for families being felt in the Establishment, a Chapel of Ease was proposed, and a subscription set on foot, but which from some cause did not succeed. It was afterwards resolved to erect a Relief Church. A small sum was raised by subscription, a suitable piece of ground was bought in the South-street, and a house built, on which a heavy debt was incurred. Mr Sangster officiated for many years, and gave much satisfaction : on his death, Mr Frew, the present incumbent, was called by a majority of the congregation. A large party soon afterwards broke off, obtained a chapel, and called Mr Arther to officiate, who, after remaining a short time, left them for Newcastle. It appeared that during his stay but a small portion of his stipend had been paid up : after his departure, actions were commenced against a great number of families who had signed the call, and poinding and captions were put in force with a severity never before witnessed in Perth. He was succeeded by Mr Bow, who has but a slender congregation : having some money of his own, he bought a small chapel, where he labours with great zeal amongst his people, by whom he is much esteemed.

About forty years ago, a schism arose amongst the Seceders about the manner of dispensing the elements at the Lord's Supper ; the consequence was the breaking off of a party who were styled the *Cap-outs.* They built a small chapel at Thimblerow ; but their members were soon so diminished, that they offered to dispose of the meeting-house as a Chapel of Ease, but a party in the Presbytery opposed this, and, with Dr Inglis at their head, moved that Mr Scott of Perth, and Mr Black of St Madoes, should be publicly censured, for preaching in the chapel. without leave from the Presbytery. Mr Scott nobly replied that he would preach from house to house in his parish, nay in a Popish chapel, if called to do so. The offer of the chapel being rejected by the Presbytery, it was sold to the Missionaries, a sect then springing into existence, who called Mr Garie to be their minister. This gentleman had not been educated for the church ; but although not deeply learned, he was esteemed a sincere christian. His sermons were full of good and homely truths, well fitted to arrest the attention of his audience. The chapel proving too small, it was enlarged to double its original size; but the congregation still increasing, they bought the ground where the Methodist chapel now stands, and built a very large house back from the street, termed the Tabernacle. Shortly after this, a difference occurred between Mr Garie and the people, which ended in a separation: Mr Garie being universally esteemed, was admitted to preach in the Middle Church on the Sabbath evenings, and the collection was given for his support. At this time he went to the North of Scotland, and applied to a Presbytery there for license; was taken on trial, and duly licensed to preach in the Church of Scotland: in a short time, by the intervention of friends, he was appointed by the Crown to the parish of Brechin. He applied to the Presbytery in due form for ordination, but here he was again met by Dr Inglis and his party, who opposed him with so much party zeal as led many to feel very much for Mr Garie, and to entertain but a poor opinion of Mr Inglis for his conduct. The ground of the opposition was, that Mr Garie was not regularly educated at the University, according to the rules of the Church. At the Presbytery, Mr Inglis carried his motion; and moved that the northern Presbytery should be censured for licensing him. The case was carried from the Presbytery to the Synod, where Mr Inglis and Mr Moncrieff of Redgorton made a stout opposition. Mr Andrew Davidson, long well known in Perth by the appellation of " black wig," for his abilities in difficult cases before the Courts, was retained for Mr Garie. While making his way into the West Church, with a large quarto bible under his arm, through the dense multitude assembled who took a deep interest in the case, he was accosted by a clergyman :—" Is this the Acts of Parliament you have got to enlighten us, Mr Davidson?" To which he sharply replied, " No, Sir, but it is the book that all Acts of Parliament, and all Acts of Assembly too, ought to be founded on." Mr Davidson's eloquence, however, was lost on the Synod, who appeared to be determined to ruin the poor man's prospects, and they succeeded in this, and also in breaking his heart, for he lost his health, and soon fell into a rapid decline, which terminated in death, leaving a widow and family wholly unprovided for. As a proof of how much he was esteemed, and how much the public felt for his peculiar situation, a subscription was soon made in behalf of his widow and family, amounting to upwards of a thousand pounds.

After Mr Garie left the Missionaries, they brought a man from England of the name of Lettle, but under his ministry they declined sadly. They introduced promiscuous exhortation into their worship. It was usual after sermon for a tailor to start up in one corner; after displaying his oratory, he would be succeeded by a sanctimonious shoemaker in another. In fact the congregation were compelled to listen to the crude harangues of self-conceited men, of whom it was difficult to say whether they were greater rogues than fools, and whose chief pride in these displays, consisted in shewing their profound knowledge of the scriptures, by raking out obscure names, and thus assuming an intimacy with passages of which the more single-minded had never heard. The house was soon found to be too large for them; a portion was then partioned off; being yet too large, they afterwards sold it to the Methodists, and built a small one in Canal-street. Mr Lettle having left them, he was succeeded by Mr Orme. This young man had been bred a joiner; he attended the Missionary seminary, where he made wonderful progress. Under his ministry, the congregation increased considerably, and their new chapel being thought too small, their old one in Thimble-row was again purchased, and here Mr Orme continued for some years to fill the house. He at one time received an invitation from a congregation in Camberwell, near London, but did not accept of it. The old chapel being thought too much out of the way, a handsome structure was erected at the foot of Mill-street. About this time one of Mr Orme's members waited on him: the result of the consultation must have been unpleasant, as Mr Orme immediately accepted another offer from the people of Camberwell. In London he distinguished himself at the Bible Society meetings, as he had done here. Mr Orme was succeeded by Mr Robertson, who continued only a short time with them. He was succeeded by Mr Machray, who was well received at first; but a coldness having arisen between him and the hearers, he determined to leave them. They have since had several young men officiating; and latterly Mr Massie, who ranks among the most able speakers in town. Their old chapel in Thimble-row was sold, and converted into dwelling houses.

Of all the mutations which it has been the fortune of this chapel to be subjected, one has been omitted which for a time made no little stir. A certain gentleman who was exceedingly fond of dipping into church matters, had advanced a sum of money when the Missionaries bought the chapel from the Cap-outs, together with a pretty large subscription. After the church had been purchased and enlarged, differences arose concerning the management, and about money matters. This gentleman insisted on holding the property for his bond, while the others claimed a right on account of their subscriptions; but he told them to pay up his bond, and then they could get the church to themselves. The bond being heavy, they declined his offer, left him with the property, and built one of the chapels already mentioned. He now became sole proprietor and patron, and it was his interest to find a man that would fill the church and its coffers. Mr Weston, from England, a person of great eccentricity in his method of preaching was invited to the pulpit. For some time the house was filled to overflowing, and the plate groaned with the extraordinary collections. In his manner of preaching, and in his prayers, Mr Weston's style was singular, frequently ridiculous. He addressed the Deity as if he had been a fellow mortal at his elbow, as much as to say that the Almighty must listen and do as he was required; yet in many of his strong expressions there was something very impressive. During the delivery, he wrought himself into a sweat, as if he had been wrestling with a Hercules. His attitudes and gestures were truly laughable; frequently he excited loud bursts of laughter, on which he would say, " Well, never mind, better a laughing congregation than a sleeping one; if I can but tickle one soul to turn to the Lord, it will be better than the tears of a hundred hypocrites." One day he chose for his text the passage relating to the cave of Adullam, " And every one that was in distress, and every one that was in debt, and every one that was discontented, gathered themselves unto him, and he became captain over them." From this passage he gave utterance to the most unbecoming exclamations. Among them were, " What a pretty company you had of them, Davie lad; there they go, tag rag and bobtail; you would have little credit of them. Tell us how you managed the buffers: a bonny regiment of vagabonds they must have been." Then addressing the congregation, " You will make me in debt and discontented too, unless you make more noise in the plate than you do with your cuddy heels. Some folks are disposed to pin their faith to their minister's coat sleeve, but do not trust to mine, for they are out at the wrist bands." Speaking of free grace one day, he exclaimed, " Our salvation is of free grace, my collection told me so this morning. I do'nt want thousands a year, to roll in my carriage like my Lord Bishop, but I want something to keep the bones green, as the sailor says of his grog." With all his drollery the people became tired of him, the plate remained empty, and he had to exercise his talents elsewhere. He afterwards came occasionally to Perth, preaching sometimes in the Theatre, but he never could obtain a numerous audience. His remarks on dress, particularly of the ladies, were often severe, with a thread of blue in them; thus no female could listen to him with comfort.

The *Methodists*, so far back as 1770, had a place of meeting here. At first they convened in a small room in the Meal-vennel, their number being limited. About the beginning of the present century, they became a considerable body ; but since then they have declined in numbers. At present, the congregation is very limited. The society in London, and some old ladies, enabled them to purchase the Tabernacle that belonged to the Missionaries, in South-street, where they held worship. This building being found, shortly after the purchase, to be in a dangerous state, it was pulled down, and the present chapel built in a line with the street, which is called Wesley Place, from the fact, that the celebrated Wesley, when in Perth, preached on the very spot. One of their preachers lately gave it as his opinion, that the Methodists would never prosper here, from the many good preachers to be found in this city !

The *Baptists* were, for a long period, very limited, but of late years have increased considerably. They perform worship in a very neat chapel in the South-street, where they have a font for Baptism. Before the font was erected, the *immersion* was performed in the river Tay, which many persons rather condemned than approved of, on the score, not of religion so much as on that of decency. For a time, there were two classes of Baptists ; but they are now united, and have got a regular pastor appointed, with a small stipend.

About the beginning of this century, there were a few *Bareans ;* but this sect lived but for a few years. About the same time, there were old wives, of both sexes, who were silly enough to listen to the absurdity of Mrs Buchan, whose doctrine was something akin to Johanna Southcote. This party also died ; more, however, through pure shame of the absurdity of their instructress, than the consequence of old age.

The *Cameronians,* or *Mountaineers,* so termed from their wandering through the mountains, during the troubles in the church, when they made a noble stand against the innovations that were attempted to be forced upon them. They never had a regular minister here ; but when one of their pastors came round, there was always a gathering in the fields, and worship performed there. On one occasion, they celebrated the Lord's Supper, on a Sabbath day, at the Muirton. The service commenced at ten o'clock forenoon ; the sermon continued until one ; the fencing of the tables occupied an hour and a half ; the first table was served by four o'clock. After the table service, the evening sermon, without any interval, continued until ten o'clock at night. In the conclusion of the evening service, fully half-an-hour was engaged in declamation against the king and government. For these forty years past, this body has been extinct.

The *Roman Catholics* had a few members in Perth ; but were too poor to procure a chapel or priest. Whilst the old Duchess of Perth was living, she maintained a priest, and the catholics here went out to Stobhall on the Sundays. After her death, it was for some years kept up; but afterwards the priest officiated one Sunday at Stobhall, the second at Dundee, and the third at Perth. They have now got a very elegant chapel in Melville-street, where worship is performed every Sunday. The congregation, of late years, has increased. Adjoining their chapel is a comfortable manse for their clergyman.

Mr Campbell of Row has lately paid the city some visits, and attempted to establish the *Rowites* here; but has, as yet, failed to make any impression.

A few years ago, another sect sprung up, under the ministration of Mr Burns. It is difficult to say what this gentleman's principles were. He commenced as a general Missionary; then became a general Baptist, and many of his followers have been, from time to time, dipped in the Tay, in the mornings. Mr Burns was considered an efficient preacher. In 1835, he left his congregation here, when the majority of them returned again to their original respective places of worship.

As early as the middle of the last century, two or three *Quakers* became residenters here; since which time, they have continued stationary. At present, they are confined to one family, who are very much respected for honesty and unimpeachable integrity. They are frequently visited by some members of their church from England and America. On these occasions, an intimation is usually sent round of the place of meeting, which are generally well attended by all classes of persons, partly from curiosity, and partly for instruction in their mode of religion. At several meetings, both old and young have delivered discourses, that would have done honour to our Theological students. The Quakers have no meeting house here.

When the Bible and Missionary Societies were formed, a spirit of christian charity and brotherly love appeared in the union of all sects for the grand object of diffusing christian truths. For many years matters went on most successfully; a friendly intercourse was established amongst ministers of all denominations; their differences were forgotten; and all mixed in acts of devotion at their public meetings. Dr Pringle, of the Secession, was repeatedly seen in the pulpit of the Middle Church, addressing a crowded meeting. In the North Secession church, Mr Esdaile, in one of his speeches, remarked, that such a spirit of christian charity and brotherly love now prevailed amongst the religious community of all denominations, that he felt himself as much at ease as if he had been in his own pulpit. This was uttered in a place where, forty years ago, he might as soon have entered a lion's den. Unfortunately, the question of voluntary churches destroyed this unanimity ; besides, it called into existence the fallacious and ill-founded whim of overthrowing all establishments. The Rev. Mr Young of Perth stood forth as the champion of the Voluntary system ; and the Rev. James Esdaile as the advocate of the established church. Pamphlets from these gentlemen followed each other with great rapidity. Whatever may be the issue of the contest, it has, in the meantime, thrown disunion into societies where union was most desirable ; besides, it is a theory which has been canvassed centuries ago, and its practical operation is, at the present day, beautifully painted to all serious thinkers, by Mrs Trolloppe, in her " Domestic Manners of the Americans."

About the year 1786, when the Catholic Emancipation Bill was first brought forward, and Lord George Gordon's riot took place in London, the question created great interest in Perth. Every association, corporation, and friendly society, held meetings, and voted addresses against the measure. At a meeting of the Presbytery of Perth, Mr Meek, then minister of Kinnoul, had the courage to stand up, almost singly, in favour of passing the measure, for which he was greatly scouted by the public ; few of his parishioners would hear him, and none of his brethren dared admit him into their pulpits. At the meeting of the Presbytery, where he declared himself, James Wilson, the barber already noticed, bawled out, " Meek, lad, you're a rank papist ; you should get the stake and faggot ; better gae hame, and set your clocking hens and your guinea fowls." Mr Meek being a naturalist, the meeting was thrown into convulsive laughter. Mr Meek was ever after styled the Pope ; and another respectable clergyman in the neighbourhood, who was by far too liberal for the times he lived in, was styled the Cardinal. During the public ferment, Lord George Gordon, the champion opposed to the bill, paid Perth a visit, and was received by the people as something more than mortal. He went both to the Established and Seceding Churches, which gained him great applause from all ranks for liberality of religious sentiments. Since that period, whenever the Catholic claims were agitated, they met with strenuous opposition. A few years ago, when the subject was before Parliament, party spirit ran high : a petition was framed privately against the measure, and laid in the Mason's Hall for signature, to which several names were very improperly subscribed ; many people openly bragged they had put down their names more than once to the petition. Not content with this, they attempted to put down a petition which was got up in favour of the measure, and signed by a numerous and respectable body of the inhabitants. A public meeting was advertised to be held in the Guild Hall, to pass resolutions and sign this petition. When the door was opened, the room was filled with a party hostile to the measure, who were determined to shut their ears to reason and argument, and equally determined to display a spirit as intolerant as ever the Catholics did in former times. A violent contest commenced for the election of preses; each party moving for one of their number. In the midst of the uproar, a gentleman friendly to the measure took the chair; but when the first resolution was read, the number of the opposition had increased so much that the hall was packed to suffocation. A general rush was made towards the chair; the furniture was smashed, the lights extinguished, and many articles belonging to the Guildry were damaged: those who had taken any lead in the business were glad to get off. During the uproar, many became alarmed for their safety, as the failure of the floor was much dreaded. For a considerable time the uproar in the dark was dreadful; but fortunately no lives were lost. Next day those friendly to the measure lodged the petition in the Hammermen hall for signature, when about 200 names were attached to it: but in the evening a mob assembled before the inn and insulted those who went in to sign it. Not content with giving every opprobrious name, they handled them very roughly, to the detriment of person and dress; many went home to their families minus their coat tails, as an evidence of their Catholic liberality.

Great efforts were made by some of the Dissenting clergy, Sabbath after Sabbath, to inflame the minds of their hearers against the measure. The deeds of ancient times were disinterred, the horrors of the Inquisition, and every malignant feature of the Catholics, were harped on to inflame the public mind.

PERTH SCHOOLS.

Perth has for ages been celebrated for its schools: here many of the wisest and bravest of the nation have received their education. The following extract from the *Edinburgh Encyclopædia*, by the Rev. Mr Esdaile, shows the importance which the Magistracy, so early as the 17th century, attached to education :—

" Perth seemed at one time in the fair way of having the honour of a University. This is a fact which seems to have escaped all our topographical writers, and we owe our knowledge of it to documents lately discovered at St Andrews, and now lodged with the Literary and Philosophical Society of Perth. They relate to a negociation which we heartily wish were resumed, of translating the University of St Andrews to Perth. The measure originated with the masters of the University of St Andrews in the year 1697, and they requested and obtained the assistance of the Earl of Tullibardine, their Chancellor, at that time Principal

Secretary of State for Scotland. They consulted Sir James Stuart, the Lord Advocate, and Sir Patrick Home, the Solicitor General, as to the legality of the measure, who gave it as their opinion that there was no objection in point of law, and that it might easily be effected by a Charter under the Great Seal, which the Earl of Tullibardine pledged himself to use all his influence to obtain. But before applying for a Charter, it was judged expedient that all matters should be arranged with the town of Perth. For this purpose the Earl of Tullibardine and the Provost of the Old College, St Andrews, stated to the Magistrates of Perth their wishes on the subject. The Magistrates met their views with great cordiality, and made what the Professors of St Andrews confessed to be a very liberal offer for promoting so desirable an object. It is but justice to the Magistrates of Perth to shew the efforts which they were willing to make in order to advance the interests of literature in the town and country. By a minute of their proceedings, extracted from the Records of the University of St Andrews, of date April 13, 1698, the Magistrates and Council of Perth declare their willingness to contract with the University to furnish them with the accommodation following, viz. :—

" ' For a divinity college, twenty convenient fashionable roumes, with kitchen, cellars, larders, brew-house, gardens double-dyked, and other appertinents necessar. For a philosophy college, sixtie convenient roumes for students, some whereof for noblemen's sons, some for gentlemen's sons, and the rest for men's sons of ordinary quality, with convenient schools, kitchens, cellars, larders, brew-houses, and other office-houses necessar, with ane double-dyked garden volary, summer-house, and houses of office, and ane convenient church for the whole universitie. And as for the other philosophy college, the magistrates and council are willing to give ane convenient spot of ground, with ane garden, in such ane place of the toune as the masters of the universitie and they shall find most convenient ; and to concur with the said masters of the universitie to address the King, the Parliament, and the countrey, and to use all methods imaginable for procuring ane fond to build that college. For procuring of which design the kindness of the nobility and gentry of Perthshire is not to be doubted.'

" Few towns in Britain at the present day would make such a stretch to obtain a University. The Professors were perfectly satisfied with the terms, and appointed certain individuals of their number to meet with the Magistrates of Perth, with a view to procure funds for building the third College, which was then judged necessary. But here the documents fail ; all farther traces of the transaction are lost ; and no light can be thrown on the subject, either from the records of the College of

St Andrews or of the Town of Perth. Should the measure of transfer-ring the College of St Andrews to any other place ever be again seriously contemplated, Perth still possesses all the advantages which formerly recommended it, with this in addition, that the necessary buildings might be furnished with no loss to the public, and little expense to the parties concerned. The Depot, within a quarter of a mile of the town, can never again be required for the purpose for which it was built; it is erected of the most substantial materials, and might supply ample and elegant accommodation for all the professors and students in Scotland.— Some of the means for transferring the College to Perth, as stated in the minutes, are curious. With regard to Perth, its central situation is ob-vious, and of course much insisted on; and then its vicinity to the High-lands would, in the event of the College being placed there, afford the means of *civilizing the Highland gentry*. With regard to St Andrews, its out-of-the-way situation is equally obvious, and is urged as a promi-nent reason for the transfer. But we sincerely hope that some other reasons alleged for the expediency of the measure have no longer an ex-istence. One of them is stated to be—

" ' This place being now only a village, where most part farmers dwell, the whole streets are filled with dunghills, which are exceedingly noisome, especially when the herring guts are exposed in them, or rather in all parts of the town by themselves.'

" Again, ' It may be considered whether the dissention between the uni-versitie and the citie at present be not a reason, seeing it may prove impos-sible for us to keep gentlemen's and noblemen's children from incurring great hazard, considering the dispositions of youth to be revenged, so that, if the magistrates should offer to meddle, they would endeavour to tumult-uate and expose themselves to the rabble of the place, or else be in hazard of burning the toune, which this last year they had certainly done in the case of Master Henderson, had not, by a particular providence, the de-sign been known by one of the masters one hour before it was to be put in execution.'

" The last reason alleged against the inhabitants of St Andrews, is—

" ' The aversion and hatred they have to learning and learned men, (so) that since our foundation, tho' there never was one farthing voted to the Universities by a burgess of St Andrews, (and) that in our knowledge there was not one capable to win his bread by learning except our pre-sent Bibliothecan. The contrair of all these may be expected in Perth.' "

During the greater part of last century, Perth contained the only se-minary in Scotland, with the exception of the Universities, where mathematics and the higher branches of education were taught. The *Grammar School*, which ranks first for its antiquity, has for ages been celebrated for its scholars. The first Rector on record was Mr Wm. Rhynd. In the register of the Kirk Session, it is stated that " the managers of the Hospital granted certain rents to William Rhynd, son to umquhil deceased Patrick Rhynd, a profitable servant to the Kirk-session of Perth, the 15th September 1589." He is mentioned as Rector of the school, 16th March 1590. So great was his reputation, that he was appointed tutor to the young Earl of Gowrie and his brother : with these young noblemen he went to Padua, and continued there three years. In 1604, we find a Mr Johnston, rector. To this gentleman the managers of the Hospital were ordained to furnish a new gown of bl   cloth. In 1622, Mr John Durward succeeded Mr Johnston. In 1632, Mr Durward was succeeded by Mr John Row, grandson to the celebrated Dr John Row, the first reformed minister of Perth; he taught Latin, Greek, and Hebrew. In 1640 he was appointed minister of Aberdeen, and was succeeded by Mr Patrick Johnston, who had a flourishing school. In 1656, Mr Johnston was succeeded by Mr W. Paton from Meigle. Besides his salary, the Magistrates gave Mr Paton a free house and a chaldron of coals, because Cromwell's army had pulled down the school-house. Mr Paton was succeeded by Mr George Paterson, in 1658. This gentleman was Professor of Humanity in the College of St Andrews. Mr Paterson was succeeded by Mr Andrew Anderson in 1668, who was succeeded by Mr Henry Cree, a native of Perth. Mr Cree was succeeded, in 1679, by Mr Guillane, from Prestonpans ; the same year he was appointed rector of the High School of Edinburgh, and was succeeded by Mr James Ross from Dunkeld, who was succeeded by Mr William Saunders from Dundee in 1690. In October 1704, Mr Saunders was obliged to resign, from old age and infirmity, and the Council appointed him a grant of 500 merks annually, from the salary of the next rector, Mr John Martin from Dumbarnie. On account of this annuity, the Council allowed him the whole Candlemas gift, instead of two thirds as formerly. Mr Martin was succeeded by his son in 1732, who was succeeded by Mr Walter Greig, from Cupar Fife. To this gentleman the Magistrates gave, besides his salary of 500 merks, the half of the quarter payments of the classes taught by the ushers. He died in 1752, and was succeeded by Mr Andrew Cornfute, schoolmaster of Dunkeld, who had been usher in Mr Martin's time, and was called to Dunkeld, where he taught with great success, and greatly raised the reputation of that school. Mr Cornfute was succeeded by Mr Alexander Watson in 1773. During Mr Watson's incumbency, the school fees were fixed at five shillings a quarter, but in addition the teachers deemed themselves entitled to a gift at Candlemas. This term was held as a sort of jubilee, at which the scholars of the different schools appeared in new clothes, to present their gifts to the masters, and received in return a few sweeties and raisins. On these occasions the Grammar-school and some of the private schools had orations delivered by the boys from a stage erected for the purpose; and frequently scenes from plays were performed, where the parents and many others attended. In the Grammar-school, at Candlemas, the rector called over the boys' names; each boy as called came forward and presented his gift, which was announced by the rector singing out in Latin the amount. There was usually an eager competition for the honour of *king*, which was usually bestowed on the highest donor. On one occasion a youth put down a guinea to ensure the honour, when the parents of a rival scholar gave their son a guinea to add to his first offering; whereupon an alternate advance of a guinea each took place, till one had laid down *twenty-four* and the other *twenty-five guineas!*—a pretty handsome tax upon the pride or folly of the parents. These scenes were of regular occurrence, though seldom to this extent.

When the fees were raised from 5s to 7s 6d a quarter, this absurd custom was abolished. Instead of the orations at Candlemas, a public examination of the classes takes place immediately before the Midsummer vacation, which is usually attended by several of the Magistrates and the clergy, and the parents of the scholars. Mr Watson was rector during a long period of last century. At that time Latin was the only classical language taught; but of late years Greek has been introduced. Mr Watson was succeeded by Mr Dick, who for many years maintained the reputation of the school; becoming infirm, he retired on a yearly allowance. Mr Dick was succeeded by Mr Moncur, from whom great things were expected; but his untimely death crushed the hopes which his talents had excited. He was succeeded by Mr Cameron, who for some time had a numerous attendance; but unfortunately he fell into irregular habits, became involved in difficulties, and latterly absconded. Mr Cameron was succeeded by Mr Muir from Edinburgh. This highly respected and learned gentleman died very suddenly; and it was believed that extreme ardour in his profession hastened his death. He was succeeded by Mr Logan, the present talented rector.

The *English Class* was taught by Mr John Reoch for upwards of fifty years. Many merchants and others, who have conducted business in Perth, and hundreds who have gone abroad, received the first portion of their education under this venerable gentleman. Latterly he has retired on an annuity, and been succeeded by Messrs Hindmarsh and

Hamilton; the Magistrates deeming it proper to divide the English school into two classes, which are taught in separate rooms.

The *Academy* has ever been noted for the eminence of its teachers and scholars. Mr Mair, the first rector, was distinguished in his day both as a teacher and an author. His "system of arithmetic and book-keeping" was very much esteemed. He was succeeded by Mr Hamilton, whose system of "arithmetic and book-keeping" is still in repute. Mr Hamilton was called to a Professorship in Aberdeen University, where he lived highly respected to a good old age. His place in Perth was filled by a Mr Gibson, who for many years maintained the respectability of the academy. During his rectorship, the academy was highly flourishing; numbers attended from all parts of the kingdom, and even from the East and West Indies. He kept a boarding house, and generally had from twenty to thirty boarders; and as many more of his scholars were accommodated in houses throughout the town. In 1784, there were upwards of 120 scholars in the rector's class. Dr M'Omie was at that time his assistant or rather second master, as his classes were entirely separate from those of the rector.

The *French Class* was usually well attended by boys: girls at that time had not begun to study French.

The *Rector's Class* was taught in the flat above the Meal-market, which was built for the purpose. The flat above that was divided between the French teacher and second master. In the rector's first class were severally taught arithmetic, book-keeping, mensuration of heights and distances, navigation, land-surveying, gauging, geography, and fortification. Those who attended the second session, which completed the course, received instructions in astronomy, and a variety of the higher branches of literature. In the assistant's class, drawing, writing, arithmetic, and geography, with book-keeping. On Mr Gibson's retiring, Dr Anderson, the present rector, a man of the highest talent both in literature and science, was appointed. Some of the greatest improvements about the city have been successfully conducted under his direction: but with all the advantages of so talented a rector, Perth Academy has not the attendance it enjoyed last century. At that time there was not a similar establishment in the country; at present there are seminaries in every quarter. Inverness, Dundee, and Dollar, have Academies of their own, from each of which places pupils were formerly sent to Perth.

Besides those above mentioned, classes for *Writing* by Mr Smith, and *Drawing* by Mr Brown, are attached to the Perth Academy; and the whole teachers are eminent in their several departments.

In addition to the Seminaries, Perth abounds in the means of instruction, and enjoys the services of numerous teachers of ability in the various branches of education.

The *Trades Free School*, taught by Mr M'Nab, is an excellent institution. It was founded by a person of the name of Stewart belonging to Perth, who bequeathed a legacy for educating the children belonging to the freemen of the different Incorporated Trades in Perth. Each trade sends ten boys; and when a vacancy occurs it is filled up by the trade in which the vacancy occurs. A neat school-room and house for the teacher has been erected in Mill-street. Mr M'Nab's system of instruction has been very successful, and he ranks high in public estimation as a teacher.

A school is established in the Hospital, and maintained by subscriptions from the manufacturers, for the purpose of educating the children of the operatives at a small expense. The teacher, in addition to the amount of subscription, receives a penny a week from each of the scholars, who are admitted by a written order from the manufacturer by whom the father is employed. This institution has been well conducted under Mr Howie, and is attended by upwards of a hundred scholars. A Charity School is also taught in the same building : which is attended by nearly one hundred children, who are taught reading, writing, and knitting. In this building there is also a female school, under the patronage of Lady Gray, Lady Ruthven, and other ladies of distinction.

The Guildry Incorporation also support a school for the instruction of the children of such of their members as choose to avail themselves of it. The teacher, however, is not restricted to these alone, but is at liberty to give instructions to other scholars on his own terms.

An Infant School, under the patronage of several distinguished individuals, has for several years been established, although not distinguished by a numerous attendance.

There are various female schools for instructions in needle-work and other necessary accomplishments. Of these, Mrs Brown's is at present the most popular for needle-work : having lately had the good fortune to execute a dress which was honoured by the notice of the Queen, she has been appointed embroideress to her Majesty.

Music and dancing masters are also abundant; vocal music, however, is very much neglected—the most able teachers receiving but little encouragement, although a piano is to be found in every house that makes the least pretensions to gentility.

A fencing academy was open many years; but it has been given up of late.

The school fees during the last half of the eighteenth century were, in the Academy, two guineas a session of ten months; the French class and the assistant's, 5s a quarter; English reading in private schools was 1s 6d a quarter; reading, writing, arithmetic, and latin, all for 3s 6d a quarter. Dancing, with the best masters, 8s a month; a ball was held every month, at which the pupils paid 1s, and a practising once a fortnight, at which they paid 6d: some very respectable teachers only charged 6s. Music was taught at from 1s to 2s 6d a month.

The following salaries are paid to the teachers of the schools under the patronage of the Magistrates, exclusive of their school fees:—

1. The Academy, ... Rector's salary, L.100
   Do.   .... Assistant, 25
2. Grammar School, ... Rector, 50
   Do.   .... Assistant, 25
3. French, ... Master, 25
4. Writing and Arithmetic, ... Master, 25
5. Drawing and Painting, ... Master, 25
6. English, L.12 10s each, ... Two Masters, 25
7. Singing, ... Master, 15

The school fees during a session of ten and a half months, are

Academy, four hours, ... L.4 6s
Latin and Greek, four hours, ... 2 12s
French, one hour, ... 3 12s
Writing and Arithmetic, two hours, ... 2 6s
Drawing and Painting, one hour, ... 3 2s
English, four hours, ... 1 8s

There are no funds mortified for the purposes of education, under the management of the Town Council.

It having been subject of murmur, that so much of the city revenue (amounting to about L.700 a year in salaries and pensions to retired teachers) should be devoted to the education of the higher classes, while the lower walks were comparatively neglected, a number of spirited individuals set on foot a subscription, which has been so far successful as to enable the town to obtain L.200 of the Government grant for the promotion of education. It is intended to proceed immediately with the erection of two school-houses. The system of education to be on a scale of economy which it is hoped will enable every parent in the city to give their children the fundamental branches of education.

2 A

CORPORATIONS.

CHARTERS.

The city of Perth lays claim to very high antiquity. The first charter incorporating Perth into a Royal Burgh is dated 10th October 1210, and is attributed to William the Lion, who is in a subsequent charter styled " The founder and instaurator of our Royal burgh of Perth, after the vastation and ruin thereof by the inundation of the said floud and river of Tay." The following charters are also held by the City :—

2d, Charter by Robert I. conferring on the burgesses the rights of guildry and of merchandize in all places within the sheriffdom of Perth, granting certain prohibitions in their favour, and certain rights of pre-emption ; also, a letter made and granted by Robert I., dated the 12th year of his reign, enforcing these rights of pre-emption.

3d, Charter by David II., dated in the 36th year of his reign, confirming these charters.

4th, Charter of feu-ferm by Robert II. in the fourth year of his reign, granting to the aldermen, burgesses, and community of Perth, their heirs and successors, in perpetual fee and heritage, the burgh of Perth, with the waters, stanks, mills, multures, and their sequels, with the Inches thereof, lying within the water of Tay, viz. the lands of Inchinnet, Inchyra, and Sleepless, with the fishings, and the yearly rent of the roods of land, and burgage ferms, tolls, and small customs of said burgh.

5th, Charter by Robert III. in the fifth year of his reign, granting to the community a sheriff chosen out of the number of their own burgesses and inhabitants, and a right to certain fines and amerciaments.

6th, Two charters granted by Robert III., both in the eighth year of his reign, giving power to the community to apprehend forestallers, and to confiscate their goods.

7th, Charter of confirmation by Robert III., 1399, ratifying and confirming foresaid letters.

8th, Charter by Robert III., 1404, granting to the community certain moneys payable to him out of the burgage ferms of the burgh.

9th, Charter by Robert III., 1405, dean of guild, bailies, and councillors, to make statutes, ordinances, constitutions, and consuetudes, for governing the burgh.

10th, Charter of confirmation by Patrick Lord Ruthven, Dec. 1450, confirming certain evidents granted to the burgh by his ancestors, of ane certain peice of land, with the pertinents, lying within the monastery of the Carmelites of Tullilum, and the common place of said burgh, selling also the said piece of ground to the burgh, and renouncing all right that he might have or crave to the said common muir, particularly to that part commonly called Gateside.

11th, Act of deliberation and declaration of the Auditors of Exchequer, contained on the back of the charter of Robert III. fifth year of his reign. This declaration is dated in the Exchequer Court of James IV., holden at Edinburgh 18th June 1474, ordaining that the fines and amerciaments of the justice ayre of Perth should be paid to the aldermen and sheriff of Perth.

12th, Indenture made by Lord Ruthven and his son to the burgh, relative to certain mill-leads and water-passages.

13th, Two charters of James VI., the one 1569, the other 1587, confirmed by acts of Parliament 29th July 1587, and 5th June 1592.

14th, A decreet of the commissioners of burghs, 1582, giving precedence to the commissioners of Perth to those of Dundee.

15th, Charter of confirmation of the whole rights and privileges of the burgh, dated November 15, 1600, by which all the privileges and powers incident to a burgh royal are granted to the fullest extent; the right to have a sheriff and coroner of their own choosing; also powers to levy duties on ships navigating the river Tay above Drumlie.

PROPERTY OF THE BURGH.

Although the burgh is still possessed of considerable property, numerous alienations have been made. The first was a gift of Gowrie house and gardens to the Duke of Cumberland, in 1746, in return for his services against the rebels. The last alienation was the ground for the water-works, in February, 1830. All the intermediate alienations, from June, 1754, to 24th December 1828, including the borough muir, were generally for a price paid with a feu-duty, but frequently for a feu-duty only. The aggregate amount of the prices for property thus alienated was £4671, 10s.; the feu-duties, principally in grain, viz. 310½ bolls wheat, 251 bolls barley, and £17 cash, making, on an average of seven years, £800, 11s. 6d. The property at present belonging to the burgh consists of lands, houses, churches, mills and water-falls, fishings, harbours, public markets, coal and wood yards, lime sheds, and dung depots. The lands are, the farm of *Nether Tullilum* and *Unthank*, *Crawhill of Dowhaugh*, which belonged to the Carmelite or White Friars of Tullilum; they were conveyed, in 1560, by the then Prior, to Patrick Murray of Tibbermuir, and were acquired by the town, partly in 1725, from Patrick Ross in Kirkaldy, and in 1747, from Patrick Davidson of Woodmill. They hold off the Hospital for payment of 16s. 8d. feu-duty annually.

The Cow Causeway Lands, let as garden ground, and partly as a brick-work. These lands were formerly an orchard belonging to the Chapel of St Laurence the Martyr, purchased by the Town in 1747, from the heirs of John Mercer, writer. They also hold of the Hospital for a feu-duty of five shillings, and one shilling of ground annual.

The Lands of Soutar Land, which at one time belonged to Patrick Anderson of Tullilum, and were purchased by the Town in 1710; hold of the Hospital for two shillings and ten pence feu-duty.

The North and South Inches, containing about 120 acres. These Inches have been the property of the community time immemorial; but they were conveyed *de nova* by James VI. 1600; and by an excambian with the Earl of Kinnoul and the Burgh, in 1803. The community are bound not to build on any part of the North Inch; and by the charters granted to the feurs of Marshall Place, they are bound, likewise, not to build within 400 yards in front of Marshall Place.

The third-part of the Sand Island.—The Moncrieff family possesses two-thirds of this island, but the Burgh has a right to remove the whole.

Maggy's Park, situated between the mills and the barracks.

Houses in the burgh, ten in number, besides the houses on the shores.

The four Churches, except the pews possessed by the Heritors and Corporations.

Mills.—Flour mills, meal and barley mills, kilns, and granaries, and oil mill, with a water-fall at the Tulloch.

Fishings.—The Weel of West, the Back-Shot, the Fourth Shot of the Ships, the fishings upon Sleepless Island, the Over and Nether Shots of Girdan, the fishings of the Loch, as also the other fishings on the said island; the fishings on the south and north sides of the Island of Inchinnet, and round about the same, with the fishings at the Island of Inchyra, called Balhepburn Inch.

The property of the burgh, including the customs, has been estimated at L.67,510, 11s 10d, after deducting debts. From this valuation, the churches, markets, customs, and other duties, must be deducted as not available to the creditors.

REVENUE.

The following items are taken from the accounts for the year, from Michaelmas 1831 to Michaelmas 1832. The annual revenue was—

Lands,	L.508	15	0
Houses,	188	5	0
Seat Rents in Churches,	765	4	3
Mills and Waterfall,	861	0	0
Fishings,	1305	0	0
Shore Dues,	200	0	0
Customs,	823	18	9
Coal and Wood Yards,	550	17	6
Feu Duties,	1053	14	2
Miscellaneous Sums,	43	17	1
Total Revenue,	L.6300	11	9

EXPENDITURE.

Debt,—Interest on Debts, and Annuities paid,	L.1640	16	3
Deduct interest received, . .	627	7	6
	L.1013	8	9

Revenue for the year ending 1832,	L.6300	11	9
Expenditure, . .	5169	4	0
Surplus,	L.1131	7	9

But the following average and comparative state of the revenue for seven years ending Michaelmas 1832, shows that there has been super-expended in those years the sum of L.1,201, 17s 6½d, or L.171, 13s 11d yearly :—

Average State of Revenue and Expenditure for Seven Years ending Michaelmas 1832 :—

REVENUE.

Customs,	L.729	12	4½
Mills,	965	7	8½
Inches,	354	16	5
Fishings,	1,291	7	9
Shore Dues,	339	7	10¼
Houses,	371	18	1¾
Arable Lands,	566	17	10¼
Burghmuir Feu-duties,	820	11	7¼
Feu-duties and Ground Annuals,	242	18	3¾
Seat Rents in Churches,	766	18	10¼
Burgess Compositions,	57	11	0
Powder Magazine,	3	13	10⅓
Miscellaneous,	39	12	5⅔
Average Revenue,	L.6,560	14	2½

EXPENDITURE.

Civil Department,	L.450	6	7
Ecclesiastical,	982	12	0
Public Education,	669	9	6
Charitable Purposes,	63	14	0
Repairs on Public Works,	437	19	2¼
Improvements and New Works,	623	14	5¾
Miscellaneous,	707	6	10¾
Jail and Criminal Departments,	338	6	9¼
Law Expenses, Clerks' Accounts, &c.	418	1	2½
Public Burdens,	194	19	6½
Finance Department,	1,452	6	3
Incidental Expences,	26	4	9½
Suspense Account,	271	11	10½
Public Entertainments,	100	14	4
	L.6,732	7	5

COMPARATIVE STATE.

Year ending Michaelmas.	*Revenue.*			*Expenditure.*			*Deficiency.*			*Surplus.*		
	L.	S.	D.	L.	S.	D.	L.	S.	D.	L.	S.	D.
1826 . .	6,650	7	6¾	5,993	2	4				657	5	2¾
1827 . .	6,715	17	0¼	7,629	11	3	913	14	2¾			
1828 . .	6,709	10	8½	8,164	12	2	1,455	1	5½			
1829 . .	6,510	8	0¾	7,232	6	0	721	17	11¾			
1830 . .	6,553	5	6¼	6,570	5	6	16	16	10¾			
1831 . .	6,454	15	11¼	6,367	15	10				117	0	1¾
1832 . .	6,300	11	9¼	5,169	4	0				1,131	7	9
Totals,	46,924	19	6	47,126	17	1	3,107	10	7¾	1,905	13	1¼

DEBTS AND CAUTIONARY OBLIGATIONS.

The amount of debt due at Michaelmas 1832, was L.41,461 15s 1d; consisting of bonds, annuities, and open accounts. The bonds are entirely moveable; the sums varying from L.100 to L.6,000, amount to L.36,673, at three and a half per cent. interest: the creditors are all private persons. The amount of annuities is small; their original value was L.2624 5s 3½d; but this is more than their present value. The rest consists in sums due to the Perth Bank, L.1444 4s 10d; to the Commissioners of the Perth Bridge, L.1060 17s 6d; incidental sums, L.119 2s 11d. Total amount, L.2624 5s 3d.

In the amount of the debt above stated, there is included a sum of L.100 given by the late Mrs Gibson of Edinburgh, on condition of the Magistrates paying L.5 yearly to have a sermon preached against cruelty to animals.

Of the sum of L.36,673 on bond, L.12,000 was borrowed on behalf of the trustees of the Bridge of Earn; this cannot strictly be considered the proper debt of the burgh. On this sum, which is to be repaid by instalments, they receive four and a half per cent. Thus deducting the above sum of L.100, the sum of principal and interest due by the Bridge of Earn trustees, and the difference arising from the reduced value of the annuities, the debt of the burgh at Michaelmas 1832 would be L.28,469 9s 6½d.— The debt has been for some years decreasing. On the 21st of October 1826, it was L.50,596 11s 8½d; and, as already stated, in October 1832 it was L.40,651 15s 2½d; shewing a decrease of L.9054 16s 7½d; and in October 1833, there was a further decrease of L.811 15s 9½d.

The administration is in general correct. The whole of the property and sources of revenue are let by public roup; with the exception of the houses and shops in town, which are set from year to year.

The books and accounts are kept with great accuracy by the City Chamberlain. At the annual election a committee of finance is appointed, who examine into the concerns of the burgh once a month. This committee examine the books of the Chamberlain, check them with the vouchers, and put their initials to the cash book. After Michaelmas, another committee make an annual examination of the Chamberlain's account; the result is then presented to the Council. The books thus docqueted, are laid on the clerks' table, open to the inspection of all concerned.

TAXATION.

Assessments and Customs are leviable at the different ports, according to a rate set down in printed tables, in which almost all necessaries and luxuries are included. Besides the special enumeration, there is an article in reference to merchants goods, by which a duty is imposed upon each pack or horse load of all kinds of goods, the manufacture of Scotland or England, not specified in the table. The duties are charged in Scots money : for some articles the inhabitants are exempted from duty, and on others a lower rate is exacted than from strangers. All landed gentlemen and ladies whose children or families reside within the burgh, are free from port and custom for all the produce of their own grounds imported for the use of their families.

Meal Market Dues are regulated by a printed table delivered by the tacksman. Under this head is included farm meal, and meal imported into the Tay ; all meal brought into the town, except wheat flour ; unground corn brought into the market ; apples and other fruit by the horse load ; salt by the same. Of late years the meal market has been almost deserted, and the trade transferred to the grocers' shops, which has rendered these dues very difficult to uplift. Many dealers have resisted payment altogether ; and at the present moment an action is pending between the tacksman and dealers on the subject.

Flesh Market Dues.—By the table, strangers pay a fourth part more for the privilege of selling in the market than freemen. The flesh market, like the meal market, has of late become nearly deserted, and shops for vending butcher meat are now opened in every quarter of the town and suburbs.

Weigh-house.—Dues are exacted on wool, butter and cheese, tallow, &c., when brought into town ; and merchants goods of every description when actually weighed in the weigh-house.

Shore Dues leviable by the Burgh.—Anchorage in proportion to the tonnage ; cess boll and shore dues chargeable on coals at so much per chaldron ; merchants goods, wood, victual of all sorts, salt, and lime, according to their weight and measure. Vessels belonging to the inhabitants were exempted from anchorage dues ; and the inhabitants from shore dues, except upon skailie and slates, and upon coals imported in vessels belonging to strangers ; but under the Navigation Commissioners, a new set of duties have been imposed.

CESS.

When a new survey is made, the assessment is so proportioned that three-fourths are laid upon the houses and lands within the royalty, and the remaining fourth upon trade. The latter portion is termed trade stent, and is laid on and apportioned yearly by twelve respectable burgesses, appointed and sworn by the magistrates. From a statement furnished by the collector of cess, the amount and application for the last ten years is as follows :—

Amount assessed,	.	.	.	£3854 0 0
Payable to Government,	.	.	3354 0 0
Amount levied,	.	.	.	3726 7 4
Allowance to Collector,	.	.	372 7 4½
Number of persons assessed,	.	14,587 0 0
Average number,	.	.	.	1458 0 0

From the foregoing state, it appears the assessment laid on for the last ten years amounted to £3854, or £385, 8s. annually ; and that the sum actually levied during these ten years, from the average number of 1458

persons, was	£3726	7 4½
The sum paid to Government during the same period,	3354	0 0
Leaving the expense of collection, ...	£372	7 4½
Average yearly expense, ...	£37	4 8

The jurisdiction of the provost, dean of guild, and bailies, extends over the royalty of the city ; but the boundary is not well defined. The property holding burgage without the line of the ancient city walls exceeds in extent that within the walls ; within the same territory the provost is also sheriff.

We have formerly stated, that the Burgh Court sits every Tuesday. Of late years, no criminal causes have been brought before this court ; these have been taken up by the police court.

From the following table it will appear how much the business of the town court has fallen off. Those cases marked pr. in the margin were decided *in fero ;* in those marked ab. the parties were absent :—

	1820	1821	1822	1823	1824	1825	1826	1827	1828	1829	1830	1831	1832	1833	Total
Pr.	75	70	69	70	38	54	39	43	23	23	27	21	17	8	577
Ab.	89	58	53	64	53	69	38	46	45	33	45	20	26	12	651
Tot	164	128	122	134	91	123	77	89	68	56	72	41	43	20	1228

The civil patronage is limited to the right of appointing the ordinary burgh officers. These officers, with their salaries, are—

City Chamberlain, - - - - -	£90	0 0
Procurator-Fiscal (exclusive of £50 for police business) - - - - - -	51	13 4
Billet-Master, - - - - - -	15	0 0
Superintendent of Works, - - -	80	0 0
Keeper of Town Clocks, - - - -	10	6 8
Keeper of Fire Engines, - - - -	10	0 0
Three Town Serjeants (£40 each, besides clothing) - - - - - -	120	0 0
Keepers of the Bells, - - - -	21	3 0

These are all paid from the common good. There are at present two town-clerks. They receive no salary; but, in 1792, the council granted them £10 yearly, which is still continued, as payment for attending meetings and writing minutes. They receive the fees of the burgh court, keep the register of sasines, take all burgh infeftments, services of cognition, and the other usual duties. The fees are regulated by a table, and amount, on an average of five years ending 1832, to £325, divisible between them. Their other emoluments arise from business done for the town, charged at the usual rates; these amounted, on an average of seven years, ending August 1833, to £238, 5s. 7d. divisible between them.

The keeper of the register of burials, the public criers, and the town serjeants, are appointed by the town. All the office-bearers are elected by the town council at large, during pleasure, except the town-clerks, who are appointed *ad vitam aut culpam*. None of them act by deputy; no price is given for them, nor any security required, except for the chamberlain.

ECCLESIASTICAL PATRONAGE

Consists in the appointment of the four ministers, precentors, and teachers in the public schools.

The parsonage teinds of the parish consists of 300 bolls of victual, of which 160 bolls, 2 firlots, 2 pecks, 2⅔ lippies meal, and 139 bolls, 1 peck, 1¼ lippy barley; the vicarage teinds amount to £7, 8s. 10½d.

The Rev. James Esdaile, East Church, draws one-half of the parsonage teinds, the whole of the vicarage teinds, and is paid in addition, from the funds of the burgh, £130 per annum. The Rev. William Thomson, Middle Church, draws half of the parsonage teinds, and £130 from the burgh funds. The Rev. John Finlay, St Paul's, receives £280 from the burgh funds, as did also the late Rev. Samuel Kennedy of the West Church.

It will be proper to remark, that £80 of what Messrs Finlay and Kennedy received were two separate grants of £50 and £30 to each of them by the council during pleasure; but the last deed of the town council under the old system confirmed these grants during the lives of the incumbents. By the deed of disjunction, the council became bound only for £200 to the ministers of the West and St Paul's Churches. Similar grants were given to the ministers of the other two churches, though not to the same extent.—The four precentors have salaries of L.5 each.

EXCLUSIVE PRIVILEGES.

The Guildry.—The exclusive privileges were important and rigid; but since the pasing of the Reform Bill a great revolution is apparently tak-

2 R

ing place in public opinion on this subject. The Guildry have already made considerable advances in liberality.

The Guildry consists of burgesses and guild-brethren, or merchant-burgesses and trades-burgesses. No tradesman can exercise his calling unless he is entered with the Guildry as well as the corporation. The Guildry are a very ancient body, in number upwards of 560 : they consist of merchants, maltmen, surgeons, and dyers. The power of administration of their public rights is vested in the Guild Court ; but since the year 1817, their pecuniary concerns have been managed by a committee distinct from the Guild Court. The Guild Court consists of the Dean, president, the Provost, the three merchant Bailies, four Guild brethren elected by the Guildry, and two tradesmen from the Court of Convenery. This court claims the sole right of admitting burgesses, and regulating the amount of entry money ; but this right was disputed by the Town Council in 1825 : the result was a tedious litigation between the Town and the Guildry.

The fees of admission consist of ten merks as upset, and L.4 Scots as foot-ball. The entry money varies according to the grounds on which the application is rested : there are three degrees of rates—1st, Sons and sons-in-law ; 2d, apprentices ; 3d, strangers. The rate also varies according to the age of the applicant : a part is paid into the common good, but much the greater part to the Guildry, the details of which are exhibited below.

The Guildry are possessed of large property, and have a considerable revenue ; their real property is valued at L.28,000, and is composed of lands at Craigmakerran, part in farms, and part feued out in small lots, where there is a thriving village built called Guildtown; besides rents and feu duties, they have interest of money lent to feuars, entry money, seats in the churches, and composition for strangers entering into business ; from the last source from L.250 to L.260 was annually drawn, but by a resolution of the Guildry, payment of these licenses (L.1 10s per annum for every stranger keeping open shop) have been suspended. Small dues are also levied for the use of planks at the Shore.

Within the last ten years the income of the Guildry has varied from L.1200 to L.1600. The expenditure is great, arising chiefly from weekly allowances to poor members, widows, and orphans. These allowances are stated at L.800 per annum : no relief is given to persons having an income of L.10. The weekly roll amounts to upwards of a hundred, ranging from 1s to 3s 6d each ; besides twelve on the quarterly roll non-resident, and twelve who receive occasional donations. Besides these, a sum exceeding L.40 is annually paid for the education of children ; the other branches of expenditure are L.117 6s payable as annuities, either purchased or granted to persons who might ultimately have a claim upon them; sums expended on improving their farms; stipend and teacher's salary payable out of these lands, L.27; officer, L.40; treasurer, L.30; clerk, L.10 10s; land overseer, L.10 10s. Total, L.114 8s. Accounts of the Clerk and Procurator Fiscal for law business: the greater part of these expenses have been incurred in a law-suit with the Town Council, and with a person who resisted a demand of thirty shillings for a license to trade, on the ground that his shop was not held burgage. The law expenses of late years have been upwards of L.300 per annum. The debts are estimated at L.2000; the expenditure and income nearly equal.

INCORPORATED TRADES.

In Perth there are eight Corporations, styled Incorporated Trades; seven of these possess the ordinary exclusive privileges. They are founded upon consuetude or immemorial usage; for the incorporations have no special charters or seals of cause, but rely first upon the general charter of the burgh; second, upon the charter granted by Queen Mary, 28th May 1556, to the Trades of Perth, reponing them against an act passed in June 1555, which prohibited the election of deacons, and granting them the same rights as merchants in the election of office-bearers within the burgh; and third, the charter by James VI., 22d July 1581, in favour of the craftsmen of the burgh.

The Corporations are the Hammermen, Bakers, Glovers, Wrights, Tailors, Fleshers, Shoemakers, and Weavers. The total number of members in 1832, was 454. The trades have a board termed the Convener Court, composed of the trades' members of the Council, and the deacon of the weavers. For many years the only business consisted in electing the Convener, and taking their dinner. There is a flag, styled "the blue blanket," of which the convener is put in possession when he is elected. When this blanket is unfurled, every tradesman belonging to the corporation is bound to turn out.

The Hammermen take the lead. This corporation consists of ten sciences, viz.: blacksmiths, farriers, gunsmiths, coachmakers, watchmakers, brass and iron founders, saddlecross and harness makers, jewellers and goldsmiths, cutlers, tinsmiths, and plumbers. The number of members is 76; their terms of entry are

Sons of Freemen,	-	-	-	-	L.3	1	0
Apprentices,	-	-	-	-	7	10	0
Strangers,	-	-	-	-	25	13	6
To each additional science,	-	-	-	5	5	0

The amount of their income in 1833 was L.194 18s. the sources are entry money, recording indentures, house rents, and seats in the churches. The expenditure for that year, consisting of pensions, repairs, salaries, and small items, amounted to L.168 8s. Balance in their favour, L.26 10s. But as there are debts due by the corporation to the amount of L.400, the interest of this sum, at four per cent. must be deducted, leaving a balance of L.10 10s. Their charities are regulated by a visiting committee, who recommend allowances according to the necessity of each case.

Under the old system, we have already remarked that the trades, besides their deacons, having a seat in the Council, the three great trades as they were termed, sent a councillor each, and the small trades one amongst them. In choosing the trades' bailie, these three trades had it each once in four years, and the small trades one year in the four : the trade that had the bailie, sent down a leet of two members from whom the Council chose one. The person the trade wished to be bailie was well understood ; the other sent down was usually the most insignificant member they could pitch upon.

It happened some years ago, that a gentleman belonging to the Hammermen got a majority of the trade, through much booing and hard eating and drinking, to vote him on for bailie : this person being obnoxious to the Council, the individual whose name was sent down with his was elected in preference, although it was well known the one they had chosen was perhaps the most unfit person they could have pitched on in Perth to perform the duties of a magistrate : and so it proved. He was a journeyman smith at a foundry, and so addicted to the bottle that he had hardly a coat to put on his back. After being sworn in, he only once afterwards made his appearance in the Council in an official capacity, being on a special emergency that required the attendance of the whole of the members.

The Hammermen tavern is a part of the property of this Incorporation, in which they have an excellent hall, which is frequently used for dinner parties, public sales, &c. The Hammermen used to be very rigid in preserving their exclusive rights, and got involved in some tedious lawsuits with individuals. Of late they came to the resolution of renouncing their exclusive privileges.

The Bakers consist of one science only : the fees of admission are

Freemen's sons,	-	-	-	-	-	L.1 18	4
Apprentices,	-	-	-	-	-	6 11	6
Strangers,	-	-	-	-	-	35 0	0

Their income arising from rents and entry money, was, in 1833,

Receips,	-	-	-	-	-	L.233 8 0
Expenditure,	-	-	-	-		176 13 8
Surplus,	-	-	-	-		L.46 14 4

They have always been bound in thirlage to the Perth Mills; at the twentieth boll. About 65 years ago, they built the range of granaries next to the Mills. The scale on which they were erected was deemed so extravagant at the time, that they were termed " the bakers' folly," a name that for many years was attached to them. So much has the trade increased, that they have lately erected another range behind, in Maggie's Park. The amount given to their poor is discretionary, and averages from 1s 6d to 2s each.

The Shoemakers number about 58 members.   Their fees are

Freemen's sons,	-	-	-	-	-	L.1 14 2
Apprentices,	-	-	-	-	-	7 5 0
Strangers,	-	-	-	-	-	20 0 0

Their annual income is L.139 13s 7d: expenditure, L.104 15s 2d.

There is a shoe market in the South-street on the Fridays, where shoemakers from the country expose their shoes. A deputation from the trade, with their officer, visit the market for the purpose of inspecting the quality of the shoes exposed, and if found insufficient they are confiscated.

The Fleshers are about 23 in number.   Fees of entry—

Freemen's sons,	-	-	-	-	-	L.3 17 0
Apprentices,	-	-	-	-	-	10 10 0

Their income, from entries and rents, amount to L.132 7s 6d: their expenditure, including L.36 of interest of money borrowed, is L157 0s 7d.

Before the present Flesh-market was built, the fleshers had their stalls in the South-street; and fleshers from the country who attended the market had to stand on the street, with the meat slung across the horses' backs, being prohibited by the corporation rules from unlading until sold. After the present market was erected, strangers were admitted on the market days on payment of the dues; but of late years butchers have commenced business in Bridgend, Pomarium, Blackfriars, and other places, which has withdrawn a great part of the business from the market; even the freemen began to take shops through the town. To this practice the Town Council some years ago attempted to put a stop. The freemen were to take up their station in the southern division of the market, and the old soldiers or strangers were to possess the north side; but the trade has extended so much in the suburbs, that the corporation have many of them forsaken the market entirely. Fifty years ago the Perth flesh-market produced a show of meat of all kinds seldom to be met with in any quarter—the stalls were almost filled with meat; now the market is almost deserted. The north side is occupied as a green market, and in the south side is to be seen a small remnant of the corporations.

The Glovers, in number about 64, consist of two sciences, viz. the Glovers and Skinners. The fees are

Sons of freemen, - - - - -	L.1	0	0
Apprentices under 30 years, - - -	20	0	0
Do. 40, and under 50, - -	27	0	0
Do. 50 and upwards, - -	50	0	0
Strangers, who must be operators, -	100	0	0

The property of the corporation consists in land, houses and shops, feu duties, interest of money lent, and seat rents in the churches. The farms of Upper Tullilum and the Leonards belong to them; Leonard Bank, Pomarium, and the east side of Leonard-street is feued from the corporation. The income from these sources in 1832 was L.1094 4s 8½d; the expenditure, L.960. There was on the poor's roll for that year 21, at a rate from 3s to 3s 6d, besides quarterly allowances for coals, shoes, clothing, and education.

On the 5th November 1829, the corporation adopted a scheme for giving annuities to superannuated members and to widows, on the principle of a legal right. The rates are

55 and under 60 years of age, - -	L.10	0	0
60 and under 65 do. - -	12	0	0
65 and upwards, - - - -	14	0	0

Widows, of whatever age, to have an annuity of L.14 so long as unmarried; but no allowances are made for children.

About the year 1786, they built an elegant hall in George-street, at that time the third house on the west side of the street: it was then the only hall in town fit for assemblies or large dinner parties. Some years ago, they sold the hall to a stock company, who converted it into a coffee room; since then the building was condemned, and rebuilt.

The *Wrights* consist of seven sciences—wrights, barbers, coopers, slaters, plasterers, glaziers, and masons. Their income arises from entries, rents, and interest of money lent out. The charge in 1833 is stated at L.774, 7s. 1d., and the discharge at L.773.

Some years ago a Mr Brown, who died in India, bequeathed the bulk of his fortune to the corporation, leaving only a small annuity to his brother. His brother and friends were so dissatisfied, that a threat was held out that they would bring the matter before a court of law; to prevent this, a compromise was made, by which the corporation gave the brother a certain sum in money, and retained the rest, which swelled their funds considerably. This corporation used to be very rigid in enforcing their exclusive rights, and frequently prosecuted individuals for doing private jobs.

The *Weavers* were once a numerous and ancient body; but the act of Parliament for the encouragement of manufactures, which gave liberty of trade to all engaged in any of its branches, rendered the corporation of little value. They had a considerable property in South-street. At one time they held a seat in the council, but they have long been deprived of it; they still, however, retain a vote in the convener court. About the time of Queen Mary, they had been esteemed an important body, as we find that she presented them with a flag of fine silk, on which the figures were wrought with needle-work of the richest pattern, by her Majesty's own hand.

This corporation was for many years very unfortunate in the management of their business. Their deacons and boxmasters came out every year defalcators, frequently to a considerable extent, until their funds dwindled to nothing; ultimately a heavy load of debt was incurred, which was followed by bankruptcy, and the breaking-up of the corporation. The consequence was, their whole property was put to the hammer; even their seats in the churches, and their ancient flag, were disposed of.

Besides their annual election dinner, the members met frequently in their tenant's house, then a respectable brew-seat, where they guzzled away their funds. They had an ancient custom of meeting there annually on Fasten's Eve, and having fortified themselves with fat brose in the morning, the rest of the day was devoted to tippling. Since their bankruptcy, a new body has been formed, rather on the principle of a friendly society than a privileged order; they, however, still retain their seat in the convener court, and elect their deacon annually.

The *Tailors*, at present about thirty-five in number, consist of two sciences—the tailors and staymakers. The income for the year 1832 was L.238, 2s. 6d., the expenditure L.275; but of this sum L.75 was expended on repairs of property. At one time this corporation strictly enforced their privileges; but this year, 1836, January 14, they came to the resolution of giving up these privileges entirely, and allowing any person whatever to begin business in that line within the town.

About seventy years ago, the tailors were in the habit of going out to their customers' houses with their men to make and mend for the family,

like the tailors in the country, for which they were paid twopence a-day
besides their meals.   This mode of doing business was both inconvenient
and expensive to the employers, which gave way to the present more
comfortable mode of making and mending at home.   Many curious anecdotes were told of the tailors and their victuals.   The guidwives could
tell well who had the best stomachs.   On one occasion, the guidwife, that
she might be revenged on the tailor for cabbaging her thread, gave him
to dinner, first kail, prepared without meat, then eggs and butter, curds
and cream, and cheese and bread.   Next day, the tailor requested that the
whole dishes for dinner might be brought forward at once, which was
accordingly done, when, to her astonishment, he proceeded to mix up
the whole in a wooden dish.   " Ods safe's, is the man mad," cried the
guidwife, " what can he mean by such a mixture as that."   " Mixture,"
replied the tailor, " I took them yesterday without mixture, and they
created a dreadful commotion ; if they are to kick up a dust, let them do
it now before I sup them."   In many houses in town they got very poor
fare, besides their twopence a-day ; at that time tailors made the women's
gowns.

Towards the close of the last century, the tailor incorporation was in
very flourishing circumstances.   Besides houses in town, they had two
fine properties in the country ; one of them, Gillon, the other beyond
Huntingtower.   They were likewise in the habit of taking in money
at 4 per cent., and lending it out at 5 per cent.; and so high was
their credit, that people who had money to lend thought themselves
fortunate if they got it into the tailors' hands.   From the flourishing state
of their funds, and handsome aliment they were able to give their decayed
members and widows, they raised their entry-money to strangers to
L.100.   The staymakers, who at that time formed a part of the corporation, employed a number of hands, until the fashion came in of wearing
very short-waisted gowns ; this was a death-blow to the staymakers, who
were thus ruined as a trade.   Besides their deacon and boxmaster,
they had an eight master court, for the management of their money concerns.   About the year 1796, a junto got into this court, who laid the
foundation of the ruin of the corporation.   Alexander Paul, tailor and
habit-maker from London, (as all their sign-boards testified), was at the
head of this corporation when the contest for member of Parliament for
the city commenced between Admiral Murray of Stanley, uncle to the
late Duke of Atholl, and Captain Campbell of Carwhin, brother to the
late Marquis of Breadalbane.   This contest was carried on with a keen-
ness never before known in Perth ; it became a common rant on the
streets, " Carwhin for ever, and Murray down the river."   If two or

three tradesmen were seen going into a public-house, they were said to be *Carwhinning.* The interest of the Murray party proved too powerful for the Campbells, and the Admiral was elected. This Deacon Paul was of Campbell's party; at the time, his second son James had just completed his apprenticeship as a writer. The father, in return for his vote, applied to the Marquis for a situation for the young writer; this was soon procured in the service of the East India Company. The Marquis sent for and kept him in London until the vessel was ready to sail.

James Paul was a man far below the common stature, of a slender make, and very much pitted with the small-pox. In disposition he was unstable and malicious. At the age of seventeen years he would have thought nothing of beating his mother, or of knocking his father on the head with the first weapon that came to his hand; and so furious was he when contradicted, that he more than once attempted to drown himself. He arrived safe in India, but, with all his faults, distinguished himself, and rapidly made a fortune; amongst the first of his good deeds, he remitted home money for the purchase of an annuity to his parents. Whilst in India, a serious misunderstanding took place between a native Prince and the British Resident. Paul took up the quarrel, challenged the Prince, met him in the field, and shot him dead. His conduct in this affair gave him much notoriety. He came home to enjoy his fortune in London; visited the first company—even George IV., then Prince of Wales, became his companion, and allowed him to ride out with him daily. Some time after his arrival, he was appointed to go out on a special mission, which he managed successfully. On his return, he was elected to Parliament for some English borough, when he brought forward an impeachment against the Marquis Cornwallis, then Governor-General of India, for taking large sums of money from some of the native Princes; but the impeachment fell to the ground, entirely through the influence of powerful friends which the Marquis had arrayed in his interest; even although Mr Pitt declared in the House that Mr Paul had good grounds to go upon. He had formed an intimate friendship with Sir Francis Burdett, but they quarrelled and fought a duel; his ambition knew no bounds. After the dissolution of Parliament, he stood candidate for Westminster at an enormous expense, was unsuccessful, and ruined in fortune. To complete the catastrophe, he cut a blood-vessel with a razor, and bled to death. Thus ended the mortal career of the great Mr Paul. During the progress of his career, the family at home appeared to be in a flourishing condition. His oldest brother, Alexander Paul, who at first kept a cloth shop, tried the manufacturing business, but

2 c

did not succeed for want of credit ; but being elected boxmaster to the
tailors, and having influence through his brother's name, he made shift
to get through ; and got into business in the spirit line, and other branches
of foreign trade. About the year 1800, when the distilleries were stopped,
owing to the dearth, he imported ship-loads of gin; and it was generally
thought he was rapidly making a fortune. Two of his younger brothers got
into extensive business in the manufacturing line ; another commenced as a
general merchant in Leith ; and the youngest went out to Jamaica as a
surgeon. Things went on swingingly. Alexander, after being some
years box-master to the Tailors, made way for his brother William to be
elected into his situation, and thus continued to keep the business amongst
themselves. They had the deacon, and the eight master-court, completely under their control. Their sittings may be said to have been
permanent, for they were every day engaged in some trifle ; and that
trifle, however small, was always finished by an adjournment to one of
their houffs, of which they had several, where they had their morning
drams of Atholl brose, porter and Atholl brose in the forenoon, and suppers in the evening, with toddy and wine ; and frequently, after a pro-
tracted sederunt, they would carry home a bottle of wine each—all at the
expense of the corporation. At length this conduct began to arrest attention. For years the two brothers had kept such a command of this
junto, that, at Michaelmas, the trades' accounts were made up in their
own way. The great man's death at London was the first blow to their
doings : it was found that he had died bankrupt, and that no support could
be obtained in that quarter. The oldest brother soon afterwards became
insolvent to a great amount, left the city, and went to Birmingham
where he got into business in the hardware line. The two manufacturers
continued to carry on business in Perth; but the time at length arrived
when all their knavery with the trade was to be exposed, and it was found
that, instead of receiving supplies from the rich Indian brother, as had been
generally supposed, they had been swinging by the Tailors' money. In
William's account of the matter, he had sent up five thousand pounds of
the Tailors' money to defray expenses incurred in the struggle for Westminster. The following circumstance, which occurred in the box-master's
absence, led to a discovery of the knavery :—A highlandman, who had
lent the corporation L.150, called for the interest of his money, when the
then deacon, who was not into the mystery of the business, after searching
the books, told him that his bill was for L.50 only. " Na, na," said the
highlandman, " her bill be an hunder and fifty." This was a sufficient

hint. An inquiry was commenced, which set matters in their true light. A great amount of the Trades' funds had been abstracted for their private purposes, and large sums borrowed in the Trades' name, that never were entered. William Paul said, that his brother, when he resigned, was seven thousand pounds in arrear, and had involved him on purpose to screen himself. Be this as it might, everything went to wreck; the Corporation became bankrupt, their country property was sold, and, having paid a composition of their debt, they obtained a settlement. The ruin of the Pauls was now complete. William, who had been bred a cork-cutter, went to Edinburgh and attempted business in that line; but having failed, he became a drunkard, and wandered the country in complete destitution. Some years ago he was seen in Perth, in so miserable a state, as to be glad to obtain shelter for the night, in the police-cells. He has been frequently detected in the attempt to commit suicide; the last attempt he made, was by cutting his throat, which he did very seriously. Being immediately afterwards carried to the infirmary, and placed under medical care, he soon recovered. He has, since, been often seen wandering in complete misery. His partner, David, who went to London under the pretence of looking after the wreck of his brother's fortune, leaped from London Bridge into the Thames, and was drowned. John, too, who was a merchant in Leith, and had failed there, went to London, and, what was remarkable, leaped from the same bridge into the Thames, and was also drowned. The youngest son, in Jamaica, ended his days in a similar manner. Their father, having for some time, along with his wife, lived on the annuities which had fortunately been secured to them, died raving mad. Thus ended the career of this unfortunate family, who suddenly rose into power, and for many years possessed great influence in this quarter. Alexander, who went to Birmingham, ended his days, it is said, by poison.

The Corporation still possess some little property, but their privileges are now little worth. Since the Reform Bill came into operation, they have no seat in the Town Council. The Trade still continues to elect their deacons and convener; but the convener's dinner, with all its glory, is departed for ever.

KING JAMES'S HOSPITAL.

This charitable institution was founded on a charter granted by King James VI., in the year 1569 ; in which his Majesty says, " It is incumbent on us to provide, by all honest means, an Hospital for the poor, maimed, distressed persons, orphans, and fatherless children within our said burgh : we have therefore given (omitting the usual legal phraseology) to the poor members in Jesus Christ, now and in all time coming, residing within our burgh, all and hail the lands, tenements, houses, biggings, kirks, chapels, yards, orchards, crofts, ground annuals, fruits, duties, profits, emoluments, farms, alms, deal silver for the dead, anniversaries, annuities, and others whatsoever which any way pertained to chapelaries, altarages, prebendaries, founded in whatever kirk, chapel, or college within the liberty and privilege of our burgh, in possession whereof the chaplains or prebends thereof were originally, the said *et cetera* are lying, or were uplifted respectively, with the manor, places, yards, lands, ground annuals, emoluments, and duties whatsoever which formerly pertained to the Dominican or Predicant friars, to the Minor or Franciscan friars, and to the White friars of our said burgh ; together with the yard belonging to the Monastery or place of the Charter-house in our said burgh : as also, all and sundry, other lands, houses, and tenements lying within said burgh, given and founded to whatever chapelaries, altarages, kirks, monasteries, or anniversaries wherever they are within the kingdom : as also, all and sundry ground annuals and other duties, which can be demanded by whatsoever kirk without our said burgh, from the provost, bailies, or inhabitants out of the revenue of said burgh, and all and sundries of the foresaid to be holden by the said members of Jesus Christ, and present being, and to be therein in all time coming of us and our successors for ever." This charter is of great length, and is dated St Andrews, 29th August 1569.

There is a second charter granted by James VI. in favour of the Hospital, dated July 29, 1587, which is a recapitulation of the former charter, now that the king was of age, " confirming the same, and giving in gift to the Hospital, all and hail the lands, tenements, houses, buildings, churches, burial places, chapels, colleges, yards, orchards, crofts, annual rents, feu ferms, canonries, pensions, mills, mill lands and their sequels, fishings and fish mercat, fruits, rents, duties, profits, incomes, emoluments, kaims, service, alms, distributions, deal silver, obites, anniversaries, and others whatsoever, which any way pertained, or are known to pertain, to said charters, altars, &c., to be holden of the poor in Perth, from the King and his successors in perpetual alms."

These charters are confirmed by an act of the eleventh Parliament of James VI., holden at Edinburgh, and dated 9th July, 1587 years.

There is a second Act of Parliament, held at Edinburgh, being the Twelfth Parliament of James VI., dated 5th June 1592, in which a privilege is granted to the Hospital of Perth, concerning "Tennant, Tennantries, and services of free tennants."

The King's Precept of Sasine upon the new gift to the Hospital, was dated at Edinburgh, 29th July 1587. The Sasine of the Hospital rent in consequence of the King's precept, was dated 13th March 1587 years.

When James VI. had attained the age of twenty-one years, and in the Parliment held in Edinburgh, 29 July 1587, had passed the famous act of the general Revocation of Church Lands and Revenues to the Crown, it became necessary that the rights of the Hospital at Perth should be renewed; especially as the former gift had been granted during his minority. Money as well as interest at Court, it might be expected, would be requisite for that purpose, both because of the composition money which the King might demand as the reparation of the gift, and because of the customary expenses of employing lawyers, and of getting deeds expedite by the officers of the Crown.

The Commissioner from Perth to the Parliament was William Fleeming, a man of great plainness and integrity, one of the most popular and respectable citizens in his time. He had the good fortune to be much in favour with the prime Manager at Court, the Chancellor Maitland, Lord Thirlestone, chiefly by means of the Chancellor's Lady, who was Jean Fleeming, daughter and sole heiress of James, the fourth Lord Fleeming, to whom William claimed kindred.

Letter of William's Nephew, Oliver Colt, advocate :—The signal services done by William Fleeming in the affair of the Hospital, and the manner in which the gift was obtained, appears from a copy of a curious letter written by his nephew, who was the lawyer employed to assist his uncle ; dated 'Edin. 22 August 1587,' directed to Patrick Ray, merchant, Perth, then Treasurer to the Hospital :—" To his well-beloved mate, Patrick Ray, Burgess of Perth, after most hearty commendation, these are to advertise you, that your gift of the Hospitality not only by act of Parliament, is confirmed with a New Gift de novo damus, and all things prejudicial thereto reduced, but also the same to be put under the great seal, and that in the same form as you and I devised often times in privy conference, and especially in the Kirkyard of Kinnoul, at Midsummer, when I was last there, and that with good convoy as you shall understand at meeting. When you see your new act of Parliment, and an

new confirmation under the great seal, I hope ye shall have occasion to
rejoice that such an good work has been done in your time.   The act of
Parliment would have served us, but the Chanceler and Trasurer would
not suffer the same to pass, except the same passed to the sealler of the
nine, and that for the commodity of the composition to the Trasurer,
and commodity of the seals to the Chanceler, which condition was accepted by the hail Barrons, and could not be refused by us, namely, that
the gift given by the King in his minority came under the revocation,
and was null otherwise ; whereas a great part of the Hospitals of the
other Burghs were granted by the Queen after her perfect age.   Moncrieff gave in an supplication to the Parliment for reducing of his twenty
bolls of victuall paid to the Black Friars for ten merks, which was refused ; therefore he had reiterate the same to the Chanceler, Trasurer,
Comptroller, and Collecter, which are the four Lords Compositers, and
he offered large composition, far above that which the toun should pay ;
and he had not failed, but would have got the same passed, if either the
Chanceler or William Fleeming had been absent ; which offer of his made
the toun's composition dearer nor it would have been, for the Lords Compositers, in respect of the Chanceler's earnestness, and of the good will
born of them all to William, whom the Chanceler calls his mate at ilk
word, and the hail rest Gentle William Fleeming, refused Moncrieff's
desire, and would not dismember the Hospitality.   But they asked an
thousand merks for the Toun's composition, which they said was over
given cheap, in respect that the confirmation of Edinburgh's gift given
in the Queen's majority, was composit for a thousand pounds, which they
alledged should have been thrice as meikle ; and so the Chanciller, sore
against the wills of the rest of the Compositors, caused your composition
to be made three hundred pound.   And when they were going to write
the same at the suit of the signatour, William prayed them to stay and
hear him twa words, and so William very lammentably deplored the
Touns estate, the decay of their brig, walls, and kirk, and common
works, the great debt the Toun were in, the great number of the poor
that were to be sustained upon the rent of the Hospitality, and how the
present commodity thereof was very small, and the parts bestowed to
bear the sick (in time of the plague) and that they had nothing to pay
the Poor's Composition but their own rent and bluid.   They answered
that William had declared the same often before, and they moved whether
his declaration had brought the composition of a thousand merks to three
hundred pounds.   Then William, with a laughing countenance replied
and said, ' My Lord Chanceler, seeing that for the causes foresaid the

composition is brought from a thousand merks to three hundred pounds, then it will please your Lordship to remember the promise you made yesterday upon your own bed-stock to my aunt, your Lady and bed-fellow, and me, at which time your Lordship promised to get an ease in the Composition, and the same being gotten to get one-third thereof discharged for her cause, and another third for my own cause, in arles whereof she gave your Lordship ane kiss, which was accepted by your Lordship, upon the same promise and condition :'—whilk moved an laughter, that they forgot the thing that was in their hand. To which the Lord Chanceler replied, that it was sure promise indeed; and he prayed the Lords Compositers to help him to keep the same, seeing it was an promise made to an Lady, which should not be broken; and was assured that Secretary Seton, Comptroller, and the Provost of Lincluden, Collector, who were both wooers, would take his part, and so they presented the pen into his own hands, and he puts in an hundred pounds for the Composition, and so they all said the dealing of William was not without the wiles of me his sister's son, who was standing at his back, indeed, and caused him keep the Secretary's promise, while the last refuge ; and I thought with myself that where all the favour was shewn that could be shewn, that the same would do no evil, and my opinion succeeded well. The hail Lords Compositers commended us to keep our composition secret, and not divulgate the same : and the Chanceler says to William, " shew your aunt, my bedfellow, that I have keepit my promise to her as an loyal Knight ought to do to his Lady.

" It was God that provided William to be in commission at this time, because he is so well known by great and small ; the hail Lords especally have been so familiar with him that they have inquired at him the whole state of your town thir years bypast, which they lament.

" So because they understand that the Princes were well served, and the town flourish'd when the same was governed by Magistrates of your own bowels, and that since the same was governed by others, the authority had gotten evil service and the town brought to decay ; therefore they desired and shew that it is the King's Majesty's mind and will that in the election of your Magistrates ye should observe the acts of Parliament, and should admit none into the sect neither to bear office or be in the Council, only these Burgesses Traffickers who dwell scot and lot within the burgh, with other good and private Council."

Mr Oliver Colt goes on to marvel " that they were so long in sending silver to outred ; albeit they should contribute greatly among themselves Will. Fleming can declare that the expense will be altogether Two Hundred Pounds." He then recommends secrecy, "praying you to keep all quiet until ye get your act of Parliment and Great Seal into your own hands, for then I count the Hasp on the Barn door, and before that time I count nothing indeed, for many things may fall between the cup and the lip." He then goes on to state the great expense William Fleeming had been at; he was in a grand estate, being one of the Lords of secret articles, and could not be absent. After commending William for his great exertions, he again says—" I pray you that some be hastened here with silver to outred the common affairs so long as he was present."

" And so ceasing to trouble you farther, I commit you and all other good friends to the keeping of Almighty God, the 22 day August 1587. Yours at your peace, Mr Oliver Colt. Read, thrive, and keep secret."

It appears that ten burghers came forward and pledged their silver plate for the sum of two hundred and thirteen pounds six shillings and eightpence, whereby they purchased the gift of the Hospital. It also appears that these ten burgesses did not get payment of that sum until the 15th April 1588; and Oliver Colt's discharge appears to be dated 1592. It appears that in May 1597, twenty-one pounds were collected for reparation of the Kirk.

From the Session Records.

In the session records there are several chasms, where the record is either lost or not been kept; some of them for months and years.

" Feb. 1578.—The Master of the hospitel to request the Bailies to clean the Cros so as the door may open and steik to by locks, for the Irons where delinquents do pennance at the Cros."

" 20 Nov. 1581.—Ordains all possessors of altarages to put up lights in the kirk, and to put on the Sunday a twopenny candle; this to be done by the sound of the bell through the town. Ordains the Bailies to purge the kirk of wood and all materials that are portable."

" 12 Feb. 1581.—Whilk day for so meikle as the Deacon of the Wrights compearing before the assembly (at that period the session assumed that name) did earnestly require in name of the hail Brethern in his craft, that place in the kirk whilk was assigned to them before betwixt the twa Pillars next the Pulpit, on the north side of the kirk. The Ministers and Elders allowing their Godly zeal and good will to decoir the house of God, grants them leave big seats in that same place to their own ease, provided always that the seats builded by them be decent and comley at the sight of the Minister and Elders, as ought to be in the Kirk of God; and moreover, because the other crafts are desirous to have places of old assigned to them, the assembly grant the same, provided every Deacon decoir the place assigned to him in a proper manner before Palm Sunday."

"2d July 1582.—Whilk day for as meikle as John Swinton of the sang school, being found not qualified for that office, and divers other faults, and disagreeing with those who held office in the Church of God, ordained that he should never pretend to such an office in time coming."

" 12 Nov. 1582.—Whilk day compeared Marjory Gibson, and being first accused of her own harlotry, and secondly, of burying infant unbaptised, without knowledge of Nicol and the bellman, which she plainly denied."

" 3d Dec. 1582.—Whilk day the friends of William Tary, who drowned himself at the head of the South Inch in the water of Tay, coming unto the Ministers and Elders assembled in their Revestry, and desiring licence at the assembly to bury the said William in the Grayfriars, whilk is the burial appointed for the faithful that depart in the fear of God, the assembly answer in one voice that they would not suffer him to be brought through the town in day light, neither yet to be buried amongst the faithfull in the place appointed for them, but ordains him to be buried in the little Inch within the water ; and this to have the strength of an act in all time coming to all such like persons; and assuring all that if any contraveens the same, the dead shall be taken up again, and the Contraveeners hereof shall make their public repentence on the stool, and pay ten pounds, to be given to the poor.

" Jan. 29, 1583.—The bell to go through the town as before, charging all who have timber in the church to remove the same out of the kirk."

" 1584, Oct. 18.—Number of elders elected ; ordained their names to be presented to the Bailies and Council, that they may desire and command the Persons written to take upon them the office of Elders for the present year."

Threat to Excommunicate the Bailies.—30 Augusti, 1585. Forsameikle as throuch the negligence off the balzies sundrie var not pwneischi yat contempnit the kirk and the ordinances thairoff, Thairfore the assemblie vith ane voice ordanit the minister to proceed vith admonitions before excommunication agains the balzies, in caiss thay pat not the kingis majesties actis off parliament to execution against Thomas Smyth on Satterday nixt, and in all tyme comming agains all sik public offendars ; and that the balzies may be foresein off this ordinance, ordains Dyoneses Conquerior and Duncan Robertson to speik tham, and to report the balzies anser to the Minister on thursday next, yat in caiss they do thair dewtie he may stay to proceed, otherwaiyis that he gyff the first admonition on thursday nixt cam, and in case of disobedience on Sounday com ought, to excommunicat thame vithout ony farther delay, and that act to haiff place not only agains the balzies present, bot in caiss thair successoris balzies do not thair dewtie, that in lyk mainer the minister of this congregation sall proceed agains them, yat gud order may be observit vithin aur burgh, and the kirk may gett obedience.

" 18 Octobris, 1585. The Sessioun appointtis Patrick Kay and Henrie Lyis to be Mrs of Hospitall for this year, ordaining thame to interpryse nathing thairin without the adwyse of the counsal and session; and because thay ar bot collectoris of the puiris liwing, quha may spair na fie for service done to thame, Thairfore the Sessioun dischargis the fornamit Mrs of Hospitall of all the fie and dewtie yr predecessoris, Mrs of Hospitall, had befoir; and siclyk ordanis yat na Mr of Hospital haiff ony fie for thair service in tyme comming, bot frelie serve and be diligent in thair calling, for thair reward they sall haiff from God.

" 27 June 1586.—For as meikle as the Minister and Elders, perceiving the ruinous, pitiful, great, and lamentable state of the kirk in all parts and places thereof, and the great decay that is still to incur thereupon, and being deeply in heart and in conscience angry therewith, in one voice and with one consent ordains the Minister to ommit his ordinary text wherein he preached before, and to chuse some portion of scripture whilk he thought most able and meet to move the hearts of the people, especially the Bailies and Magistrates, whatever bearing rule and authority in the said burgh, to provide that the same were repaired in all honest and decent form, whilk failing and not being in no wayis done, all should return to ruin."

"10 Jan. 1589.—By aet of Parliment and General Assembly, it is ordained there shall be no more burials within the kirk, nor the floors to be broken or altered; and ordains that the kirk floors shall not be raised or broken in all time coming.

" Whilk day Will. Rhynd, son of Sir Robert Rhynd, resigns the altarages of St. John, St. Laurence, and St. Michael Arch Angel to the Hospital."

" 27 March 1592.—David Jackson, subtennant of the Lands of Black friars, by command of the Ministers and Elders, did advance to Collin Eviot of Balhouse altogether and at once in advance, 900 merks, being three years rent of, excepting 120 merks; the whole rent for three years being 1040 merks."

" 19 Jan. 1596.—The Session appoint Thomas Gall and Donald Johnston, Elders, to compear before the Council, that the common seat of the Provost, Bailies, and Council, may be builded."

It appears that several collections were made on the Sabbath for repairing the kirk. One of them, " 14 April 1600—The Bailies and Elders collected last Sabbath for repairing the kirk, six score and two pounds twelve shillings and ninepence."

" 23 Sep. 1605.—Because the sins of Fornication and Adultery does encrease more and more, to the great offence and dishonour of God and slander of this congregation, the Session ordains that a more public place of repentance be bigged, and to contain degrees that therein Fornicators and Adulterers may be distinguished both by their place and habit."

" 6 March 1609.—There was collected at the Church doors for repairing the roof of the kirk, one hundred and twenty pounds fifteen shillings; and on the 11th of September same year, for the kirk and steeple, one hundred and eighteen pounds."

" 10 January 1616.—Halkerston's tower (above the West Church door) to be repaired with strong bolts and locks, of the penalty of five merks of fines received."

" 5 June 1616.—Gregory Johnston has promised to bring cake lead from Dantzic for the reparation of the steeple."

" 4 Novem. 1616.—The Session finds that the Bailies contemn the Session, because by the space of five weeks past none of them has compeared before the Session to report of the visitation on the Sabbaths, and to put in execution the ordinances of the Session, as they should so conform to old use and wont, and therefore protest for remeed as effeires."

" 20 Jan. 1617.—For as meikle as the Session understanding that Gilbert Robertson, tennant in a laigh house in the South-street pertaining to the Hospital, whilk wants a chimney, and yet has daily ingill therein, to the perriling of the hail tenement to be set on fire, ordains that no ingill be kindled nor used in said house hereafter ; and the Bailies are requested to inforce their authority for that effect."

" 5 May 1618.—The Session ordains John Brown to make an substantious common Mort Kist, for burying the corpse of the Poor."

" 15 May 1620.—The Session ordains the Master of the Grammar school to be admonished to cause the Bairns of the Grammar school come two and two in order therefrom to their seat in the kirk, and make no tumult or perturbation at their coming and sitting down in their seat, and for that efficit go before them, and at their going back again to the school to give their notes, the going back to be in the same manner ; with certificates that if Mr Johnstone fail in doing this, the bairns will be reduced to their old seat, and the new one made common.

" 17 Nov. 1620.—Agreed with Robert Doig, that he shall pas doun to Kingudie, and there wyle twenty-six sufficient stones, summer-won, to be thirteen ovals to the Barmiken of the steeple ; cause bring the same up the river, and hew them sufficiently, according to the form of the old work of the Barmiken, and sicklike ; to wyle fourteen rough stones, for Aislers to said work ; the same to be transported up the river,—for which he shall have fifty-four pounds, thirteen shillings, and four pennies."

Inundation.—" It is to be noted, and put in register in this book, the great and miraculous deliverance that the Lord gave to this burgh of Perth, an fearfull inundation of waters, compassing the same on all parts therethro ; the Brig of Tay was haillilie dung down, except only ane bow thereof left standing ; none could get forth it, nor yet come within it, to make any relief thereto.   The manner of the rising of the waters was this :—The rain began on Friday the 12 of October 1621, about ten hours of the day ; it continued that day and Saturday ; and in the night, un-looked for, the water increased, so that all those that dwelt outwith the Castle Gavel port in low houses, behoved to go to high houses for pre-servation of their lives : and being in high houses, the water rose to the laftings in the highest mid-house in the Castle Gavel before six hours in the Sunday morning ; and the wind and wet continuing, the water came up to Gilbert Henderson's yett in the Castle Gavel, and to Margret Mo-neypenny's yett in the fish mercat, to Donald Johnston's yett in the High-gate, to the Meal Vennel in the South-street ; and the water ran like mill-slouses at the yetts of divers parts in the north-side of the High-gate. An great tempestuous wind blew all this time from the east ; the waters also came above Henry Sharp's shop in the Speygate. The like fearful inun-dation of waters was never seen in Perth, in no living man's remem-brance,—whilk brought the people under such fear, that they looked to have been destroyed.   Whereupon Mr John Malcolm, minister, power-fully endowed with God's Spirit, caused ring the preaching-bell on Sun-day at seven hours in the morning ; and the haill inhabitants came to the kirk, and there he exhorted them to repent of their sins, whilk had pro-cured the said judgment of God to come upon the city, assuring them that if they were truly penitent therefor, and would avow to God to amend their lives, God would avert his judgment, and give them deliver-ance ;—whose powerful exhortation moved the people to cry to God with tears, clamours, and cries,—to hold up their hands to God, to amend their lives, and every one of them to abstain from their domestic sins.   The like humiliation, both of men and women, had not been seen in Perth be-fore. Fasting, preaching, and prayer, continued all that week, our pas-tor continuing to exhort them to true repentance and amendment of life.

The waters began to assuage after noon on Sunday ; but after day-light passed, there arose an greater tempest of wind and rain, whilk so afeared the people that night, that they looked for nothing but that the waters should have risen to greater height. Notwithstanding thereof, miraculously, the waters decreased, whilk in the morning moved the people, in the kirk and all other places, to give hearty thanks to God for [his] mercy towards them. Great plenty of corn, in all parts, both stacks and stooks, on haughs and valley-ground, were carried away by the waters ; and divers sheep by tempest perished, and horse, nolt, and kye, and sheep [were] drowned.''

" 14 Jan. 1622.—The Session sets down eleven merks to be taken from John Lamb and John Brown, per ilk boll of their farm-bere of the crop 1621, on the farm of the Blackfriars," (equal to 12s 2¾d sterling per boll.)

" 31 Jan.—The Council and Session agree that they shall have a second minister.''

" 21 Feb. 1621.—Andrew Conquerour, overseer for the reparation and theiking of Mercer's Aisle, produced his accounts, whilk being read, were found equitably given, and admitted, whilk amounted to eight score eight pounds, sixteen shillings, three pennies."

" The 7 March 1622.—Mathew Lamb obtained a tack of the lands of Blackfriars, 71 bolls and 71 pecks of bere."

23d May 1631.—From a minute and receipt of a ground annual from Lord Sanquhar, it appears that his lodging was in the Speygate. From several other minutes, it appears also, that the power of appointing the town bellman, and a person to ring the church bells, was invested in the Kirk Session. In one clause it is enacted, that " one-third of John Tenender's Wage shall be given to three honest misterful persons therein named.''

From the year 1590 to the year 1616, there had been no less than twenty public collections for repairing the kirk, and four for repairing the steeple.

" 30 Dec. 1616.—In the new kirk, with the Bishops and Council present—the Archbishop of St Andrews, the Archbishop of Glasgow, Bishop of Dunkeld, Bishop of Galloway, Bishop of Dunblane, Lord Sanquhar, Lord Scone, John Malcolm (minister), the Bailies, Council, Deacons of Craft, and Elders there,—of whilk day it is agreid, for better ordering of all matters in the Kirk and Session, that the Provost and Bailies hereafter shall always be elected and chosen members of the Session."

From the year 1569 to the year 1616, it appears that several orders had been issued to certain individuals to provide a house for the poor ; but nothing further was done during that period, nor indeed until the year 1750, when the present Hospital was built. Upon the completion of this erection, an hospital-master, an hospital-mistress, and a teacher (who also acted as chaplain), were appointed ; and a certain number of aged persons, male and female, and children, were admitted to the establishment. About the year 1784, when the cotton-jennies were introduced, the boys and girls of the hospital were employed in reeling the copes, which they held between their knees by a pin, with their legs inclining outwards on each side. In consequence of close confinement to this awkward position, the children became knock-kneed, whilst their feet were more than twelve inches asunder. Some of these individuals are yet to be seen in this distorted condition. About the period alluded to, the managers began to make strict inquiry into the state of the inmates, and the funds expended on them, the result of which proved very unsatisfactory. The hospital master was expelled, and another appointed in his place, who proved a tyrant,—on his death it was found that the accounts were three hundred pounds in arrear. The person next appointed was much esteemed, but did not long enjoy his situation, being removed by death a few years after his appointment. His successor, on the contrary, was distinguished for his haughty deportment to the poor under his charge, who were removed from the hospital, some time before his death, and a weekly aliment in money settled on them. When the Depot was built, and a large garrison established here, Government took a lease of the hospital buildings, as a military infirmary ; but the general peace having occurred before they had been occupied as such, a great part of the hospital was then let as an extensive manufacturing establishment, and one wing of the building is still occupied in that line. The first two flats of the centre are occupied as schools, and part of the ground floor of the west wing as a charity school, above which are the hospital master's dwelling-house and offices. The principal income arises from the rents of the lands of Lethendy, the feu-duties of the gardens recently laid out in building-stances, and ground annuals of a number of houses in Perth, which last, being paid in Scots money, yield little revenue.

OTHER CHARITIES AND PROVISIONS AGAINST DISTRESS.

The Session funds have always afforded a very slender pittance to the poor. In ordinary cases the allowance weekly is to each from 6d. to 9d. Besides the above allowance, there are several heavy burdens that fall upon the session funds—coffins and winding sheets, and burial charges for the destitute. Foundling infants form another heavy charge, for nurses' fees, and maintenance until they arrive at a certain age; add to these, the maintenance of lunatics, and the wonder will cease that the weekly allowance is so small.

Besides the session funds, there is an assessment laid on annually on all the lands and houses within the parish, of about 4d. to 5d. a pound of the rent, from which the poor receive   a-week. The indigent are allowed to beg from door to door on the Saturdays, but not through the week.

Besides these funds, there are other establishments of a voluntary description that have done infinite good to the poor and distressed. Amongst these, the Destitute Sick Society, originally established for the relief of industrious families who were, by severe distress, deprived of their means of subsistence. It often happened that, when a tradesman was laid up by distress, the family were reduced to a state of destitution; to relieve cases of this kind was the original intention of this institution, but of late years the managers, from a kindly feeling, allowed many infirm persons, who had been long in distress, and would continue to be so for life, to come on the society, where they remained. Persons of this description became so numerous on the list, that the directors saw clearly they were departing from the original intention of the institution, and that persons of this description were proper objects for the common funds for the poor. They have, therefore, begun to act on the principle of confining their aid to industrious families in temporary distress, and until they are fully able to resume their usual occupation. By this line of conduct, they are now saving a vast sum annually for the original purposes of the institution.

The Indigent Old Men's Society is another institution formed lately for the relief of old decayed men, rendered incapable of labour from age and infirmity, who have nobody to take charge of them. During the winter season they are served with articles of clothing, meal, and coals, so far as the funds will allow, which, with the exception of some small legacies, are all voluntary.

The Ladies have formed a society amongst themselves on the same principles, for the relief of indigent old women. Both societies have the town divided into districts, which are visited by the members appointed to that duty. These societies have been of immense benefit to many poor families.

Until of late years, there were a number of friendly societies formed amongst the different working classes, who, by paying a certain sum annually, were entitled to an allowance weekly during distress; and on their death, or that of their wives, the survivor was entitled to a sum for funeral expenses. For many years they continued to act on this principle, but it was uniformly found that the sum paid quarterly was inadequate to keep up the funds, and pay the usual allowances.   Of late the Highland Society framed a set of tables of annuities upon correct principles; but it appearing from these tables that it would require a considerable addition to their quarter payments, a great proportion of the members became clamorous for breaking them up, and dividing the funds.   In most instances this was accomplished, and men who had arrived at an advanced age were left destitute, after having paid into these funds for upwards of thirty years, in the fond hope that they were securing an independence in sickness or age; all they received was a few pounds from the division of the funds, which, in too many instances, lasted only a few days.   In some instances, societies have been formed on the new principle, according to the act of Parliament, which, in all probability, will succeed well.

The Savings Bank, established of late years under the direction of a number of disinterested gentlemen, has afforded an opportunity to industrious individuals of depositing weekly any little savings they can spare.

There is, besides, the Mason Lodges; these afford relief to their members.   The Royal Arch Lodge was long eminent, many of the most influential gentlemen in town being members; but about 1780, a number of worthless characters got into office, which caused many to retire in disgust.   Thus left to themselves, they wasted the funds until the Lodge was deeply in debt.   Within these twenty years, the management fell into better hands—respectable members again attended, by proper management their debt has been liquidated, and they now again maintain their former character.   The Perth and Scone Lodge is chiefly composed of operatives; they have a hall at the foot of the High-street, and are a numerous body.   St Andrews' Lodge is of great antiquity, and has now many of the most respectable gentlemen, both in town and county, enrolled as members.

The following Incidents connected with Perth are extracted from a rare Volume now out of print.

1537.   The deir symmer, quhen the bow of maill guift 26 shillings 8 pennies; Alexander Blair than Provost of Perth.

1537.   Mallochis post in September.   Jhone Denying than Provost.

1541.   Quene Margaret, mother to King James fyft, deciesit on Sanct Manokis day, buriet in the Charter hous besyde Perth, the King's majestie, nobilitie, and baronis being present.

1543.   The execution of James Hunter, Robert Lamb, James Ranaldson, and his spous, in Januar, on Sanct Poulis day.

1544. The conflict or battle of the brig of Tay, on the Magdalene day, the 22d of July.

1560. The reform of the Charter hous and friars, beside Perth, the 10 day May.

The burnyng of Scone on Twysday after Midsamer day, 27 Junii.

The downfalling of the bridge of Almond, the 23d day of November.

The Kat harrow in Perth 22 May.

1568. The Queenis passing forth of Lochleven on Sonday, 2d of May.

1580. The entrie of the worthie and nobill King James the Saxt within Perth, the 28 day of Maij.

Mr John Row departed, minister of Perth, Oct. 16.

1581. Mr Patrick Galloway, minister, admitted there to 25 Apryle; he tuik his voyage to be minister to his Majesty the 11 Februar 1580 zeeris.

1582. The downfalling of five bows of the brig of Tay on the 11 day of Januar.

The justice air holden at Perth by King James, the saxt of Jullie.

1584. Pest in Perth, 24th day of September 1584 zeeris, continued to the 24 August 1585 zeeris, quharin, at the plesore of God, departed this lyff fourteen hundred and twenty seven persons, young and auld, thereby·

1590. A plauge among the bestial.

1592. The raid of Falkland by the Earl of Bothwell, quha assailit the king. The town of Perth were down for his defence for feir of weir.

Upon the 16th day of August the Laird Clackmannan tuik William Englis, decone of the hammermen, and Jhone Caskie, decon of the wrights, coming from Dundee, captives into his house of Gaskinhall.

The town of Perth, mair raischelie than na vyslie, unvilling to abyde the indignitie, that samen night, with all diligence, past to the said Gaskenhall in armes, releevit their nechbours, and broch the laird with theme to Perth. They vair thereafter agreit upon the toun's large charges. The laird remanint, not being a free man, 1593.

1594, Jhone Erle of Atholl decesit in Perth on the penult day of August. Conwayit honorablie to Dunkeld, and buried there the 11 September therefter; the Queen's majestie being in Perth, in William Hallis chamber, beneath the Croce, beholding the conway of the corps.

1597. Ane trouble betwixt certaine of the servants of the Drummonds and Oliver Young, than ane of the bailizies of Perth, within the Hiegate of the said burgh, quhan the greatest number of the persewars leap the town's wall; and so few number of them as remainent came to the tolbeuth

2 E

on Setterday the 27th August. The agreement was made in the South Inch on Wednesday the first day of September thereafter following.

1597. The eclips of the sone on Setterday calit the merk Saturday, 25 Februar 1597 (8), at half hour to 10 morning.

1597—8, March 21. The Countes of Montrose, dame Jeane Drummond, conveyed through Perth to Abruthven.

1598. The Duck of Holstein, brother to the Quene, come to Perth, and received a banquet frae the toun be his Majesty's directions, and conwayt be 100 horsemen of the toun to Abruven, and receavit by Tullebardin.

April 10, being Gude Fryday, Henrie Adamson, dene of guild, slain be Thomas Pebles, and was buried on peax (pasch) day. The execution of Thomas Pebles for the slaughter of the said umquile Henrie on Tuys-day the penalt of May, at the Mercat Croce.

Sept. 9. The witches brunt in the South Inche, betuix the Buttis, called Janet Robertson, Marion Macause, and Bessie Ireland.

The fische merkat was removed from the Schoar Head to the North Gaet Port be act of Counsell.

Nov. The town began to repair the new kirk in wall and windows.

Feb. 16. The slaughter of William Hey, sone to the gudeman of Gourdie, in Andro Gibis hous in the Kirkgate, be the Laird of Craighall, Rattrace, and his accomplices. Thomas Lafrew, chyrurgione, was there, wha sufferit for it.

The toun began their voluntar contribution for reparation of the bridge of Perth, and left in August 1600.

1599. Ane great dead among the pepell.

1600. The Erll of Gowrie cam to Perth after seven zeirs peregrination in other countries.

June 28. The execution of David Drummon for the slauchter of George Ramsais man, the first court that ever the Eril of Gowrie held efter his return.

Aug. 5. The slaughter of John Eril of Gowrie and Mr Alexander, his brother, in the Eril's own lodgings in Perth, be John Ramsay and Douchter Herrees, his Majesties servanties. Praesit be God, the King was saiff. The toun knew nothing till the common bell rang. The toun of Dundie being adverteisit, come all up in armes to have spoilant the toun of Perth, but praisit be God, the King knew the part to be sure.

1601. The King's Majestie come to Perth, and was made burges at the Mercat Croce. Thair was ane punscheone ot wyne sett there, and all drunken out. He receevit the banquet frae the toun, and subscrivit the gilde buik with his awin hand, *Jacobus Rex parcere subjectis et debillare superbas.*

Sept. 22. There fell a nich of the tymer bridge of Tay, with tua men, ane horse, and ane lead; ane of the men was goten safe again, with the horse and the lead, but the ither man, callit Lamb, drownit in the water.

Nov. 1. Henry Balneavis and William Jack, maid their repentance in their ain seats in the church eftre sermone, for making lybell against Mr Henry Coupar, minister, and Henrie Elder, clerk. " As King David was ane sair sanct to the crown, so is Mr Will Coupar and the clerk to this poure toun." An act of council against them, that none of them sould be an officer or gett honourable in the toun thairafter.

July 12. The laird of Ballendene, quha was slain in Dundee, was buriet in the kirk of Perth, be eist the counsel house door, under a blue stone of the Ryne.

1604, Jan. 24. The stepell of stone fell.

March 27. The toun's burrow muir was sawin with eattis.

June 15. The men of black Ruthven and Huntingtower cuist turffs on our burrow muir at command of the comptroller. Sir David Murray, captain of his Majesty's guard, and our provost for the time. The toun raise aught hunder men in arms to put them off. Angus Caerdene died of the apoplexie thair. No more harm, but great appearance of skaith,

July 3d. An parliment houlden at Perth be John Erill of Montrosce. Viceroy Kathones buir the suord, Argyle the septer, Angus the crown. My Lord Flemying maid Erl of Wigten, Glamis Earil of Kinghorn, Tullibarden made Eril; my Lord Newbattle maid Eril of Louthiayne. This parliment was ridden by the nobilitie all in robbis of red scarlet, with quhite furris, and the bishopis in black.

At this tyme there fell ane pley betwixt the Eril of Eglinton and the Eril of Glencairn. It lasted frae sevin till ten houris at night, with great skaith ; ane man of Glencairn was slane. The toun raise in arms an pot doun the assaulters, to their great commendation.

July 17. John Mylne and his men entered to the bridge work.

August 9. The laird of Auldie's lodgeing beneath the Croce fell in ane Saturday at nicht. The fair land of Andrew Roy, next to James Drummond's land, took fyre, and brunt all ane the same night. There was blude, fyre, and the pest come in, quhilk contineweit till May thereafter.

1607. The tree bridge was taen away betwixt twelve and ane on ane Sunday in tyme of denner.

March 2. There raise ane great extraordinarie wind, that blew the lead off the steepel to Mr John Malcolme's back yett, callit the Bishop Murray's house.

April 8. Ane synodall assemblie haulden in the new kirk of Perth. My lord of Scone came in and dischargit them, and threw over the tabells amongs them, and pat them forth of the kirk, wha yet held thair assembly at the kirk door, wi joy that the peopell were so well affected to them. Mr Hary Livingstone was moderater.

Sept. 23. The reid of Carpen, quhen the hail inhabitants of Newburgh cam out against our baillies and counsall, that war singell on our part; there wis sundrie hurt on baith sides. Thomas Cobraits was slain to them of Newburgh.

Dec. 1. There wis ane continual frost from said day untill the 23d March, and passage upon the yce over Tay all the tyme, and passage owre and owre at the mill of Errol.

1608, April 8. Patrick Eviot, brother-germane to the laird of Balhousie, was murtherit in Blilok bi his wife Jannet Ross, quha was air to the lairdschip of Craigie and Kynfaunis baith; he was shot in his bed with ane gun while sleeping, be James M'Nair. Thereefter they were both takin and execute, and brent after they were hangit, in the Playfields of Perth, 17 May 1608, his head an arm put up on the Castel Gavel Port.

1654, May 12. This day Cromwell was proclaimit Lord Protector of the three nations, Ingland, Scotland, and Ireland, upon ane stage of timber right beneath the court guard, being hung in with tapestrie, being present thereon Collonel William Daniel, governor of Perth, the maer ane Inglis, capitaine of horse, John Mill, master of wark for the masons, Andrew Butter, present provost, William Roche, baillie Andro Read, Robert Arnot, Henrie Jackson, glover, Mr John Nairne, sherriff deput, Mr William Ord, sherriff clerk, with diveris others.

The act of gras, with som utheris paperis, alse red be Patrick Ross and Henrie Broune, notaris, proclaimed be Andrew Henerie Baxter, be sound o trumpetis.

Ane troup of horse and some troupes of dragoones staid beneath the court guard, fairanent the stage, and efter the proclamation endit, gaif fyre thrice; the hail fute regiment that stude in armes above the meane guard gaif fyre. Cannons wir shute and bonefyres set furth that nycht by the garrison.

1658, Jan. 7. Lord Richard proclaimit Protector of Ingland, Scotland, and Irland, and dominions thereto belonging, be sounding a trumpetis on ane stane beneath the court of guard.

Oct. 22. Captain Forde, brother-in-law to Collonel William Daniel, govirnour of Perth, about eleven hours before noone, nane being present except Docter Beaten and the Collonel's eldest dochter, being setting in a chair fornent the fyre, efter taking a cup of bear going to breakfast, sattled down presently to the ground, and departed presently, but ony words spyking, Bang of wynd, efter some physic he had taken ; he had been imediately in the guarding walking a little befoir.

LETHENDY MORTIFICATIONS.

Besides the charitable institutions already mentioned, there is the Lethendy Mortification, under the patronage and conditions as stated under :—

1. By Mr Butter, 1660. Two-fifths of Lands of Lethendy, to maintain four poor persons of the Burgh of Perth, aged 60. Patrons—the Provost, Bailies, and Ministers.

2. By Mr Jackson, in 1686. One half of one-fifth of the Lands of Lethendy, to support one poor relation, whom failing, one of the name of Jackson, whom failing, any other. Patrons—the Provost, Bailies, and Ministers.

3. By Mr Cairnie, in 1743. Two-fifths of the Lands of Lethendy, to the poor of the Burgh of Perth, reserving two-thirds of the free rent to two of his descendants nearest the age of 14 years, one half to be paid them annually for 10 years, and at the expiry of 10 years, the reserved half to be paid in full, but without interest : the other third annually to the poor.

The Ministers and Elders trustees of all these Mortifications.

For many years the first bequest was confined to four decayed burghers, above the age specified, which, prior to the beginning of the present century, yielded them five pounds each. The enormous rise which took place in the price of land about the beginning of the present century, raised the available funds to each of the four to about L.32 per annum ; and for some years it was even higher. The patrons, conceiving that it would do more good to divide the bequest among a greater number of deserving objects, the four original ones were continued, but were burdened with riders, some of whom received one half of the amount. After this plan was introduced, the charity was not confined to decayed burghers alone. Frequently a majority of the annuitants were widows and old maiden ladies, who, according the terms of the original bequest, had no right to be admitted to the benefit of the fund. At one time there was on this fund a Robert Foggo, one of the four to whom the fourth part of the income was granted, without any riders. Shortly after he was admitted, the funds greatly advanced, and the surplus above L.32 was given to others. To this Mr Foggo objected, and for several years would not take a farthing, until they should pay him in whole. The consequence was an arrangement, by which he received a handsome sum in hand for the bygone years, and an augmentation to a considerable amount during life.

Owing to the defalcation of a tenant on the Lethendy property, who made a voyage to America without previous notice, the funds were for some years greatly reduced, but they have again considerably recovered. At the present time there are as many females as males on the fund.

TITLE AND STATUS OF THE CHIEF MAGISTRATE OF PERTH.

The reader is perhaps aware that the right of the Chief Magistrate of Perth to assume the title of " Lord Provost," was lately challenged by the Lord Justice Clerk and Lord Meadowbank ; and that Mr Patton was called upon, as Counsel for the Magistrates, to show by what right the designation was assumed ; the former learned Lord remarking that, a good many years ago, the Court had refused to acknowledge any such right. Mr Patton, although unprepared for such an objection, with his characteristic promptness, stated various grounds which occured to him at the moment, resting chiefly upon consuetude, and the recognition of the title in various late Acts ; which operated so far on the Bench, that a minute was ordered to be given in, stating the grounds, to be communicated to the Lord Advocate, in order that the matter might be finally set at rest.

Although it is considered that the question was one not competent to be entertained by the Court, the Magistrates departed from such objection, and a minute having been given in, in terms of their Lordships' appointment, it came under discussion on the 12th of March 1836. The Judges present delivered their opinions seriatim, and, with the exception of Lords Meadowbank and Medwyn, unanimously agreed to sustain the title. The two dissentients founded their objections on the ground, that it required an express Charter to warrant the assumption of the title.

As the discussion involved matters of interesting historical record, a copy of the prepared minute by Mr Patton is subjoined :—

" I. The burgh of Perth is of high antiquity. It is one of the most ancient in Scotland, and at a very early period enjoyed distinguished privileges. It was the residence of the early Scottish Monarchs, the seat of the Court, of the Parliament, and of the National Councils of the

Clergy. The earliest charter in favour of the burgh, which is extant, was granted by William the Lion, in 1210. This charter, which is *verbatim* narrated in a subsequent charter, granted by King Robert III. in 1399, itself narrates a prior grant in favour of the burgh, by King David, the grandfather of King William, who died in 1153, dated on the 10th of April, in the 36th year of his reign. It was the residence of William the Lion, the granter of the charter foresaid, and the seat of his his Court. A cotemporary writer testifies to its importance and opulence at that early period, and describes it as a main support of the kingdom. It was in like manner the seat of the Court of Malcolm the Fourth, who, in a charter addressed to the monks of Scone, in the neighbourhood, describes that place as the principal seat of his kingdom. It was the favourite residence of other Monarchs, and received charters, containing additional grants of land and of immunities, from various kings. In addition to the charters already referred to, it received grants from Robert II. (charter dated the 4th year of his reign, 23d July.) Robert de Bruce. David II. (36th year of reign, 10th April.) Robert III. (5th year of reign, 10th April.) Robert III. (10th year of reign, 6th May.) Robert III. (15th year of reign, 21st January 1404.) Robert III. (16th year of reign, 1st March.) James II. (25th March 1451.) James V., (10th March 1527.) James VI. (9th August 1569.) James VI. (29th July 1587.) Its latest and most important charter, by which all of the preceding are confirmed, was granted by King James VI. on the 15th November 1600."

" II. Perth enjoyed this pre-eminence until the middle of the fifteenth century, at which time Edinburgh became the capital. Of the thirteen Parliaments held in the reign of King James I., eleven were held at Perth, one at Stirling, and one at Edinburgh. The National Councils of the Scottish Clergy were held there uniformly till 1459."

" III. Though losing its pre-eminence by the selection of Edinburgh as a capital, Perth has uniformly and constantly maintained the second place in the order of burghs, and its right to do so has been repeatedly and solemnly acknowledged. Attempts were made to question its right by Dundee, which is the third in order ; but these attempts uniformly failed. Upon reference to the King and the Estates of Parliament, by the royal burghs, it was ' ordained, That the burgh of Perth, their procurators, and commissioners of the same, shall be preferred in order of antiquity and dignity to our said burgh of Dundee, inhabitants, commissioners, and procurators of the same ; and shall give place to them in order of priority of place and dignity ; and that in all our successors'

Parliaments, and public meetings of our States in all other Convention of Estates or Burrows and Councils, the foresaid, our royal burgh of Perth, their procurators and commissioners, shall have and enjoy perpetually, in all time coming, the principality, prerogative, first place and order, and shall be preferred, in giving of votes and suffrages, before the said burgh of Dundee, their inhabitants, procurators and commissioners, shall altogether, and in all things, give place to our said royal burgh of Perth, inhabitants, commissioners and procurators of the same, as being long before them in order of antiquity and dignity, and that they altogether cease, for that cause, to contend with our said royal burgh of Perth, inhabitants, procurators and commissioners thereof.' On the 30th May 1594, this order was renewed by a precept under the hands of King James VI. The precept is as follows :—

" ' REX.

" ' George, Erl Merschell. We greet you weill. It is our will, and we command you that ye place the commissioner of our burgh of Perth in ye second place, and next ye commissioner of our burgh of Edinburgh, ye haill tyme of yis our Parliament, and in tyme coming, that yer may have ye priority, first rank, place and vote before ye commissioner of Dundee, according to yaer antiquitie and decreet of our haill burrowis, geven yeanent, as ye will ansr to us upone your office and duetie in yt respect, kepand yir p'nts for your warrant. Subscryvit wt our hand, at Huliruid House, ye penult dey of May 1594.

JAMES R."

" A decreet-arbitral of the King and his Lords of Session, confirming the right, was ratified by Parliament, upon the 9th July 1606. Since that period the right of priority has been enjoyed and exercised."

" IV. The order of the principal burghs in the Rolls of the Convention is as follows :—Edinburgh, Perth, Dundee, Aberdeen, Stirling, Linlithgow, St. Andrews, Glasgow, Ayr, &c.—So in the Rolls of the Scottish Parliament,—-Edr., Perthe, Dundie, Striveling, Sanctandrois, Aberdein, Montrois, Dumbartane, Glasgow."

" V. On the 15th April 1601, King James the Sixth accepted the office of Chief Magistrate of Perth. This acceptance of the office is thus described in the Diary of Mr Dundee, a burgess of the town, and an eyewitness of his induction into the office :—' Item, On the xv. Apprill, in anno a thousand vi. hundred ane yeir, the Kingis Majestie came to Perth, and that same day he was made Provost, with ane great scerlane of the courtcoures, and the bancait was made at the crois, and the Kingis Majestie was set down thereat, and six dozen glasses brokine, with money owdir pissiz and pewdir vescilles ; and thair the King made ane greit solleimne aith to defend the hail libertie of this brouche.' His Majesty was enrolled as a burgess and guild-brother, and he himself inscribed his name in the Guildry Register. Adamson, the author of the Muses Threnodie, also witnessed the King's induction into the office, and describes it in the poem bearing that name. The poem was published in 1638, and is dedicated ' To his Native Town of Perth, THE LORD PROVOST, Bailies and Council thereof, his worthy patrons.' Cant, who published an edition of the poem in 1774, with extensive notes, similarly dedicates his work to ' THE LORD PROVOST, SHERIFF and CORONER,' and to the other Magistrates of that day."

" VI. The charters of the burgh give a right to the burgesses to appoint a Sheriff, having, within the town, power and authority co-extensive with the Sheriff of the county. The office has been uniformly held by the Chief Magistrate, as is that of Coroner, and the appointment to those offices is annually made. The Chief Magistrate of Perth has exercised, in various instances, the power of trying crimes punishable by death, and sentences of death pronounced by him have been carried into execution."

" VI. For a very long period, a use and consuetude has existed, of addressing the Chief Magistrate of Perth by the title of the Lord Provost. He has uniformly enjoyed the title in the burgh, and in correspondence on the affairs of the town. He has been called, under that designation, to attend the annual Convention of Burghs. He communicates with Secretaries of State, and other public officers, under that designation, and is so addressed by them in their communications to him. He holds various powers and functions, conferred on him under that designation by various Acts of Parliament, and was introduced to the King at Holyroodhouse, in 1822, by the Lord Lieutenant of Perthshire, under that title, while the Chief Magistrates of Aberdeen, Dundee, &c., were presented as Provosts of those towns only. The Gazette of that time contains the address of the " Lord Provost, Magistrates, and Council of Perth," which was presented to his Majesty, and which was acknowledged by the Secretary of State to have been received by the King in the usual form.'

" VIII. Further, and what is humbly thought to be absolutely conclusive, he has received the title and designation under a deed granted by the Crown, and bearing the sign manual of his Majesty. In the precept for passing a warrant under the Great Seal, for the Incorporation of the Royal Lunatic Asylum at Perth, he is expressly directed and appointed a director, under the title of Lord Provost ; and in the charter passed upon this precept or warrant, and passing the Great Seal, the designation is repeated."

" In England the title of Lord Mayor is assumed by the Chief Magistrates of London and of York. In neither case was it given by any ex-

press grant.   The title of Lord Mayor was assumed by the Chief Magistrate of London about the year 1354."

" In Edinburgh, the title of Lord Provost in like manner does not
stand upon any grant, but upon prescriptive usage and incidental recognition alone.   Maitland, the historian of the burgh, thus speaks of it :—
" Having given a list of the Provosts of this city, I think it will not be
amiss to observe, that the title of Lord annexed thereto *being by prescrip-
tion and not by grant*, every Provost within the kingdom has as great a
right to that epithet as the Provost of Edinburgh hath.' "

The appendix contains copies of the documents referred to in the
Minute, from which are extracted the following proofs of the exercise of
the Lord Provost's jurisdiction as " Sheriff :"—

" 15th April, 1523. Alexander Chambers, Depute-sheriff of the burgh,
(and then ane of the Bailies), by an assize of seventeen burgesses, found
Margaret Lockart guilty of stealing from John Ramsay's wife a silver
belt and pot, and proved a known thieff, was discerned to be drowned
under the water till she be dead."

" 1524. Provost Macbreck Sheriff, by the verdict of an assize, condemned to be hanged on a gallows, and doom given thereon, John Hutch-
son, for breaking proclamation made upon him banished this burgh, never
to return, under pain of death, and for the theftuous stealing of certain
wool apprehended upon him, hand howand, and for a known thieff ; also
John Paterson, for stealing two cows, which he sold to Halkarston the
flesher, and for a known thieff."

" February 6. The same Sheriff, by assize of fifteen men, convicted
and condemned to be hanged on the gallows, John Brown, for stealing a
cow, and tane howand therewith, stolen by him from William Williamson,
in Drumcowan, east from Falkland, and for ane common thief."

" May 25, 1524. The same Sheriff, by an assize of fifteen, convicted
and condemned to be hanged on the gallows, John Butcher, for stealing
a grey mare, tane hand howand, and for ane common thieff."

THE GENERAL TRADE.

THE Trade of Perth, about the middle of last century, was at a very low ebb. The only traffic of importance consisted in foreign spirits. Great quantities of gin and brandy were smuggled in from the north coast; and the boat-house, where the church of Kinnoul now stands, was a well-frequented rendezvous for smugglers. The old gentleman who at that time possessed the boat-house, bought largely from the smugglers; and having an extensive garden on his premises, he concealed the ankers under ground, and planted kail over them, which were frequently observed, during the season, to be but newly planted. This individual realized a fortune in the illicit traffic, and left considerable property in Bridgend. These smugglers brought home large cargoes of wine and spirits, direct from Spain and France, and supplied Leith and other places with these articles, at a rate below what the merchants there could afford to sell at. This created a strong suspicion that all was not fair. On the arrival of a vessel at the North Shore, with wine, after she had cleared the custom-house, and her cargo had been partly delivered, an officer from the custom-house at Edinburgh made his appearance, who inspected matters, and found that the vessel had been entered at less than one half the amount of duty chargeable upon the cargo. It now appeared that the officers of the custom-house had gone hand in hand with these traffickers in defrauding the revenue, and they were consequently dismissed from their situation. When the Trustees for the Encouragement of Manufactures gave premiums for the cultivation of flax, several vessels were freighted with lint seed and lint, from Rotterdam. In the spring, grocers, cloth-merchants, and others, speculated very largely in this trade, which at some seasons paid pretty well, while at others it was a dead loss. One old merchant, who, for upwards of thirty years, dealt extensively in lint-seed, has been heard to say, that, taking the one year with the other, he had not saved a penny by it. About the year 1784, there were upwards of 3,000 hogsheads of this article imported, besides some hundreds of barrels from Riga, but the latter was considered of coarser quality. Oatmeal and corn was also imported. At that time agriculture was in such a low state, that the produce of this country was not adequate to its consumption. No potatoes were cultivated, and but little wheat. A great deal of the corn sown consisted of grey oats, which yielded little meal, and that of an inferior quality. Corn and meal was brought from the Continent, which was imported without being kiln-dried, and had an exceeding bad flavour. The meal, on its arrival here, was put into damp girnals, which made it

much worse, and frequently it became so polluted by mites and wevils, as
to be unfit for human food.   Many of these girnals were on the ground
floors of houses in the Meal Vennel, from which that street derives its
name.   Great quantities of meal were sent to the Highlands.   The natives
came down in bands, with their shelties, bringing linen yarn with them,
and small kegs of whisky of the finest quality, for which the excisemen
were constantly on the look-out, and fierce struggles for possession frequently occurred.   The Highlanders sold their yarn and whisky.   The
price they received for their goods was carried home with them to pay
their rents, whilst they purchased their meal on several months' credit,
for which they granted their bill—accepted, perhaps, by a dozen of
names.   The meal merchants, also, were in the habit of going up to the
Highland markets to purchase yarn and collect the price of the meal then
due.   One of these gentlemen went regularly and collected his money,
but always forgot to take the bills along with him, assuring the parties
that he would mark on their bill the amount of money received.   After
his death, his son, who was a " limb of the law," summoned hundreds to
make payment of the bills for which his father had already received the
money ; and, their oaths not being taken, they were forced to pay their
bills a second time.   Many an imprecation, both in English and Gaelic,
was pronounced on sire and son.   These Highlanders, when on a journey
to the low country, formed themselves into bands, accompanied with perhaps a hundred little ponies for the purpose of carrying back meal.   On
their return, the ponies were loaded each with a boll of this commodity,
and travelled in a line, the head of the one animal being fastened to the tail
of the other.   The Highlanders also came down sometimes, in hundreds,
with small tumbrels of a primitive construction, for the purpose of taking
home the lairds' coals.   Each cart consisted of a rude frame of birch, with
rungs set into it, at distances of about nine inches, the interstices being
filled with ferns, which were warped through the frame-work; the sides
of the cart were composed of upright spars of the same material, but the
back and front were quite open.   A circular piece of wood, with a hole
in the centre for admitting the axle-tree, which was also made of birch,
constituted the wheel.   In one of these hurleys they would take home
about twenty stone of coals.   As the wooden trundles soon became ellip-
tical by the action of the rough road on the side-wood, they communicated
an up-and-down motion to these vehicles, which resembled that of a fleet
of cobles in a storm.   The less provident took only a sack with them,
which they laid across the pony's back.   Except for the lairds' fires,
little or no coal was used in the Highland districts ; peats and wood constituted the principal fuel.   The peat reek, however agreeable as a fla-

vour in their whisky, smelt horribly rank in their clothes. About this time, there being no duty on the importation of grain, but premiums rather given to those individuals who imported the highest number of cargoes, great quantities were brought into Perth. Mr John Richardson obtained the premium one year for sixty ship-loads. Provost Ramsay, in another year, had freighted fifty-six vessels with grain. It is not to be understood, however, that these were all brought to the port of Perth.

Fishings.—These, for ages, have been a source of much income to the proprietors, and have afforded employment to many individuals. The salmon of the Tay are highly esteemed for their superior quality throughout the whole of Europe. During the last century, vast quantities were exported to different ports in the Mediterranean, and to Spain and Portugal. Previous to being exported, the salmon were cut in pieces, boiled, pickled in salt and vinegar, and packed up in small kits. which employed a great number of coopers, and men engaged in boiling and packing. In the operation of dressing the fish, the back-bones were extracted : these were sold to the inhabitants for a trifle, and supplied a good and cheap dinner to many a family in Perth. Twopence-worth of these " sheens," as they were called, would have abundantly served a large family, and imparted an excellent relish to a *pundie* of ale. Salmon was then in such universal repute, that it was used at every diet. It was not unusual for people to eat salmon, " bite and sup," with their morning brose. Were we to judge by the present diminished produce of the fishings, we could form no idea of the great quantities of salmon caught in former times. It may be safely asserted, that more fish were taken at the North Inch fishing stations, at that time, in the early part of the spring, than what are at present caught in the whole river during the same period. The fishermen had then liberty to consume as much as they choose for their own use. An instance is on record of one hundred and fifty fish being taken at one draught; and from fifty to sixty, and even seventy, were not unusual. Cart-loads were, every morning, driven from the Inch to the boiling-house. Frequently, when the coopers could not get a sufficient number of kits ready, the Maltmen's cobles were packed full of pickled salmon. There were two establishments for curing them, both of which were on an extensive scale. The roans of the fish were thrown into the river, which attracted vast numbers of large eels, and thus afforded fine eel-fishing to those who were fond of that amusement. Mr Richardson, who had the largest of the two curing establishments, kept two smacks for carrying the fish to the London market. These vessels sailed at stated periods for London, and took with them, besides their regular cargo of fish, other descriptions of goods destined for that quarter. They were loaded on their return with goods for the Perth merchants; and frequently brought with them a plentiful supply of London porter, which Mr Richardson sold on favourable terms to the publicans, at from 50s to 56s a hogshead, who retailed it in their houses at four pence a bottle.— When the method of packing salmon with ice commenced, the boiling and cooper-work entirely ceased—ice-houses were built, and a large supply of ice collected in due season, to the mortification of the lovers of skating, who used to have fine scope for that amusement over the hollows of the Inches. The salmon of the Tay have diminished of late, both in size and number. Many instances are on record of fishes of 60 lbs. weight being caught, which seldom occur at the present day. On the lower part of the river, all the way down to the mouth of Tay, numerous stake-nets were set up, which caught immense quantities, and deteriorated the upper fishings exceedingly. This gave rise to contention between the parties, and a law suit was carried on for many years, which, after much expense, was decided in the House of Peers against the stake-net proprietors. Since that period, the fishings have still continued to decline, and of late years have been a heavy concern to the tacksmen, although the rents have been much reduced. Within these few years, another kind of nets, which do much injury to the upper stations, has been introduced by the fishermen on the lower parts of the river. These nets are fixed in peculiar situations, where they remain till the reflux of the tide, when they are drawn on shore. The salmon get entangled in these nets while they are endeavouring, by entering the shallow water, to escape from the numerous porpoises which pursue them up the river. The value of the fishings having much increased, new shots were multiplied to a great extent, which has rendered many of them not worth attendance. The former proprietors of the North Inch fishings, fearing that the consequences arising from the building of the bridge would be ruinous to these fishings, sold them for a sum of money not equal to half the amount of their present annual rent.

Gloves and Breeches.—The Glovers during the last century carried on a very extensive trade in these articles. Perth-made gloves were celebrated all over the kingdom: numerous hands were employed in the cutting department, and a vast number of women earned a comfortable living by sewing them. Old Bailie Gray alone had seventeen men cutting gloves to keep his sewers in work, his son Robert for many years carried on a considerable trade after his father's death. The Glovers occupied almost the whole of the shops in the Skinnergate, besides several very respectable shops in the High-street. Bailies Grant, Gray, Robertson, and Mr John Pirie were all extensive dealers in that line, besides the father of Mr Rough, who has at present rendered Dundee gloves so famous. This gentleman began business in Perth, but went to Dundee in his young days, whence his fame for gloves has spread far and near; while in Perth the trade has altogether ceased to exist. The last of the operative glovers, a William Prop, died a few years ago. The cloth merchants have now got the glove trade into their hands, with the exception of Bailie Young, who continues to sell gloves in the shop formerly occupied by Bailie Gray. In those days buckskin breeches were much in fashion, and the Perth glovers were esteemed for the tight neat manner in which their work was cut and sewed. Their usual sign was a pair of breeches, with a buck between the legs. A curious anecdote is told of a late glover, famous for making tights, and equally distinguished as a knight of the trencher. This gentleman having been employed to make a pair of buckskins to a dashing officer belonging to a regiment of fencible cavalry then quartered in Perth, had been too successful in making a close fit. The officer, while at mess in the George Inn one day, was cursing the glover, in the hearing of the landlord, for making his buckskins too tight; and swore he would make him eat them if he had him in his power. To which mine host replied, that Mr —— was very fond of a feed. This hint was enough; a note was sent requesting him to call at a certain hour to get his money. In the mean time all the buttons were cut off, the seams ripped up, and the leather cut in slices and boiled until it was quite soft, and afterwards done up with butter and rich sauce. The glover came punctual to the time, and was introduced into the room where all the officers were assembled for the occasion. That nothing might be suspected, they were apparently occupied at play with cards. On producing his account, he received the money, and was complimented on the very tight finish he had made. Calling in the landlord, the officer inquired if he had anything handsome with which he could treat Mr ——: he replied, his cook had just finished a dish of very fine tripe, done up in an entire new manner. "Bring it up," said the officer, "and let Mr —— have a lunch and a glass of brandy." The cloth was spread on a table in the room; the breeches and the brandy brought up; and the whole were soon dispatched with the usual dexterity. On rising, he returned thanks to the officer for his kindness; and was told in reply that he was particularly fortunate, for he had got his money in his pocket, and the buckskins in his belly. The poor glover was dumfoundered at the information, and went away in a rueful state, to the great amusement of the assembled party. The thing took air, and many a hard rub was given to the poor dealer in buckskins by his bottle companions.

Besides the trade of gloves and breeches, the glovers carried on an extensive business in dressing sheep and goat skins, and employed a number of hands on their extensive premises beside the mill lade, which they still retain, where a few individuals do a little in the skin trade. The goat skins were dressed with the hair on, and sent to the London market with the sheep skins, where they were used for knapsacks for the army, and for covering saddles. Several individuals concerned in the trade made large sums of money. One old glover built a house on the side of the lead where the spinning mill stands, and put upon it as a motto— " Wha would have thought it, that skins would have bought it." To this trade was attached a manufacture of glue from the scrapings of the skins, but this has gone with the glove trade. Their works on the lade and in the glover's yard were then in full employ, and exhibited a scene of great activity. Now the whole is deserted ; not a single individual is employed about the place.

Shoes.—Before the year 1770, the trade was confined entirely to the manufacture of shoes of a heavy description for the home market ; many of these were made by shoemakers in the country, who had a pit or two for tanning their own leather. About that period, some companies with capital started, and built that large tannage on the Blackfriar's ground, now in Mr Johnston's possession. For many years this company did a great deal of business, and entered into the shoe trade for exportation and the London market. This company employed several hundred shoemakers in making light shoes for these markets. Bailie Bell, a shoemaker, erected another tannage on the grounds at County-place, and did a good deal of business both in the tannage and the shoe trade. Mr Robertson had also a tannage to the south of St Paul's Church, that gave employment to a number of hands. The operation of the Excise laws did up all the small tannages through the country, but created a new trade in that line. Shops for the retail of leather to small dealers became general. Another tannage on an extensive scale was established in Bridgend, also with a view to the export trade of shoes ; and about the beginning of the present century, a second one was started in that quarter, on a smaller scale, but which has lately given up. For a number of years the property between the Tannage-bridge and the Glovers'-yard, which formerly was all occupied in the malting line, was converted into a tannage. The exportation of light shoes having been given up, anything that is now done in the shoe line is for home consumption, and shoe shops now abound in every street. There appears some mystery about this trade. A heavy duty was put upon the leather, and the business was fettered with many absurd excise restrictions as to the manner of tanning the hides. Shoes immediately rose in price from 4s 6d to 8s and 9s a pair. The duty on the leather was all the cry. The men's wages were reduced, but still the price advanced, the duty forming the excuse. The duty, which was declared to be so oppressive, was at length repealed, but the price has not fallen, and the men's wages are still miserably low. Tanners have failed in every quarter, and the shoe shops are still complaining of bad trade. The import duties on foreign hides may perhaps explain this anomaly.

It has been already stated that a great deal of flax-seed was imported. Very fine flax was raised in the Highlands; and as there was then no out-door work for the women, spinning formed their constant employment. A number of merchants in Perth who dealt in the yarn trade, attended the Highland markets, and bought up the yarn, brought it down to Perth, and with such as they bought in the neighbourhood, which was spun by the women, who had little other employment, was packed up in bags and conveyed on pack horses to the Glasgow market for sale. About the year 1780, great quantities of 2 lb. yarn were spun for the Dundee market, where an extensive trade for coloured thread was carried on. About the same time a manufactory of dyed thread was established here, on a pretty extensive scale, which was given up in a few years as a bad concern, more on account of the bad management and villany of the acting partner, than by the failure of the trade. A system of pilfering was detected in this concern which made considerable noise in Perth at the time. The house where Malloch's warehouse stood in Canal-street, and several houses behind, were built for this establishment. A rumour arose that the place was haunted by a ghost; lights were seen in it during the night; and so strong was the impression amongst the workmen who were not up to the secret, that none of them would enter the premises alone in the morning. It was discovered, when too late, that a system of embezzlement had been carried on by the men who had the charge of the work, and the foreman of Mr Young's yarn-boiling work, next door. These individuals, with some accomplices, had carried on their depredations to a ruinous extent before detection.

Hat-making.—Before the year 1784, the whole supply of hats came from England. About that time a Mr Saunders from Glasgow settled here, and carried on the business for a number of years to a considerable

2 G

extent. Two of the workmen whom he brought with him also got into business, but on Saunders' death the trade fell off, and is now extinct in this quarter. We had a bonnet-maker fifty years ago, but bonnets falling out of fashion, he turned grocer.

Rope-spinning.—There has been from an early period a number of hands employed in this line, chiefly for small twine for fishing nets, and ropes for country purposes. About forty years ago, Messrs Dow and Davidson attempted the manufacture of ropes of a heavy description for the shipping, but did 'not then succeed. The increase of the shipping at Perth has since enabled Mr Buik to establish a considerable trade in tarred ropes and cordage ; and a number of individuals are also employed in making small cordage.

Mr Buik has also a number of hands employed in sail-making, and pre-paring rigging and ships' stores of every description. Another gentleman, Mr Durie, has opened a large establishment for supplying vessels with stores. Being an experienced seaman, he is well qualified for providing articles of the best description.

Blacksmiths.—Before the year 1770, this trade was very limited, and the articles made were of the most ordinary description. At that time a smithy exhibited but a meagre appearance. A forge, bellows, study, and vice, with a couple of hammers, and a few files, comprised the whole of the working tools. In this branch of trade there has been an amazing increase, as also in the variety and elegance of the articles manufactured. The introduction of turning-laths into smithys has made a complete change in that line of business. The late Bailie Gray and his brother, were the first who improved the trade in that line. After his brother's death, the bailie built extensive premises at the foot of the High-street, where the different branches of smith work and brass-founding are still carried on. Other manufactures of the same kind have lately sprung up, where machinery of the most complicated description is pro-duced. Fifty years ago, four blacksmiths, one coppersmith, one tinsmith, one jeweller, and three watchmakers, comprehended the working trade in the metals. Since that period each of these trades have greatly increased.

There was formerly a considerable trade in the tobacconist line. The mill at the foot of Charlotte-street was kept constantly employed in grinding snuff, and three houses kept a number of men spinning tobacco. Robie Davie's rappee was widely known both in town and country ; but this trade is now entirely lost in Perth. Gillespie's rappee and plain brown came into repute, and fairly drove the Perth snuff out of the market, by the sale getting into the grocers' hands.

The manufacture of starch was another branch of trade, now extinct in Perth. There was an establishment in the Watergate on a pretty extensive scale for this article. Although it did not employ many hands, it was of considerable benefit to the poor, as the pourings were sold for a mere trifle, which were boiled into sowens for their families. Mr Miller, the proprietor, was such an inveterate smuggler, and was so often detected, that the Excise put him out of the trade, and no one has since attempted it here.

Soap was manufactured by William Arnot on a great scale. Besides the supply of his own shop, and the country sale, he sent considerable quantities to the London market. He had also a candle work, in which line he did much business, and also sent large quantities of rendered tallow to the London market. This gentleman was a general merchant, wholesale and retail, both in hardware and groceries, and enjoyed a vast run in his shop; and through the Highlands he was so universally known and esteemed by the country people for his easy terms in dealing, that his name among the Highlanders passed into a bye-word. When any person refused trust, the common phrase was, " You be no good Willie Arnot."

Besides Mr Arnot, there were several others in the candle line, who did much business ; but of late years this trade has fallen off considerably, and is at the present time limited to two individuals. The introduction of gas has not only reduced the sale, but a considerable supply of candle are brought from Aberdeen, and many genteel families, where gas is not yet introduced, use wax and sperm candles.

The *Dyers*, who form a part of the Guildry, were, during the last century, employed in dying wool and yarn for the manufacture of cloth spun and made by each family for their own use. The men's coats were all hodden grey, which were spun in the house, given out to the weaver, and then sent to the dyer to be finished. The dyers had a wauk-mill where Mr M'Farlane's foundry is now erected, which was kept in constant employment. A finer kind of cloth was made for the gudeman's Sabbath-day coat, and was dyed of a very light blue colour, called Dunblane blue. The women wore camblet gowns and petticoats, also of their own spinning. From these sources the dyers had a pretty fair business ; but as these fabrics were afterwards superseded by English cloths, and the spinning of wool given up in families, the dyeing trade for many years greatly declined, but of late has again recovered in another line, which shall be noticed in due time.

Milliners.—Sixty years back, this branch of business was entirely confined to the Misses Cornfute, who had a shop in the High-street below the Perth Bank, where St John-street now enters. Their trade was chiefly confined to head-dresses for balls and assemblies. Mantua-making was confined to two or three ladies, who were employed only by the first families—the tailors engrossing the gown-making trade.

Comb-makers.—For many years a very considerable branch of this trade was carried on by a Mr Marshall. Circular combs were long fashionable, both for boys and girls. These went round the forehead from ear to ear, and laid back the hair, which was worn very long, flowing over the shoulders, and required many combs to keep it in order.

Barbers were a numerous branch of the Wright Incorporation, and each of them employed a number of boys. Shaving, except in a very few instances, was all done by the barbers : and before the hair-powder tax was imposed, the hair of the respectables was dressed and powdered every day. Many of the ladies heads were dressed daily by the barbers, and even the humblest tradesmen had to get their hair dressed and powdered on the Sundays. The old men wore enormous bag wigs, which required constant powdering and curling. The lads, when their apprenticeship was out, went up to London, and returned, dubbed " wig-maker and hair-cutter, *from London.*" Some of these barbers were most barbarous in their operations. One of them in particular, who was known by the name of " Skin-him-alive," often brought tears into the eyes of his customers. Shaving old Mr Jervie the minister one day, the worthy clergyman exclaimed, " Saunders, if this be skinning, it is tolerable, but if it be shaving, it is dreadful." The tax on hair powder ruined the hair-dressers, as a trade. To make up for the loss of the principal branch of their business, they advanced the price of shaving, which to customers had been previously as low as a farthing. This induced many to shave themselves. Of late years they have recovered a little by the making of fancy curls.

Wrights.—Formerly the work in the cabinet line was confined to very ordinary articles. Much of the elegant modern furniture was then unknown; there was no such thing as a cabinet wareroom with ready-made furniture till the year 1784, when Mr Wm. Gowrie opened one in Blair's-close. The journeymen had but very low wages, most of them not more than five shillings a week, and even this limited income was farther encroached upon by the pernicious practice then prevalent, of paying the men's wages in public houses, where they were frequently kept waiting until ten at night, which placed their families in a very miserable condition. For a long period there appeared to be a fatality attending this class of tradesmen. With few exceptions, they took to the bottle when they got into business, and tippled away their time about public houses, conceiving, when they were enabled to employ a couple of hands, that it was beneath their dignity to be seen working at a bench. Many thus soon became embarrassed, and died bankrupt. To this class old Mr George Sandeman, then at the head of the trade in that line, was an exception. He possessed that proparty in the Watergate now occupied by Mr Hewat, and the back ground, used as a coal-yard. He had also a saw-mill on Annaty-burn, opposite the white dyke, and enjoyed the patronage of many of the county gentlemen, and genteel families in town.

The *Joiners* were in a similar situation. The same person generally carried on both branches, when he could find employment.

Masons,—The same also may be said of the masons. From the year 1745 to 1780, but few buildings were erected in the town. Many old houses had been allowed to remain in ruins, half pulled down. In every direction these unseemly ruins met the eye, particularly in South-street. The masons wrought on day's wages, and took especial care not to hurry the job. From those who employed them they daily expected a morning dram, and their " eleven hours" in the forenoon. Such was their trifling, that it became a by-word, " That it was easy getting into the mortar tub, but ill getting out again." Amongst the master masons of that day, Daniel Scott was remarkable for keeping a job long on hand. One of his customers who had a job to do, was aware of this, and resolved to have it done by contract. Rather than lose the job, Daniel engaged with it, but soon found it would not suit. The men could not be pre-vailed upon to move beyond their deliberate habits, which were so inve-terate, as to give rise to the proverb, that " An ounce of masons' sweat was worth an ounce of gold." Daniel explained to the men hourly that he had the job by the piece, but finding all would not do, he told his em-ployer that he must give it up, as it would not pay. The employer gave in, and allowed Daniel to go on in his old way. On his next visit to the men, he told them that "it was now old use-and-wont, and that they might take it canny." About 1784, new streets and buildings in various directions were contemplated, men who were not masons by trade began to speculate in buildings. They bought ground, and contracted with wrights and masons for the work, closing with those who undertook to do it on the lowest terms. Wages were then low, and material cheap, which was a great inducement to build. A mason's wages was seven shillings a week, a wright's amounted only to five shillings, and the best Memel logs could be purchased at nine pence per solid foot. Amongst these speculators, Mr James Mitchell, a manufacturer, took the lead. His first operations were in Blair's-close, where he built several houses, and the lofty one fronting Mill-street. Having sold these, he bought the ground in George-street between the Glovers'-hall and the close leading to the Skinnergate, then the only entrance from George-street to Mill-street. He built these three stances all at once. The season was very wet. At that time a custom prevailed of running up the vents with circular cases, which were pulled up as the work advanced. As no pains were taken to bind the building round the case, in a high house, with a double set of vents, the greater part of the walls were little better than a rickle of rubbish. In these houses of Mitchell's, this scheme, added to the effects of the wet season, proved fatal to the building, and at same time opened the eyes of the public to the worthlessness of the plan. The workmen were just finishing the chimney tops of the gable of the centre house, when the whole gable came down with a tremendous crash, carrying with it the men on the scaffolding, and driving out the front wall into the street. Four of the men were dug out of the ruins dead, and others were severely bruised. One old man, a labourer, fell from the top, and lighted on his feet on the pavement opposite, at the shop door of Mr Richardson, miraculously escaping almost unhurt. The noise resembled a peal of thunder, and alarming the whole town, thousands were soon on the spot. The standing portion of the front wall being considered dangerous, beams of wood were set up against it, and the street railed in for the winter season. This misfortune for a time damped Mitchell in his speculations, but he afterwards built three houses in Atholl-street, and three in Methven-street. At this time a stir was made about opening a better access to the south than the Watergate, afforded, and parties were divided as to whether they should open John-street, or widen the Watergate. Mr Mitchell made the town an offer to purchase the whole of the property on the west side of the Watergate, to pull it down, and rebuild it forty feet farther back, and lead a line from the bottom of South-street in a direction to meet Princes-street at the

English Chapel. Had this been then adopted, it would have made a far better thoroughfare than that of John-street, with its numerous quick turns. Interested parties, however, overruled the plan, and got John-street formed; and it was by means of this party interest that it was made so narrow. Bailie M'Ewen, mason, also began in the building line about this time. He had previously been employed by Mr Mitchell as his mason. He built the Horse Barracks and St Paul's Church, and erected several houses in John-street and on the west side of St Paul's church, and also a number in Marshall-place. Bailie Hepburn also entered extensively into this trade. About the year 1800, he built the whole of Atholl-place, the greater part of the Crescent, the north half of Rose-terrace, most of Barrosa-place and street, a number of houses in Marshall-place, and the west side of John-street north of the Church. He contracted for the Tabernacle meeting-house, which the Methodists purchased, but which had to be taken down and rebuilt. He erected the two houses in George-street south of Bridge-lane, and all the south side of that lane. Extending his operations to the other side of the river, he built Garie Cottage and three others, and also a number of the villas on the banks of the river, north of the bridge. During the war, the price of wood rose to an enormous price, Memel logs selling as high as four shillings and ninepence per foot. This led the builders to use much home wood, which in a short time will tell severely against the owners. Of late years a number of individuals have been engaged in this trade, who have erected the greater number of the houses in several of the new streets.

About the year 1770, a printing press was first established in Perth by Mr Johnston. At that time its operations were very slow and clumsy. A magazine was attempted by this gentleman, but it did not succeed. Mr Johnston shortly afterwards removed to Edinburgh, when the printing business fell into the hands of the Morisons, who continued the trade with great success. These gentlemen have published numerous excellent works, which conferred at the time of their publication a high literary character on Perth. Among these the Perth Encyclopædia was esteemed the best work of the kind in its day. It was edited by Mr William Morison, and is a noble monument to his memory, and a lasting honour to the city. This highly esteemed gentleman was cut off in the meridian of life. He lived to correct the last sheet of this work, and there is reason to fear that he sank under the excessive application called forth by the magnitude of the undertaking. Some works have been edited and published by his brother, Mr David Morison, in a manner which reflects much credit on his literary talents.

The *Perth Courier*, a weekly journal, was begun, in 1809, by the Messrs Morison, and is still conducted by them. Its principles have been moderate Tory. It enjoys a moderate circulation, and is well advertised.

In the year 1829, the *Perthshire Advertiser*, another weekly journal, of liberal principles, was established by a number of gentlemen. This paper enjoys an average circulation, and is also well advertised. It is printed by Mr Taylor, and is thrown off on a machine which was invented and constructed by Mr James Bogle, brother-in-law to the printer. The peculiarity of this invention is great simplicity, combining in its principle all the excellences of the most expensive and complex printing machines.

In 1835, the *Constitutional*, a weekly journal, of extreme Tory politics, was established ; but its success has hitherto been aught but satisfactory to the proprietors.

The printing business has been an increasing one in Perth for some years back, and it is probable that the proposed alteration in the newspaper stamp duty, and the reduction of the excise duty on paper, will stimulate it still farther. Besides the newspaper offices, there are at present two others on a smaller scale.

Copperplate and lithographic presses are also in operation.

Previous to the middle of the last century, there were no cloth manufacturers in Perth. The weavers were then generally employed in what was called customer work ; that is, by taking in yarn to weave, and returning the cloth. At this period each family span their own yarn, and got it wove to order. Even the nobility took a pride in having their linen and napery spun in the family. Amongst the master weavers in this line at that time, Deacon Vallance was famous throughout the country for his elegant patterns and skilful workmanship. He executed the greater part of the work for the neighbouring gentry, and ornamented their napery, by weaving their respective coat-of-arms into the fabric. Some of his looms could produce cloth two-and-a-half ells wide. At that period, two webs of damask table-cloths, ten quarters wide, were wove by two brothers, for the Earl of Kinnoull. In weaving these immense sheets, a man was placed at each side of the loom, each having a separate set of treddles, the one throwing the shuttle to the other. For their workmanship, the brothers received L.72, and Mr Vallance received a similar sum for his share. Besides table napery and towelling, very fine linen, termed Hollands, was manufactured. Mr Vallance had long enjoyed the Duke of Atholl's patronage ; but, unfortunately, in one account which he presented, the cloth was called *linen* instead of *Holland*, hence the Duke's housekeeper maintained that the cloth had never been wove with a Holland reed. This inconsiderate expression in the account lost the Duke's custom. Mr Vallance, who had his factory where the Methodist chapel now stands, and occupied all the property south to Canalstreet, was an original in his way, and possessed considerable genius for almost every mechanical operation. He took an active hand in every thing that occurred about Perth, and was always consulted in general matters. He did not confine his activity entirely to Perth, but extended it on many occasions in other quarters. He was one of those who went over to Edinburgh at the Porteous affair, and took an active part in the administration of that remarkable instance of retributive justice. The good old custom of making family cloth having decayed, Vallance became reduced in his latter days. The following acrostic record in the Grey Friars still honours his memory :—

> " Muse here assist me ; now I surely must
> Relate brave Vallance' character that's just.
>
> Renowned much ; justice will join his cause ;
> Of tradesmen he in Perth deserves applause ;
> Betrayed no trust was put into his hand—
> Endeavouring always by the truth to stand :
> Ready he was, and that at any hour,
> To make redress, or to relieve the poor.
>
> Vallance, whose virtuous actions shone so bright,
> Always did stand up for the People's right.
> Let monument, or some recorded verse
> Loud unto ages his bright fame rehearse.
> All craftsmen who him knew will yet declare
> None in the country could with him compare.
> Grief now, nor pain, no more his peace annoys,
> Entered the choir, he lives in perfect joys."

Besides the above-mentioned cloths, a kind of thin ell-wide linen, spun and bleached by families in the country, was made. This was sold in a half-bleached state to merchants in Perth, who sent it to the London market. There was also some linsey woolseys made by families for their own use; indeed the most becoming gowns were made of a species of this fabric termed fingering. Weaving at this period (1760) was esteemed both an honourable and lucrative calling : so much so, that a young nobleman, who afterwards succeeded to the estate of Kinnaird, wrought as an apprentice under Mr Vallance. Some time afterwards he paid his old master a visit, and went on one of the looms on pretence of trying if he could still weave; knowing it to be an established rule that none of the men durst take money from any of the gentry who came to see the work, he took the opportunity of leaving a guinea under the temples, to enable the men to drink his health. About 1766, silesia linens were introduced by George Penny, who had accidentally met with a piece of that kind of cloth. This fabric succeeded for many years: at first they were bleached and sent to the London market, and thence to the West Indies. A few years afterwards the trade became general in Perth; numbers of weavers got a few looms and a warping mill, bought yarn, and sold their cloth for ready money, as fast as it could be produced. In this way a steady man, with six or eight looms, made out to live in competence. A number of houses got into the line of buying from the weavers and sending the work to the London market. Amongst these may be stated, Anderson and Lindsay; Provost Caw; Young, Ross, and Co.; Messrs Thomas and John Barland; Mr John Ross of Balgersho; and several others. Besides the silesias made in Perth, numerous weavers throughout the country were similarly employed, who brought their cloth into Perth for sale, on the Fridays, there being several houses where they were sure of finding a ready money market. So eager were these merchants, that they frequently employed men to intercept the weavers on their way. This system led to the formation of a new species of dealers termed hawkers, who bought from the weavers and sold again to the merchants. Besides this method of sale, they contracted with weavers who had a few looms, supplied the yarn, and took back the cloth at five per cent. commission. This trade was very steady for some years, but there were times, during the war with the Colonies, in which the merchants suffered severe losses. One of these occurred on the taking of St Eustatia, when many of the Perth manufacturers were much injured, and had to hold heavy stock for a long period. They never then thought of reducing the wages of labour, or turning off their men; though they might sometimes advise them to go to the harvest. After the introduction of block printing, this trade took a wide range. Vast quantities of silesias were sold in a green state for the Glasgow printers. These fabrics were wove in 700 to 1400 reeds, and averaged from 23 to 30 inches in breadth. About the year 1780, small spinning jennies were introduced, which led to the introduction of a new fabric called blunks. These goods were a combination of linen warp and cotton weft, and being preferred by the printers, their manufacture took a number of hands from the linen trade.— About the year 1782, the father of the writer introduced the cotton manufacture into Perth. The first piece of cloth made was six quarters muslin, wove in an 1100 reed. Part of this was bleached and sold for ladies' gowns, at five shillings a yard : (it would now scarcely bring five pence.) Part of the same fabric was printed into shawls; common colours brought ten shillings each, and chintz patterns a guinea.

At this time the erection of Stanley Mill was contemplated. The late Duke of Athole took great interest in the establishment. The celebrated Arkwright was to be one of the partners. Mr William Sandeman, the proprietor of Luncarty Field, a gentleman of great enterprise, had seen and admired the muslins referred to. The Duke of Athole and Mr Arkwright, having met at Perth, at the King's Arms Inn, Mr Sandeman introduced Mr Penny, and recommended his fabrics to the notice of these distinguished individuals, who expressed themselves highly delighted with his success. They inquired if he could weave them himself and teach others ? On his answering in the affirmative, Arkwright said, that was all they could desire ; that the erection of the Mills might be immediately proceeded with ;—there could be no fear of success. The building was forthwith commenced ; and a number of boys and girls were sent up to Manchester to learn the spinning trade. Mr Penny afterwards introduced the manufacture of calicoes for the printers, which soon became general. Various fabrics were by times introduced in the cotton line. As the trade was at first very prosperous, a manufacturing mania seemed to pervade society. Every gentleman who had a second son of the requisite age, put him apprentice to the loom. The individual so often referred to, had at one time ten apprentices, the sons of gentlemen and merchants. Manufacturing establishments continued to increase till the year 1810, at which time upwards of sixty houses in that line were established in Perth, who not only employed the looms in town, but also most of those in the country within twenty miles. As this year produced a crisis in the manufacturing history of Perth, we shall go back to other branches that had previously sprung up.

About the year 1765, a company was formed for the manufacture of fine linen, which did not flourish long, being ruined by the ignorance of the manager, who took it into his head to make the cloth super-excellent, by picking out every thick thread or lump. To such a length did he carry this taste, that the weavers were terrified to take in their cloth, being certain of a day's work at picking. When the cloth went to market, the injury thus done to the fabric rendered it unsaleable.

Both the Mill-wynd and New-row company started with the manufacture of linen sheetings. The buildings and houses on the east side of the Mill-wynd were erected for the purpose, and filled with looms. In these establishments sheets were made of all descriptions from 1000 to 2400 reed, and were wove from five quarters to four ells wide. For many years these houses carried on a steady trade in that line, the New-row company also extended their business to the manufacture of diapers and damasks, which they carried on a few years. Being outstripped in this line by the Dunfermline manufacturers, the New-row company directed their attention to the cotton trade, and launched extensively into the manufacture of cambric, book, and mull muslins, and calicoes; but in these branches they were also outstripped by the Glasgow people. The concern thus turning out unprofitably, was abandoned. Messrs Stewart and M'Naughton, who were bred to the business in this house, then commenced on their own account. About the year 1785, a new branch of the linen trade was introduced. These were thin five-quarters wide fabrics for umbrellas, which were filled with wax. As the cotton trade increased, they were superseded by green cotton ginghams. Before the introduction of cotton twist, a considerable trade was carried on in coarse stripes, checks, and napkins of blue and white, with linen warp and cotton weft, which were chiefly sold about Dundee, Forfar, Montrose, and along the east coast. So generally were these napkins in repute in that quarter, that at a *penny wedding* to which Mr James Mitchell, a manufacturer of these fabrics, was invited, of 400 persons present, all the women had on Perth made napkins.

Previous to the year 1800, the introduction of the inkle manufacture was unsuccessfully attempted. An abortive effort was also made to introduce the carpet manufacture. About this time a mill was built at the foot of Mill-street, for spinning cotton, which was afterwards converted into a wool-spinning mill. For many years this business was carried on to considerable extent, giving employment to a good number of hands. The company having suffered some heavy losses, were compelled to stop payment. Soon after this, the building being found to be in a very crazy condition, was pulled down.

About the year 1806, Mr George Smith introduced the manufacture of imitation shawls; many of which were of very rich patterns. For some years much business was done in this branch, and the weavers obtained high wages, but the fatal 1810 overwhelmed Smith amongst the rest of our manufacturers. Before this period nearly 3000 weavers were employed in Perth, and great numbers of webs were also sent to the country. During the progress of the linen trade, there were six establishments for boiling linen yarn, each of which employed four hands, and averaged from 60,000 to 70,000 spindles of yarn annually. From this data it would appear that about 400,000 spindles of linen yarn were annually manufactured in Perth and neighbourhood, independent of the vast quantities of silesias bought from the country. These goods were required by law to be measured and stamped : the stamp indicated the length and breadth of the piece, and also contained the stamp-master's name. Two-pence half-penny was paid for stamping each piece ; and if not of sufficient quality, the stamp-master had it in his power to cut it in pieces and stamp each portion which was of the proper quality. This establishment employed a few hands, but is now given up. On the introduction of cotton goods, it became of little value ; these fabrics not being in existence when the law was made, were not liable to its scrutiny. Every piece of linen finished at the bleachfields had to be stamped in the same way.

Bleachfields.—The Tulloch was the first work of this kind in the neighbourhood. Luncarty was established shortly afterwards,—about 1760. Vast quantities of cloth were bleached at these fields : Luncarty soon became distinguished over the kingdom for superior finishing, and cloth was sent there from all quarters. At this field several hundred men were employed. For many years the whole Dunfermline manufactures were sent to this field to be finished. After the year 1775, Huntingtower and Ruthven bleachfields were established, and the whole found ample employment. About this period, the proprietor of the Tulloch introduced cloth printing ; a few tables were set up, but this branch was entirely confined for some time to jobbing work. Books of patterns were lodged with their agents in various quarters, where women brought the cloth for their gowns, and chose the pattern. The printing of these averaged from 1s 6d to 3s 6d a yard, according to richness of pattern. The present generation, who have been accustomed to obtain the richest prints wonderfully cheap, will be astonished at the cost of a gown in those days. Say for instance, six yards of ellwide linen at 1s 6d a yard, 9s ; and printing ditto at 3s 6d,—making 30s for a gown piece of only six yards. As business extended, the proprietors of the Tulloch began to work for the general market ; and when calicoes came in they did a good deal in that trade.

About the year 1782, Mr M'Alpin came from Glasgow and established a printing concern in this quarter, on an unprecedented scale of magnitude. He bought the grounds at Cromwell Park, built a large dam-dyke across the Almond, and dug a mill lade down to his works at great expense. Machinery and printing shops rose like magic ; printers and print-cutters were brought from Glasgow ; and business commenced on a very extensive scale. A large house was built for spinning cotton twist ; he bought largely from all the Perth manufacturers, and for some

time his business appeared to be extremely flourishing. Finding the
grounds of Cromwell Park too limited for his operations, he bought the
ground of Stormont-field; and cut a mill lade along the bank of the Tay
at an enormous expense. Besides buildings for printing, he erected a
large twist spinning factory; but by the time these various operations
were completed, he was so completely embarrassed as to be compelled to
abandon his property to his creditors, who brought it to the hammer.

After this, a company, comprising a number of the monied men in
Perth, purchased Ruthven bleachfield, and converted it into a printfield.
For many years this concern flourished, and became the greatest printfield in Scotland. Some years eleven hundred individuals were employed
in the works, which contributed to the revenue £54,000 a year of duty.
This company had a branch in Manchester, and agencies in various
quarters of the globe. Immense quantities of goods were brought from
Manchester: their man of business there had always a great command of
cash, and when a bankrupt estate came into the market he was enabled
to purchase on very low terms. They also bought from those in needy
circumstances, who often made great sacrifices to keep their credit. Heavy
lots of goods were thus obtained at twenty or thirty per cent. below prime
cost. In Perth they went regularly round the manufacturers, and purchased once a month; and as their bills were always taken at the banks,
the manufacturers were enabled to push business to any extent, as they
had their yarn at six months' credit, and sold their goods at four months.
For many years this company continued to flourish; but having latterly
speculated very extensively in indigo and other Eastern produce—and although they could have realized a handsome profit, owing to a fatal error
in their manager, they did not embrace the favourable opportunity of
disposing of it, but continued to hold stock in the prospect of a further
rise in the market, which the altered state of the currency rendered it
hopeless to expect. These articles having fallen more than fifty per
cent. below what they had cost, the company were at length constrained
to part with them at what they would bring. By these untoward circumstances, they abandoned the printing business. The field was sold,
and is now in the hands of a Glasgow company, who do a good deal of
business, but owing to the facilities of the cylandrical press and other
improvements, the number of hands is not half what was formerly required.

Cromwell Park, which M'Alpin established, was sold by his creditors
to Andrew Mellis and Son, who for some time carried on the business of
bleaching, printing, and cotton spinning. Andrew Mellis's was one of

the oldest established houses in Perth; he had been long in the white cloth line, had for many years carried on an extensive thread manufacture, had a principal share in the Ruthven work when a bleachfield, and was considered one of the richest men in Perth; but the fluctuation of the times had such an effect on business that the firm became bankrupt, and the whole property was brought to the hammer. The father having previously died, was spared the misery of seeing the wreck of his fortune. The son got no settlement with his creditors, and seeing no prospect of doing anything in this quarter, removed with his family to Manchester. The printfield was again sold, and purchased by Hunter, Burt, and Co., who carried on the printing basiness extensively. The other field that M'Alpin set a-going at Scone was purchased by Messrs Thomas and John Barland, who carried on the business of cotton spinning and bleaching. Stanley mill was in full operation by this time. An unsuccessful attempt had also been made to spin linen yarn. In this state was the trade of Perth before the year 1810. During the war, the fluctuation in business had been so great, that commerce had assumed more of the hazardous character of gambling than of fair trade, often overwhelming merchants in the most inextricable difficulties. It was emphatically remarked that business was driven at the point of the bayonet. The news of a victory or defeat, or political convulsion, were alike the harbingers of ruin to many, by the fall in the price of goods on the one hand, or the entire loss of them on the other. The regular channels to the markets were often shut up by the exclusion of British goods from the continent; and the general chances of the war, had an irresistible tendency to involve in difficulties those engaged in trade. But in spite of these difficulties, a class of men got into business on the credit of others, who obtained material on long credit, and sold their goods on short bills; often sacrificing largely to obtain cash to keep moving. These people scrupled at no hazard; they had to go on, and sell at any price. The system of accommodation bills was greatly resorted to by these individuals; an instance of this may be quoted, which was witnessed by the writer. On a certain day, a knot of these worthies had a number of these bills to pay: every expedient was resorted to to raise money; each of them ranged the public houses which he frequented, in order to raise the necessary funds, it being common in these cases to apply in such quarters. At this time several individuals who sold a dram always kept a sum at command, lending a few pounds for a few days only, by which means they drew a pretty constant run of customers. A dram was always expected when the cash was borrowed, and another when paid; the individual thus paying dear for the accommodation. On the present occasion the party had been pretty successful, and a supper was ordered in the Hammermen tavern, with wine and other things in accordance. In the course of the evening, the conversation turned on the means for getting the borrowed money paid up. One of the company who held a hundred pieces of cambric, offered to sell them to his right hand neighbour at 32s a piece, and take his bill for them at three months; which offer was instantly accepted. The purchaser immediately offered them to his neighbour; and in this manner these hundred pieces were sold sixteen times, and sixteen bills granted on a fictitious sale; for these very goods were sold next day by the original holder to the Ruthven company, and their acceptance discounted. But this system was suddenly brought to an end. The great political revolutions that were taking place on the continent, the Berlin and the Milan decrees, and Buonaparte's burning system, gave trade and credit such a shock, that many of the oldest established houses were overwhelmed; and in no place in the empire were these disasters more severely felt than in Perth. The company at Cromwell Park had a branch in London who suffered most severely. They had goods to the amount of nearly L.100,000 value burnt at Cadiz. In their ruin many of the Perth manufacturers were involved. The banks in the general alarm were constrained to withhold their discounts. Failure on failure was daily occurring; and manufactured goods fell at once to less than half their former value. Those holding large stocks thus saw their capital melt away as if by magic. For some time previous the cotton manufacturers had flourished beyond example, giving employment to an immense number of hands, at very high wages. It was not uncommon for one manufacturer to coax away the weavers employed by another, giving them either a premium or an advance of money, in some instances to the amount of fifteen or twenty pounds. An ordinary workman could earn from four to five shillings a day; and a woman a shilling, at winding yarn. Such was the demand, that not a herd boy could be found in the country; all flew to the loom. Farm servants' wages rose to L.30, besides meal and milk. In 1810, the price of weaving a certain quantity of cloth, fell suddenly from fourteen shillings to five shillings, and even at this reduction work was not to be procured. Fortunately for the weavers in this quarter, the building of the Depot was commenced in the midst of these misfortunes, and afforded employment to several hundred weavers. Even several manufacturers, who had previously been paying upwards of one hundred pounds a week in wages, were themselves reduced to the necessity of earning a subsistence by labouring in the quarries. In the midst of the general disaster, there were individuals who scrupled not to aggravate the evil by the most dishonourable conduct towards their creditors. Amongst these, one individual was distinguished : when he stopped payment, having a large stock on hand, he agreed to pay twenty shillings a pound by instalments, and granted mere nominal security for the fulfilment of the engagement. By the time the instalments fell due, he declared his inability to meet them, and offered a composition of nine shillings a pound. Goods having now advanced somewhat in value, and being likely to rise still more, he prevailed on two individuals to pay his composition, agreeing to share with them the profit on the goods when sold. By this manœuvre they realized more than would have paid the creditors in full. Having got into business again, by assiduous attendance on bible society, missionary, and prayer meetings, he acquired a high odour of sanctity in the kirk, whilst in private he was equally fervent in his devotions to the brandy bottle. In the course of a few years he had acquired considerable wealth ; but at his death, instead of assisting any of those individuals whom he had formerly ruined, and some of whom were actually living on charity at the time, he left several hundred pounds to bible and missionary societies ; besides handsome sums to his wife and friends.

The upright conduct of Mr Cleland, another gentleman who was overwhelmed in the general ruin, stands in honourable contrast to the above. Having got a settlement with his creditors, and again entered into business, he was so far successful, that, finding himself equal at the end of a few years to meet his former deficiencies, he called his creditors together, and paid them in full. The unpretending virtue of rigid honesty thus stands in bold relief above the subterfuges of pious fraud.

This unfortunate period, 1810, made a complete revolution in the trade of Perth. About sixty of the small manufacturers were driven out of business, leaving only about eight firms who were able to carry on business. The weavers were now obliged to apply for work from Glasgow, in which quarter an endless variety of cotton fabrics had been introduced. Perth had allowed the linen trade to pass into the hands of the inhabitants of Fife, and the power looms were beginning to take the calicoes from the hand-loom weavers, who felt their situation daily becoming worse. The Perth manufacturers began to feel that they were unable to compete with the Glasgow people in light fabrics, because a change of patterns and fabrics continually taking place, before the Perth manufacturers got into the line, the demand was filled up : they turned their attention therefore to the production of heavier goods, amongst which the manufacture of umbrella ginghams has for many years been one of the staple branches, and for which Perth has acquired a distinguished character.

Imitation shawls, scarfs, and robes, have of late years been extensively manufactured, and a few houses do a good deal in pullicates, ginghams, and crams. The manufacture of these fabrics has given an impetus to the dyeing business, which otherwise would have been nearly extinct in Perth. The whole yarn wove in this quarter being either dyed or bleached in the neighbourhood, a considerable source of employment is thus opened up. Several establishments put as much as 500 lbs. of yarn through hands per day. Of the houses employed in the light fabrics there are two, Messrs Cornfute and Blair, who carry on an extensive business in ginghams, crams, pullicates and fine muslins, employing a great number of weavers. These goods are chiefly made for the South American market, and are sent direct to that quarter by these gentlemen. Only a very few linen fabrics are at present manufactured in Perth. Mr Fleming's lint-spinning mill being now in successful operation, with the prospect of several others being speedily erected, it is to be hoped the linen manufacture will be again revived. Prior to the year 1810, the number of weavers in Perth amounted to about 3000; at present they do not exceed 1800. When hand-loom calicoes were in demand, they afforded employment to aged people, whose sight had become unfit for the finer fabrics. This and similar work being now engrossed by the power loom, these tradesmen have in consequence experienced very great distress. Agents are now established in Perth who give out work for Glasgow houses in pullicates and ginghams. Some very fine imitation harnesses are employed for Paisley and Edinburgh work; but the moment trade declines, these houses withdraw their agencies, and the men are left in a state of destitution. There are two houses in Perth who keep a great number of hands at work on harnesses of various descriptions, which gives employment to a corresponding number of boys and girls.

Within the last sixty years a rapid improvement has been made in the working of the metals; and the number of people employed in the various lines have been vastly increased. Formerly the coppersmiths were chiefly employed in making small stills for the Highlands; but the various alterations in the excise laws gradually destroyed this trade. Prior to the year 1793, distillation from large stills was confined to the south of Scotland. At these great establishments, a coarse spirit was made from a mixture of malt, raw grain, pease, beans, corn, potatoes, and turnips, all mashed together. Great quantities of this spirit were retailed in Perth, some of it as low as a penny a gill. It was exceedingly harsh to the taste, but to a certain class its pungency was as great a recommendation as its cheapness. To the north of an imaginary line, drawn by the excise laws, small stills were allowed to be wrought. Perth lying in the privileged section, a number of forty gallon stills were erected. During the last year of their existence, twenty-three distilleries were in operation in Perth and vicinity, each containing two stills of that capacity, one for singling and the other for doubling. By the act they were allowed to distil 300 bolls of malt, duty free, in the course of the year,—a duty of forty pounds a year being paid on the still. When more than the 300 bolls was distilled, the malt duty was paid on the extra quantity. For some years this was a lucrative business to those engaged in it; the grains and lees, which were freely bought up by the cow-feeders, more than paying the duty on the still. They were thus enabled to sell whisky of the very best quality at fourteen-pence the pint, with an additional pint to the score, or twenty pints. This trade was alike profitable to those concerned, and beneficial to the community; milk, in consequence of the distillery refuse, being of excellent quality and abundant; and the bakers were also provided with an ample supply of the finest yeast. Owing to a little party spite, this trade was suddenly destroyed. It has been previously stated, that the *Friends of the People* maliciously burnt the effigy of the Right Honourable Henry Dundas, secretary of state for the time being. This gave so much offence to his lordship, that the excise line was immediately thrown eight miles further north than Perth, and thus these twenty-three distilleries were immediately stopped. Several were removed to Auchtergaven, but then they durst not bring any of the spirits beyond the prescribed line. This was a new source of evil. The people in Perth, who had been accustomed to drink whisky of the best quality, could not tolerate the idea of being restricted to the *liquid fire* then produced by the large distilleries. A bold and extensive contraband traffic was the consequence. The excisemen, who were always on the alert, seized great quantities, which were frequently sold by public roup. At these sales the publicans bought the whisky frequently much beyond its value, but with it they got a permit, and it was entered to them as stock; which they contrived to keep up with constant additions of smuggled whisky, taking especial care to bring it forward in quantities proportioned to their stock. Many and ingenious were the devices by which they contrived to elude the excisemen. Tin vessels were made like a case, to clap to the person's sides or round the body; bladders were hung from women's haunches; even beggar women were pressed into the service : but each of these shifts were frequently detected, and constant brawls occurred between the excisemen and the smugglers, frequently ending in serious disasters. This state of petty warfare—of collision and collusion between the smuggler and the excisemen, continued for several years, to the detriment of the morals of the people.

We have already stated that Perth was at one time famous for fine beer. Alterations in the excise laws drove the small brewers out of the trade ; and for some time the whole business on the old system was confined to Mr Hugh Cameron in the Watergate. Breweries on a large scale being given a preference in the duty, Craigie, Clocksery, and Perth breweries for many years engrossed the whole of this business. Of late several others have commenced ; there being at present, in addition to these, St Katharine's, St John's, the South Inch, and Westley Place breweries. Considerable quantities of beer are also brought frem Inchture, Scone, Methven, and Auchterarder. Of late a considerable trade has arisen of sending strong ale to London ; and at each of these places ale of excellent quality is now made. In place of the smuggled, the town is supplied with very fine malt whisky from entered stills in various parts of the country.

Though the making of malt for the London market, formerly a staple branch of the trade of Perth, is now at an end, large quantities of barley are still shipped for various quarters. Owing to the improved state of agriculture, the importation of meal or foreign corn is but seldom required. Formerly the bakers considered the wheat grown in the district as unfit for their purpose, without a mixture of English flour. Both wheat and flour are now frequently shipped at Perth for the London market.

Previous to the year 1800, when St John's Foundry was established, Perth was supplied with cast metal articles from Carron and other quarters. There are at present three founderies in town, in apparently prosperous circumstances, with extending business. St John's has recently fitted up a new steam engine for their work, with the view of entering upon the machinery line ; and Mr Macfarlane is endeavouring to establish a trade in building iron boats ; he is presently engaged on a steam vessel of this description, in size nearly equal to the Tay steamer, to be propelled by an engine of sixty horses power.

To many intelligent people it has been matter of surprise that the woollen manufacture has not been attempted in Perth. The situation could not be better for procuring the raw material, being at the very mouth of the Highlands, where the stoutest wool is produced ; and the surrounding strath and carse lands producing abundance of the finest quality. The price of labour is cheap ; and there being an unlimited command of water, mills and power looms to any extent might be wrought by steam. Coals can be had as cheap as in Dundee ; the freight of vessels is much the same to any foreign port, with an equal facility to the London market. Perth only wants a few men of spirit to set the linen and woollen manufactures agoing, to ensure its prosperity.

SHIPPING.

During the early part of last century, the shipping belonging to the Port of Perth was very trifling. Peats and wood from the Town's Muir, Craigie, and Kinnoul hills, were much used ; such quantity of coals as were then used were all brought from the Frith of Forth by vessels belonging to Alloa and Kincardine. When the vessels arrived, the seamen, if there was no vessel ready to take them, travelled home on foot, as their vessel had to lie until the cargo was sold from the hold. The coal shore was covered with weighing apparatus; for each of these, a man, under a *coal deacon,* was stationed, who sold the coals for the owner, and weighed them for the purchaser, for which a certain rate of dues was paid by the former. This obnoxious tax was kept up even after this mode of sale was abandoned. When the coal trade was thus conducted, there was a chance of getting coals cheap in the summer season ; but sometimes in a severe winter, the price rose to the enormous sum of fifteen shillings per boll. In the winter of 1794, when the river was closed by ice for three months, and for many weeks when the roads were blocked up with snow, even at that price it was considered a great favour to get them from a cellar where a stock was laid in for a bleachfield. English coal were scarcely known in this quarter ; they came in trifling quantities by the Newcastle traders, laden with crockery ware. A few metts of coals were with difficulty sold for baking fires in genteel families. There was then a duty of two-pence a bushel on them, which made the price about two shillings and four-pence a mett. About the year 1796, this duty was taken off, when the price was reduced to eighteen-pence and lower ; but although the price fell, a considerable time intervened before people could be induced to use them generally, from not knowing the method of burning them. By degrees, however, they came into general use, and a trade of bringing vessels fully loaded from Newcastle commenced. It has been observed that the coals were sold from the vessel on arrival, but after the scarcity of that article during severe winters, the price rose so high that several individuals filled cellars with coals to sell out during the winter : it so happened that a season or two gave them a handsome return for their money. A young man named Inches took the whole of that ground now occupied as coal slips, as a coal yard, and freighted a number of vessels with Scots and English coals ; but as the old practice of selling from the vessels still continued to be extensive, this person was, from the heavy rent of L.160 per annum which he paid, joined to slow sales, obliged to relinquish what was called a bad speculation. The hint was improved on by the Town Council, who let the ground out in lots at high rents, which caused yards to be opened in other parts of the town.

About the close of last century, when the improvements in agriculture commenced, a new trade in lime began, and increased to an amazing extent. Every farmer freighted a vessel, some of them even two, for a number of seasons, until their farms were limed. During the summer months, these vessels would average between twenty and thirty every spring tides. When a farmer's sloop arrived, he mustered all the carts in the neighbourhood to drive his lime home, and he in turn gave his carts to all who aided him ; they were thus enabled to have the whole cargo laid down on the farm within three days. Formerly there was a lime shed on the shore, where lime was kept to supply the masons ; but now a practice commenced of selling lime to farmers who did not bring a vessel of their own ; and thus a number of sheds were built for this purpose, and a successful trade established.

About the year 1774, a carpenter introduced the trade of ship building here. The first vessel he launched was about 25 tons burthen, called the Busy Bee of Newburgh. Immediately after this, the business was taken up and carried on extensively by Mr David Gibson for a long period. This gentleman, who was considered one of the first in the trade, built several vessels, many of them upwards of 300 tons register. Before the late Provost Robertson's time, it was thought impossible to float a vessel of that size down the river. Ship building was briskly carried on, and numbers of large vessels constructed, some of which were wrecked in the American trade, and others were, during the greater part of the late war. employed by Government as transports. The building yard was then in front of the Alloa coal yard, the road leading down within a few feet of the Grey Friars', and turning round the carpenter's yard, to the east of the alley, one side of which was lately cut down. Mr Gibson got this ground gratis from the town ; also the ground lately taken into the Grey Friars' on the south side, which was bounded by an alley of trees that ran right west by the back of Marshall Place from the shore road, having the north trench of Cromwell's Fort on the south. Besides these advantages, he received a sum of ten pounds a year from the town for his great enterprise and public spirit. A few years before his death, he sent in a petition to the Town Council for liberty to build a house on the ground he possessed ; but the Council considered, if he had made money by his business sufficient to build a house, that he had no need of a bounty—and withdrew it.

This piece of ground having soon afterwards changed possessors, several coal slips were erected on it; part was also taken into the Grey Friars'; the trench was filled up; the building yard demolished, and the road straightened to the new shore. On Mr Gibson's death, the business was taken up by Mr James Brown, who has for some years carried on an extensive trade. Since the year 1815, he has launched 76 vessels, some of them upwards of 400 tons burthen ; several steam-vessels have also been built by him ; amounting in whole to about about 8000 tons register, and averaging 93½ tons each, which, at L.9 per ton, amounts to L.72,000 ; being nearly L.2,600 a-year during the time he has been in business. Mr Brown is the gentleman who so greatly distinguished himself by his success in raising the Comet steam-vessel, after she had been long sunk in the Clyde. The late Duke of Athole, who was very anxious to introduce his larch into ship building, employed Mr Brown to build a brig entirely of his own fir—a vessel of about 200 tons. At the launch, the Duke and a number of nobility and gentry assembled on the ground, where a large marquee was erected, and an elegant entertainment provided. The Duke himself christened the vessel " The Larch ;" she went off in fine style, in the midst of a vast concourse of spectators. This vessel kept the sea for many years, and was found to answer the Duke's most sanguine expectations. Some years ago she sank in the Black sea. Last year she was raised, and is again active in business ; and what is singular, after lying upwards of two years at the bottom of the ocean, her timbers have been found to be as fresh as the day she was launched. About the same time, the Duke prevailed on Government to introduce larch into the navy. The Athole, a frigate of 36 guns, was built of the Duke's larch, and sent out on foreign service. After having been for a number of years in various quarters of the globe, she was on her return taken into dock, and her timbers narrowly inspected. Another frigate of the same class, built the same year of English oak, was also taken into dock ; when it was found that the timbers of the Athole were quite sound, while those of the other were completely rotten.

A few years ago, Thomas Graham and Sons, general merchants, commenced ship building, chiefly for their own trade. They have already built seventeen vessels, amounting to 1334 tons register, some of which have been to the West Indies. These gentlemen lately sent to Jamaica singular article of export, namely 100 barrels of Perthshire potatoes, which brought a fair return. Mr William Taylor has also engaged in ship building, within these few years, and has built a number of vessels.

It has been already observed, that most of the shipping engaged in the Perth trade belonged to the Frith of Forth. A few vessels, however, belonged to the port, of small tonnage, the owners and masters of which were so cautious, that they never ventured to sea after the month of November. Some were regularly laid up from that time until spring set in, when they made a trip to Rotterdam for flax, and various descriptions of seeds. At this period there was much smuggling in gin, spices, &c. Various methods were resorted to, the best of which were frequently detected; the vessels sometimes being seized and sold by the custom-house. One season a flaxdresser brought in 300 ankers of gin in one vessel, which were all safely landed, and sold at a high profit. Not contented with his success, he imported another large cargo; but, unfortunately for him, an information having been lodged with the custom-house, the ship and cargo were both seized, condemned, and sold. This put an end to his smuggling, and rendered him a beggar. Another bold attempt was made by Mr Robert Foggo. This gentleman had been bred to the sea in his youth, but had long been settled here in the manufacturing line, though he still retained his rambling propensities. Whilst in London on one occasion, he took it into his head to attempt running a cargo of gin from Holland to Perth. Having fallen in with the master of a small vessel belonging to Perth then in London, he procured as many porter hogsheads as filled the vessel; filling a few with porter and the rest with water, he got them on board the vessel and cleared out at the custom-house as with a cargo of porter for Perth; but instead of steering for Perth he sailed to Rotterdam, filled his water casks with gin and arrived at Perth shore with his clearance from London with porter. The few hogsheads of porter were placed nearest the hatches. Some of these on being brought ashore were pierced and tried as to quality, and being found all right, it was deemed useless to pierce any more: the whole cargo was thus safely landed without exciting suspicion. Previous to the year 1800, one or two vessels were anually freighted from Oporto with wine and fruit for the merchants. Vessels were freighted from Petersburgh with hemp, tallow, &c.; from Riga, with flax, flax-seed, wood, and iron; from Dantzic, with deals, battens, black beer, and honey; from Gottenburgh, with wood and iron; from the Danish and Prussian ports, with grain; and from Bremen, with bark and hides. From Memel and other Baltic ports, a great deal of logs were imported. A Mr Campbell contracted with Mr Gibson the ship carpenter, in 1785, to build a vessel for the wood trade, of upwards of 300 tons register. Since that period the wood trade has greatly increased : in place of one yard, as at that period, there are now a number of houses in the line. Many cargoes of American timber are also imported.

It has been already remarked that Mr Richardson kept several vessels for conveying his fish to the London market, which he often freighted in the return voyage with London porter. About the year 1780, the fishing company built two beautiful smacks for this trade, with cabins fitted up in a superior manner for passengers. The charge for a cabin passage was one guinea; steerage, half a guinea : these vessels brought goods from London to the shore. Since that period, by the junction of the Perth and Dundee Shipping Company, the trade has been completely altered. The Perth goods are now brought down in Dundee vessels, and transferred to lighters at Dundee, which are towed up the river by a steamer. About twenty years ago this trade greatly declined, a number of grocers having got into business who were compelled to take their goods at second hand from merchants in Leith and Dundee. Of late the London trade has again revived. Two Newcastle traders were formerly pretty regularly employed in bringing down English goods, great part of which consisted of crockery ware, grinding stones, spades, shovels, and such like; but for these articles other channels have been opened, which has had the effect of putting down these regular traders. The vessels going up with wood for pit props and bringing down coals, afford the most ample opportunity of conveying all kinds of merchandise. At the period we speak of, the vessels loaded with coals came all up to the coal shore, where there were scales for weighing them. Merchant vessels were all delivered at the lower pier, and lime vessels in front of the lime sheds. Near the top of this shore, and all the way up behind the barracks, now the county buildings, the water was of sufficient depth to float a vessel of large tonnage even at low water, and the only ford of consequence was right in front of the recently erected water house.

Since the potato trade for the London market commenced, there has been a rapid increase of the shipping belonging to the port. Sixty years ago, the tonnage of the vessels belonging to the port would not amount to 600 tons; it may now be taken at upwards of 6,000. This increase, independent of goods carried by passengers in the steam vessels plying between Perth and Dundee, shews that Perth has advanced her shipping trade extensively : and it is not improbable that a few years will find the average of goods nearly doubled. Upwards of 90,000 bolls of potatoes are now annually shipped from the port.

About forty years ago, the communication between Perth and Dundee was kept up by means of a caravan. This diligence held four passengers, was drawn by one horse, and went daily; though not always successful in obtaining passengers. The first attempt to establish steam communication on the river was on a very limited scale. It was predicted that the projectors would never find passengers. Since that period large and elegant boats have been put on the passage. During the summer months upwards of 1200 persons have been known to sail down the river in a day.

Since that period, the fords on the river have shifted amazingly. At various times, plans have been proposed for removing these obstructions to the navigation. The first attempt was made under Provost Allison; but the means employed were so inadequate to the end, that the project was speedily abandoned. During the time Thomas Hay Marshall, Esq., was at the head of the magistracy, it was proposed to excavate a dock at the back of the lime sheds, to communicate with the Tay, at the Friarton, by means of a canal through the old water course, termed the Gulloch. This plan lay over until a few years ago, when P. G. Stewart, Esq., was chief magistrate, when the proposition was taken into serious consideration; and it was at length determined to carry it into effect. But here a difficulty occurred,—the Council were inclined to improve the river by deepening the fords, and building a new pier; whilst a party among the inhabitants were for a dock and canal, under a set of commissioners. The Magistrates, as conservators of the river, were inclined to maintain their rights; whilst the others were as determined to carry their object. Application was therefore made to Parliament, and a bill obtained for deepening the fords, and building a new pier, under a set of commissioners; but, unfortunately, the bill was so defective, that the operations under it were confined between the Friarton-hole, and an imaginary line, drawn 450 yards below the County-buildings, without any reference to to the fords below; although it was well known that these fords had become an almost insuperable bar to the navigation of the river. During the progress of the bill in Parliament, in consequence of the numerous objections that were started, and the opposition given by each party to their antagonists' views, as well as from those connected by the fishings, or otherwise with the river, an immense expense was incurred. The new pier was intended to be carried up in a line to the north shore.

Dredging the fords was commenced under this act, with a kind of levelling-boxes, about 3 feet wide, which were dragged by two horses, followed by a man guiding it. In the operation, the horses and the man crossed the river in perhaps ten minutes, bringing ashore as much gravel as would fill a couple of wheel-barrows. After much expense, and the loss of a whole season, the absurdity of this plan was sufficiently manifest. Punts were then got, with capsterns, two of which were placed at a certain distance from, and opposite to, each other. From one of these, a box, shod with iron, was let down into the river, which was dragged across the bottom by a number of men working at the capstern on the opposite punt. After a heavy and tedious pull, the apparatus was landed with a modicum of shingle, when the empty box was drawn back to be refilled. If the other plan was absurd, this one was still more rediculous, as the horse machine did more work, at a tithe of the labour.

It was soon found that this farce could not continue long. In working this wonderful engine, about twenty men were employed; in the course of thirty minutes, these twenty men brought up just as much shingle as would load a very small cart. This trifling was at length seen in its true light. At same time, the new pier had been proceeded with on a scale as if it had to withstand the fury of the Northern Ocean. It was also extended into the centre of the river, thereby exposing the shipping to the whole force of the mountain floods, which, on the breaking up of the ice after a severe storm, is sufficient to do much injury to the vessels exposed to the drifting ice. The whole plan soon came to be denounced by the public, as useless and most expensive.

Another eminent engineer was consulted, who gave it as his opinion, that the plan of thus deepening the fords and building the new pier, was impracticable, recommending the formation of a dock behind the lime sheds, to be entered by a canal from the Friarton, with the addition of a large tide harbour at the lower end of the canal, immediately above the Friarton. A new bill was obtained for this purpose, by which the commissioners under the act are empowered to deepen the lower fords. This bill met with much opposition from the proprietors of the fishings, during its progress through the House of Commons, which involved the commissioners in much expense. A compromise which they were obliged to make with the fishing proprietors, has been the source of much delay and expense; and, in addition to these difficulties, they have been dreadfully annoyed and subjected to great expense, by the litigious conduct of the trustees on the estate of Moncrieff.

A dredging machine, for clearing the fords, was built at a great expense, but which has been found to work most effectually. It is understood that two feet of water has been gained on the lower fords, and this branch of the operation has every appearance of doing much good. For the dock and canal a contract was entered into with two individuals from England, who were to complete the whole work in a given time; but, unfortunately, in consequence of the differences which arose between the

Moncrieff trustees and the commissioners, followed by interdicts, and other machinery of the law, the progress of this important part of the work has been completely arrested during the past half-year. The commissioners have been placed in such difficulty, that it is now doubtful whether they would be justified in proceeding further under the present act ; the opinion being that they should rather go again to Parliament to get either a new bill, or the present one amended.

BRIDGEND.

This important suburb was but a sorry village, at the time the bridge was built. The road to Dundee passed down the narrow street of Bridgend, which consisted of a few thatched hovels, except the house at the shore, now in ruins, where the ferry boats for some time landed : this, and the houses of Rosemount and Potterhill, were the only respectable buildings in that quarter. The road leading to Scone ran through a dirty narrow lane, sunk about eight feet below the upper bank on the side, which was lined with very mean clay huts. The building of the bridge made a complete revolution in the place. New lines of roads were formed to Scone, Coupar-Angus, and Dundee, and good substantial houses, many of them elegant, were betimes reared. About 1786, the toll on the bridge was removed. At the same time, ground was feued, and beautiful villas built, along the side of the hills as far east as Barnhill, where the most of Mr Moncrieff's property is laid out in small possessions, yielding a very high rent.

Bridgend, or Kinnoul, is a burgh of barony, under the Earl of Kinnoul, and is entitled to hold a weekly market, and four annual fairs; but owing to its identification with the city, by the erection of the bridge, these markets are not held. Shortly after the completion of the bridge, a nursery was begun in this parish, opposite Perth, by Messrs William Dickson and James Brown, which has continued as a very extensive and useful establishment of the kind in this part of Scotland. The ancient church of the parish was long a rectory in the proprietary of the monastery of Cambuskenneth, and was dedicated to rather a rare saint, Constantine, who was a king of Scots in the tenth century, and who became a monk among the Culdees of St Andrews. The new church of Kinnoul is a neat edifice, built on a bank, overhanging the Tay, south from the bridge. Among other establishments are a tannage and a brewery (Clockserie). The latter in connection with a distillery, at one time, did much business. The bridge, though justly admired at the time it was built, is found to be too narrow for the intercourse of the county, and several unsuccessful attempts have been made to widen it. The people in business meet annually, and elect magistrates from among themselves; after which they dine together. These magistrates, although not legally constituted, have frequently been very successful in healing differences.

Murray's Royal Lunatic Asylum, an establishment which is one of the most perfect in the kingdom, is situated in a park of 12 acres, on the declivity of Kinnoul-hill, and has a delightful view of the Grampian mountains, the Tay, and surrounding country. The house, which was built from a plan of Mr Burns, architect, consists of three floors, 256 feet in length; and was opened for the reception of patients in 1827. This establishment, the admiration of strangers, and allowed to be the first of the kind in Britain, both for cleanliness and attention to the unhappy inmates, has just been extended by an additional building, calculated to accommodate about 80 additional patients. The extensive inclosures afford ample room for exercise to the inmates, and where those able to work are employed,—a course which has been found to be attended with the most salutary effect in restoring bodily and mental vigour. During the winter season, and in rainy weather, the patients promenade in ong galleries, open on one side to the air. The meanest patient is well ed and clothed, and those from among the higher classes who can pay for it, are as well lodged and cared for, as they could be in a palace.— No coercion is used; everything is mild and soothing to their feelings. On Sundays, the whole are assembled in a chapel, divided by a partition about 6 feet high, the men on the one side, the women on other; so that the inmates do not see each other; the desk from which the governor reads the service, being so placed, that both parties see and hear him. Each person has a separate room. To frustrate any attempt on their lives, the curtains of the beds are hung from the roof in such a way, that if eight pounds weight were attached to them, the whole would come down. This excellent establishment was founded on a legacy by one of two brothers, of the name of Murray, who were day labourers in Perth, at the time it fell into their hands; which was left to them by a brother in India. Mr James Murray having no family, bequeathed his portion for the purpose of founding a lunatic asylum, which has since obtained a Royal Charter. It is governed by a patron, David Beatson, Esq., one of the trustees, and a number of directors appointed by the charter. Mr Simmonds, the present governor, has much credit for his manner of treating the unfortunate individuals under his care.

The Hill of Kinnoul, rising from the Tay, opposite, and within view of the town of Perth, is one of the very finest objects of the

kind in great Britain.   It is crowned and highly embellished with
wood, and has a variety of villas environed in shrubberies and gardens of the most exuberant description, the whole only paralleled in
beauty and salubrity of situation by Richmond Hill.   The eastern
part of Kinnoul-hill is the property of Lord Gray; the centre, which
contains the most elevated point, belongs to the Earl of Kinnoul; and the
western promontory, to Matthew Moncrieff, Esq.   Thomas, late Earl of
Kinnoul, planted his part of it with spruce and larch fir, which, for many
years, had a beautiful appearance.   Of late a great part of the wood has
been cut and sold, at good prices.   Earl Thomas caused a carriage-way
to be made through the plantation to the top of the hill, which he annually
visited.   This road was termed the serpentine walk, and was considered
one of the most delightful trips that could be taken in the whole country.
The late Earl Robert, caused a large stone-table to be placed on the top.
For many years his Lordship and family with a few friends made an annual
visit to this delightful spot, and dined at the table.   Until recently, this walk
was open to the public, and was visited by great numbers, to enjoy the
magnificent view commanded from the summit—a view which perhaps is
not surpassed in the world, and only equalled by the prospect from the
opposite eminence of Moncrieff hill.   Lord Gray has also ornamented
the highest point of his property, by erecting a building which represents
a ruined tower.   At the close of the last century, the face of the hill below the rock was covered with sloe bushes and brambles, and was much
resorted to by the youngsters from Perth, in search of wild fruit.   The
brushwood has since been rooted out, and replaced by a thriving plantation, which adds much to the beauty of the scenery.   Lord Gray has
also cut some delightful walks at the foot of the rock, which traverse the
the hill at different heights.   In the face of the rock is a cave called the
dragon's hole, which, like the human stature, is related to have been formerly much larger.   At present it is capable of holding about a dozen of
people, the height being about ten feet : it used to be reckoned no small
feat for the boys to scale the rock up to this hole.   To the eastward is a
deep hollow in the hill, named the *windy gowl* from the currents of wind
constantly blowing up the ravine; at one point there is an echo which
repeats a syllable several times, with great distinctness; although by no
means equal in politeness to the celebrated one in Ireland, which, on any
one saying " How do ye do, Paddy?" replied, " Very well, I thank you !"
Before the front of the hill was planted, many beautiful peebles were
found amongst the soil at the foot of the cliffs.   Several people obtained a
living by digging for them, and carrying them to Edinburgh for sale.
Hawks, kites, ravens, and hooded crows, build their nests in the face of

the rocks. Huge masses of stone, by the action of the weather, have, from time to time, been detached from the rocks, and precipitated with tremendous velocity. We remember of a small house standing on the farm of Lairwell, which one of these large boulders had struck, and, breaking through the back wall, killed a woman within. A number of medicinal herbs formerly grew on the face and top of Kinnoul-hill : amongst these, agrimony, hoarhound, lady's thistle, spleenwort, mountain flax, wild thyme, dwarf elder, &c.

On an eminence to the north of Captain Moncrieff's house of Woodend, stood the castle of Kinnoul. This place has given the title of Earl to the family of Hay of Errol, the first of the title being ennobled in 1627, as Lord Hay of Kinfauns, and elevated to be Earl of Kinnoul, Viscount Dupplin, in 1633. Here James the I. had an interview with the lady of Kinnoul, who was then above 100 years old, and blind. The king was very fond to hear her account of the changes and events, to which, in early life, she had been witness ; having seen five kings, his predecessors, besides Wallace, the governor. She related the history of Wallace and Bruce, whom she had seen, and described both as being strong and handsome ; but added that Wallace exceeded Bruce in fortitude. The king departed highly delighted with the old lady's narrative. So late as the year 1773, the remains of this old castle were to be seen.

About the year 1793, the western division of Kinnoul hill, at that time belonging to Sir Stewart Threipland, comprehending the lands of Bellwood, and all the Moncrieff property, was planted down to near the Dundee road. Mr Moncrieff rented the house and land below the road, on a life rent, lease and nineteen years thereafter ; a large portion of the hill, indeed all he now possesses, was included in the lease, at a very moderate rent, with liberty to clear out any part of the planting, upon payment of three half-pence for each tree taken out. This property having come into the market, John Young, Esq., bought that portion on which the house of Bellwood is erected. Mr Dickson bought the land which he now occupies as nursery grounds ; and William Stewart, Esq., bought the lot below the road on which Garry Cottage and other buildings are erected. The grounds under lease to Mr Moncrieff fell into his hands at a very low price, owing to the terms of the lease which he held. About 1800, when the different garden grounds about the town began to be feued for building, the lands of Barnhill came to be a speculation amongst gardeners, which, owing to the light soil and southern exposure, was found to be admirably adapted for raising early crops of vegetables. Lots were let at from L.8 to L.12 an acre, planted with trees and bushes. Encouraged by this, the proprietor built houses ; and as fast as he cleared

out the wood, got it let at very high rents: at the same time the restrictions and total shutting of many of the Baltic ports against the British
traders during the war, caused such an advance in the price of wood, that
many of the fir trees grown on the Hill of Kinnoul were sold as high as
3s 6d the foot. The Hill of Kinnoul appears to consist of a mass of blue
whin stone, interspersed with veins of fine limestone, part of which was
at one time wrought, and burnt on the bank of the river below the old
church.

The Boatlands consisted of that piece of ground on which Mr Paton's cottage now stands. It belonged to the Town of Perth, and was
sold by them to Mr Chalmers in perpetual feu. Sheriff Chalmers sold it
to Provost Marshall, who built the present cottage, and died just at the
time he was about to take possession of it. Since the year 1800, many
lots of ground have been feued out by the different proprietors, on which
some beautiful villas have been built, adding much to the ornament of
the city and vicinity. In Bridgend there are now some very elegant
well filled shops, and commodious inns. Mr Joseph Clark's establishment has stabling for nearly 200 horses, and can furnish a dinner table
equal to any inn in the country.

It has already been observed that the noble family of Kinnoul took a
warm interest in the bridge. A circumstance occurred some time after
the toll was taken off, which deserves to be noticed When the post-
horse duty was first farmed out, the contractor, deeming the Bridge of
Perth a most eligible place to collect the duty, erected a mean-looking
gate in the same place where the former handsome one for collecting the
pontage had stood. The late Earl Robert on receiving notice of the circumstance, came personally, with men provided with spades and picks,
and with his own hands assisted to pitch the obnoxious obstruction into
the river: declaring that, whilst he lived, a gate should never disfigure
the bridge for that purpose. At the back of what was once the old
church of Kinnoul (lately pulled down) stands an aisle, formerly the
burying-place of the Kinnoul family. A beautiful piece of statuary, in
white marble, size of life, of Chancellor Hay in his robes of state, is preserved here. The adjoining nursery, now the property of Archibald
Turnbull, Esq., has been famed throughout Britain during the last half
century, for the culture of fruit and forest trees, ornamental shrubbery,
and flowers in endless variety. Vast quantities of plants are annually
sent from this nursery to England. The late Duke of York, when laying out his pleasure grounds, procured the greater number of his ornamental shrubbery from this quarter.

D. Mackenzie

Joseph Swan

River Tay and Kinnoull Hill from East of Craigie.

James Stewart

Joseph Swan

Kinfauns Castle, The Seat of the Right Hon. Lord Gray.

James Stewart

Joseph Swan

Elcho Castle.

James Stewart

Scone Palace, The Seat of the Right Hon. Earl of Mansfield.

Joseph Swan

D. Mackenzie

Ruthven Castle.

Joseph Swan

William Brown

The Grave of Bessy Bell and Mary Gray.

Joseph Swan

J. C. Brown

John Smith

Dunkeld from Torrhill.

VICINITY OF PERTH.

The Parish of Perth, which was subdivided a few years ago for ecclesiastical purposes, into four parishes, is about four miles in length, and three in breadth, and forms a beautiful semi-circle on the banks of the Tay. It is bounded on the east and north by the Tay; on the west by Tippermuir and Aberdalgie; and on the south by Dunbarney and Forteviot. The surface is flat on the banks of the Tay, and the lands are of excellent quality, and well cultivated. In the parish are situated the ancient castles of Balhousie and Pittheavles; and the villages of Craigie, Tulloch, and Muirton of Balhousie.

From the year 1750 to 1780, the vicinity of Perth formed a wonderful contrast to its present appearance. Except the house of Balhousie, the castle of Pittheavles, and the old Palace of Scone, then standing, there was scarcely a slated or two storey house to be seen. The farm steadings were all low thatched hovels, with a stable and byre on the one side, and the barn on the other; with the midden hole in the centre, in front of the house, through which it was often necessary to pass by the aid of stepping-stones, before access could be obtained to the house. The maids slept in the kitchen, the master and mistress in the ben-room; all in close beds, with lids or doors on them. The back of the two kitchen beds formed the partition or one side of the pantry; the ends of the beds in the room, with the back of the gudewife's aumry, forming the other, the door being between them. The rafters were bare above, encrusted with soot, and dripping with condensed evaporations. The floors of the ben-house even were of earth. The kitchen fire was often placed out from the wall, leaving a considerable space behind; here sat the ploughman and herd on one side, and the farmer and colley on the other.

During the winter evenings, the maids were ranged in front on each side, plying the spinning wheel with eident thrift; the gudewife in the centre being occupied with the reel. When a maid was fee'd, the quantity of yarn she had to spin each day, besides doing the work of the house, was stipulated. Their meals were all taken in the kitchen; the contents of the pot being dished up in one large cogue, and placed on a stool, beside which were set an abundance of pease bannocks; the whole family supped from one dish. When there was flesh in the pot, which was rarely the case, the gudeman cut a piece to each one and handed it to him; some had a fork for this purpose, others adhered to the more primitive mode of using their fingers; when there was no meat, a slice of cheese was given to each. In the morning the porridge were dished up in the same way, and all supped from one dish; the same in the evening with the sowens. After the introduction of potatoes, the pot in which they were beat was set in the centre, all sitting round and digging away with their spoons; after supper the whole joined in family worship. As the towns increased, the population of the country diminished; the cottars melting away rapidly as the farms were increased in size. At the Muirton, upwards of forty cottars' houses were demolished, and the families turned adrift. Each of these kept a cow, and worked to the farmer for their rent. The Friarton and other parts of the parish, as well as the country in general, shared the same fate.

Old Earl Thomas of Kinnoul was the first who set the example of improving the houses of his tenantry. He built houses of two storeys covered with grey slates, and gave the farmers three nineteen-year tacks at a moderate rent. It was his chief pride to see his tenants thriving, and with a good coat on their backs; some of these steadings may yet be seen on the Kinnoul farms. However much these houses may in the present day be despised by our wealthy farmers, they were thought exceeding grand when built. This excellent nobleman was much esteemed: after being engaged abroad in a diplomatic situation, he retired in his old age to Dupplin, where he took great delight in improving his property, and spending his income in the place. His only care being not to run in debt, wishing at the same time to spend his whole income within the year. On one occasion, when settling the year's accounts with Mr Keir, his factor, there was a balance in his favour of *four-pence half-penny;* on which the Earl facetiously observed, " Eh! George, if we go on at this rate we'll save money !" This old nobleman exhibited many fine traits of generosity; but like other great men, he had his weak side, and those who knew it might lead him like a child. The Earl was exceedingly careful of his health. So apprehensive was he on this score, that it is said, on one occasion he was persuaded to keep his room till a new garden dyke, which was blown down one night, was rebuilt, and the damage repaired; the mason who had built it being terrified to meet his Lordship's anger. On one occasion, at rent day, the widow of one of his tenants sent her son to pay the rent of the farm and mill which her lately deceased husband had possessed. The factor having represented to his Lordship that the widow was unable to manage the farm and mill, had got a three-nineteen-years' lease made out in his own behalf. The Earl, on seeing the youth, inquired of the factor who that fine young man was? This was a thrust for which the factor was not prepared. " Heigh! George," exclaimed the Earl, " I did not know that Mrs ——— had a son come this length; he's a fine young man that, we must not let him go, he must have his father's farm." A new lease was accordingly granted to the son, for behoof of his mother, to the great mortification of the factor. Another of the tenants had a couple of very fine pointers, which had taken his Lordship's fancy, and for which he offered a very high price. The owner, however, was not disposed to sell them; but if his Lordship pleased they were at his service. The proffer being graciously accepted, the dogs were sent to Dupplin. When the tenant laid down his rent at the term day, the Earl handsomely returned the whole sum as a recompence for the pair of dogs. Mr S———, the principal wright in Perth, was the Earl's man of business in the cabinet line. The Earl having sent for him one day in haste, when he was not at home, was quite irritated at the delay. When Mr S——— arrived at Dupplin, the Earl being busy in a small closet at a writing desk, ordered him up. Mr S——— was a venerable looking gentlemen about seventy years of age. On his entrance, the Earl, in his usual hasty manner, chid him for not coming sooner; concluding with " Sit down, sir, until I finish my letter." Mr S———, seeing no chair in the room to sit upon, squatted down on the floor behind the Earl to await his pleasure. On finishing his letter, he turned round, and, perceiving Mr S——— sitting cross-legged like a tailor, booted and spurred, and with a huge snuff mull in his hand, burst into a fit of laughter; but checking himself, begged a thousand pardons; trusting Mr S——— would forgive him, as he did not mean to insult him. His Lordship was extremely regular in his attendance at the parish church of Aberdalgie, where he built an aisle for his family seat, with a funeral vault underneath; behind were erected a suite of rooms for the convenience of dining between sermons—the dinner being sent up the previous evening. One Sabbath morning, the clergyman, as was his custom, went into the apartments to wait his Lordship's arrival, before beginning service. The Earl was late of coming;

and the clergyman, either to prevent ennui, or in a fit of abstraction, ventured to taste a fine roasted fowl which lay invitingly upon the table. Eating and drinking, it is said, only need a beginning, and so it proved in the present case ; for having once begun, he made short work of the whole fowl, and washed it down with a bottle of wine. It was usual for the clergyman to dine with his Lordship after service; but it is easy to conceive, that on this occasion the dessert would be less palatable than the diet, when called upon to account for his fit of abstraction ; and to acknowledge, that while his mind was absorbed in the contemplation of the sublime doctrines of truth, his carnal man could not resist Adam's temptation of the forbidden fruit.

The greater part of the splendid castle of Dupplin, which contained a most extensive collection of books of all ages, and a good gallery of paintings, was burnt down in September 1827. It has since been rebuilt in a style of great magnificence, after the style Inigo Jones, the celebrated English architect. Such of the paintings and antique furniture as escaped the general conflagration, have been restored to their places in the new edifice, the interior decorations of which are exceedingly elegant and chaste. The policies around the castle are truly delightful, and command one of the most enchanting views in Scotland. The estate is distinguished for the size and excellence of the timber produced upon it. The battle field, in which the covenanters were so completely vanquished by Montrose, lies at a short distance, being partly in the parish of Aberdalgie and partly in that of Tippermuir.

Kinfauns.—This remarkably fine edifice occupies a delightful situation on an elevation overlooking the Tay, and the Carse of Gowrie to the east. In the castle of Kinfauns is kept a large two-handed sword, probably made five hundred years ago. It is shaped like a broad sword, and is five feet nine inches long, two and a half inches broad at the hilt, and of a proportionate thickness, with a round knob at the upper end, near eight inches in circumference. This terrible weapon bears the name of *Charteris' Sword*, and probably belonged to Sir John Charteris, commonly called Thomas de Longueville, once the proprietor of the estate of Kinfauns. Sir Thomas Charteris, *alias*, Longueville, was a native of France, and of an ancient family in that country. If credit can be given to accounts of such remote date, when he was at the court of Phillip le Bel, in the end of the thirteenth century, he had a dispute with, and killed a French nobleman in the king's presence. He escaped, but was refused pardon. Having for several years infested the seas as a pirate, known by the name of the *Red Reaver*, from the colour of the flags he carried on his ships. In 1301, or 1302, Sir William Wallace, in his way to France, encountered and took him prisoner. At Wallace's intercession, the French king conferred on him a pardon, and the honour of knighthood. He accompanied Wallace on his return to Scotland, and was ever after his faithful friend, and aided him in his exploits. Upon that hero's being betrayed and carried to England, Sir Thomas Charteris retired to Lochmaben, where he remained till Robert Bruce began to assert his right to the crown of Scotland. He joined Bruce, and was, according to Adamson, the first who followed that hero into the water at the taking of Perth, January 8, 1313. Bruce rewarded his bravery, by giving him the lands in the neighbourhood of Perth, which appear to be those of Kinfauns, and which continued in the family of Charteris for many years. It is to this ancient knight, and to the antique sword above mentioned, that Adamson refers in his Muses Threnodie :—

> " ———— Kinfauns, which Thomas Longueville
> Sometime did hold, whose ancient sword of steel
> Remains unto this day, and of that land
> Is chiefest evident."

About fifty years ago, upon opening the burying-vault under the aisle of the church of Kinfauns, erected by this family, there was found a headpiece, or kind of helmet, made of several folds of linen, or some strong stuff, painted over with broad stripes of blue and white, which appears to have been part of the fictitious armour, wherein the body of Thomas Longueville, or Charteris, had been deposited.

Lord Gray, the present noble proprietor, is perhaps the most liberal and enthusiastic patron of science and the fine arts now alive. His collection of paintings, by the first masters, is immense, while the visitor is altogether bewildered with the variety, number and beauty, of his splendid collection of statuary. His Lordship, however, is generally understood to pride himself more on the extent and excellence of his philosophical and mechanical apparatus, which is extensive, and of the most perfect description, collected entirely by himself, or made to his directions ; his lordship's genius being chiefly inclined towards scientific, and the more elegant mechanical, pursuits. The library is also extensive : the catalogue, a copy of which was recently presented by his lordship to the Literary and Antiquarian Society of Perth, occupying a large folio volume.

Seggieden lies about a mile east of Kinfauns. This family still possess their celebrated drinking-horn. This venerable relic is about fourteen inches deep, straight, and tapering, with ornamental rings round it. The principal use of this heir-loom seems to have been similar to that of the horn of Rorry More, as described by Dr Johnson : every successive heir of the family on his succession to the estate, had to prove his being a worthy representative of his ancestors, by drinking its contents at a draught. There was a rhyme used on this occasion :—

> " Sook it out Seggieden !
> Though it's thin, it's well pledged."

And the young laird had to sound a whistle at the bottom of the horn, after having *sooked out* the liquor, to signify that he had redeemed his pledge. The same ceremony was gone through, to prove the powers of the laird's guests.—The proposed line of railway between Perth and Dundee, passes immediately in front of this mansion.

Elcho Castle.—On the opposite side of the Tay stands the ruinous castle of Elcho. It once contained a nunnery ; and is celebrated in the achievements of Wallace, as frequently affording shelter to the Protector of Scotland. This edifice still confers the title of Lord on the eldest son of the Earl of Wemyss.

Bridge of Earn, some years ago, consisted of only a few thatched cottages, with an ancient bridge, which was one of the principal passes in Scotland. Recently this place has been completely revolutionized. The old bridge, which, in the time of Bruce, had been a landmark in the popular mind, is broken down, and half swept away ; the remaining ruins forming no inapt illustration of the Vision of Mirza. The beautiful new bridge, of three arches, erected farther up the river, has done much to effect a change in the character of the place ; and its prosperity has been greatly promoted by the recent removal of the foot pontage. The principal street consists of a row of very neat houses, many of which are let as summer lodgings, for valitudinarians attending the neighbouring mineral springs. The hotel will vie the largest and best appointed inns in the country.

Pitkeathly, situated about a mile from the Bridge of Earn, is yearly becoming more frequented by parties in pursuit of health and pleasure ; and if the loveliness of the scenery, or the beauties of a highly cultivated and fertile country, can restore vigour to the jaded mind, or enervated frame, it would be difficult to point to a more eligible spot. The time when these celebrated mineral waters were discovered, cannot be ascertained,—even tradition says nothing of their discovery. There are five distinct springs, all of similar quality, but of different strength. The water is considered efficacious in curing or alleviating scrofula, scurvy, gravel, dispepsia, and divers internal complaints. The mineral is gentle in its operation, has an agreeable effect in relieving the stomach of crudities, procuring an appetite, and exhilarating the spirits ; and instead of weakening, tends to strengthen the constitution. The water is of a cool-quality, and very efficacious in removing all heat and foulness of the blood. The promenades around Pitkeathly are extensive and agreeable, and there is no lack of accommodation. The waters are allowed to be most beneficial when the valitudinarian resides in Perth ;—the patients walking to the wells, and back again, *before breakfast*.

Martyrs' Graves.—In a secluded glen, a short distance from Pitkeathly house, are the remains of the old house of Ecclesiamagirdle, formerly inhabited by the family of Lennox. A few paces distant are the ruins of the small chapel and burial-ground of Ecclesiamagirdle : here, a rude stone, recently cleared of the turf and moss that concealed it, points out the grave of "a village Hampden," by the following simple, but nervous inscription :—

" HEIR LYIS ANE VERTOUS HUSBANDMAN, THOMAS SMALL, WHO DIED FOR RELIGION, COUENANT, KING, AND COUNTRIE, THE 1ST OF SEPTEMBER, 1645, OF HIS AGE 58.—*Memento mori*."

In the neighbouring burying-ground of Dron, a stone points out the resting place, and records the sufferings of another martyr for the cause of truth.

The Rocking Stone of Dron.—On the south side of the hill of Ecclesiamagirdle, which rises from behind Pitkeathly, and affords a view little inferior to that from the hill of Mordun, stands this celebrated relict of a rude and superstitious age. It is about ten feet in length, and seven in breadth ; and so poised, that upon its higher end being slightly pressed, it vibrates in an arc of between two and three inches. In contemplating this witness to the ordeals of Pagan barbarity, we cannot but execrate the damnable villany, that would subject the simple inhabitants to a test which involved the immolation of its shrieking victims on the altars of Baal ; and which the officiating fiends could regulate at their pleasure, by the simple expedient of inserting a wedge under the poised stone.

Abernethy.—This place is connected with the early history of Scotland. Its name is derived from *Obair Neachtain*, signifying in Gaelic, the work of Nethan or Nectan, who was a Pictish king, A.C. 456, and constituted this town the capital of his dominions. He founded a church, dedicated to St Bridget. The town was subsequently created an archepiscopal see, but on the Picts being subjugated by Kenneth II., King of Scots, he removed the episcopate to St Andrews, 840. After this the cathedral became a collegiate church, and a university for the education of youth, in the possession of the Culdees, that class of christians who were in the island prior to the assumption of universal power by the Bishop of Rome. The glory of Abernethy is altogether gone. The whole of its ecclesiastical structures, once so eminent, are now utterly obliterated; and a single round tower of about 75 feet in height, and 48 in circumference, built of solid hewn stone, only remains as an evidence of the Pictish reign. It stands in an angle of the church yard, and serves the purpose of a steeple for a clock and bell to the adjacent plain modern church. On the one side of the church has been attached during the times of religious severity, an iron collar and chain, ready for the pilloring of persons convicted by the kirk sessions of infractions of church rules. Abernethy is a burgh of barony, and occupies a pleasant site in the south verge of the vale of Strathearn. It consists mostly of thatched houses; and is more irregular and dirty than almost any other inland town of Scotland. It is supported chiefly by linen weaving. It has also been rendered of late more isolated, by the alteration of the highway, which formerly led through the town.

Lindores Abbey.—About two miles from Abernethy, and immediately to the eastward of the flourishing town of Newburgh, are the remains of this once extensive abbey. It is situated beyond the verge of the county; but as the steam vessels, which daily ply between Perth and Dundee, pass within sight of the ruins, the following brief account may not be deemed out of place:—" This establishment was founded by David, Earl of Huntingdon, brother to King William, upon his return from the Holy Land, about the year 1178; he bestowed it upon the Tyronenses of Kelso, whom Boethius highly commends, as being 'morum innocentia clari.' There is a bull of Pope Innocent III., granted at Lateran in the year 1198, confirming all the lands and privileges granted to this place; it is addressed, ' Guidoni abbati monasterii Sanctæ Mariæ de Lindores, ejusque fratribus.' Johannes Scotus, Earl of Huntingdon, confirms likewise to the monks all the donations which had been made to them by his father. From these and other grants, the monks of Lindores had twenty-two parish churches, and were otherwise very rich. In the course of fifty years after the erection of the abbey, a similar establishment for Cistertian monks was erected a few miles to the east, at Balmerino. The readers of Scottish history will perhaps remember that it was within the abbey of Lindores that the body of the Duke of Rothesay, eldest son of Robert III., was interred, after being cruelly starved to death by his uncle in the dungeon of Falkland palace; and it will not be forgotten that it was within this monastery, that James, the ninth Earl of **Douglas,** spent the four last years of his existence (1484-88) in penitence and peace, after many vicissitudes, and an unsuccessful rebellion against his sovereign. At the Reformation, the abbey, as a matter of course, was destroyed, and its property sequestrated. In 1606, it was erected into a temporal lordship by James VI., in favour of Patrick Lesly, son to Andrew, Earl of Rothes. Among the last seized moveables belonging to the establishment, was the bell of the church, which, in 1585, was removed to Edinburgh and placed in the spire of St Giles. Such has been the dilapidation of the buildings of the abbey, that some fragments of the walls alone remain standing, testifying the former extent of the sacred precincts. "Within these walls, and for a small space beyond them, on one side, the ground continues to be occupied by fruit trees, which having been long since planted, exhibit appearances of decay, that, viewed in conjunction with the mouldering fragments of structures, half covered at top with ivy, and surrounded at bottom with thorn and hazel, give an air of melancholy grandeur to the place at large. Formerly, strangers who visited the ruins had a stone coffin pointed out to them, which was placed within the area of the church, on the north wall, towards the east end, which was said to have contained the remains of the Earl of Douglas, but in consequence of depredations lately made upon the walls, it is now covered with rubbish. Whether this coffin did in fact contain the bones of this person, or of the Duke of Rothesay, or perhaps of some dignified ecclesiastic, no certain information can be procured, as there is not a single inscription on any part of the church, or of the other buildings."

Besides the ruins of Lindores abbey, the parish contains two crosses of very ancient erection. One of these is placed on a rising ground a little westward of the town of Newburgh, and within a few yards of the Tay, on the grounds of Mugdrum. It consists of one large stone placed upright on another, and exhibits the mutilated forms of animals carved upon it. The other, called Macduff's cross, is much more interesting, though less entire, and is situated on the high grounds south-west from Newburgh, near the side of an obscure road leading across the hills to Auchtermuchty. The site of this object of antiquity is a hollow in the face of the hills, commanding an extensive prospect of the lower part of Strathearn, and when the cross was in complete condition it must have been seen at a very great distance. All that now remains of the cross is a mass of freestone measuring about three feet square, resting on a mound of earth: from its appearance it is impossible to say what was its original figure; it is reputed by tradition, however, to have been of considerable

2 M

height, and covered with a rude inscription.   This cross of Macduff was
in early times a potent sanctuary or place of refuge, the origin and qua-
lification of which will be best described in the language of Sir Walter
Scott, who thus notices it in the Minstrelsy of the Scottish Border :—
" When the Revolution was accomplished, in which Macbeth was de-
throned and slain, Malcolm, sensible of the high services of the Thane of
Fife, is said by our historians to have promised to grant the first three
requests he should make.   Macduff accordingly demanded, and obtained,
first, that he and his successors, Lords of Fife, should place the crown on
the King's head at his coronation ; secondly, that they should lead the
vanguard of the army, whenever the royal banner was displayed ; and,
lastly, this privilege of clan Macduff, whereby any person, being related
to Macduff within the ninth degree, and having committed homicide, in
hot blood, or without premeditation, should, upon flying to Macduff's
cross, and paying a certain fine, obtain remission of his guilt.   Such, at
least, is the account given of the law by all historians.   Nevertheless,
there seems ground to suspect, that the privilege did not amount to an
actual and total remission of the crime, but only to a right of being exempted from all other courts of jurisdiction, except that of the Lord of
Fife.   But the privilege of being answerable only to the chief of their
own clan, was, to the descendants of Macduff, almost equal to an entire
indemnity.   The tumuli around the pedestal are said to be the graves of
those who, having claimed the privilege of the law, failed in proving
their consanguinity to the Thane of Fife.   Such persons were instantly
executed.   The people of Newburgh believe, that the spectres of these
criminals still haunt the ruined cross, and claim that mercy for their souls
which they had failed to obtain for their mortal existence."

Scone.—The Parish of Scone is one of the most beautiful districts of
Perthshire.   The land rises from the banks of the Tay, and composes
part of that splendid amphitheatre of hill and dale, in the centre of which
stands the city of Perth.   The surface, where not planted and disposed
as gardens and pleasure grounds, is mostly under cultivation.   The objects
most worthy of consideration are the palace and village of Scone.   During the middle ages of the Scottish monarchy, Scone was the residence of
the kings, in which respect it divided their favour with Dunfermline and
other places.   Independently of being thus to Perth, what Windsor in the
present day is to London, it was from an early age to a comparatively
recent date, the appropriate place of the royal coronations.   The crowning of the Scottish kings at Scone, was for a long period intimately connected with the famous Black " *Stone of Dunstaffnage,*" sometimes called

the " *Stone of Scone,*" on which, by an ancient usage, it was customary for the kings of Scotland to be crowned. The history of this famous palladium of the Scottish monarchy, whether fabulous or real, is replete with interest, the more especially as the stone exists at the present day, and must have been used as a coronation seat for upwards of thirteen hundred years. It is related in the fabulous chronicles, that the Stone of Dunstaffnage was originally brought from the East, having formed the pillow of Jacob when he slept on the plains of Luz, an event recorded in the tablet, by which Edward accompanied this trophy when he carried it away :

> " Si quid habent veri vel chronica cana fidesve,
> Clauditur hac cathedrâ nobilis ille Capis,
> Ad caput eximius Jacob quondam patriarchi
> Quem posuit, cernens numina mira poli." &c. &c.

From Syria the Stone was brought to Egypt, by Gathelus, the son of Cecrops, King of Athens, a person who entered into the service of Pharaoh, and married his daughter Scota. Having consulted with Moses, he was desirous to be out of the way of the impending plagues, and accordingly, sailed from the Nile with his wife and the curious stone, the trophy of one of his victories. Gathelus, we are next told, landed in Portugal or Spain. Acquiring an equally successful settlement in either of these countries, he at last bethought himself of invading an " islande opposite to Spaine, in the north, which a rude people inhabited, having neither lawes nor manners," and fitted out an expedition of which Hiber was made admiral. On the 5th day he landed in Ireland, which thus came to be called Hibernia, though the descendants and retainers of Gathelus received the name of *Scots.* According to the Irish records, the Stone was brought thither from Spain, by the colony of Tuath de Danan, and it was placed on the hill of Tara, where the kings of Ireland were wont to be installed in royal authority. Its names, with them, were *Lagphail* and *Clach-na-Cineamna,* signifying the " Fatal Stone," or the " Stone of Fortune." A superstition is said to have prevailed regarding it in Ireland, that at the inauguration of kings, it had the property of emitting a sound indicating the estimation in which it held the election. On all occasions of installation, which ceremony was performed by the Druids, the following rhyme in the ancient Irish Gaelic tongue was repeated by the officiating priest :—

> " Cioniodh scuit saor on fine,
> Man ba breag an Faisdine,
> Mar a bhfuighid an Lia-fail,
> D'lighid flaitheas di ghabhail,"

* Which has been thus translated by Wantoun :

> " But gif werdys falhyand be,
> Quhare-evyr that stane yhe segyt se

> Dare sall the Scotes be regnand,
> And lordys hale our all that land."

And some English poet has rendered it thus :

> " Should Fates not fail, whene'er this stone is found,
> The Scots shall monarchs of that realm be crown'd."

This stone, it is alleged by the fabulous chroniclers, was brought from Ireland along with Fergus I. in the year 330 before Christ, though, as other and more acute historians insist, it was not till 503 after Christ, that Fergus, the first Scottish king of Irish origin, began to reign in the western parts of this country. Towards the ninth century the history of the Stone of Fortune begins to clear up. It was deposited in the palace of Dunstaffnage, where it remained till the year 834, when it was carried by Kenneth II. to Scone, " there to remain thenceforth, as a sacred token for the establishment of the Scottish kingdom in that countrie," which had before appertained to the Picts. At Scone all the Scottish kings were crowned on it, till the time of John Baliol, when Edward I. seized upon it and carried it off to Westminister, under the idea that he would thereby acquire more easily and permanently, a right of governing the Scots. By the treaty of Northampton, 1327, it was to have been restored to Scotland ; but this was never done.

The Scots however were supposed to have asserted their indefeasible right to it, and to have at the same time proved the truth of the prophecy connected with it, when James VI. on acceding, in 1603, to the English throne, used it at his coronation. In the present day this stone remains in Westminister Abbey. It is of an oblong form, but irregular, measuring 26 inches in length, 16¾ in breadth, and 10½ in thickness, of a dark appearance, and is in some way fixed to the bottom of the chair in which the Kings of Great Britain are crowned. This chair stands in the east end of the Minster, and is exhibited to strangers. It is itself of oak and is still firm and sound, though much disfigured by wanton dilapidations rather than the effects of time. There can be no doubt, from the character of its construction, that it belongs to the reign of Edward the First, and that it was made for the reception of the highly-prized relict which it now encloses. The form of the heads and turns of the panelled arches which ornament the back and sides, prove the age to which it belongs. The back is terminated by a high pediment along each angle, of which were five crockets on a scotia or concave moulding. The whole chair has been completely covered with gilding and ornamental work. The tradition invariably describes the stone to be of marble ; but this is not correct. It is of a peculiar kind of sandstone, and there is much reason to suppose that it is merely a fragment of the rocks on which Dunstaffnage is built, as these are said to be precisely of the same quality. There is another theory,—

namely that it is a meteoric stone which, having fallen from the clouds, might easily excite the superstitious feelings of a rude people.

The last monarch crowned at Scone was Charles the Second, January 1, 1651, when on his expedition into Scotland. We are informed by different chroniclers, that on the occasion of crowning Kings at Scone, the Barons who assisted performed the strange ceremonial of casting together a portion of the earth of their respective estates, as a species of offering or corporal pledge of their fealty—Hume in his history of the Douglases, mentions, "that when Robert the Bruce was crowned in 1306, Sir James, the eighth Lord Douglas, assisted and cast into a heap, as did the other Barons, a quantity of the earth of the lands of Douglas, which, making a little hill, is called *omnis terris*" We are farther informed that the Barons of Scotland could receive investiture of their lands as lawfully, by delivering earth and stones from this spot, as from their lands. The hillock of earth which is reported to have been formed in the manner described, is still observable on the north side of the palace; in ordinary language it has been called the *moat hill* of Scone.

It would seem that Scone was also for many ages, the seat of a distinguished religious establishment, at which councils of the Scotian church were held. Whatever was the character of the first religious house, which, we are told by Buchanan, belonged to the Culdees, it was superseded in the year 1114, by Alexander I. who founded here an abbey which was dedicated to the Holy Trinity, and St Michael the Archangel, and furnished with monks or canons, regular of the order of St Augustine, After the confiscations consequent on the Reformation, the abbey was erected into a temporal baronetcy, by James VI., in the year 1604, in favour of Sir David Murray, a cadet of the family of Tullibardine. The abbey itself was demolished along with the palace, by a mob from Perth and Dundee at the Reformation. On the site of the ancient palace a splendid edifice, though of heavy architecture, has been reared by the Earl of Mansfield, who represents the ancient family of Stormont. In this modern structure,—to which access is seldom refused to tourists and others, on making application through Mr Condie, his lordship's agent in Perth,—much of the old furniture has fortunately been preserved; in particular a bed that had belonged to James VI.; and another, the curtains of which had been wrought by the fair hands of Queen Mary when prisoner in Lochleven Castle. The music gallery occupies the same site as the noble old hall in which the coronations were performed. The view from the windows of the drawing-room is exceedingly beautiful, though inferior to that commanded from the neighbouring castle of Kinfauns. About 50 yards from the house there is an old aisle,

the last remaining portion of the Abbey of Scone, containing a magnificent marble monument to a Viscount Stormont, who died about two centuries ago.   At a little distance farther stands the old Market Cross of
Scone, surrounded by a wilderness of pleasure grounds, which has come
in place of the ancient village.   There is many instances of towns losing
their market crosses, but this is perhaps the only instance of market cross
losing its town.   The burying ground of the old village is also embedded
in these plantations ; and although every inducement was held out when
the village was removed to the other side of the hill ; nothing could prevail with the inhabitants to forego their right of sepulture with the remains
of their fathers.

• The occupations of the inhabitants of the New Village are of a mixed
character, between the manufacturing and agricultural ; a great proportion are weavers, principally employed on the plainer fabrics ; but as each
house has a piece ground attached, its cultivation necessarily occupies a
good deal of attention ; much of the fruit and vegetables brought to the
Perth market, are grown in this quarter.

Huntingtower.—This venerable ruin is entitled to some attention, as
being the ancient seat of the Gowrie family, and the place where James
VI. was sometime confined by the Earl of Gowrie and others, who had
entered into a combination for taking the young king out of the hands of
his two early favourites, the lately created Duke of Lennox and Earl of
Arran.   This enterprise has usually been called by our historians, the
Raid of Ruthven.   After the forfeiture of the last Earl of Gowrie, this
castle and the adjoining manor were bestowed by King James the VI. on
the family of Tullibardine, now united by marriage to the family of
Athole, in whose possession they still remain.   The last noble occupier of
this seat was a Dowager Duchess of Athole.   It was also employed some
time as a hunting lodge.   The building consists of two square towers,
one of which is called the *Maiden's Leap,* from the following romantic
occurrence :—" A daughter of the first Earl of Gowrie was addressed by
a young gentleman of inferior rank in the neighbourhood, a frequent
visitor of the family, who never would give the least countenance to his
passion.   His lodging was in the tower, separate from that of his mistress.
The lady, before the doors were shut, conveyed herself into her lover's
apartment; but some prying duenna acquainted the countess with it, who,
cutting off as she thought, all possibility of retreat, hastened to surprise
them.   The young lady's ears were quick : she heard the footsteps of
the old countess, ran to the top of the leads, and took the desperate leap
of nine feet four inches, over a chasm of sixty feet, and luckily alighting

on the battlements of the other tower, crept into her own bed, where her astonished mother found her, and of course apologized for the unjust suspicion. The fair daughter did not choose to repeat the leap; but the next night eloped, and was married."

Such has been the change of circumstances of the place, concurring with the genius of the times, that the same castle, in which the haughty Ruthven once confined his king a prisoner, has been converted into a house for the reception of a colony of calico printers. The bleachfields and printfields of Ruthven and Huntingtower lie at the foot of the bank on which the castle stands, and are well supplied with water from an artificial canal from the Almond to the town of Perth, which is of great antiquity, having been formed previous to the year 1244, it being distinctly mentioned in charters of that date.

Graves of Bessy Bell and Mary Gray.—Within the grounds of Lynedoch is Burn Braes, a secluded spot on the banks of Brauchie Burn, made classic by the song of Bessy Bell and Mary Gray. These were two beautiful young ladies, who, dreading a plague which raged in that neighbourhood in 1666, retired to this spot,

> "And biggit a bower on yon burn brae,
> And theekit it o'er wi' rashes."

Here they were visited by the lover of one of them, who communicated the infection to both, and all three fell victims to it. The grave of those ill-fated beauties is still pointed out at Dronach-haugh, about half a mile west from Lynedoch Cottage, and near to the banks of the Almond.

Luncarty.—This locality is celebrated as the battle-field of that name, in which the Scots, under Kenneth III., obtained a decisive victory over the Danes. A great many *tumuli* appeared, until lately, upon this field and its vicinity; and from their scattered positions, the conclusion may be drawn, that both armies had successively retreated and rallied. On levelling some of those *tumuli*, human skeletons and bones, mingled with the bones and teeth of horses, have been found. About 700 yards south upon the Tay, stand eight *tumuli;* and in front of them, nearer the river, is a larger *tumulus.* At a little distance is a large unpolished stone, said to mark the grave of the Danish general; and, on the land-side, are the remains of a long oval rampart of earth, which was probably intended to strengthen the Danish encampment. At the east end of the *tumuli* stand some cottages, which are still called Denmark.

Dunkeld.—The parish of Dunkeld consists of no more land than that which is covered by houses of the town, which is the chief and central point in the tract of beautifully romantic scenery, which constitutes the upper part of Perthshire. It is situated fifteen miles distant from Perth, twenty-four from Kenmore, and twelve from Blairgowrie. In ascending the banks of the Tay from Perth, Dunkeld is found nestling in the bosom of an amphitheatre of hills, exactly at the place where the Highlands and Lowlands seems to meet, and where the noble river first emerges from its mountain fastnesses, into the fertile land to which it contributes so much additional beauty. The first peep of Dunkeld, as obtained from Birnam hill, is exceedingly striking. Deep under the brows of the lofty woody hills, lies the little Highland city, rendered in itself worthy of the pic- turesque scenery around and above it, by the fine antique effect of its ruined cathedral, rising above even the lofty trees that encompass it, and the modern elegance of the bridge over the Tay, by which the town is approached. Dunkeld is chiefly interesting as the object of a pleasure tour, or as a point in Highland scenery from which radiate many lines of route. Being thus a place of infinite resort in summer, it is provided with two inns, upon a first rate scale, both as to extent and quality of accommodation. At Birnam, about half a mile south of Dunkeld, is an- other excellent and well appointed inn. As those who put up here escape the heavy pontage of Dunkeld Bridge, it is much resorted to by visitors from the south. The origin of the place as a settlement of population is lost in the mists of antiquity. The Gaelic name of the place, Dun- chailledun, seems to indicate a fort on the top of some one of the neighbouring woody hills; but the earliest authentic notice speaks of nothing but a retreat of the early religious order, called the Culdees. This ancient monastery, which authentic history notices so early as 729, was, in 1127, converted into the seat of a bishopric, by David I. on the country passing from the Culdee to the Roman Catholic establishment. How a religious institution of this order could exist in such a spot, at such a time, is matter of astonishment. We find, in Spottiswood's Church History, that the poor bishops had dreadful battles to fight occasionally, with the lawless clans around them. The clan Donnachy, or Robertson, seems to have been a dreadful source of annoyance to the holy men. It is, at the same time, amusing to find, that the terrors of the church would sometimes assert their sway over the superstitious and half-instructed minds of the savage chiefs, compelling them, perhaps only a short time after they had attacked the prelate and his vassals with sword and buck- ler, or stolen his cattle and burnt his stack-yards, to come in hair-cloth shirts to the altar, and implore the forgiveness at once of heaven and his lordship. The first bishop of this see whose name appears prominently in history, is the famed William Sinclair, brother of Sir Henry Sinclair of Roslin, who assumed the mitre in 1312. He distinguished himself by repelling a body of English, who landed near his palace at Auchtertool in Fife, and who had previously driven back a band of regular soldiers under the sheriff. King Robert Bruce was so much impressed with the gallantry of this action, that he used ever after to call Sinclair " My own bishop." At his death in 1327, he was buried in the choir of the cathedral, which he had himself built from the ground ; and there still exists, on the top of that building, a fluted cross, which was part of the armorial bearings of his family. Bishop Brown, who flourished in the end of the fifteenth century, rendered himself equally worthy of the praise of history, by sending preachers, who understood the Erse language, into the Highlands, to instruct the benighted Gael. In the early part of the sixteenth century, the see of Dunkeld was honoured by no less distinguished an occupant than Gawin Douglas, a younger son of the Earl of Angus, the translator of Virgil into the Scottish language, and author of many beautiful original poems. At the epoch of the Reformation, the revenues of the see amounted to upwards of L.1600. In the period of Episcopacy prior to the Revolution of 1688, so poor was the benefice, that the king, as is understood by an entry in the secretary's books, had to make a gift of L.100 to the incumbent. Since the Reformation, the cathedral, has gone, in a great measure, to ruins. The architecture is partly Saxon, and partly Gothic, like most of the abbeys. The choir, which was built, as just mentioned, by King Robert's bishop, is still entire, and converted into the parish church, and very elegantly fitted up. The pile of building is about two hundred feet long, and sixty feet wide. On the north side of the choir is the charter-house, built by Bishop Lauder in 1649 ; the vault of which is now used as the burying place of the Atholl family. In the porch of the present church is the tomb of Alexander Stewart, a younger son of Robert II., and called, on account of his ferocious character, the Wolf of Badenoch. Among the departed who repose in the consecrated earth of the cathedral, lie the remains of Mrs Margery Scott, who died in 1728, on whom Pennant wrote the following epitaph :—

" Stop passenger, until my life you read ;
The living may get knowledge from the dead ;
Five times five years unwedded was my life ;
Five times five years I was a virtuous wife ;
Ten times five years I wept a widow's woes ;
Now tir'd of human scenes I here repose.
Betwixt my cradle and my grave was seen
Seven mighty kings of Scotland and a queen.
Full twice five years the Commonwealth I saw,
Ten times the subjects rise against the law,

And, which is worse than any civil war,
A king arraign'd before the subjects' bar;
Swarms of sectarians, hot with hellish rage,
Cut off his royal head upon the stage.
Twice did I see old Prelacy pull'd down,
And twice the cloak did sink beneath the gown.
I saw the Stuart race thrust out ; nay, more,
I saw our country sold for English ore ;
Our numerous nobles who have famous been,
Sunk to the lowly number of sixteen.
Such desolations in my days have been,
I have an end of all perfection seen."

The situation of the cathedral, in the midst of a fine grove, on the left
bank of the Tay, and just within the whisper of the town, and yet seques-
tered from its gaze, is well calculated to delight the imagination.   The
bridge of Tay, at this place, is a splendid structure of seven arches, built
in 1809, and the expense of which was chiefly disbursed by the late public-
spirited Duke of Atholl, government contributing only L.5000, while
fully six times as much was given by his Grace, not to speak of a great
sacrifice of property made by the latter at the same time.   A secondary
seat of the Athole family stands near the town, connected with which are
a series of pleasure grounds, and succession of walks and rides, which
may well be pronounced without parallel in Scotland for the many beautiful and romantic, or wild and grand prospects, which they open up.   A
splendid mansion, projected by the late Duke, was stopped in consequence of his death, after considerable progress had been made in
the building, which it was supposed would cost about L.100,000.   The
Bran, a tributary of Tay, runs through the grounds, forming at one spot
a cascade of famed merit, which is rendered additionally attractive by a
beautiful and elegant erection called Ossian's Hall, built by the late Duke
for the convenience of seeing the natural wonders of the scene to the best
advantage.   The tourist is brought into Ossian's Hall before he knows
that the fall is near, and then, upon a shutter being withdrawn, the tremendous scene of cascades thunders before him in all its magnificence.
About a mile farther up the stream, a chasm of fifteen feet wide is span-
ned by an arch called the Rumbling Bridge, above which the water pours
down over a bed charged with massive fragments of rock, making that
peculiar sound which is indicated by the name given to the arch-way.
The lines of walk through these delightful pleasure-grounds are said to
be altogether about eighty miles in length.   Many objects of course are
pointed out in them by guides, which we do not find it necessary to allude
to more particularly ; but it is impossible to omit noticing the extensive
and enchanting prospects which are obtained by climbing the neighbouring hills, particularly that called Craigie-Barns.   Dunkeld was the scene

of a remarkable historical incident, which took place on the 21st of August 1689. A single regiment (the Camerons, now the 26th) having been absurdly exposed here, to garrison the place against the remains of that Highland army with which Lord Dundee had endeavoured to oppose the revolution settlement, the mountaineers came down in great numbers and attacked it. Being chiefly Scottish Presbyterians, and therefore inspired with strong sentiments of antipathy against the cavalier Highlanders, these poor men fought most desperately, and finally maintained their post in Dunkeld house, though at the expense of their brave commander, Lieutenant-Colonel Cleland. A handsome new edifice is occupied by a branch of the Central Bank of Scotland.

THE COUNTY.

Perthshire is one of the largest counties in Scotland, and one which contains a much greater variety of territory than any other. Situated in the centre of the kingdom, it may be said in some measure to connect its great northern and southern divisions. It may also be considered an inland district, because, although it comes into contact with the estuaries of two great rivers, it in no quarter extends to the shore of the ocean. Extending from the Firth of Forth on one hand, to the wilds of Inverness-shire on the other, and from the eastern district of Angus to the western one of Argyle, it measures from east to west seventy-seven miles, while its extreme breadth is not less than sixty-eight miles. Altogether it comprehends 5000 square miles, that is 3,200,000 Scottish, or 4,068,640 English acres. It is bounded on the east by the county of Forfar; on the south-east by the counties of Fife and Kinross,—the Firth of Tay causing a considerable separation between it and Fifeshire. It is further bounded on the south by the Forth and the county of Stirling, and also by the small county of Clackmannan, which it embraces on two sides. It is bounded on the south-west by Dumbartonshire; on the west by Argyle-shire; and on the north-west and north by Inverness-shire. In every respect, situation included, Perthshire may be regarded the *Yorkshire* of Scotland. Like that immense county, it is subdivided into districts, which were formerly stewartries under the jurisdiction of different great landed proprietors, but which, since the abolition of the heritable jurisdictions, have only been preserved in popular parlance. The names of the various districts are Monteith, Gowrie, Perth proper, Strathearn, the Stormont, Breadalbane, Rannoch, Balquhidder, and Athole; and all these give, or have given, titles to various noble families. These districts do not include the portion which lies on the Firth of Forth.

This large county, in a general sense, rests upon a south-eastern exposure, as the whole of its waters flow in that direction. From its high western boundary the whole waters of the shire descend towards the German ocean on the east, whereas the waters of Argyleshire flow in an opposite direction to the Atlantic. Thus the western boundary of Perthshire appears to have been pointed out by nature as a line of separation between the eastern and western sides of the island.   With the exception of that portion on the Forth, the whole of the county may be described as that territory in Scotland whose waters descend into the river Tay, and by their confluence form that mighty stream.   The heads of this river, and of the waters which flow into it, do indeed, in almost every direction, constitute the boundaries of the shire.

As regards physical distinction, Perthshire is divided into highland and lowland districts.   The vast range of the Grampian mountains runs along the northern and north-western part of the county, and a large portion of the area of Perthshire is occupied by these mountains.   The territory to the south-east of the Grampians is considered as belonging to the Lowlands.   Eighteen parishes in Perthshire belong to the Highlands, and fifty-eight to the Lowlands ; but the Highland parishes are of great extent, and some of them cover a tract of country equal to eight or ten parishes in the lower and more fertile districts.   Thus the parish of Blair in Athole is not less than thirty miles in length and eighteen in breadth, and the parish of Fortingal is fully thirty-seven miles in length, by seventeen in breadth, including the districts of Glenlyon, Rannoch, &c.

In regard to its natural features, Perth is esteemed a county of first-rate interest.   Lying, as we have said, partly in the Highlands and partly in the Lowlands, it comprehends scenery of every description of excellence, from the wild and romantic, down to the beautiful and champaign.   On account of its inland situation, it of course does not comprise any specimens of that singular combination of marine and mountain scenery, which forms the great attraction of the West Highlands.   Yet, as it abounds in inland lakes, and possesses rising grounds of fully as stern and grand a character as that district, it is in no respect inferior as the object of " a tour in search of the picturesque," while its splendid plains may be said to form an additional attraction.   Among the more striking scenery of the county may be noticed the famous Pass of Killiecrankie, in the district of Atholl, formed by a narrow vale or chasm, through which flows the tumultuous river Garry, a tributary of the Tay, and which, moreover, forms part of the great access to the Highlands between Perth and Inverness.   Previous to the general revival of the Highland roads, this pass was the most wild in appearance, and the most dangerous, in the whole of the north of Scotland ; the road being led along a narrow tract on the left bank of the river, with a stupendous precipice rising almost perpendicularly above it.   Here the bold dark hills which range along the banks of the Garry on both sides, advance so near, and start up with such perpendicular majesty, that the eagles call to each other from their various tops, and the shadow of the left range lies in everlasting gloom upon the face of the right. The road now passes along the brink of a precipitous brae on the north-east side, the bare steep face of the hill rising above, and the deep black waters of the Garry tumbling below, while the eye and the imagination are impressed by the wildness of dusky foliage which clothes the opposite hills. This road, formerly so difficult and dangerous, is now no longer terrible, unless to an imagination unaccustomed to such wild scenes. The Pass of Killiecrankie, which extends two or three miles in length, is remarkable as giving name to a battle fought on the rough ground at its north-west extremity, July 27, 1689, between the forces of General Mackay, commander of the government troops for the protection of the Revolution settlement, and the Highlanders, who assembled under Viscount Dundee, in behalf of King James VII. The former being defeated, were driven back through the vale, amidst whose tortuous and contracted recesses great numbers were slain by the pursuing Highlanders. On the other hand, the cause of King James suffered more by the death of Dundee, who was killed by a musket ball near Urrard House, while cheering on his men to victory. So dreaded was the Pass of Killiecrankie by regular soldiers after this event, that, in 1740, when the Hessian troops, furnished to this country to assist in the suppression of the insurrection, were brought to enter the Highlands at this point, they started back and returned to Perth, declaring it to be the *ne plus ultra* of a civilized country.

The soil of Perthshire consists of all the varieties known in Scotland, the carse and loamy being prevalent on the banks of the rivers, and sandy and tilly soil on the sides of the hills. In many parts of the county are extensive mosses, particularly in Monteith, in which is situated the moss of Kincardine or Blair Drummond. In former times the greater part of Perthshire, like the adjacent county of Fife, was covered with woods, which the progress of agriculture has in many districts removed; but in every moss, in the flat land, in the valley, or on the tops of hills, roots and trunks of large trees are found. Besides the detached woods in the country, there are extensive forests in Breadalbane and in Monteith. Within the last sixty years, there has been a great deal of planting in Perthshire, greatly to the advantage of the climate and agriculture. Of the different noblemen and gentlemen who devoted their attention to this species of improvements, none acted so distinguished a part as the late Duke of Athole. It appears from an abstract made in 1830, of this nobleman's woods and forests, that they consist of 13,378 Scottish acres—of which the whole, except about 1000 acres, were planted by the late Duke after his accession in 1774. Thus, his Grace planted the enormous quantity of 15,473 English acres; and allowing 2000 plants to a Scottish acre, the number of trees planted will amount to 24,756,000. But the number in reality is much more, as ten per cent. may be allowed for making good; so that the number may be stated at 27,231,600. Of these plantations, the principal portion, to the amount of about 8600 acres, are of larch; about 1000 acres are of oak; the remainder are of Scottish fir, spruce fir, a few acres of birch, &c. The same patriotic nobleman exerted himself to improve the roads of Perthshire, and by his means the road affairs of the county were brought into excellent condition.

The loftiest mountains in Perthshire are Ben Lawers, 4015 feet in height; Ben More, 3903; Schihallion, 3564; Ben Gloa, 3724; Ben Ledi, 3009; Ben Venue, 3000; and Ben Chonzie in Strathearn, 2922. The classic Hill of Dunsinane lies about eight miles north from Perth. It is of a conical form, and rises 1034 feet above the level of the sea. The top is flat and verdant, as are also its sides, though much broken by projecting masses of rock. There is now very little trace left of the immense stronghold built there by Macbeth for protection from the indignation of his people, and the attack of King Malcolm. The ascent is exceedingly difficult on all sides, except that leading from Collace. Birnam Hill is situated about twelve miles north-west from Dunsinane, in the parish of Little Dunkeld.

The chief lakes of the county are Loch Katrine, Loch Achray, Loch Ard, Loch Voil, Loch Lubnaig, Loch Dochart, and Lochearn, in the south-west quarter; Loch Tay in the centre of the western mountainous district; and Loch Rannoch, Loch Ericht, and Loch Lydoch, (the two latter in part only), in the north-western districts. In the lower divisions there are numerous smaller and less important lakes. Immediately to the east of Loch Katrine is the singular piece of scenery called the Trosachs, which may be described as a valley covered with large fragments of rock, and flanked with naked precipices, amidst which grow many beautiful trees and shrubs, giving a delightful air of softness to what would otherwise be a scene of untamed and savage magnificence. The banks of Loch Katrine consist of slopes descending from the neighbouring mountains, the most of which are covered with beautiful natural woods, and supply innumerable picturesque points of view to the tourist. Formerly, the extraordinary beauty of this Highland paradise lay entirely concealed and unknown; but since the publication of Sir Walter Scott's poem, the Lady of the Lake, of which it was the scene, it has become a favourite object to tourists, and is daily visited by multitudes during the summer and autumn. A good road is now formed between Callander and Loch Katrine, and also along its northern bank; and the conveniency of a boat to traverse the lake from one end to the other may at all times be had by tourists, whether they approach from the east or west extremity. A tract of three or four miles of mountain road intervenes between Loch Katrine and Loch Achray. There is also an excellent inn at the latter, near the east end of the lake. It affords a curious notion of the late indifference of the people of Scotland to their own beautiful scenery, that a place of such transcendant loveliness as this should have continued, till a recent period, to exist within sixty miles of the capital, and between twenty and thirty of Stirling, without being accessible by a road. Near the east end of Loch Katrine is a beautiful little island, which has evidently supplied the poet with the imaginary residence of his fair Naiad of the Lake. The neighbouring country was formerly possessed by the Macgregors.

The chief running waters of Perthshire are the Tay, the Earn, the Dochart, the Almond, the Garry, the Tummel, the Bran, the Bruar, the Ericht, the Ardle, the Shee, and the Isla, besides innumerable third and fourth-rate rivers, and streamlets of all sizes. The river Forth, from rising in Stirlingshire, is not considered a Perthshire river, though it flows along a large portion of its south-west quarter.

Perthshire abounds in game of nearly every description, though the larger species are now considerably diminished in numbers. The red deer or stag may be said to inhabit the forests and mountain glades in the most perfect state of nature and wildness; it is cautious in the extreme, and singularly jealous of the human form, eluding with wonderful effect the wiles of the sportsman. A variety of other game are also inhabitants of these wilds. Among the rest the roe, a much more familiar animal than the stag, appearing, even in summer, in the woodlands and plantations of the valleys, down to the habitable places; nevertheless, their aversion to restraint is such that they may be said to be untameable.

The subject of the mineralogy of this county affords sufficient materials to excite and to reward the curiosity of the scientific student of the works of nature; but in a political or economical point of view, its minerals are of no great importance. At Culross, upon the Forth, coal has been wrought for ages; but as it is situated at a detached corner between the counties of Fife and Clackmannan, it is of little importance to Perthshire. The Carse of Gowrie, and the country around Perth, are supplied with coal by sea from the southern coast of Fife, or from England. From the ports of Dundee and Perth, coal is conveyed overland, along Strathearn and Strathmore, to a great distance. The districts of Monteith and Strathallan are supplied from the coal-works in Clackmananshire. In consequence of this want of coal, by far the greater part of the county is exposed to great disadvantages. Peat is the fuel generally consumed by the common people in all the inland districts, together with such brushwood as can be obtained. In such a northern climate, the difficulty of obtaining fuel operates severely on all sorts of arts and industry. Even agriculture proceeds under great disadvantages where it is not easily obtained; a great part of the summer is consumed in the Highland and all upland districts, in digging, drying, and carrying peats. Neither can that important ingredient, lime, be obtained for carrying on improvements in agriculture where coal is wanting. Limestone rocks are found in a variety of districts, both in the Highlands and in the low country; but the use of lime is greatly restrained on account of the difficulty of calcination, peat being a weak and ineffectual agent for this purpose. Limestone is found in the Highland districts, such as Rannoch, Glenlyon, and Breadalbane, and the head of Strathearn. In Monteith is a quarry of beautiful limestone, of the density of marble, of a blue ground, variegated with streaks of white; it is found on the estate of Leny. Marble of a superior quality is also worked on the property of the Duke of Athole, near Glentilt. Large beds of fire clay have been discovered near Culross; and in that neighbourhood, on the Devon, there is abundance of ironstone. Slates are found in a variety of situations. Of these, the blue slates have been found at Birnam near Dunkeld, in Monteith, and along the north side of the Ochils; also in Monteith, as well as in Strathallan and Strathearn, gray slates are abundantly diffused. Near Drummond Castle, and more particularly near Callander, that species of rock called *brecia* or *plum-pudding stone*, is frequent. It is a composition consisting of a great variety of small stones of different colours and sizes, so firmly cemented together by a brown substance, that when used in buildings it resists the influence of the weather for ages. This kind of stone, together with the slate and limestone, run in three parallel veins, at the distance of a mile from each other, to a very great length in a north-eastern direction from Dumbartonshire. There seems to run parallel to these on the east, a chain of sandstone from Gartree to the vicinity of Crieff. At the south-east corner of the county, upon the Tay, is one of the best and most celebrated stone quarries in the country. This stone, called the Kingoodie stone, is of a greyish colour, difficult to work, and hard and durable in an uncommon degree; so much so, that the fine old tower, the steeple of Dundee, built with it, has, after the lapse of so many centuries, scarcely shown any symptom of decay. The principal stone of which the Grampians consist is granite; and it is remarkable, that as the coal field of Scotland terminates to the southward of the Ochils, the sandstone, or freestone, seems in a great measure to terminate at the next parallel ridge northward, that is, the Grampians. It is not a little singular, that the

2 o

same territory formed in ancient times the boundary between the forests of fir-trees, which in ancient times covered the north of Scotland, and the forests of oak, and other deciduous trees, that covered the whole of Scotland to the south of the Grampians.

The monuments of antiquity in this county are sufficiently numerous to afford a field of curious investigation. Lying to the northward of the Roman wall, Perthshire was the scene of the last struggle for independence which the inhabitants of the low country of Scotland made against the Roman arms. The last and most distinguished battle fought by the Britons was that against Agricola, under a leader to whom the Romans have given the name of Galgacus. The scene of this struggle, is, however, much disputed. The Roman road along Strathearn towards Perth is still to be traced, and also from Perth along Strathmore to the northern extremity of the county. The remains of several camps are still to be seen, in particular at Ardoch, this being the chief in Scotland. The station is on the right of the great military road from Stirling, through Crieff, to the north Highlands, and close upon the little river Knaick, or Knaig, a feeder of the Allan, which falls into the Forth. This station is supposed to have been founded by Agricola in one of his northern campaigns, perhaps in his fourth. It was on a road carried by the Romans from the wall erected by them between the Firths of Forth and Clyde into Strathmore beyond the Tay, and which crosses the river Knaig immediately below the station. The west side of the camp is protected by the river Knaig, the banks of which are very steep. The level of the camp is sixty feet above the river. The prætorium, which has from time immemorial been called Chapel Hill, has been at some time enclosed with a stone wall, and has the foundations of a house ten yards by seven. The whole station has been of late years enclosed with a high stone wall, There is said to be on one side of the prætorium a subterraneous passage, supposed to extend under the bed of the river; but the entrance having been closed about 1720, to prevent hares, when pursued, from taking refuge there, it is not known where the passage is. Search has been made for it, but in vain. Previous to its being closed, a man who had been condemned in the baron court of some neighbouring lord, consented, upon condition of pardon, to explore it; but after bringing out some Roman spears, helmets, and bits of bridles and other things, he descended again and was killed by the foul air. These interesting articles to the antiquary, were carried off by the Duke of Argyle's soldiers after the battle of Sheriff-muir, and were never recovered. The camps are a little way north of the station on the way to Crieff, and are of different magnitudes. The largest of them has a mean length of

2800 feet, and a mean breadth of 1950, and was calculated to hold be-tweem 25,000 and 26,000 men. The military road enters the camp by the south gate, and has levelled half of the small work which covered it, leaving the other half of it standing.

The county also possesses antiquarian remains of a later age and his-tory, in the shape of ruined towers and religious structures, the district having once been the residence of a number of powerful chiefs, and of a large body of churchmen. Before the Reformation, and while Episcopacy was established, Perthshire formed the ample diocese of a bishop, whose seat was at Dunkeld, as well as another diocese of a bishop at Dunblane.

Within the last half century a prodigious improvement has taken place in the agriculture of Perthshire, the lower parts of which, especially in the Carse of Gowrie, and in the lower part of the Earn, vie in rural wealth, cultivation, and beauty, with any district in Scotland. Owing probably to the flat clayey land, and the almost impassible state of the roads, the inhabitants of the Carse were noted in public obloquy for their stupidity and churlishness; and "Carles of the Carse" used to be a com-mon appellative for them not more alliterative than true. Pennant records a proverb respecting them that supports the same theory, namely, "that they wanted fire in the winter, water in the summer, and the grace of God all the year round." Whether there be now, or ever were, any real grounds for these charges against the people of this blessed and beautiful spot, we shall not take it upon us to determine, but shall relate an anec-dote, to prove that examples of retributive wit were not unknown among them. A landed proprietor in the Carse used to rail in unmeasured terms against the people, alleging that their stupidity was equally beyond all precedent and all correction. "In short," said he, "I believe I could make a more sensible race of people out of the very soil which I employ them to cultivate." This expression having got wind amongst the people, excited no little indignation. Soon after, the gentleman in question had the misfortune to fall from his horse, into a clayey hole or pit, from which, after many hours' struggling, he found it impossible to extricate himself. A countryman coming past, he called to him for assistance. The man approached, took a grave glance at his figure, which presented a complete mass of clay, and coolly remarked, as he passed on, "Oh, I see you're *making your men*, laird; I'll no disturb ye."

The upper county is still, of course, devoted to the pasturing of sheep and cattle, which are chiefly driven southward for sale and consumption. The agricultural character of the county has in recent times been much enhanced by the active exertions of various local associations. The prin-cipal object of industry in the villages and towns of Perthshire is the linen manufacture, of much the same fabric as that which forms the staple manufacture of Forfarshire. In aid of this branch of industry, there are a considerable number of bleachfields in the county.

Perthshire contains only two royal burghs, namely, Perth and Culross, the latter a small decayed town on the Firth of Forth : but it possesses many considerable towns or large populous villages, including several burghs of barony. The following places may be noticed, among many others :—Auchterarder, Blackford, Auchtergaven, Stanley, Blairgowrie, Comrie, Callander, Crieff, Coupar-Angus, Doune, Bridge of Earn, Dunblane, Dunkeld, Dunning, Errol, Fortingal, Kenmore, Killin, Kincardine, Meigle, Methven, Muthil, Rattray, Tibbermuir, Scone, Thornhill, &c. Of these, Blairgowrie claims to be distinguished. Situated at the foot of the Grampians, it commands a delightful view of the noble valley of Strathmore, its elevated situation rendering the air very salubrious, while the impetuous current of the "ireful Ericht" yields a never-failing source of wealth to its enterprising inhabitants, by affording water power to impel numerous lint spinning-mills. Fifteen of these are in full operation, and some very extensive ones are in course of erection, in the immediate neighbourhood ; and at a short distance on the Lochty, several others are established. Blairgowrie is perhaps the most flourishing town in the county. The railway now forming between Newtyle and the neighbouring town of Coupar Angus, by connecting it more intimately with the flourishing port of Dundee, will still add to its prosperity. Blairgowrie was made a borough of barony by a charter from Charles I. in 1634. There are the remains of several Druidical temples in the parish. At the back of the manse, in 1796, there was a moat-hill or circular mound, where, it is said, Earl Gowrie held his regality courts. There are also some cairns, in one of which, when opened, a small stone coffin was found at the bottom ; and many tumuli run through the parish. Not far from the village, commanding a fine view of Strathmore, is Newton House, built somewhat in the style of a castle, on the foundation of the old house, in a vault of which many gentlemen were saved while it was burned down. The scenery in the neighbourhood of Blairgowrie, and along the banks of the Ericht, combine the beautiful and romantic. The neighbouring cliffs of Craighall would amply repay a day's journey, by a view of their wild grandeur.

The county is divided into ten districts, each under the jurisdiction of a justice of peace court, and a body of deputy lieutenants. The county is further divided into two sheriff-substituteships, the seat of the one being Perth, the other Dunblane. In the shire is a large association of landed gentlemen for the protection of game, woods, and plantations. The county gentlemen also form a Hunt, having races at Perth. Besides this, there is the Strathearn Coursing Club, and the Doune Club. Of those valuable associations, already alluded to, established for promoting improvements in matters connected with agriculture, the following may be named,—the Perthshire Farming Society, which meets at Perth four times in the year; the Strathearn Agricultural Society, which meets once a quarter; the Athole and Weem Agricultural Club, which meets annually in October, and has instituted annual competitions all over the Highlands of Perthshire; the Dumblane Farming Society, which meets in July to receive the report of the state of farms and crops, and in November to hear the report of stack-yards, turnips, &c., and holds a ploughing match in spring, when six prizes are distributed; the Carse of Gowrie Agricultural Society, which meets in the spring and autumn; the Strathmore Agricultural Society, which holds its numerous and respectable meetings in Coupar-Angus; and the Burrel Agricultural Ploughman Society. The present Noble Marquis of Breadalbane, since his accession to the title and estates, has laudably endeavoured to promote the improvement of the upper district of the county, by holding out every encouragement to industry and enterprise. Among others, two agricultural societies have recently been established, which hold their annual competitions at Kenmore and Killin. In the parish of Killin, on the river Fillans, or Water of Dochart, lies the village of that name. St Fillan was a pious abbot or friar, who, according to Keith, flourished in Scotland at the beginning of the eighth century, and was some time superior of a religious house at Pittenweem in Perth. It is told by the chroniclers that the miraculous powers of this person were of no ordinary kind. When at the priory of Pittenweem he engaged himself in transcribing the scriptures, and while doing so, his left hand was observed to send forth such a splendour as to afford him sufficient light to write with the other; a miracle which saved many candles in the priory, as the holy man used to spend whole nights at that exercise. He afterwards, for the sake of more perfect seclusion, and undisturbed devotion, retired from Fife to this wild vale. Here the saintly monk performed innumerable miracles through the excess of his devotion. On the top of a conical hill, named Dun-Fillan, a little way east from the village is shown a rock, called St Fillan's chair, from which he use to bestow his blessings on the country; and near it are two small cavities in the rock, said to have been worn out by his knees in his almost incessant praying. Adjacent, in the low ground, is also shown a pool, called the Holy Pool, which, through the saint's power, had the virtue of curing madness in persons bathing in it, provided a certain ceremonial was used. The Highlanders continued to dip lunatics in the sainted spring until a very late period. There is a bell belonging to the chapel of St Fillan, that was in high reputation among the votaries of that saint in old times. It seems to be of mixed metal: is about a foot and a half high, and of an oblong shape. It usually lay in the church-yard. When mad people were brought to be dipped in the Saint's Pool, it was necessary to perform certain ceremonies, in which there was a mixture of Druidism and Popery. After remaining all night in the chapel bound with ropes, the bell was set upon their head with great solemnity. It was the popular opinion, that if stolen, it would extricate itself out of the thief's hands, and return home ringing all the way. For some years past this bell has been locked up, to prevent its being applied to superstitious purposes. The origin of the bell is to be referred to the most remote ages of the Celtic churches. Six hundred years after the epoch of St Fillan, his memory and powers of intercession were vividly retained in the country. In the heat of the battle of Bannockburn, Robert Bruce invoked his aid, which, as he imagined, was granted, to the discomfiture of the English; and out of gratitude for such assistance, the patriotic king founded a priory near the ancient residence of the saint, which was dedicated to his service. At the dissolution of the religious houses, this priory, with all its revenues and superiorities, was given by the king to Campbell of Glenorchy, ancestor to the Earl of Breadalbane. The houses of the village have all gardens annexed to them, and are even in many cases surrounded more immediately by sweet shrubs and flowers. There are also a few villas built, for families who may be inclined to settle in this delicious spot. It is annually, in autumn, rendered the scene of high festival, by a meeting of the St Fillans' Society, which was instituted in 1819, for the purpose of giving prizes to successful competitors in certain national sports, and as a benefit society for imparting aid to indigent and distressed members, widows and orphans. Their festivities are usually attended by hundreds of persons of distiction, male and female, from all parts of the Highlands.

Upon the whole, it may be remarked of Perthshire, that this large and important district of Scotland exhibits every where striking manifestations of being in a thriving and prosperous condition, and offers a forcible example of what has been effected in meliorating and civilizing the country—in the exchange of a life of almost savage strife, ignorance, and poverty, for one of intelligence, peace, and all the comforts to be procured by industry—within the brief space of little more than a century.

For several years prior to the passing of the Reform Bill, the county was represented in Parliament by Sir George Murray; and, politically speaking, Perthshire was considered eminently a stronghold of Conservatism. The Marquis of Breadalbane, then Earl of Ormelie, by carrying the first popular election, succeeded in wiping out this obnoxious appellation. On the accession of his Lordship to the peerage, Sir George succeeded once more to the representation of the county ; but his triumph on this occasion was short-lived, having within a few months, to give way before a liberal candidate, in the person of the Honourable Mr Maule.

APPENDIX.

No. I.

BRIEF HISTORY OF PERTH.

In order to connect the reminiscences of the manners of the inhabitants, and occurrences, which have been detailed in the foregoing chapters, the following brief history of the city is appended : For the information contained in this and some of the preceding sketches, we have been greatly indebted to Chamber's excellent Gazetteer of Scotland :—

Perth occupies a low situation on the right bank of the Tay, almost twenty-eight miles above its confluence with the sea, and at the distance of 43¼ miles north from Edinburgh, by the Queensferry road, 61 from Glasgow, and 21¼ west from Dundee. It is situated near the southern boundary of a very spacious plain, and is surrounded by soft and far-stretching acclivities, whose sides, thickly ornamented by bower-like villas, hedge it in with a splendid cincture of picturesque and beautiful scenery. Boasting of the most remote antiquity, Perth is hallowed by many delightful recollections ; and it is almost impossible to say whether, by a visit to it, sight or sentiment is most to be gratified. The origin of Perth is as obscure as the etymology of its name, both being the subject of contest by antiquaries and philologists ; and out of the vast mass of disputatious matter it is difficult for the statist to extract any thing distinct or satisfactory. From the notices of early historians, we are led to suppose that the Romans had a settlement in or near the spot where the modern city of Perth now stands. Adamson, in his Muses' Threnodie,—or Metrical History of Perth, written in the year 1620,—embodies the current tradition of the origin of Perth, of which the following is the purport :—" Cneius Julius Agricola, in the third year after Vespasian had sent him to be governor in Brtain, namely, about the year 81 of the Christian era, led a numerous army round by the pass of Stirling into the country on the north side of the Forth. Penetrating northwards, they approached the place on which Perth is now built, and when they first came in sight of the Tay and this beautiful plain, they cried out with one consent, " Ecce Tiber ! Ecce campus Martius."—Behold the Tiber ! Behold the Field of Mars ! comparing what they saw to their own river, and to the extensive plain in the neighbourhood of Rome. Agricola pitched his camp in the middle of that field, on the spot where Perth stands. He proposed to make it a winter camp, and afterwards built what he intended should be a colonial town. He fortified it with walls, and with a strong castle, and supplied the ditches with water by an aqueduct from the Almond. Also, with much labour to his soldiers, and probably to the poor natives, a large wooden bridge was constructed over the river at Perth."

Whether Perth originated in a settlement of the Romans, or arose from the gradual erection of the aboriginal Picts, it made no figure as a town till the Scoto-Saxon period. To render its early history still more obscure, a story is related by Boece, and other venerable romancers, about a place called Bertha, a Roman town, said to have been situated on the point of land formed by the confluence of the Almond and Tay, a few miles above the present Perth. " This city," we are informed, " was swept away by a flood about the year 1210. after which the modern Bertha or Perth arose under the auspices of William the Lion." Fordun, with an equal claim to credit, tells us that the Tay was for ages called the Tiber by the Italian writers, which he proves by saying, that hence arose the name Tibbermuir, a place in its vicinity; whereas, had he understood Gaelic, he would have known that Tibber-muir, or Tipper-muir, simply signifies " the well in the muir." If we discard Bertha as an etymology, there is none other left; the Highlanders, it is true, always called Perth *Peirt*, or *Peart*, which by some is construed into " finished labour," or " a complete piece of work;" but this hardly clears up the etymon. Much of the fable and conjecture of the antiquary connected with Perth, has been overthrown by the reverend and learned Mr Scott, author of the Statistical Account, who mentions that " it is certain that the town had the name of Perth, long before the year 1210. There are many hundreds of charters, from the year 1106 to the year 1210, still extant. Any person who will take the trouble of looking into these charters, will find, that whenever there is occasion to mention the town, its name was always written Perth, or Pertht, or by way of contraction, Pert. There was no noble person who gave his name to Perth: but there were some persons who took their surname from the town. It is also certain, that tenements and streets in Perth are described in charters prior to the year 1210, the same as they afterwards were." Until the period of the murder of James I. at Perth, in 1436-7, the place enjoyed in many respects the character of a capital, or seat of government. It having been found that neither Perth nor Stirling, Scone nor Dunfermline, had the power of protecting royalty against the designs of the nobility, Edinburgh and its castle were chosen as the only places of safety for the royal household and functionaries of the Scottish government. Until this event, Perth was deemed the first town of the kingdom, the sovereign residing very frequently in the place, and being crowned at the neighbouring palace of Scone. Perth was, on these accounts, the appropriate place where great national councils were held, from the time of Malcolm IV. until the second of the Jameses, and occasionally till the era of James IV. Perth was likewise the chosen seat of national assemblies of the church, some of which were called or presided over by nuncios of the Pope. It seems that before and after the contests for the crown, by the demise of Alexander III., the town possessed the popular name of St Johnstoun, an appellation derived from the saint to whom the principal church and the bridge over the Tay were dedicated; but though this name appears to have been common enough, and was even used by some historians, the place was never so called in any of the public writs. In allusion to the patron saint of the church and the bridge, if not the town also, the common seal of Perth prior to the year 1600, as appears from impressions appended to charters, represented the decollation of St John the Baptist; Salome standing by with a platter in her hand to receive the head. On the reverse, it represented the same saint enshrined, and a number of priests or other persons kneeling before him. The legend round both sides—*S. communitatis villæ Sancti Johannis Baptistæ de Berth*, "the seal of the community of the town of St John Baptist of Berth." This "superstitious seal" was laid aside after the Reformation, and that since used refers to the Roman origin of the town, being a double imperial eagle, charged with a Holy Lamb passant, carrying the banner of St Andrew, with the legend, *Pro Rege, Lege, et Grege.* Perth was in early times a place of great trade. Alexander Neckham, an English writer, who was abbot of Exeter in 1215, takes notice of Perth in the following distich, quoted in Camden's Britannia :

> " Trans ampli Tai, per rura, per oppida, per Perth :
> Regnum sustentant illius urbis opes."

Which has been thus translated by Bishop Gibson :

> Great Tay through Perth, through town, through countries flies;
> Perth the whole kingdom with her wealth supplies.

It seems, an extensive commerce was carried on during many ages between Perth and the Netherlands. The merchants of Perth visited in their own ships the Hans towns. And it is a part of the eulogium conferred on Alexander III., that he devised successful measures for securing these and all other Scottish trading ships from pirates and foreign detention. The German merchants, or Flemings, as they were called, very early frequented the port of Perth; and not a few of these industrious foreigners fixed their abode in the town, and introduced the manufacture of woollen and linen goods. As may be supposed, the intrusion of these peaceful artizans alarmed the natives of the place, and excited the ignorant legislature of the period. David I. laid restrictions on their traffic, and his grandson William the Lion, perhaps to procure the favour of the burgesses, denied them the privilege of entering themselves freemen of the corporations. The Flemings, however, found favour with the more enlightened monarchs of England, who, by encouraging their settlement, laid the foundation of the cloth manufactures of that part of the island. Perth comes prominently into notice in the history of the war of Scottish independence, or struggle for the crown between Bruce and the Edwards. After the unfortunate battle of Falkirk in 1298, Edward I. reduced all the fortresses in Scotland, but fortified Perth, and rebuilt the walls in the strongest manner. It was often the residence of his deputies, and his son Edward lived here some years. On the return of Robert Bruce from his expedition into England, in 1312, he again turned himself to the conquest of his castles, and the expulsion of the English garrisons. Of these places of strength, Perth was found to have the most impregnable fortifications, and the largest garrison. Although repeatedly assailed by the Scottish forces since their first successes in the north, it had still withstood all their efforts, unassisted as these were by the military engines then in use for battering or scaling the walls, and for discharging stones and other missiles. In the end of the year of his first expedition into England, Bruce again invested the town of Perth with the most powerful force that he could muster. For a considerable time he pressed the siege with the utmost vigour, but still ineffectually, because he wanted the necessary engines ; and because the garrison, and the rest of the people within the town, were too vigilant to be surprised by stratagem. Again he was reluctantly obliged to withdraw his troops, and to retire, lest famine, and the diseases occasioned by long encampment on low marshy ground, in an inclement season, should cut off the flower of those brave and faithful followers, by whose aid he had now nearly reconquered Scotland. But no supplies came from England, to relieve or reinforce the garrison of Perth ; and Bruce would not desist from his purpose, or suffer this single-walled town to baffle him for ever. Providing himself with scaling ladders, and such other instruments as he could find, he speedily renewed the attack, at a time when those within the town were pleasing themselves with the persuasion, that they were inclosed within impregnable walls, and had no future siege to fear. He chose a dark night, and, in its silence, with a chosen band, conducted them in person, partly wading, partly swimming, across a ditch, deep, broad, and full of water, that surrounded the walls. The rest were animated on this, as on many other occasions, by the example of the daring valour with which the king exposed himself foremost to the danger. The contest among them, was who should first cross the ditch, and, by the scaling ladders which they carried with them mount the walls. This gallant and perilous enterprise succeeded. The king himself was the second to enter the town. The garrison and the townsmen were easily overpowered. In the castle, and in the stores of the merchants was found a supply of those things which the captors wanted most, for the relief of their own necessities. The slaughter of the vanquished was humanely stayed, as the resistance ceased. The houses were burnt, and the walls and fortifications levelled with the ground. By this happy achievement, all Perthshire and Strathearn were freed from servitude to the English, and reduced under the authority of King Robert. In the year 1332, Edward Baliol, after his success at the battle of Dupplin, had taken possession of Perth, and was crowned at Scone. Immediately after his coronation he returned southward, to open a communication with the English marches, and a party of loyal adherents to the interests of David Bruce concerted a sudden enterprise against the slender garrison left by the usurper in the town of Perth. Its temporary fortifications were unfit to resist a siege ; it was garrisoned by few else besides the family and vassals of the Earl of Fife, who, from being the prisoner had become the partisan of Baliol. By stratagem, however, probably, rather than regular assault, it was quickly taken by the besiegers. Perth was again the scene of some stirring events in 1339. In the beginning of that year, after the death of the Regent, Andrew Murray, the regency was conferred on Robert, the Lord High Stewart, afterwards king, who was but a youth. He resolved to distinguish himself by opening the siege of Perth, which Edward and his engineers had fortified with uncommon skill, and provided with an excellent garrison. The defence they made for three months was so brave, that the High Steward was about to raise the siege, when Douglas, Lord Liddesdale, arrived from France, whither he was sent on an embassy to David Bruce, bringing with him five (Fordun says two) ships, with a supply of men and provisions. The siege was renewed with vigour. Douglas was wounded in the leg by a shot of a cross-bow, while he was going to the escalade. When the siege had lasted four months, and was likely to have continued much longer, the Earl of Ross, by digging mines, drew away the water, and dried up the fosses and ditches, so that the soldiers, approaching the walls on dry ground, beat off the defenders with arrows and darts shot out of engines made for that purpose. The governor, Sir Thomas Ochtred, with his garrison, seeing the city untenable, surrendered, having stipulated for the safety of their lives and estates. Some marched off by land, and others were provided with shipping to England. Douglas rewarded the French liberally and sent them back to France well pleased. He caused also to be delivered to Hugh Hambel, their commander, one of the best of his ships, which was taken by the English during the siege. Hambel had adventured to approach the town with his ships, to give an assault ; one of which was taken, and now restored.

A singular combat took place on the North Inch at Perth in the reign of Robert III., which, from the singularity of the circumstances attending it, has furnished the Author of Waverley with a theme in the novel styled " the Fair Maid of Perth."   There was a dreadful feud between the clan Kay and the clan Chattan, which both parties at length agreed to decide by a personal combat of thirty picked men, in the presence of the king, at this public place.   When the combat was about to commence, it was discovered that one of the clan Chattan had absconded through fear ; but the dilemma thus occasioned was obviated by a saddler of Perth, by name Harry Wynde, who offered to take the place of the runaway for half a French gold dollar ; terms to which the clan Chattan were obliged to accede, because no individual of the opposite party would retire in order to bring the parties upon an equality.   The combat was commenced and carried on with fearful fury on both sides, until twenty-nine of the clan Kay were slain.   The remaining single combatant, then wisely judging that he could not resist the impetuosity of Harry Wynde, and the ten of the clan Chattan who were left alive, jumped into the river Tay, swam to the other side, and escaped.

It appears that the reformed doctrines were early embraced by many of the citizens of Perth, and that few places suffered so severely from the vengeance of the Romish church.*   The following extract from the

---

* It would appear from the following passage, in Professor Tullideph's M. S. account of the Reformation at Perth, published in Colonel Murray's splendid work on the National Views of Scotland ; that Perth, at this time, must have been nearly overwhelmed with the extent of her saintly blessings.   The place seems to have been a perfect nest of monkish establishments.   Their numbers are monstrous, when we take into account the limited size of the town at the time :—

" The religious communities with which Perth is surrounded are tearing asunder the bonds which erst united her citizens together, and those gorgeous buildings you now admire, are become the pest houses from which evils innumerable are creeping out upon the land.   Yet there are not wanting moderate men amongst them who would willingly allow us liberty of conscience, if the more bigotted would but listen to them.   The Warden now of the Franciscan Observantine or Grey Friars' Monastery, that building you see nearest us outside the walls, (the parties are supposed to be looking from the south eastern shoulder of Kinnoul Hill), is well known to be the secret favourer of the new doctrines.   There are but eight of them in that huge house—good canty fellows all of them—known too, privately, to keep an excellent table, and willing to let all the world alone so that they are not disturbed at dinner time.   But then they are in constant dread of the fire-brands in that princely building you see on the same side of the town further to the west, who can write although their rules forbid them to speak.   Austere fellows they are these Carthusians—and pride themselves not a little on this, their only establishment in Scotland, and on the odour they and it are in with the Queen Regent.   But for all their austerity, there are queer stories told of them and the nuns in the Convents of St Leonards and the Magdalenes, both of which are a short distance to the southward ; they are hid from us just now by these trees on the left.   Certain jolly skippers, too, from the coast, from whom I sometimes get a keg of Nantz, under cover of a few oysters or haddocks, and who take my gloves and other leather articles of dress to Dundee—wink and glance knowingly towards this ' Monasterium vallis virtutis' as the monks call it, while they hint about the many good and ghostly customers they have in Perth.   Then there are these Dominicans, beggars they profess themselves, like the Franciscans, and sturdy ones they are ; see how comfortably they have set themselves down in that palace you see, without the walls, on the north side of the town—just over the Castle there.   Ah! these Black Friars are your men for the pulpit.   If you want a good easy confessor, go to the chapels of St. Paul's or St. Katherine's, you see peering above the trees, on the west side of the town, and there find one of the Carmelites, or White Friars, from Tullilumb, a

Memorabilia of Perth will fully illustrate the conflict of opinion on matters of religion in the town, and the severities practised :—" 1544. This was a busie year. Cardinal Bethune, in the last convention, having obtained an act in favour of the bishops and clergy, to persecute and punish heretics to death, came in January this year to Perth, with the Regent Hamilton, Earl of Arran, who was a weak man. Friar Spence accused Robert Lamb and his wife Helen Stark, William Anderson, James Ronald, James Hunter, and James Finlayson. Lamb and his wife were accused of interrupting Spence in a sermon, in which he taught that there was no salvation without intercession and prayers to the saints. They confessed the charge, declaring that it was the duty of every one who knows the truth to bear testimony to it, and not suffer people to be abused with false doctrine as that was. Anderson, Finlayson, and Ronald, were indicted for nailing two ram's horns to St Francis' head, putting a cow's rump to his tail, and eating a goose on All Hallow eve. Hunter, a butcher, simple and unlearned, was charged with haunting the company of the heretics. Helen Stark was further charged with refusing to pray to the Virgin Mary when in child-birth, and said that she would only pray to God in the name of Jesus Christ. They were all imprisoned in the Spy Tower, being found guilty and condemned. Great intercession was made to the Regent for them, who promised that they should not be hurt. The citizens, who were in a tumult, relying on a promise of Arran, dispersed and went peaceably home. The cardinal, who had the Regent in his power, had taken his measures. Determined to make an example

---

monastery still farther to the west, hid from us by the wood ; but if you want a discourse that will keep you quaking for a week, go to the church of the Dominicans. And well worthy, let me tell you, it is of a visit, such halls, such aisles, such windows :—the gardens too, and the gilten arbour ! No wonder our monarchs forsook that old gloomy Palace you see at the end of the bridge for the sweet arbours and soft beds of the Blackfriars, although James the First of blessed memory found it any thing but secure. But come," added the good humoured old man, " I forget that neither of us have broken our fast this morning yet. Let us be moving onwards, and as we descend the hill, I shall try to make you acquainted with others of these stately edifices, which you will, I hope, take many days to examine and note. There now, where will you find in Scotland, letting alone your Cathedrals, a more graceful fabric than the church of St. John, towering above all the other buildings, in the very centre of the town. It is well worthy of being dedicated to our tutelar Apostle, although, in truth, so many altars have been reared within it to other saints, that our great patron has scarcely been left a niche he can call his own—as if there were not chapels enough in the town beside. There you have the chapel of the Virgin close by the end of the bridge, where no traveller, however wearied, omits in passing to put up his Ave. Our own craft have a chapel dedicated to saint Bartholomew, whose flaying alive, strange enough, finds more sympathy among those who live by flaying than among any other craft. It is hid from us by the Castle walls, and there the bell which warns the inhabitants to go to bed betimes is hung. St. Anne, the mother of the Virgin, is honoured under those pinnacles you observe near the church of St. John. The School-house is just at hand, and in the sanctuary of this patroness of instructors, the little urchins are taught to mumble their paternosters, and receive a weekly lecture from some of the Friars appointed by the patrons. To the west again, besides the chapels of St. Paul and St. Katherine, already pointed out to you, outside the Walls, there is a Chapel of the Cross or Holyrood at the South-west Port—the resort of those who have heavy consciences and light purses. Nearer us, and not far distant from the Chartreux or Charthusian Monastery, you may observe a building with a spire in the form of a crown : that is the chapel of Loretto—like its prototype in Italy, famed for its riches and for having come through the air from the Holy Land, at the intercession of all the Friars in the town ; and a capital speculation they have made of it, for who can expect to have an Ora or an Ave put up for him in a place so far travelled —without paying handsomely for it ? Some of the populace have long had their eye on the gold and silver which is lying useless there."

of these heretics, he brought them forth next day to the gibbet, January 25th, being St. Paul's day, and feasted his eyes from the windows of the Spy Tower with their execution. The men were hanged, and Helen Stark was drowned. Robert Lamb, at the foot of the ladder, made a pathetic exhortation to the people, beseeching them to fear God, and forsake the leven of popish abominations. Helen Stark earnestly desired to die with her husband, but her request was refused ; however, they permitted her to accompany him to the place of execution. In the way, she exhorted him to constancy in the cause of Christ, and, as she parted with him, said, ' Husband, be glad we have lived together many joyful days, and this the day of our death we ought to esteem the most joyful of them all, for we shall have joy for ever ; therefore I will not bid you good-night, for we shall shortly meet in the kingdom of heaven.' As soon as the men were executed, the woman was taken to a pool of water hard by, where, having recommended her children to the charity of her neighbours, her sucking child being taken from her breast, and given to a nurse, she was drowned, and died, with great courage and comfort." This barbarous execution, instead of quenching the ardour of Protestantism, increased it, together with a settled aversion of the priests and their superstitious usages. Matters now came to a crisis. On the 11th of May 1559, John Knox having arrived in Perth, preached a zealous and animated sermon against the follies of the church of Rome. After concluding his sermon, the congregation quietly dispersed; but the people had hardly left the place when a priest, most indiscreetly, proposed to celebrate mass, and began to decorate the altar, for that purpose, whereupon the persons who remained were precipitated into action with tumultuary and irresistible violence ; they fell upon the churches, overturned the altars, defaced the pictures, broke in pieces the images, and proceeding next to the monasteries, in a few hours laid these sumptuous fabrics almost level with the ground. This riotous insurrection was not the effect of concert, or any previous deliberation : censured by the reformed preachers, and publicly condemned by the persons of most power and credit with the party, it must be regarded as an accidental eruption of popular rage. The queen having heard with concern the destruction of the religious houses at Perth, the Chartreux monastery especially, as it was a stately pile of building, and a royal palace, and the repository of the remains of the first James, she determined to inflict the severest vengeance on the whole party. She had already drawn the troops in French pay to Stirling ; with these, and what Scottish forces she could levy of a sudden, she marched directly to Perth, in hopes of surprising the Protestant leaders, before they could assemble their followers, whom, out of confidence in her disingenuous promises, they had been rashly induced to dismiss. Intelligence of these preparations and menaces was soon conveyed to Perth. The Protestants, animated by zeal for religion, and eager to expose themselves in so good a cause, flocked in such numbers to Perth, that they not only secured the town from danger, but, within a few days, were in a condition to take the field, and to face the queen, who advanced with an army seven thousand strong, commanded by D'Oysel, the French general. Ultimately a treaty betwixt the belligerants was concluded, by which it was stipulated that both armies should be disbanded, and the gates of Perth set open to Mary, the queen-regent, who entered the town on the 29th of May. It seems that no sooner were the Protestant forces dismissed than the queen broke through every article of the treaty, introduced French troops into the town, dismissed the magistracy, and established the old religion. She had, however no sooner left it than the inhabitants again broke out in a ferment, and implored the assistance of the Lords of the Congregation. Argyle, Lord Ruthven, and others consequently marched to their relief, and on a refusal of the garrison to surrender, prepared to besiege the town in the usual form. In this emergency the queen employed the Earl of Huntly and Lord Erskine to divert them from this enterprise; but her wonted artifices were now of no avail; repeated so often, they could deceive no longer; and, without listening to her offers, they continued the siege. Lord Ruthven attacked it on the west, and Provost Hallyburton, with his people from Dundee, fired with his artillery from the bridge, and obliged the defenders to capitulate, upon the 26th of June 1559. After the reduction of Perth, the populace went to Scone, to destroy the abbey and palace. Patrick Hepburn, Bishop of Moray, son of the first Earl of Bothwell of that name, held the abbacy in perpetual commendam, and resided in the palace. He had been a severe scourge to the Reformers, and was obnoxious to them ever since the death of Walter Mylne, who, at his instigation, was burnt at St Andrews; they with assistance from Dundee, attacked the abbey and palace, though guarded by a hundred horsemen. Hallyburton, Provost of Dundee, with his brother, and John Knox, hearing of this tumult, went and entreated the people to spare the edifices, to whom they hearkened, and separated, after they had destroyed the monuments of idolatry; but the next day, a citizen of Dundee was run through the body with a sword, by one of the bishop's sons, while he was looking in at the door of the bishop's granary, which so enraged the people both of Perth and Dundee, that they quickly repaired to Scone, and, notwithstanding the entreaties of Argyle, Ruthven, the Prior, and all the preachers, they pillaged and set fire to these noble edifices, and burnt them to the ground, on the 27th of June. After the loss of Perth, the queen endeavoured to seize on Stirling. On hearing of this movement, Argyle, and other leaders of the congregation, marched out of Perth with three hundred citizens, who, having felt the severe yoke of the French government, resolved to prosecute the Reformation, or perish in the attempt. To shew their zeal and resolution, instead of ribands, they put ropes about their necks, that whoever deserted the colours should certainly be hanged by these ropes; from which circumstance arose the ordinary allusion to " St Johnston's ribbons." A picture of the march of this resolute band out of Perth, is still to be seen in the town-clerk's office. Advancing towards Stirling, they secured that town, and demolishing every monument of the popish worship, as they proceeded, they, in a few days, made themselves masters of the capital.

The dark tragedy of the Gowrie Conspiracy, which is connected with the memorabilia of Perth, need not be here recited, as it is sufficiently known to the readers of history. After this period, the historical memoirs of Perth are not fruitful in interest, though the place was visited by Cromwell, and in more recent times was a temporary rendezvous for the Highland troops of Prince Charles Stewart, on his untoward insurrection of 1745. Passing, therefore, to a description of the town :

In ancient times, Perth, as has been seen, was surrounded by walls for its protection, but these emblems of a turbulent age have now altogether disappeared. The internal structure of the town was also at one time mean. Numbers of the houses were faced with wood, and were so close to each other that the thoroughfares were of the usual breadth of lanes. At the same period, the town generally stood at a lower level, so much so that the streets were continually liable to be inundated by floods of the river. To guard against this evil, the streets have been raised from time to time to their present elevation. In the present day, Perth is the handsomest town of its size in Scotland. More than one bridge of Perth has

given way to the impetuosity of the floods.   The great inundation in the
thirteenth century, (which Boece fabled to have destroyed ancient
Bertha), swept away a bridge; and in 1621, a building of ten spacious
arches, which stood opposite the east end of the High Street, below the
present bridge, was carried off.   By far the most pleasing characteristics
of Perth are two large expanses of green parks, one on the south and one
on the north side of the town.   These beautiful pieces of public ground,
which are devoted to the recreation of the inhabitants, having been formerly insulated by the waters of the river, on which they now only border, are respectively called the North and South Inch.   The latter was
in former times the scene of the various athletic sports and games of the
citizens, as well as often the active theatre of military movements.   Perhaps the community of no city in the kingdom are in possession of a finer
or more extensive green than the North Inch, on the west side of which
stands the ancient mansion of Balhousie, environed by some fine aged
trees.   Behind the house, secluded from view, is a flour mill, driven by
the notable boot-full of water.   The streets of Perth are preserved in a
cleanly condition, and have excellent side pavements.   The water-works
is a beautiful building, having a chimney in the form of a circular column
130 feet in height; it is situated at the eastern extremity of Marshall
Place near the river.   The water is raised by steam, and the building
and machinery were erected at an expense of L.11,000.   The town and
shops are tastefully lighted with gas.   Here and there are public edifices
of good and tasteful construction, calculated to attract the notice of
strangers.   At the extremity of South-street stands King James the VI.'s
Hospital, on the site of the Carthusian monastery, a large and handsome
structure.   The principal and most ancient public building is undoubtedly St John's church, situated in the centre and oldest part of the town.
This edifice, the precise origin of which is uncertain, but which seems to
have been built at different times, and to have undergone many modifi-
cations, now contains three places of worship.   It was in this church
that the demolitions of the Reformation commenced, and before that
period it was the scene of some remarkable events.   In 1336, according
to Fordun, a remarkable incident occurred within it.   Edward III. was
standing before the high altar, when his brother, John Earl of Cornwall,
a minor, came to inform him that he had travelled through the west of
Scotland, marking his journey with devastation and flames; in particular,
that he had burnt the church and priory of Lesmahago, besides other
churches, with people in them, who had fled thither for refuge.   Edward,
indignant at his cruel conduct, reproached him bitterly, and the youth
replied with a haughty answer, to which the king rejoined with a stroke
of his dagger, that laid his younger brother dead at his feet.   The English
writers say, that this young prince died at Perth in October 1336; but
they take no notice of his having received his death in this manner.—
St John's church has a conspicuous tower, from which springs a pointed
spire, containing some fine bells,—the great bell being the same which
called the people to prayers before the change of religion at the Reformation.   The spire also contains a set of fine music bells, which play every
hour at the half-hours.
    Of Gowrie-House, the ancient manson of the Earls of Gowrie, and the
scene of the well-known mysterious incident in Scottish history, most unfortunately for the antiquary, not a vestige now remains; the whole,
which stood near the entrance to the town from the south, with its back
part to the river, being recently taken away, to afford room for a splendid
suit of county buildings and jails, in the Grecian style.   The chief of
these new erections is a large handsome building looking to the Tay, be-

tween which and it there is a promenade. The structure has an elegant portico with twelve columns in front. Opening from the portico there is a large entrance hall; to the back of which stands a flight of steps leading to the gallery of the Justiciary Hall. The Justiciary Hall occupies the back part of the centre of the building, and is 66 feet by 43½ feet in the upper part. Under the gallery there are jury and witnesses' rooms. Behind the Judges' bench are the Judges' rooms, also witnesses' rooms. From the prisoners' box a flight of steps leads down to a passage communicating with the prisons. The County Hall, which occupies all the south wing, is 68 by 40 feet; in it are portraits of the late Duke of Athole, and Lord Lynedoch, by Sir Thomas Lawrence, and one by Wilkie, of Sir George Murray. To the right of the entrance to the County Hall is a committee room 30 feet square, and above, a tea or card room 44½ by 30 feet. The Sheriff's Court and Clerk's Office, are contained in the north wing. Above the north entrance is an office for the collector of cess. The building cost £22,000. Behind these county buildings is the new city and county jail, enclosed by a high wall. In the north area is situated the felons' jail, and in the south that of the debtors. The felon's jail is in two divisions; the one for males, and the other for females. The division for the men contains ten cells, and one large day-room. The division for the women, three sleeping, and one day-room. Each division has an enclosed airing-ground adjoining. The south, or debtors' jail, is likewise divided into two,—one part for debtors, and the other for misdemeanors. The debtor's department consists of four large sleeping rooms and a day-room. The jail buildings, altogetner, cost £10,000, £6000 of which was contributed by the town, and £4000 by the county. The town pays two-thirds, and the county one-third of the current expenses. The remains of the old chapel which stood at the gate of the bridge, dedicated to the Virgin, has been recently converted into a Police Court and Bridewell. Excepting the church of St John, this is the only vestige extant of the numerous ecclesiastical structures of Perth.— The other public buildings are as follows:—A house with a tastefully built front, of a peculiar construction, in George-street, near the end of the bridge, to commemorate the public services of the late Thomas Marshall, Esq. of Glenalmond, Lord Provost of the town: the monument contains halls for the Public Library and Museum of the Perthshire Antiquarian Society. The new Coffee-room, in George-street. The classes of the High School of Perth, a distinguished provincial academy, are provided with ample accommodation, in a large building forming the centre of Rose Terrace, adjoining the North Inch: on the ground floor are the English, drawing, and writing class-rooms, and above are the rooms for the academy, grammar-school, and French classes. A neat Theatre is erected at the junction of Kinnoul-street and Crescent, which has been but little encouraged: it was reared by subscription among the gentlemen of the county and town, in 100 shares of 25 guineas each. On the north-west side of the town is a spacious suit of Barracks, in which a certain number of troops are generally stationed. In the environs on the south, and adjacent to the South Inch, stands a most extensive suit of Government Barracks, or Depot for prisoners of war, still kept in the best state of repair. In the High-street, and facing Methven-street, stands St Paul's church, which is rather a modern and elegant structure of stone, with a steeple surmounted by a spire. Farther east, in King-street, the new Chapel of Ease, or church of St Leonards. A little west from this will shortly be erected an Infirmary for the town and county. Although the project of opening up the excellent line of street from the Shore to the Bridge, appears to have been again abandoned for the present, it is to be regretted that new buildings have been allowed to be erected on the very breastwork of the line, and so near the Fish-market; as it is probable that the new flat-bottomed iron steamer will be able to land passengers at this upper quay, and thus greatly add to the convenience of the public, and stimulate the trade by bringing it nearly into the centre of the town. Besides various private, Perth possesses several public libraries, some of a general character, others congregational. An institution was established in 1784, under the title of the Antiquarian Society of Perth. The chief design of this association was to promote the investigation of the History of Scotland, and to collect and preserve manuscripts, books, coins, and all other relicts illustrative of the antiquities of Scotland, and all other nations. They were also to receive geographical maps and descriptions, whether ancient or modern, and curious natural productions of the animal, vegetable, and mineral kingdoms. In 1787, the plan was enlarged : the name adopted was, " The Literary and Antiquarian Society of Perth ;" and the communications now extend to every subject connected with philosophy, belles-lettres, and the fine arts. The hall of the Society is situated in Marshall's monument. The city is governed by twenty-five popularly elected Magistrates, and the Dean of Guild : this body electing the Lord Provost, four Bailies, and Treasurer, from among their number. The peace of the city is more immediately preserved by a body of police, established by act of parliament. Under this establishment the town is divided into nine wards with commissioners. The executive is under the charge of a superintendant; and the quiet and good order of the city is greatly increased by a clause in that act, authorizing the magistrates to punish summarily by fine and imprisonment, in the case of petty offences. The expense of the police establishment is defrayed from the increased rent derived from the public dung, by the operation of the amended act, without any additional burden being imposed on the community. The town has, besides, a body of high constables. Prior to the passing of the Reform Bill, Perth joined with Dundee and the Fife burghs in returning a Member to Parliament. By considerable exertion, Perth succeeded at that time in establishing her claim to send a member to the legislature, since which time she has been represented by Mr Oliphant of Condie. who has given general satisfaction to his constituents—although, perhaps, more to those who opposed his election, than to the party who supported him. Before the passing of the Burgh Reform Bill, the force of public opinion had succeeded in a great measure in breaking up the close system and beautiful order which previously existed in the municipal affairs of the city. The following gentlemen had the honour of being selected as the first Reform Magistrates of Perth.

> ADAM PRINGLE, Esq., Lord Provost.
> ROBERT BOWER, Esq., Dean of Guild.
> T. R. SANDEMAN, Esq., Bailie.
> DAVID CLUNIE, Esq.,   do.
> JOHN GRAHAM, Esq.,   do.
> JAMES M'LEISH, Esq.,   do.
> JAMES DEWAR, Esq., Treasurer.

Perth has recently been stigmatised, in one of the leading monthly magazines, as being highly Conservative in its principles. In every community. where freedom of thought and expression of sentiment is tolerated, all views of politics must necessarily exist : but from the period of the declaration of war against France, in the year 1793—a war evidently entered into for the purpose of arresting the spread of the French doctrines in this country—down to the present day, there has not been want-

Ing a proper expression of public opinion on every occasion demanding it.* During the struggle for Reform in Parliament—which (like the important measure for uniting England and Scotland, and that appointing the succession of the present family to the British throne,) was carried in one of its stages by a majority of *one*,—Perth was as eager, and struggled as ardently, as any portion of the empire. But these things are still fresh in the memory of our readers, and therefore need not be detailed here.

---

* The following protest against this impolitic war was passed at a meeting on the South Inch of Perth, January 1793. The meeting was held in face of a proclamation, which was issued to prevent an expression of popular opinion :—

SOLEMN PROTESTATION AGAINST WAR.

The Friends of the People in Perth, and its neighbourhood, solemnly declare to the world, that a sense of duty alone prevented them from joining in the late rage, of resolving and anathematising republicans and levellers ; because we were convinced, that no seditious spirit prevailed in the country, and that the whole furor was the effect of a gross political delusion, cruelly and artfully played off by designing men, with a view to throw the public mind into that state of confusion and incapacity, in which it is best prepared to receive the idea of war with the least possible hazard of its revolting against it. Recent informations justify our suspicions ; and an awful crisis is now at hand. The Country is about to be plunged into a War, so wholly unprecedented in our history, that even with success itself, no man can say it will be productive of advantage to the British nation. Let every man, therefore, ask himself, why it is that we are plunged into a War ? Is it to defend us against invasion ?—none is threatened. Is it to vindicate our National honour ?—that is not called in question. Is it to defend our Trade?—there is at present no dread of its being injured. Is it to preserve the faith of treaties ?—none which are founded on the unalterable laws of justice have been invaded. We ask, then, why is the country to be plunged into a War, in favour of which none of the ordinary pleas of justification can be set up. To sacrifice the lives of fellow-citizens, to sport with the tenderest anxieties of families, to interrupt trade, and encrease the public debts of a people, already over-burdened, without any just reason, is surely the very consummation of national folly. Anxiously would we call upon the monied interest, the landholder, the merchant, the manufacturer, and the tradesman, seriously to weigh in time the dreadful calamities which must be the inevitable consequences of the threatened war ; earnestly would we conjure them to think in time, by every consideration which is near and dear to them, were it not that we know our feeble voice would be of small avail. There is one consideration, however, which presses so powerfully upon our minds, that we consider ourselves called upon by the strong obligations we are under to our country, to our king, and to our constitution, to come forward to the world with our solemn protestation against a War with the French. It is this, that besides being convinced that we have every thing to lose, and nothing to gain by such a quarrel, we perceive it possible that the very existence of our Constitution and Civil Government may be endangered. This we deprecate of all things ; and in entering this solemn protest, we give the best refutation to those calumnies of our enemies, by which we have been represented as void of loyalty, and secretly aiming at the overthrow of the British System of Government. By this, we evince that true loyalty, and genuine patriotism, which, though too discerning to be imposed upon by delusions, is very prompt to step forward, and avert real dangers. By this declaration, we wash our hands clean of any share in the innocent blood which may be shed, by plunging our country into the most unpropitious war into which it ever entered ; and if any dangers accrue from it to our happy Constitution, (which may God, of his infinite goodness, avert) no part of such calamities can be ascribed to us ; but must and ought to be charged equally to the account of those who publicly approve of the measure ; and those who, by their silence, afford Government a pretence for saying, as was done in the American War, that they have thereby given their acquiescence and consent to it. Let every Briton seriously ponder these things in his mind.

PATRICK GRANT, *Preses.*
WALTER MILLER, *Sec.*

At the present time, Perth is not what is usually styled a manufacturing town ; although many manufacturing establishments in the country adjacent are connected with it, such as Luncarty, Stanley, Stormont Field, Tulloch, Almond Bank, Huntingtower, Cromwell Park, Ruthven, Pitcairn Green, &c. The distinguished loveliness of the city, its situation, and the excellence of its schools, have conspired to render Perth the residence of a great number of affluent people. Like Edinburgh, it is pre-eminently a *genteel* town, and like it, has its more bustling trading neighbour; for, if Edinburgh has Glasgow, Perth has Dundee, between which places there exists a sort of rivalry from their opposite manners and character. Dundee is usually understood to have injured the trade of Perth, by intercepting its foreign commerce, from being in a more accessible situation for general trade. Although Dundee lies nearer the ocean, and of course is better suited to be a port for large vessels, yet Perth has a more extensive country to supply, and is the magazine or store-house of the centre of Scotland, and better adapted for internal commerce—the roads radiating from it in every direction being both numerous and excellent, and the neighbourhood being so populous, that a circuit of little more than four miles includes about forty thousand souls. Among the proprietors of the Dundee, Perth, and London Shipping Company, are a great proportion of Perth merchants, the chief part of that concern depending on Perth. Their London and Dundee steamers are allowed to be unequalled by any afloat; the *Perth* being distinguished by the proud title of " *The Queen of the Seas.*" Many also hold shares in the whale shipping companies of Dundee, and a number of vessels belonging to other ports are freighted by Perth and unloaded at Newburgh. Moreover many of the vessels coming into Dundee harbour have cargoes partly belonging to Perth. Betwixt Perth and Dundee steam-vessels ply daily, touching at the intermediate port of Newburgh on the Fife side of the Tay. There are a variety of stage-coaches leaving Perth daily, running to and from Edinburgh, Glasgow, Inverness, and Aberdeen. In summer the place is visited by a great number of tourists, who never fail to be delighted, as the Romans are said to have been, with the perfect beauty of the scenery around. Pennant calls the view from the hill of Moncrieff, where the first sight is got of Perth, in journeying from Edinburgh, " the glory of Scotland ; and truly, there could hardly be a more charming prospect. The town is not alone visited for its own sake. It forms the threshold of a series of scenes in the romantic regions of the surrounding shire, which are now the objects of attraction to tourists. The population in 1831 amounted to upwards of 23,000.

APPENDIX.

No. II.

The status of the Incorporations in the municipal government of the Royal Burghs in Scotland, being extinguished by the Burgh Reform Act, their importance in this respect must now become matter of history. It will be particularly gratifying to many of our readers to know that we are enabled to record the following interesting notices, of one of the most important Incorporations of the City of Perth, through the kindness of one of the most intelligent and upright members of that Incorporation. They were drawn up a few years ago by Mr ANDREW BUIST, *Deacon of the Glover Incorporation.*

ORIGIN OF THE SKINNERS AND GLOVERS.

When were the Skinners and Glovers formed into a corporation in Perth ? is a question that has likely suggested itself to many of our brethren, both now and in former times, but which has never been satisfactorily answered. It is certainly much to be regretted that the origin and early history of our ancient craft is involved in such darkness and uncertainty, owing to a blank in our corporation annals. One reason which may be assigned for it is this : that when Edward the I. of England, in the end of the thirteenth century, subdued the greater part of Scotland, he, with a refined skill, I call it of state policy, for the purpose of destroying every trace of Scotland as an ancient and independent nation, commanded all the archives of the country to be ransacked, and all the valuable and important national and public documents—every thing that was connected with the history and doings of Scotland as a nation, were ordered, under heavy penalties, to be delivered up to him. Whether he intended to destroy them, or merely to keep them as trophies of his conquest, is not known, as, unfortunately for poor Scotland, the ship that had the greater part of these truly valuable documents on board, was wrecked on its passage to London (where they were to have been kept to wait his pleasure as to their ultimate fate), and thus much that was of such essential importance to our country was lost for ever.

Perhaps it may be said by some, all this may be true ; but what connection has it with the history of the Glovers ? Why, it bears most strongly on the illustration of our subject, for we have the Glovers at this period in the full possession of extensive political privileges. They were admitted, a century before this, by King William the Lyon, to the free right and privileges of being merchant burgesses, in addition to their own peculiar rights as incorporate craftsmen ;—now it is well known, that when an individual or public body is raised to dignity and honour, that the charter conveying these generally narrates the reason for doing so, and services performed to entitle them to these distinguished marks of their sovereign's approbation ; therefore I think it highly probable that the Glovers, when Edward issued this tyrannical mandate, had, in their possession, not only this charter of William the Lyon, with the royal signet attached to it, or the official seals of his ministers of state, but that they would also have the original charter of their formation as a corporate body. Now, as it was evidently the intention of Edward to make Scotland not only tributary to, but a part and portion of, England, and Edward entertaining such views, and residing with his army at Perth, the metropolis of Scotland, would he not make it his particular study to collect every document within its walls that, in the smallest degree, bore upon the history of Scotland as a free and independent nation ; therefore, I firmly believe, from all these circumstances, that our city would be more completely stript of its records, both public and corporate, than any other town in the kingdom ; and of course all the Glovers' papers would share the same fate. This is my opinion, and one of the strongest reasons that can be adduced for the records of Perth being so particularly barren in charters, and every thing connected with its ancient history.

While we mourn over the loss of these valuable parchments, there is an event that has happened in our day, that far more than compensates us for this depriva-tion, an event which has immortalised our ancient and worthy craft, and spread its name in connection with every thing beautiful and virtuous in female character— upright, affectionate, and honourable in the conduct of the purest citizen and crafts-man, not only over the British dominions, but also over the whole of the polished and enlightened population of Europe and America, so that the Glover craft of Perth is now a part and portion of public history. I know that I will be anticipated when I state, that it is Sir Walter Scott (a name now as generally known and celebrated over the world as that of Napoleon Buonaparte), who, in his admirable and interest-ing work, " The Fair Maid of Perth," has honoured our craft by making the heroine of his tale the daughter of one of our calling of Glovers. The manner in which he has portrayed the characters, and the fidelity of the description of the times in which the scene is laid, have met with the unanimous approbation of the enlightened and impartial literary world, which sufficiently proves the estimation in which this work is held ; and I hope that no circumstance will ever occur in the *real history* to tarnish the fair fame with which this beautiful and interesting fiction has adorned the *imaginary history*, of the doings and conduct of the members of our calling in former days.

I may only remark, in illustration of the accuracy with which our author has described that part of the " Fair City" in which Simon Glover dwelt, that by far the greater part of the property that was burdened for the maintenance of St Bar-tholomew, then belonged to the Glovers, and was situated in the Curfew Row or Castle Gable, which may be said to be a continuation of the same street ; and that the *Gilt Arbour* was a place where the Glovers held many of their meetings in ancient times, and is thus described in one of our old charters, dated 26th May, 1534, " The *Vindaris*, now the said Burgh, vulgarly called the Gilt Arbour of the Silver Book or Missal ; Palia Vestimenta Sacerdotalia, and other ornaments of the Altar of St Bartholomew, founded by the said Crafts (Skinners and Glovers.)"

SAINT BARTHOLOMEW.

St Bartholomew, the Patron, was one of the twelve apostles,—the evangelical history being most express and clear as to that matter ;—but he being no farther taken notice of than the bare mention of his name, many, both anciently and of later times, have supposed that he lay concealed under the name of Nathaniel, one of the first disciples that came to Christ ; because, St John never mentioned Bar-tholomew in the number of the apostles, so the other evangelists never took notice of Nathaniel ; and as in St John, Philip and Nathaniel are joined together in their coming to Christ, so, in the rest of the evangelists, Philip and Bartholomew are constantly put together ; and afterwards we find them joint companions in the church. Nathaniel is particularly reckoned up with the other apostles to whom our Lord appeared at the sea of Tiberius after the resurrection, where there were together Simon Peter, Thomas, and Nathaniel of Cana in Galilee, and the two sons of Zebedee, and two other of his disciples, who were probably Andrew and Philip. Besides, if Nathaniel had not been of the twelve already, no tolerable reason can be given why he, who was so eminently qualified, was not pitched upon to fill up the place of Judas.

The word Bartholomew imports a relative capacity, either as a son or a scholar, rather than a proper name. As a son, it denotes his being born of Tholmai ; as a scholar, it may relate to him as a disciple of some particular sect among the Jews ; and, among several other institutions of that nature, some learned men reckon the Tholmeans from Tholmai, of which order Nathaniel seems to have been, and hence called Bartholomew, the son or scholar of the Tholmeans. And many of the learned concur in the opinion, that it is the same person under two names, the one proper and the other relative. This character was given by our Saviour, that he was a man of true simplicity and integrity,—" an Israelite, indeed, in whom was no guile, no art of hypocrisy and deceit." He travelled as far India, that part of it that lies next to Asia ; for, as Eusebius relates, when Pantaemis, a man famous for philosophy as well as christianity, desiring to imitate the apostolical zeal in propagating the faith, travelled as far as India itself; there, among some that yet retained the knowledge of Christ, he found St Matthew's gospel written in Hebrew, left as the tradition asserts, by St Bartholomew, one of the twelve apostles, when he preached christianity to these nations. He afterwards returned from thence to the more northern and western parts of Asia, instructing the people of Thirapolis in the doctrine of the gospel ; from thence he went into Lycaonia, where he employed himself upon the same account ; and, at last, removed to Albanople, in Armenia the Great, where, endeavouring to reclaim the people from idolatry, he was by the governor of that place put to death.

How did he suffer martyrdom ? He was crucified, some say, with his head downwards ; others, that he was *flayed, and his skin first taken off,* which might consist well enough with his crucifixion, excoriation being a punishment in use, not only in Egypt but among the Persians, next neighbours to these Armenians, from whom they might easily borrow it. He cheerfully bore their cruel usage, and comforted and confirmed the christian converts to the last minute of his life.

GLOVES.

Who was the first Glover ? was a question propounded a few years ago at the annual Michaelmas dinner of the calling, and which puzzled the meeting to solve, although, among the strangers present, there were several belonging to the three learned professions—church, law, and physic ; but which was, I think, at last satisfactorily answered by the chairman (Deacon A. G—y), who replied, " Rebekah," who is the first glover mentioned in either sacred or profane history. But I have no doubt " our skinner craft" was of a much earlier origin, for our great progenitor, Adam, being clad in skins, it is very probable that, to preserve these from decay, which they were very liable to in that warm climate, would steep them in those saline or aluminous springs, which were so abundant in that region of the globe, and which process would be continued and improved upon by his descendants ; but whether these be counted satisfactory explanations of the origin of " our ancient craft" or not, is of no great importance to our subject, but I hope it will not be considered as out of place here, to give a short account of the use and importance of the glove in ancient times.

The *hand,* that important member of the human frame, is often referred to in scripture as emblematical of honour, strength, protection, power, and friendship : among the Egyptians as a symbol of strength ; and among the Romans, as a symbol of fidelity ; and has been held in high estimation by all the nations of the world. For its covering, adornment, comfort, and protection, the *glove* was invented and used, and is described as " a habit or covering for the hand and wrist —used both for warmth, decency, and as a shelter from the weather.

" *To throw the glove,*" was a practice and ceremony very usual among our forefathers, being the challenge whereby another was defied to single combat. It is still retained at the coronation of our kings ; when the king's champion casts his glove in Westminster Hall. This custom is supposed to have arisen from the Eastern nations, who, in all their sales, and deliveries of lands, goods, &c., used to give the purchaser their *glove* by way of livery or investiture. To this effect is Ruth, iv. 7, the Chaldee paraphrase calling that *glove,* which the common version renders *shoe ;* and the Rabbins interpret by *glove,* that passage in the cviii. Psalm, ' over Edom will I cast my *shoe.*' Accordingly, amongst us, he who took up the *glove,* declared his acceptance of the challenge ; and, as a part of the ceremony, took the *glove* off his own right hand and cast it upon the ground, to be taken up by the challenger. This had the force of a mutual engagement on each side to meet at the time and place, which should be appointed by the king, parliament, or judges.

The custom which still prevails of "*blessing gloves*," in the coronation of the kings of France, is a remnant of the Eastern practice of giving possession with the *glove*.

Anciently, it was prohibited for the judges to wear *gloves* on the bench.

The *gauntlet* is described as a " large, strong glove, made to cover the arm or hand of a cavalier, when armed at all points." The gauntlet was of iron, and the fingers plated, and was always borne in the ancient marches in ceremony. Gauntlets were not introduced till about the thirteenth century, and were frequently thrown like the glove by way of challenge.

About a century ago, the manufacture of gloves appears to have reached to a high pitch of perfection, they were made of " velvet, satin, taffetty, silk, thread, cotton, and worsted ; leather gloves were also made of chamois, kid, lamb, doe, elk, buff, &c. There were also perfumed gloves—washed, glazed, and waxed gloves ; single, lined, top'd, laced, fringed with gold, silver, silk, fur, &c. ;" and it was a proverb, that for a glove to be good and well made, three kingdoms must contribute to it— " Spain to dress the leather, France to cut it, and England to sew it."

PAGEANTS AND PROCESSIONS.

During the domination of the Popish church, full and ample leisure was given to her votaries to indulge in every species of splendid shows and processions ; and our citizens of Perth do not appear to have been behind any in their love and indulgence in these often expensive, but always popular entertainments ; and it is very likely that a considerable part of the revenue of the Incorporated Trades of Perth, was directed to defray the expenses incurred in the getting up of these exhibitions.

I cannot trace, in the records of the calling, the particular part that they took, and the manner in which they conducted themselves in these pageants ; but I have no doubt they would vie with the other trades in the splendour of their processions, and would spare no expense to make these as attractive and popular as any in the town, for the honour of "St Bartholomew," and the " honour and great commendation" of the Glover calling. I hope the following instance or two of the manner in which these processions were conducted during that period, will not be counted as out of place. The personage whom the Baker calling were pleased to honour, by adopting him as their patron saint, was a St Obert, Berth, or Burt, a gentleman, whose origin and history completely baffled the researches of the Rev. James Scott, founder of the Perth Library and Antiquarian Society, and for many years a very highly respected clergyman of Perth. He could find no trace of his saintship in any of the popish calendars now extant. Whether a real or imaginary personage was the patron saint made choice of by the Baker incorporation, does not appear ; but for the purpose of celebrating the annual festival of their saint they composed and acted a play, or dramatic performance, called "Sanct Oberti's Play." A very great number of persons were engaged in this play, and on the 10th of December, which was wont to be called " Sanct Oberti's Eve,' they passed through the town in disguise dresses, with piping, and dancing, and striking a drum, carrying in their hands burning torches. One of the actors was clad in the devil's coat ; another rode upon a horse, which went in men's shoes,—probably the horse and its rider represented a part of the legendary history of the saint.

At the Reformation (1560) our reforming ancestors were very anxious to wean the citizens from these absurd, expensive, and often licentious pageants ; and the kirk session, or weekly assembly, as it was then called, issued an act, dated 27th November 1574, " against superstition," and ordered this act to be published on certain Sundays that none should pretend ignorance, but that all should conform to its enactments. The whole of the incorporated trades of Perth appear to have given due obedience to this mandate, and to have discontinued whatever was popish or superstitious in their processions, with the exception of the Bakers, who appear to have been a " tap thrawn, and camstarie sett ;" and who, for fourteen years after the passing of this act, continued in the face of all the expostulations and threatenings of the reformed church, to celebrate as formerly the festival of their saint: But in 1588, the Baker incorporation enacted in their books, that such persons as should play, in any time to come, Sanct Oberti's Play, should " be debarred from all the liberties of the craft, should never have entry to the same again, and should be banished from the town for ever." An attested copy of this act was sent to the minister and elders, that it might be inserted also in the book of the weekly assembly. This act of the Baker calling appears to have completely put an end to Sanct Oberti.

I may mention another instance of ancient pastimes ; and as the Glovers were as fond of diversion as their neighbours, it is very likely that the youths of both sexes, connected with the corporation, formed a part of the procession of the young people, in the summer dresses, who went annually, in the month of May, to the " Dragon Hole," a cave situate in the hill of Kinnoul. It appears to have been a very joyous festival, and of very great antiquity, as the young people of both sexes in Perth and its neighbourhood, in the popish times, and most probably also in the times of heathenism, resorted to it in companies at "Beltaine," or "Bel Fire Time," in the month of May. The festivities in May, which were once general over all the kingdom, are justly supposed to have had an idolatrous origin, and to have been instituted by the Druids; who, as the sun, under the name of Bel, or Baal, was an object of their worship, welcomed his new approach to the earth with demonstrations of joy, and with sacrifices, to conciliate his favour. The rejoicings were continued in the after ages in different forms, and under various pretences. The cave had been known by the name of the Dragon's Den a thousand years previous to the year 1380.[*]

But as this was one of the superstitious pastimes, as they were called by our reformers, for the purpose of putting an end to it, they issued an edict, dated 2d May 1580, entitled " The act anent passing to the Dragon Hole," which states, " because the assembly of ministers and elders understand, that the resort to the Dragon Hole, both by young men and women, with their piping and drums striking before them through the town, has raised no small slander to their congregation ; statute and ordains, that no person, either man or woman of the congregation shall resort or repair hereafter to the Dragon Hole, as they have done in times past, namely, in the month of May ; nor shall pass through the town in their way to it with piping and striking of drums, as heretofore they have done, under the pain of twenty shillings to the poor ; also, that they shall make their public repentance upon a Sabbath day, in presence of the people." This ordinance having

---

[*] The following passages relating to these observances occur in Principal Tullideph's manuscript, before quoted:—"At the opening of a dark but narrow fissure in the rocks, stood a figure fantastically dressed and adorned with garlands of flowers. Several young men and women were clambering up the rocks towards the cavern, while a knot of spectators stood below, whose shouts rent the air, as occasionally some unlucky aspirant missed his or her hold, slipped down again into the crowd, or more unlucky still, regained not their footing until they had toppled down the steep bank beneath, which was formed of small stones too recently dislodged from the parent rock, to admit even of a handful of furze or fern to break the fall of the unskilful. Beyond this crowd, a long line of people in their holiday attire, among which many religious habits were visible, extending along by the foot of the cliff until lost to view within a ravine—out of which the procession seemed still slowly advancing. As Oliver drew near, he observed an elderly respectable looking citizen standing aloof from the rest. To him he advamced, and, after the usual salutations of the morning, inquired what this concourse meant. "You are surely a stranger in these parts," replied his informant, " not to have heard of the Festival of the Dragon on May morning?" " I had heard of such a custom being observed at St Johnstoun, but knew not that a spot so wild and romantic had been chosen for its celebration. I think it is said to have had its origin in the rejoicings which were instituted, after the slaughter of a dragon which long infested the neighbourhood?" " And a dragon of no contemptible taste," rejoined the citizen, " for the virgins he kept in durance here were remarkable for beauty. Between ourselves, I suspect the true monster lived on the law below us, while the inhabitant of the rock was the offspring of the Priests who wished to cloak the misdemeanors of their patron under the wing of this dragon. But the mummeries to which the fable has given rise will soon, like many others, be rooted out of the land."

the sanction and approbation of the magistrates of the town, was published at the "Mercat Cross," and from the pulpit, and was the means of finally putting an end to this ancient and popular pastime.

I have already stated, that it is very probable that the Glovers had had their full share in these ancient revelries, and now come to an amusing document which fully bears us out in our opinion upon this point, and throws considerable light on the manner in which our ancestors amused themselves in former times. Is is styled in the Calling's records, "Memorandum of his Majesty's coronation, and coming to Scotland, his entry to Edinburgh; and Perth, 15th of June 1633, which day our dread Sovereign, Charles, King of England, France, and Ireland, came to Edinburgh. Being accompanied with the Nobalitie of Scotland ryding before, and the Nobalitie of England ryding behind him. Desired out of his gracious favour and love with his Nobalitie of both Kingdoms, to visit his own city of the burgh of Perth, upon the eight day of July; and come to his lodging (formerly Gowrie House, and the site presently occupied by the County buildings), and went down to the gardine thereof; his Majestie's chair being sett upon the wall next to the Tay, whereupon was ane flatt stage of timber, clead about with birks, upon the which, for his Majestie's welcome and entry; thirtein of our brethren of this our calling of Glovers, with green caps, silver strings, reid ribbons, white shoes, with bells about their leigs, schering rapers in their hands, and all other abulziment, danced our sword dance, with many difficult knotts and allafallajessa, five being under and five above upon their shoulders; three of them dancing through their feet; drink of wine and breaking of glasses about them (which, God be prased,) wis acted and did without hurt or skaith to any,—which drew us to great charges and expences, amounting to the sum of three hundred and fifty merks (yet not to be remembered), because wee was graciouslie accepted be our Sovereign and both estates, to our honour and great commendation."

These extracts shew that the Glovers bore a very prominent part in these festivities, and that they were the only craft in Perth that was honoured on this occasion to appear before "royalty."

This dance appears to have been the ancient Morris Dance, which was popular throughout Europe for several centuries previous to the visit of King Charles the First, and seems to have been a great favourite with the Glovers. I, perhaps, need not explain to many of my brethren the origin of this dance. It was first introduced into Spain by the Moors, a bold and warlike race, who inhabited the southern shores of the Mediterranean, and who invaded and conquered the most fertile provinces of Spain; after occupying these for a considerable time, they were at last. After many a severe and sanguinary conflict, driven out of that country into Africa, from whence these bold and enterprising tribes had issued. But during the period they occupied these southern provinces of Spain, they introduced many of the fashions and customs of the East, and particularly the Morocco or Moorish Dance, generally known in Britain as the Morris Dance. It cannot now be ascertained when and where the Glovers first practised this amusement. It is not unlikely that some of the brethren, in their travels through foreign lands—especially if any of these had joined the ranks of the Crusaders—had learnt this dance, and, on their return to their own country,—seeing the rivalry that existed among the Trades of Perth to outvie one another in the splendour and novelty of their pageants, had taught this dance to the members of their own Corporation, in the manner and way in which it was performed in the East. And it appears to have been the amusement which they particularly studied and excelled in, for it is called "our sword dance"—(and one of these silk dresses, cap, and bells, which still form part of the curiosities in the possession of the calling, is a proof that it must have been a showy and expensive exhibition,)—that is, a dance which was their peculiar province, and in which none of the other Crafts could pretend to cope with them. They must have been complete masters in that profession, and quite confident in their own powers, or they never would have volunteered to exhibit, not only before the King, but also before the travelled and polished nobility of his Court, who had most likely seen this performed by the most celebrated dancers in Europe. And although the age of chivalry was past, the spirit of chivalry still retained its influence in the breast, and regulated the conduct of many of those gallant and high-minded Noblesse who graced the Court of Charles at that period, and who would view with interest an exhibition which reminded them of those scenes and pastimes which had often contributed to the amusement, and refreshed the spirits of their warlike ancestors, in the days of chivalry and war. But little thought these joyous spirits, while engaged in these coronation revelries, that in a few years many of them would lose their lives in defence of that ill-fated Prince with whom they were now so heartily rejoicing.

How long the Glovers continued to practise this amusement, after such a memorable display, is not stated; but it is likely the disturbances that arose in the country shortly after this period, and continued for nearly fifty years, had put a stop to that, and to many others of a similar nature throughout the kingdom, for there is no further mention in the Calling's records of *" our sword dance"* having been exhibited in public again; and the only other reference to any thing like public processions, is in an act dated July, 1665, wherein the Auditor Court enacts, after " Having heard explained to them the act of the Convener Court anent the going about the Town with the Provost and the rest of the Town in Midsummer yearlie, the Court ratifies and approves the same; and that yearlie, in time coming, those that are warned, and are absent from conveying their Provost, Council, and Deacon, and accompany them, for that effect shall pay fourteen shillings the piece of unlaw;" " As also not to absent themselves from ryding of the Marches yearly."

From the great change that has taken place in the manners and taste of the public, especially within these last forty years, almost all these processions have fallen into disuse; and what was formerly looked forward to with peculiar interest, enjoyed with such a relish, and, when properly conducted, added so much to the simple and innocent enjoyments of our ancestors, (I speak only with respect to these as they were practised after the reformation,) is now, in this age of the " march of intellect," as it is called, looked down upon with contempt, and, when spoken of, as being only fit for children, or a barbarous age. But I really cannot view them in that light; for although we live in an age of more knowledge and general information, we should not treat with contempt, or speak of with scorn, that which was probably one of the means of exciting a spirit of honest emulation to improve and excel in the different arts and sciences exercised by the respective Incorporations: it is well known, that in these processions there was often displayed specimens of great ingenuity and skill, either invented or perfected by some of these craftsmen—for talents and genius have never been confined to one age or nation. But, however superior we may consider ourselves to our forefathers, we should never forget that to them we are indebted for laying the foundation, and furnishing the materials, which has enabled their descendants to carry on the fabric to its present state of improvement and perfection.

Among the ancient pastimes, " Archery," and the " Noble Game of Golf" were held in high estimation, and much practised by our ancestors. The latter being so well known in the present day, it would be out of place here to say a word about it; and as to the former, the account of it more properly belongs to another branch of our subject, to which we shall afterwards direct our attention.

But there is one very ancient amusement, the origin of which I cannot trace, but which undoubtedly must have been a favourite diversion with our forefathers, and that is the " Foot-Ball." How this game was played in former times we are not informed. Whether it was the bachelors of the Calling against the married brethren, or the Glovers against any of the other Crafts, is not known; but it is likely that the contest was among the members of our own calling, as a sum was levied on all the new married brethren to defray the expenses attending it, and which still forms part of the dues paid by these to the calling at the present day It sometimes is called the " Wife's Foot-Ball," as probably being given in name of the bride, either as her entry money, or as a marriage gift to the brethren, that they might enjoy themselves on that occasion.

Cards and Dice, Quoits and Pitch-and-Toss, appear to have been games in which several of the younger brethren and apprentices sometimes engaged, and which was, as is too often the case with these enticing games, at times carried to excess. To put a stop to this, the calling, in 1664 and 1784, imposed certain penalties on those who indulged in these amusements. As an instance of the excess to which they were carried in 1784, they followed the moon-light from one outside stair to another, of the malt-barns, &c. in the Curfew Row and Lead-side, playing at cards until midnight on these stairs.

Some one will perhaps say,—What do you think of the Michaelmas Saturday Dinner as an amusement ? Why, I think it is a very friendly and social meeting, and also of great antiquity ; and I hope will never be given up, (although the day of the week might be altered,) as long as the Glovers are an incorporated body, but always be enjoyed in a rational, prudent, and becoming manner.

OSTRICH EGG.

Whether the " Blue Blanket," the banner of the incorporated trades of Perth, ever waved over the plains of Palestine, as its namesake of Edinburgh is said to have done, is a question that history or tradition does not solve, but I think the one is as likely as the other ; for Perth was the capital of Scotland during the time of the " Holy Wars," and it is very probable that some of its citizens joined the ranks of the Crusaders, anxious to rescue the Holy Land and Jerusalem from the polluted and tyrannous sway of the infidel Saracen : and of the many hapless individuals who embarked in these dreadful and sanguinary wars, few indeed ever returned, to tell their eventful tale to those friends and companions of their youth whom they had left at home ; but when any of them returned, along with the trophies of the battle-field, they usually brought home specimens of the productions of the strange lands which had been the scenes of their toils and warfare—and amongst these, *ostrich eggs* often formed a part of their collection, which they presented to their friends, or to the societies of which they were members.

From the circumstance of the Glovers having in their possession *one of these ostrich eggs*, which has been suspended for centuries from the ceiling of their hall, and the iron chain of which bears such evident marks of great antiquity, we have every reason to suppose that the Glovers were inflamed with a portion of that enthusiasm and zeal which at that period overspread Christendom, and that one of their number, on his return from the " red field of fight," had brought with him, and presented to the calling, this specimen of the produce of the " Holy Land," as a small tribute of respect and attachment to the corporation of which he was a member, and which shewed that, amid all his wanderings and perils, he had never forgot the land of his fathers, or the scenes of his youthful and happy days.   But perhaps all this may be called the reveries of a warm imagination,—be it so,—and that this specimen is of a far more recent date.   Probably it may—as there is no authentic account of the Glovers being a corporation at the period of the Holy Wars ; but when we see the crafts of Edinburgh claiming to be ranked amongst the Crusaders, why may not we, who ranked higher, and can boast of as ancient a genealogy, as "Auld Reekie," be permitted also to claim our share in the doings of these noble and chivalrous times ?

FUNDS.

In the illustration of this important branch of the subject, so essentially connected with the prosperity and stability of the incorporation, I intend to give a short sketch of the origin, uses, and application of their funds, so far as I have been enabled to trace these in the records of the calling ; and more particularly to prove that these funds are not " poor's funds," a very prevalent but most erroneous view of the nature of corporation funds, and a view which so many in the present day entertain.

I have already stated the most probable way in which these funds were originally formed and accumulated, now let us go more particularly into the illustration of this subject.   The meaning and intention of the constitution of a society can only be ascertained by tracing it through its charters, acts and bye-laws, minutes and proceedings ; and in these, I think, it will clearly appear, that the idea of the funds of the calling being called " poor's funds" was never for a moment contemplated by our ancestors ; and although, no doubt, they always applied *part* of these funds towards the support of their poor brethren, yet they considered the legitimate use of these same funds to be for maintaining the rights and privileges, promoting the respectability and influence of the calling, the comfort and social enjoyment of the members, and also for the encouragement and cherishing a proper spirit of industry and independence among the brethren.

But to prove this, out of 35 charters and grants, conveying certain sums to be paid annually to the calling, out of lands and houses, only one, for 30s. yearly (dated 1569), is stated to be for " *an annivesarie and*   for the maist puir and indigent of the said craft," the other 34 charters being chiefly intended to maintain the altar of St Bartholomew, of which the calling were the founders. And would our ancestors have expended such large sums in 1633, when they danced before King Charles I., which amounted to 350 merks, or would they have paid (in 1655) six hundred pounds Scots for a matchlock, a sum equivalent to the value of two acres of their lands of St Leonard's at that period, had it been " poor's funds"? Surely not. But what places it in a still stronger light, and proves to a demonstration that these funds were never intended to be styled " poor's funds," is this, that the sums paid by freemen's sons at their entry to the incorporation, are as follows :—" *Four pounds Scots to the calling, and eight pounds Scots in lieu of the banquet and wine, conforme to ancient practice of the calling.*" (See minute book, 12th September 1737.) Also one freeman's son is stated to have paid, at his entry, " *as an freeman's son, twelve pounds Scots for the banquet and wine,*" and other " *twelve pounds Scots for his freedom, banquet, and wine.*" (See minute book, 29th September 1726.) And the last instance that I shall mention is 23d November 1762, where the freeman's son, at his entry, " *payed to the box-master, for the use of the calling, four pounds Scots, and eight pounds Scots in place of a dinner, as the ordinary dues.*"

Now, had these funds been originally intended as " poor's funds," or had the idea of ever turning them to that purpose been entertained by our ancestors, would they have allowed such an important and permanent part of their revenue, as the entry money of freemen, to be applied to such purposes?—surely not. But perhaps the best way of knowing exactly the uses and purposes of the funds, is by taking an abstract of the accounts for ten years, at the period when the affairs of the calling were managed with the greatest propriety, and attention to the interests of the incorporation, and when the calling were possessed of all the landed and heritable property that they have at present,—the period I allude to is from 1750 to 1760 inclusive. I have subjoined in the appendix a table shewing the income and expenditure of the calling for those 10 years, to which I beg to refer ; but I may be allowed to state, that at that period the number of members were about 80, that is, nearly a third more than they are at present : and one thing is certain, that among that number there must have been many indigent families, for sickness, disease and death, were as prevalent at that time, as they are in our day. Well, how were these distressed members, widows, and orphans supported ?—I cannot tell,— but one thing is clear, that they did not derive the whole of their support from the funds of the calling, but only a small and scanty allowance, as during that period the average eleemosynary roll was only £55 sterling, while the average income, during the same period, was £245 sterling, which was applied in paying the interest of their borrowed money, the ordinary expenses of the calling, such as entertainments, public burdens, &c., and a considerable part applied to paying off their debts ; but perhaps it may be said, that living in these days was very different from the present, as provision, and all the other necessaries of life, were so very cheap. No doubt that was the case, but not to the extent that many suppose, as meal was $7\frac{1}{2}$d a peck, and barley averaged 11s per boll. I have already stated, that the acts and bye-laws of the corporation are excellent guides for leading us to a true and accurate knowledge of the doings of our ancestors, and the nature and design of a corporate body ; and I have attentively gone over and studied the whole of these from 1593 to the present day, and I cannot find even in a single one of these any thing that countenances, in the most remote degree, the idea that the corporation funds are " poor's funds." No doubt there are several of them that prescribes the manner, and lays down rules, how the poor are to be attended to, and the way in which these poor should act; but even in these very acts, there is nothing that can be interpreted as furnishing grounds to suppose that the calling's funds are " poor funds."

In the acts and laws we have, as it were, the rules and regulations for the government of the calling embodied in a judicial form; but in the *minutes* of the calling, which we are now about to take notice of, as throwing so much light on this branch of the subject—in these minutes we have the spirit and meaning of these laws reduced to practice, and brought into the active business of life, and which present to us a faithful and striking delineation of the doings and conduct of our ancestors; and, I may almost say, exhibits before us their inmost thoughts, desires, and feelings, and the motives by which they were influenced in conducting the affairs of the corporation.

I can only speak with certainty as to the minutes which commence in 1719, and which are continued in an uninterrupted series to the present day, all of which I have most carefully gone ever, and endeavoured to make myself fully acquainted with their contents, and I can honestly and conscientiously state, that there is not a single word (with the exception of one word that was inadvertently introduced into a minute a few years ago), that in the slightest degree countenances the idea of the funds being " poor's funds." And nothing more clearly illustrates this, than that the calling were often engaged in tedious and expensive law suits. The propriety of engaging in many of them was often questioned by a considerable minority of the corporation, who, to express their disapprobation of such proceedings, entered their protest, and reasons of protest, in the minutes: these, with the answers to such protests, often occupy a considerable space in these minutes. Yet in any of these reasons and answers, and reasons of dissent, there is not one that ever states that the money which was expended in these law-suits belonged to a " poor's fund," or that it was injuring the poor; but only states, in this general way, that they either injured, or tended to waste, the " funds of the calling," or " calling's funds."

Had any of these protestors conceived the calling's funds to be " poor's funds," and waited for a favourable opportunity to record these views, this would have been the time which he would have seized upon to have expressed his solemn dissent at seeing what he considered the money that should have been solely directed to the support of the poor, squandered away in expensive law-suits: this surely would have been a subject on which he would have expostulated in the most feeling and eloquent manner; but however much inclined he might have been to have given a high colouring to his reasons of dissent, by using such a strong appeal to the benevolent feelings of his brethren, yet this natural, and what would have been indeed a strong reason of protest, was never in any one instance resorted to—for this very plain and obvious reason, that our ancestors never for a moment entertained the idea of the funds of the calling being " poor's funds," and therefore never used an argument which they well knew was so untenable. This view of corporation funds being " poor's funds," is a discovery which has been reserved for the " learned" of the present day, but which has no countenance or support from the records of the doings and proceedings of our ancestors.

I might multiply instances to establish the truth of this position; but I shall only state one or two more. In the title deeds conveying the valuable landed and heritable property that the calling has from time to time acquired, one would naturally expect to find the uses and purposes to which the revenues or rentals arising from these were to be applied, the more especially if they were to be held in trust for the benefit of the calling. Now, let us for a moment enquire into the manner in which these properties were conveyed to, and held by, the calling. When the calling gave orders to purchase those lands, it was " *for the use and behoof of the whole members and community of the said Glovers' calling*," and " *in name and for the use and behoof of the calling.*" The extracts from the title deeds are as follows :—The title deeds, conveying the Lands of Pomarium (1642) mention that it is to the " Deacon of the Glovers of Perth, for himself, and in name and behoof of the remanent brethren of the said craft." The title deeds of Leonard's Ley (1646.) " Disposition by John Anderson, glover, burgess of Perth, and deacon of the Glovers, with consent of Euphan Johnston, his spouse, *to the auditories and positories* of the said incorporation, *for themselves and remanent members of the calling*," and " *in favour of the brethren of the Glovers' calling.*" The title deeds of Tullilum (1684): " *In favour of the dean and box-masters of the Glovers' calling of Perth, for themselves, and in name and behalf of the whole remanent bre-*

thren and fraternity of the said incorporation," and *" for behoof of the calling."* The title deeds of Souter Houses (1740): *" In favour of deacons and box-masters of the Glover incorporation of Perth, in name and for behoof of the calling."* The title deeds of St. Leonard's Hall and Willsland (1742): *" In favour of the deacon and boxmasters of the Glover incorporation of Perth,"* and *" in favour of the Glover calling."*

Now, in all these extracts from the title deeds of these lands, there is not a single syllable that conveys the idea that they were held in trust for behoof of " poor's fund," but " for behoof and in favour of the calling," that is the revenue derived from these lands to be applied to, and issue for, such purposes as the members for the time being considered to be for the good of the calling.

The only other instance that I shall state, is the manner in which the calling acted in regard to their seats in the churches. If any species of property more than another might be considered as peculiarly belonging to the poor, and any revenue derived from that source applied solely towards their support, it surely must have been this, had the corporation funds been solely intended for the poor. But let us judge by facts on this point. I have therefore only to remark that the calling never derived a fraction from their seats in the churches (with the exception of a seat in the East Church, which they acquired by special compact, the manner of which will be afterwards stated) until 1773, when the Middle Church was new seated at a considerable expense, and the calling, from a wish to accommodate the families of the brethren allowed them to hold particular seats, on paying a trifle, more like a small feu than a rack rent.

FLAG.

Whether the calling had a flag or banner, previous to 1604, is not stated, but it is highly probable that they never would be without this ornamental and characteristic ensign of their craft. There is no trace in any of the records of the purposes for which it was used, but from a tradition that is still current among the brethren, that the youngest member is always styled the standard-bearer, or the one whose duty it is to carry the flag—from this tradition we naturally draw the conclusion, that the flag was used as a rallying point when the brethren were called to arms, and also used, and that principally, in the pageants and processions of the calling in former times. The one that is presently in possession of the calling is made of yellow silk, with a square of blue persian in the centre, with the arms and motto of the calling emblazoned in gold, surrounded with an inscription in an elliptic or oval form, but as the gold had eaten away the blue silk where the letters and arms have been inscribed, it was renewed three years ago, and is now in a complete state of repair, the original yellow silk being still in excellent preservation, and very little injured by time or tear and wear, although it is now 226 years old.

The calling, in 1648, were presented by one of their old apprentices, who had been an " Ensign Lieutenant under my Lord Banff," with the flag or ensign that had belonged to his company of the army of the Covenanters, with this inscription on it, " Carrying for Religion, King, Country, and Covenant;" but what became of it is not known, as there is no further notice taken of it in the calling's records, and none of the present generation of Glovers ever saw it, or heard what had become of it.

COATS OF ARMS AND MOTTOES.

" Arms are used in heraldry for marks of dignity and honour, regularly composed of certain figures and colours, given or authorised by Sovereigns, and borne in banners, shields, coats, &c., for the distinction of persons, families, and states, and passing by descent to posterity." " It is a rule that the simpler and less diversified the *arms,* the more noble and ancient they are."

" Stars are one of the three forms of *blazon* chiefly used for empires, kings, and princes."

" The shorter the motto, the more beautiful."

The arms of the calling, as blazoned on the flag, are a pair of gloves or gauntlets " *displayed,"* in a shield, with three green-painted stars surmounting the shield, with the motto " *Grace and Peace*" carried in a scroll over the arms, and the whole encompassed with these words in an ellipse or oval, " The perfect honour of a craft, or beauty of a trade, consists not in .... whereby virtue gains renown." The blanks shew that certain words are awanting, which cannot now be supplied, in consequence of the gold letters having corroded the silk, or rather the substance that had attached the gold to the silk had been the cause of destroying that particular portion of it, and which, in consequence, had allowed certain letters to drop away, until it was too late to restore them. But although we may regret the loss of these words as a matter of antiquarian research, to complete the sentence, yet they do not affect the proper decyphering of the arms, which fortunately are yet entire on the flag.

The other coat of arms, as painted on the calling's seats in the Middle Church, and dated 1773, the Dictionary of the Acts 1793, the Glover seats' minute-book 17—, the calling's seat in East Church 18—, and also the painting in the hall 18—, is quite different from the arms on the flag, for they are a pair of gloves " displayed," with the branch or cane of five balls or nut-shells between them, the large shears for cutting gloves, the skinners' paring iron, and pair of glove sticks, all under the gloves, and emblazoned in a shield, the field blue (" azure") ; the supporters are a stag " rampant" on the right, and a goat " rampant" on the left, with a ram " passant" for the crest; but the arms in the Middle Church have for the crest a stag " salient," the motto " To God only be all glory."

From such a difference in the coats of arms, I am inclined to think that we are indebted more to the imagination of the painters of these modern arms, in the churches, books, and hall, than to any accurate copy from the real and genuine arms and motto of the calling ; for I am firmly convinced that the ancient and genuine arms and motto of the calling are those that are on the flag, and not those modern ones which are to be seen in the places already referred to, for I cannot find any trace of the arms with the supporters and crest of a more ancient date than 1773, which was the period when these were painted in the Middle Church, where I suspect the painter had devised and executed these arms from his own fancy.

We also find portions of the arms scattered over different parts of the old furniture belonging to the calling. On the front of the old oaken charter-chest, we discover, deeply indented, the pair of gloves " displayed," and the skinners' paring iron ; also on the old picture of St Bartholomew, that formerly graced the old hall in Curfew Row, we find in the corner one bunch of nut-shells or balls.

By the way we may remark, that the five balls or nut-shells were used for the purpose of containing specimens of the manufacture of certain descriptions of remarkably fine gloves in ancient times ; for they were made of such fine materials that they were folded in pairs, and inclosed in these nut-shells, which were often sent as presents, by the cavaliers of olden times, to the fair sex, as tokens of affection and love.

But to return : One weighty reason that should induce us to adopt, as the genuine arms and motto of the calling, those that are on the flag (1604), as being, as far as we are enabled to judge, the most ancient, and, of course, the most genuine, but also as, according to the laws of heraldry, the most honourable, for " the simpler and less diversified the arms, the more noble and ancient they are," and " the shorter the motto, the more beautiful." Now, all these marks of ancient and honourable bearing are fully exemplified on our flag ; and, therefore, we should, without hesitation or doubt, receive them as the real, genuine, and ancient arms of " our ancient craft."

And when we also recollect that our motto was the apostolic salutation to the Christian churches—St Paul using the identical words in almost all of his epistles, the beloved disciple in his second epistle, and in the Revelation—St Peter in his epistles—also James and Jude—all the books of heraldry cannot furnish us with one more expressive or becoming ; and, in conclusion, I sincerely wish that it may not only be the motto, but that " *Grace and Peace*" may always be the portion of the Glovers.

POLITICAL RIGHTS AND PRIVILEGES.

At what time the Glovers, along with the other Trades, first sat in the Town Council, cannot now be ascertained. It must have been at a very early period, very probably coeval with the Town Council itself, as from the numbers, respectability, influence, and importance of the Craftsmen of Perth, and from the respect that the Sovereigns of Scotland always shewed to these Craftsmen, I think there can be little doubt that they were entrusted many centuries ago, (along with the Guild or Merchants,) as Magistrates and Town Council, with the civil government of the city—our city being amongst the earliest or most ancient of the royal burghs of Scotland, upon which important political rights and privileges were conferred ; as Perth, previous to 1482, was the the metropolis of Scotland, and for many centuries occupied a distinguished place in the history of our country.

The Glovers appear to have always had two representatives in Council, viz.—the Deacon and Trades' Councillor, and every fourth year, when they had the Trades' Bailie, three members.

To be a Deacon, Bailie, or Town Councillor, and as such to have a seat in Council, was an honour that was very highly prized by our ancestors, and was to them an object of honest and laudable ambition,—as in it they had an opportunity of promoting the welfare of their fellow citizens, and advancing the interests and respectability of their Incorporations. To give an instance how they estimated that honour, I quote an extract from an act of the Convener Court, dated 15th October, 1653,—" Anent unbrotherly conduct betwixt members of crafts, and that due respect should be shown to such as had been office-bearers in their respective Incorporations ;" Statutes and ordains, " that for encouragement of those members of any of the said Incorporations who have carried public office, and have been admitted within the Council House : *And to the effect a tender and reverend respect may be had of their persons in time coming,*" ordains " that whatsoever private member, of any Incorporation, who shall be found guilty of any miscarriage against any of the said members, (who has been in public office, or in the council as said is,) either by reviling words, or calumnies, or by any hostile action, private or public, offered to their persons, his fault shall be esteemed double to that which is committed against private persons, and shall be ordained and censured in a double fine and punishment accordingly."

When this act of the Convener Court was passed, the Incorporated Trades enjoyed a full and a fair share in the management of the public affairs of the burgh ; as at that period the Town Council consisted of fourteen Merchants and fourteen Tradesmen, and the Treasurer every alternate year being taken from the Trades, gave them in that year the majority in Council. But the Merchant side of the Council, by a deep-laid and politic manœuvre, applied to the Convention of Burghs, and most probably suggested the plan to that Convention, which plan was to eject from the Town Council the Trades' Deacons of the Weaver and Wauker Incorporations, which was accordingly done, by an act of the Convention of Burrows, dated 19th July, 1658 ; not for any acts of delinquency on the part of these two Incorporations, or deficiency in their titles, but solely on these grounds,—"*for settling of peace betwixt the Merchants and Tradesmen of the said Burgh of Perth at present, and for avoiding all controversys in future.*" Really this was one of the most despotic and iniquitous acts, all the circumstances of the case considered, that ever was passed. Upon the same principle, any Prime Minister might request his Sovereign to expel from the House of Peers any nobleman, who, in the conscientious and upright discharge of his duty, found himself compelled to oppose those measures of government that he thought hurtful to the best interests of the country. And the Premier, in getting rid of such obnoxious members, might think it quite sufficient to state to the country, that these Peers were expelled solely upon these grounds—" for settling of peace at present, and for avoiding all controversies in future." Strong and important reasons indeed ! And the two cases I consider as exactly parallel ; for these two Incorporations held their seats in Council by royal charters, and were, like the seats in the House of Peers, hereditary.

The Convention of Royal Burghs, who were both the judges and jury in this case, being all merchants, and having to decide whether merchants or tradesmen should have the superiority, of course, all their *clanish feelings* were decidedly in favour of the Merchant side of the Town Council. Clanish feelings, did I say; I am assured there was something worse that influenced these merchant judges ;—a narrow-minded jealousy and envy of the peculiar privileges at this time enjoyed by the craftsmen of Perth. And a strong proof of such feelings influencing these merchants in the Royal Burghs of Scotland, is—that in the dispute for precedency, or priority of place, betwixt the Burghs of Perth and Dundee, in a memorial dated 31st December, 1602, presented by the Magistrates and Council of Dundee to the Royal Commissioners appointed by James VI. to decide this question betwixt these two burghs, they plead the following as one of the grounds on which they should be preferred to Perth, viz. :—" *Dundee is more civillie governed than Perth, in respect the haill Magistrates of Dundee are of the merchant state, except two of the Council for the crafts, and the equal half of the Council of Perth are craftsmen.*"

" More civillie governed ;" indeed, it really showed that these proud and self-important merchant burghers of Dundee were sadly in want of argument to support their claims, when they were reduced to use such unworthy and unbecoming language towards the Incorporated Trades of Perth. How different is the language used by Mary Queen of Scots regarding these same Trades ? In a charter dated 28th May, 1556, and fourteenth year of her reign, specially granted in favour of the Trades of the Burgh of Perth, the following expressions of respect and regard to these crafts occur :—" Mary, by the grace of God, Queen of Scots, to all good men to whom thir presents shall come, greeting,—Forasmuch as, we, understanding that our noble progenitors, Kings of Scotland, *having regard and respect to the common well and policy of our kingdom, and that good manners and order did arise therein, and increase by tradesmen, without whom no kingdom nor city could stand or be in esteem,* did give and grant sundry privileges and libertys *to tradesmen* of burghs and citys of our kingdom, *especially to our burgh of Perth ;* ' "*and moreover, we, having respect that the said burgh of Perth doth daily increase, and is chiefly upheld by the fortune, order, and policy of the tradesmen,* and that they exceed the rest of the inhabitants and indwellers of the said burgh *in number,* and do equal the merchants themselves thereof in paying all manner of stents, taxations, and impositions whatsoever imposed on the said burgh, *and that they are perpetually ready with their bodys and goods to defend our authority* as the rest of the said burgh,—We, therefore, desiring peace, friendship, and good will betwixt the merchants and tradesmen of the said burgh may for the future appear, and be ceremoniously observed, and that every one of them, according to their several fortunes, have the equal use and enjoyment of their privileges for the future within the said burgh." " *Moreover, we, by these presents, ratify and approve all other privileges, libertys, and facultys, given and granted by our noble progenitors to the said tradesmen in times bygone.*"

And King James VI. in his charter, dated 22d July 1581, in favour of the craftsmen of burrowes, thus speaks of tradesmen, " Witt ye, because we, understanding that our noble progenitors, kings of Scotland, having ane good mind and respect to the common well of our realm ; *and that without honest craftsmen the common policy well composed could not stand long.*" What a contrast does these extracts from the charters of these two sovereigns of Scotland exhibit, when compared with the taunting and insolent language of these merchant burghers of Dundee ; and by merchants entertaining almost similar sentiments were the rights and privileges of the tradesmen of Perth brought under review, and a sentence passed by them depriving two incorporated trades of their privileges, the injustice of which has scarce any parallel in history. But it may be said, was there no appeal from the Convention of Burghs to a higher tribunal. Unfortunately for the trades at that period, none ; for Oliver Cromwell being then in the zenith of his power, it being the last year of his Protectorship, how could the trades expect to be heard by an appeal to him, when they had nothing to produce in their own favours but *royal charters*—all which authorities Cromwell despised. And it most unfortunately happened for the Trades, that for thirty years afterwards, the whole country was in a state of anarchy and confusion, in consequence of the oppressive and cruel treatment that the Presbyterians—Covenanters as they were called—endured at the hands of a tyrannical government, in their attempts to force upon the consciences of the people a religion that they considered as too nearly allied to Popery, and which they could not approve of. And at the Revolution (1688), time, which blunts the feelings, and reconciles the mind to deprivations, and also many of those whose feelings had been so deeply wounded by seeing these *trades* degraded in the town, being gathered to their fathers, and their descendants, from various causes, perhaps from not having a proper opportunity for urging their claims before a higher court, were obliged to submit to an act of injustice, which they must have felt, but could not remedy. And although it may be considered a digression, I cannot help taking notice of an individual, " John Davidson, one of the hammermen of the said burgh," who, along with Patrick Cree, deacon of the skinners, had been deputed to attend the Convention of Burghs, to advocate the cause of the trades before that court. From many collateral circumstances, I have every reason to believe that he was that celebrated personage who, when Cromwell invaded Scotland in 1651, acted as the Lieutenant of the division of our citizens who marched by orders of King Charles II. to oppose Cromwell's landing at Burntisland, and who, after fighting heroically, were defeated, and obliged to retreat to Perth, where Cromwell followed them, and sat down before the town walls with his army, having found the gates shut. " *John Davidson,* a bold and enterprising gentleman, ordered carts to drive up and down the streets, and a drum to beat continually through the town, and at all the ports, to deceive the English general. The town being summoned to surrender, Cromwell offered honourable terms, which were accepted, and the gates thrown open." " The Provost attended the English officers, and conducted them to John Davidson's house, where, after an entertainment, Cromwell asked the Provost how, in his defenceless situation, he proposed to keep him at the gates ; the Provost simply answered, that they designed to stand out until they heard that the King was in England. Cromwell, with a sneer, called him a silly body, and below his notice; but said, if he had time, he would hang *Davidson.*" " Immediately after Cromwell's departure from Mr Davidson's house, the side wall fell down ; and Davidson said, he wished it had fallen a quarter of an hour sooner, though he, Sampson-like, had perished in the ruins. Davidson had great possessions in the town, was a public notary, and fiscal of court. He translated and illuminated the town's charters ; some copies, written by his hand, are extant among the incorporations of trades, with gilded capitals His progenitors founded the chaplainry of St Leonard's, and endowed it with a stipend out of their lands. The lineal representatives of that family are called Vicars of St Leonard's, and reserved their title to that benefice. John Davidson gave a tack of the lands of St Leonard's to Campbell of Aberuchill, for a charging horse to fight against Cromwell." Amongst the calling's papers, there is an " Assignation by John Davidson, chaplain of the chaplainry and altarage of St Leonard's, to Colin Campbell of Aberuchill, of said chaplainry, and annual rents thereto belonging, for his life, and three lives after, and then for eleven times nineteen years, dated 17 March 1660, and registered at Edinburgh, 12 August, 1734." This is very probably the tack previously alluded to, as said to have been given for a " charging horse." The calling have also in their possession one of the copies of these illuminated town charters, with gilded capitals, written by the said John Davidson, bound in vellum, and in very good preservation.

But, to return to our subject—perhaps it may be asked, why attach so much importance to that act of the Convention of Burghs, depriving these two incorporations of their seats in the Town Council, seeing that the Trades have still such a respectable minority, being 12 to 14 guild members in Council, their influence and importance appear to be very little less than formerly ? But, alas! from a system that was introduced, either at that period or very shortly afterwards, among the Guild side of the Council, of the minority being obliged to fall in with the majority upon every question of importance brought before the Council, such as voting for a member of parliament, clergymen of the established churches, teachers, &c., and which system has been acted upon with more or less severity against the Trades ever since ; it was indeed a masterly stroke of policy. I do not speak as to its morality, for every person in efficient situations should be allowed to vote according to their conscience, and for what they really believe to be best for the interest of the community over which they are called to preside. This system, in fact,

rendered the twelve trades' representatives in Council of no more value or importance than so many cyphers—a degradation which our ancestors felt most keenly,
and made many a severe struggle to break those chains, and abolish what they
considered a most iniquitous system.   Some of the steps they took, and the results
that followed, I cannot describe in more appropriate language than in the following
extract from the calling's minutes of 29th September, 1740, which gives a most
masterly and graphic description of that system, or " beautiful order," as it is
called in modern times:—" Perth, 29th Sept. 1740, at six o'clock afternoon.
Which day, convened in the ordinary meeting-house of the Glover calling of Perth,
in ane general court, John Miller, present deacon, (and convener of the trades),
together with the remanent brethren and freemen of the incorporation, being fifty
in number, when the deacon represented to the calling, that for several years
byegone, those of the guild side in the Town Council have had combinations
together, wherein six of them, with the preses, oblige the rest of their number to
vote in elections, and in all other matters of moment in the Town Council, according to the minds of the majority, (though never so contrary to their inclinations),
which majority these seven are, the preses always having the casting vote ; and
none are admitted to the Council on the Guild side but upon making such promises,
and conforming to this arbitrary practice; and any who saw the unlawfulness of
these promises afterwards, and did not continue to follow these engagements, at
very first election were turned out of their offices, or out of the Council.   By which
illegal combination, seven men, of which the preses being one, overrule the whole
Council, consisting of twenty six members, whereof fourteen are of the Guildry,
and twelve of the Trades ; and by virtue thereof, several worthy and useful members
have been frequently turned out of Council, to the great loss both of the Guildry
and Trades — thereby both their privileges come to be in great hazard—elections,
with all their votes of moment, have been carried as these seven desired."

" For remedying of which, he the said deacon, and his brethren in the convener
court, after duly considering the above, and consulting the same, thought it their
duty to join with three of the guild side at that day's election, (left the council-
house, and adjourned to the tolbooth, where the last year's elections were made),
and having chosen a preses and clerk, proceeded to elect magistrates and councillors
for the ensuing year.   " All which the deacon laid before the calling, to know
their approving or not approving of his conduct ; and they did unanimously
approve of his and the convener court's conduct in all the above mentioned proceedings, also of the magistrates chosen by them ; and did, and hereby do enact, if
any process or lawsuit shall happen, any manner of way, on account of the above
election, that the expense of such process shall be defrayed out of the public stock
of the trade, in proportion with the guildry and other trades, and that their box-
master may advance money accordingly when called for.   Likewise the court
ordered the thanks of the house to be returned to the deacon and councillor for
their steady conduct and behaviour in Town Council, which they look upon as
very much conducive for supporting and vindicating the rights and privileges of
the trades and whole burgh, which was done accordingly ; they also appoint this
narrative, and this their act, to be insert in the trade's book, and the deacon
and clerk to sign the same.   (Signed) JO. MILLER, JAMES SIBBALD, Clerk."

Another meeting of the calling took place, 5th November 1740, on the same subject, forty-eight of the brethren being present, when Bailie William Barland (in
absence of the Deacon) being chosen preses, stated to the meeting that James Cree
and his adherents (that is, the eleven guild members, who were left in the minority) had presented a petition to the Lords of Council and Session for sequestrating
the common good of the burgh, and taking the management of it out of the hands
of Provost Ferguson and the other Magistrates and Councillors (that is, those who
were elected by the other fifteen members of Council, who formed the majority),—
" and also that mutual summonses of declarator and reduction have been raised by
the said Provost Ferguson and his adherents, and James Cree and his adherents ;
and, as we have formerly approven of the election of the said Provost Ferguson,
and of the Magistrates and Council adhering to him, therefore we hereby unanimously empower John Miller, present deacon, Thos. and William Barland, late
bailies, and Alexander MacEwen, or any one or more of them, to apply to the Lords
of Session by a petition in our name by themselves or any other proper person, for

preventing the sequestration, and to keep the management of the said common good in the hands of Provost Ferguson, and the other Magistrates and Councillors adhering to him, and appoints the preses and electors to sign this act and sederunt." (Signed) " WILL. BARLAND. JAMES SIBBALD, Clerk."—There is no other minute in the calling's records that I can trace relative to this important case, but from all that I could learn from authentic sources, the issue of this plea was against the Magistrates and Council chosen by the twelve trades' members, and three guild members of Council, who formed the majority—in consequence, chiefly, of the said majority having left the Council House and completed their elections in the Tolbooth. It was most keenly contested, having been carried by appeal to the House of Lords, and cost both parties upwards of two thousand pounds sterling, an immense sum in those days; but it showed the great importance and deep interest felt by the trades of that period, in every thing connected with the free and unfettered exercise of their civil and political rights and privileges, and we cannot but honour the memories of our patriotic ancestors, in having thus, although unsuccessfully, made such a glorious struggle to shake off the yoke of an oppressive and unjust system, and to restore the Incorporated Trades to that place and influence in the Councils of the City, which it was originally intended by the Sovereigns (who conferred upon them these honourable situations in the government of the city) that they should hold.

The only other attempt to break the " beautiful order" was in 1774, when the Convener Court, along with certain merchants and guildry, resolved to oppose the right of the Magistrates to roup " the Town's salmon fishings till such time as they agreed to serve the inhabitants, and expose the same to sale each day in the public market, and expected the calling would approve of it, which the calling accordingly did; and also agreed to join along with them in a petition to the Court of Session, " not only to insist upon salmon, but also to break the " beautiful order;"—but this plea fell to the ground, the calling some months afterwards having declined to middle any farther with it, in consequence of the said plea (salmon) being "jumbled with other matters."

WARS, &c.

Although the history of the last fifty years is perhaps the most eventful and interesting that ever happened in the world, and has been productive of such important consequences both to nations and individuals; and while wars and desolations have raged with the most tempestuous fury over almost all the countries of the earth, —yet we in this highly favoured island have lived in comparative peace and security, listening to the details, and watching with deep and heart-felt interest, the progress of these mighty events, which were apparently changing the destinies of empires and nations, and completely altering the constitution of civilized society. Although we have never experienced the horrors of domestic wars or foreign invasion, our ancestors in this country, and in our own city, were often exposed to these calamities, and lived in troublous times, when they were obliged to learn the art of war as a profession, along with the arts or sciences of their own peculiar crafts; and, like the Jews of old, while rebuilding the walls of their beloved city, were obliged to wear the sword in one hand, while they wrought with the other. Thus, as it were, being always cased in armour, they felt a keen interest in every thing connected with the science of war; and to render themselves masters in the use of the different warlike weapons was their constant and anxious study. Amongst these instruments of war, the bow and arrow was the favourite, and our citizens were long celebrated as first-rate bowmen. One of our townsmen, in his History of Perth, thus speaks of this warlike science :—" Archery, of which the gentlemen of Perth were great masters, was made an indispensable article of education, from the days of James the First. This most accomplished and wise Prince passed an act *forbidding the favourite diversion of foot-ball*, substituting in its place that of shooting with bows and arrows. Every boy, when he came to the age of thirteen, was obliged at stated times to practice archery at certain bow-marks." " The strong and expert archers had their bow-marks in the South Inch. Near the south end of this Inch stands yet a stone, which, tradition says, was the southern mark; the northern is near to the north-west side of the ditch that surrounds the mount. It was fixed on a rising ground, called the " Scholars' Knoll." The stone was but lately carried off. The distance betwixt these marks is about 500 fathoms. They must have been very strong and expert archers who could shoot an arrow between these marks! But it was not solely as a sport or pastime that our ancestors practised archery, but chiefly as one of the means of resisting their enemies, either in the battle-field, or defending our city when besieged by a hostile army. I need not state that the English were more celebrated for their skill in archery than any other nation in the world ; and, from the Scotch being so frequently at war with them, they had often experienced the fatal effects of that mode of warfare ; and, as our countrymen, previous to King James the First's time. had not cultivated that branch of the art of war so assiduously as the English, although they were by no means strangers to it, but on the contrary many of them excelled in archery ; but it was only in James the First's time that it was made an " indispensable article of education." And our townsmen had better opportunity of making themselves masters of this branch than any of the citizens of the other Scottish burghs ; for, not only being the metropolis and, as such, the chief residence of our monarchs previous to James III., the flower of the Scottish nobility, with their numerous retinues, must have often taken up their residence in our city ; and even after the royal court was removed to Edinburgh, yet Perth was not deserted by our nobility, but was still the place in which many of them abode. But Perth was also often garrisoned by the English army, who, while they occupied it, would undoubtedly practise that science for which they were so celebrated, and our citizens would not fail to embrace such a favourable opportunity to perfect themselves under such able instructors. And more especially in 1298, when Edward I. of England, after having reduced all the fortresses in Scotland, rebuilt the fortifications of Perth, and placed in it a strong garrison of his English troops ; and when James I., about 120 years after this, issued the act ordering the more genuine cultivation of the science of archery, he would find his citizens of Perth, among whom he lived, particularly zealous in seconding his views in this matter, for they must have been well trained to this exercise, especially while the town was occupied by the English under the first three Edwards. And what furnishes us with a strong proof of their great proficiency in this " noble art" is, that in a contest of archery held on the Links at Leith, our townsmen triumphantly carried off the prize, and offered the odds of ten to three, a challenge which their opponents appears to have declined.

And as the Incorporated Trades of Perth have long been known as the " sheaf of arrows," not only as an emblem of their union and strength, but also, I should suppose, for their superior skill and dexterity in archery ; for it is highly probable that, in the numerous competitions that took place on the South Inch, the craftsmen were often pitted against, not only the trained and expert marksmen who often formed the retinue of the great men of the Scottish court, but also the soldiers of the English and Scottish armies that either garrisoned the city, or attended their sovereigns or commanders while residing there. And it was not only in archery that the citizens excelled, but history informs us of their being well skilled in the other weapons used in war, and also conspicuous for their bravery ; as in the memorable combat in the reign of Robert III. (1400), betwixt the two Highland clans in the North Inch, where the victory was achieved chiefly by the prowess and strength of Henry Wynde, a saddler in Perth, who espoused the cause of one of these clans, and was the principal means of their gaining the day. The other weapons of war in most common use by our ancestors, previous to the invention of gunpowder, were the sword, spear, battle-axe, and pike, or partizan as it is sometimes called ; and it was the practice at the election of every new deacon and boxmaster, for them to present to the calling a new pike ; but, in 1631, the deacon presented a musket, staff, and bandolier, and the calling made this a law afterwards for his successors in office to do the same, and which was continued until 1710, when, " taking to their consideration the little use the calling has for firearms, they therefore statute and ordain, that, for the future, each new elected deacon pay five pound Scots in place of his gun ; and each new box-master, four pounds Scots, as the value of his gun, for the use of the poor of the calling."

From what has already been stated, it clearly appears that our ancestors were regularly trained to military exercises ; and that the citizen of former times was the soldier and craftsman combined. Now let us shortly take notice of a few of those scenes of strife and war in which the Glovers bore a part ; and although there can be no doubt that they must have often been called upon to defend, with their lives and property, their rights and privileges both as citizens and Scotsmen, previous to 1559, we shall confine ourselves to a few instances that took place at this period, or shortly afterwards. The first we shall mention is that memorable one in 1559, when, in consequence of the duplicity and perfidity of the Queen Regent, who had violated the most solemn promises to protect the Reformers, and who was taking measures to root them out of the land, and re-establish Popery. The leaders of the Congregation, as they were called, the Earl of Argyle and James Stewart, Prior of St Andrews, having received intelligence that the Queen designed to take Stirling, marched out of Perth with *three hundred citizens*, resolved to prosecute the Reformation or perish in the attempt. To shew their zeal and resolution, instead of ribbons *they put ropes about their necks*, that whoever deserted their colours should certainly be hanged by these ropes : from this circumstance arose the proverb of " St Johnston's ribbons." With this inconsiderable force they advanced, and wherever they came the people joined them in a body. Their army was seldom less numerous than five thousand men. The gates of Stirling, and every other town, were thrown open to receive them, where they took care to destroy every monument of Popish superstition ; and, without striking a blow, they took possession of the capital of the kingdom ; and, having purged the kirks of idols, they placed the reformed preachers in them.

It is not stated in any document that I have seen, the number of the Glovers who formed a part of these three hundred citizens ; but I have no doubt, from the circumstance of the craftsmen at this period forming the majority of its citizens (as Queen Mary in her charter, granted only five years before this, states " that they exceed the rest of the inhabitants and indwellers of the said burgh in number"), that they also formed the majority of this heroic band, who were so instrumental in planting and establishing the Reformation ; and I think it highly probable that the Glovers would furnish at any rate from twenty to thirty of the brethren as its quota, of this brave and gallant band. What strengthens this conjecture is this, that in a case almost similar that happened about eighty years after this, there were fourteen of the Glover calling, whose names are on record who formed part of that army of the Covenanters, who were defeated at Tibbermuir, in 1644, by Montrose, who commanded the Highlanders and Irish, three to four hundred of our people being left dead on the field of battle, and a great many more of our Covenanting army were slain in their retreat to the town.

The only other instance that I shall mention is, in 1651, when, by order of the King (Charles II.), the whole citizens of Perth marched out to the South Inch, where they cheerfully made choice of a hundred men, who were to march to Burntisland to watch the motions of Cromwell's fleet and army. This company joined a detachment from the army at Dunfermline of 3000 men, and were attacked near Inverkeithing, and defeated by a superior number of Cromwell's army ; 1600 being killed, and 1200 taken prisoners. The Perth officers marched with the remains of their company to Perth. There is no account given of the number of Glovers who either joined this company or fell in battle ; but it is very probable that some of our brethren perished, for more than one-half of our force engaged appear to have been slain in this sanguinary conflict.

I need not give any further account of the troublous times in which our ancestors lived, suffice it to mention, that it was only in 1710 that they began to throw off their armour, and allow the soldier to merge into the quiet and industrious craftsman ; and long, very long, may these peaceful times continue.

> " They hung the trumpet in the hall,
> And study war no more."

In corroboration of what has been stated as to the share the Glovers have taken in defending the liberties and privileges of their town and country, I have been favoured with a copy of a very old march, " The Perth Glovers' March," said to have been played in 1559, before that gallant band of 300 patriots, who marched from Perth to Stirling and Edinburgh, with ropes round their necks, to prosecute the Reformation, or perish in the attempt.